D1212346

VERBAL STYLE AND THE PRESIDENCY

A Computer-Based Analysis

HUMAN COMMUNICATION RESEARCH SERIES

PETER R. MONGE, Editor

VERBAL STYLE AND THE PRESIDENCY

A Computer-Based Analysis

RODERICK P. HART
Department of Speech Communication
The University of Texas
Austin, Texas

1984

ACADEMIC PRESS, INC.

(Harcourt Brace Jovanovich, Publishers)

Orlando   San Diego   San Francisco   New York   London
Toronto   Montreal   Sydney   Tokyo   São Paulo

Quotations from Theodore H. White, from *The Making of the President 1964*. Copyright © 1965 Theodore H. White. Reprinted with the permission of Atheneum Publishers.

Quotations from *A Thousand Days* by Arthur M. Schlesinger, Jr. Copyright © 1965 by Arthur M. Schlesinger, Jr. Reprinted by permission of Houghton Mifflin Company.

COPYRIGHT © 1984, BY ACADEMIC PRESS, INC.
ALL RIGHTS RESERVED.
NO PART OF THIS PUBLICATION MAY BE REPRODUCED OR
TRANSMITTED IN ANY FORM OR BY ANY MEANS, ELECTRONIC
OR MECHANICAL, INCLUDING PHOTOCOPY, RECORDING, OR ANY
INFORMATION STORAGE AND RETRIEVAL SYSTEM, WITHOUT
PERMISSION IN WRITING FROM THE PUBLISHER.

ACADEMIC PRESS, INC.
Orlando, Florida 32887

United Kingdom Edition published by
ACADEMIC PRESS, INC. (LONDON) LTD.
24/28 Oval Road, London NW1 7DX

Hart, Roderick P.
    Verbal style and the presidency.

    (Human communication research series)
    Includes bibliographical references and index.
    1. Political oratory--United States. 2. Presidents--
United States--Language. 3. Persuasion (Rhetoric)--
Political aspects. I. Title. II. Title: Computer
assisted analysis of persuasion. III. Series.
PN4055 .U53P643 1984   815'.01'0923512   83-21512
ISBN 0-12-328420-1 (alk. paper)

PRINTED IN THE UNITED STATES OF AMERICA

84 85 86 87   9 8 7 6 5 4 3 2 1

To
Dorothy A. Sullivan
and
James F. Sullivan

For their love and wisdom, but mostly for their love

CONTENTS

PREFACE

In 1984, as in all election years, we become especially aware that presidents speak. This book is based upon 6 years of research focused on the speaking styles of the nation's last eight chief executives. It presents previously unpublished findings about the American presidency that are based on the analysis of political messages by a computer program (DICTION) written expressly for this purpose. Over 400 speeches of presidents Truman through Reagan have been processed by the computer, and the result is a broad-based look at the modern presidency as well as a detailed understanding of the most recent occupants of that office. *Verbal Style and the Presidency* therefore examines what presidents do most frequently and most avidly—talk.

Although academic and popular writers comment upon presidential discourse constantly, this, to my knowledge, is the first book-length, long-term study of presidential communication based on systematically collected factual information. Thus, this book presents a large amount of information previously unavailable, but has been written for the general, serious reader. Most of the scientific data are placed in the appendixes, which frees the various chapters to tell the eight individual stories of the recent presidency. Technical language has been kept to a minimum, and all observations are accompanied by anecdotes or by quotations from the speeches themselves.

The book therefore presents a "rhetorical history" of the modern presidency. Such a history is necessarily both a modern and a public history. Americans now seem to feel that only by listening to their presidents on radio and television can they know them in suitably intimate ways. And with television, modern Americans listen to their chief executives more frequently, if not more carefully, than ever before. As a result, voters' interest in the human qualities of their leaders is pronounced. This "personal" contact has given rise to the various presidential exposés that so often top the bestseller lists, the constant stream of chatter about presidents on television and radio talk shows, and the fascination with First Families, White House staffers, and Oval Office furnishings. Because presidents now talk to us virtually whenever they wish, we have become accustomed to both their faces and their voices.

With this new (some would add, false) sense of intimacy comes the great danger that the nation's citizens will fail to take all of this talk seriously. *Verbal Style and the Presidency* shows that a new way of studying presidents is mandated in our media-suffused age, that much has been hidden within public utterances, that entire presidencies sometimes die or are reborn because of presidential speechmaking, and that clever speechwriters cannot, ultimately, sanctify whited sepulchers with dead men's politics if the nation's citizens know how their presidents persuade them.

The book begins with a discussion of the rhetorical character of the modern presidency and then explains how forces centered in the Oval Office make presidents speak in institutionally distinctive ways. Thereafter, the presidents and their presidencies are discussed serially, from Harry Truman's folksy certitude through Ronald Reagan's uncertain folksiness. Each of these stories is at once unique and yet also part of the evolving presidency. While a rhetorical view of the American presidency is but one view of that complicated institution, it is a view that increasingly dovetails with our everyday experience as citizens, which is to say, with our experience as consumers of political persuasion. As citizens, we could choose to ignore presidential speechmaking, but to do so would be to take refuge in ignorance, a sorry haven indeed for thinkers and voters, and thinking voters.

ACKNOWLEDGMENTS

I alone am responsible for any inadequacies in this book, but several people have gone out of their way to keep such inadequacies to a minimum. I am particularly indebted:

To my former colleagues at Purdue University, who proved consistently willing to help me resolve those research problems that tire the mind. For the efforts of Donald Ellis, Henry Ewbank, Robert Norton, Linda Putnam, Charles Redding, and Charles Stewart, I am indeed thankful.

To my present colleagues at the University of Texas, who encouraged me to think aloud about the things I was writing. For the help of Richard Cherwitz, Robert Hopper, Fredric Jablin, and, especially, John Daly, I shall always be appreciative.

To fellow scholars who study political discourse and who stimulate me to think harder about the things I think about. Persons like Ernest Bormann, Edwin Black, Karlyn Campbell, Walter Fisher, Richard Gregg, Bruce Gronbeck, Kathleen Jamieson, Herbert Simons, and David Swanson make me happy that I am part of their scholarly community.

To my research assistants, particularly Tommy Barron, Robert Carlson, Mark Comadena, Kunio Ishida, Patrick Jerome, Craig Roberts, Rich Sorenson, Kari Whittenberger-Keith, Charla Witosky, and Roxanne Zimmer, who cheerfully did things I did not wish to do.

To professionals like Carol Buckman, Diana Cable, Kaye Draper, David Frame, Jo Hansen, Sharon Hartman, Carol Hatfield, Deanna Matthews, Peter Monge, Laura Stevens, Charlie Watkins, and G. Morgan Watson, who made my work infinitely easier because of their expertise.

To former students who have taken special interest in me and my work. I especially appreciate the kindnesses of William Eadie, Michael Hyde, Carol Jablonski, Jill McMillan, David Sinclair, Kathleen Turner, and Rob Wiley.

To the four most talented university administrators I know—Lear Ashmore, David Berg, Robert Jeffrey, and William Livingston—who in ways equally tangible and intangible have encouraged my efforts and made it possible for me to work unfettered.

To Peggy and Chris, who constantly help me know the difference between being serious and taking myself seriously; and finally,

To Kathleen Mary Hart, who now, at last, has her name in a real book.

CHAPTER
ONE _____

THE CHIEF EXECUTIVE
AS CHIEF PERSUADER

Just before Thanksgiving Day in 1971, President Richard M. Nixon and the usual retinue of aides and security personnel drove the short distance from 1600 Pennsylvania Avenue to the training camp of the Washington Redskins professional football team in Loudoun County, Virginia. Once there, Richard Nixon made a speech. What prompted his speech, he told his sweaty (and undoubtedly curious) audience, was their loss the previous Sunday to the Dallas Cowboys. He had come to share "a couple things that, to a lot of old pros, probably don't need to be said." Continuing, he exulted: "I am sort of an old pro, too, in my business. . . . I, speaking as one who heard a few of those boos—and I have heard a few myself in my lifetime—but I heard a few, the great majority of the people of this town are back of this team." He then went on for what must have been some 15 minutes to talk of spirit, of his college experiences, of the relative value of sportswriters, of General Pershing, of the Kansas City Chiefs, of Charley Taylor (a wide receiver), of the salaries of professional athletes, and of a salad of other topics. At one point in his speech the leader of the free world became quite specific: "And then, when you look at Larry Brown, now he was really playing. He didn't have as sharp a cut as he usually has when he was playing on Sunday. Harraway was really not up to par. And basically, when Brown or Harraway are going, you gain 150 to 200 yards. When they are injured, you gain 60 yards. That puts an enormous amount of pressure on the passer."[1]

It is possible, perhaps even likely, that the nation's chief executive had few better ways of spending his time on that November afternoon. Vietnam was then mostly behind him; his reelection seemed assured; and the tribulations (and later trials) of Watergate had not yet, in the words of his predecessor, "hunkered him down." It is really not the banality of the president's remarks which merits attention here. Surely Harry Truman committed greater rhetorical excess during his years in the White House. What is important is how unremarkable all of this appears. It is, after all, just another U.S. president giving another speech.

But certain questions beckon: Why would Richard Nixon choose to spend his off-hours speaking in public? Why did the national press not think it important to cover this presidential event? Why, on the other hand, did the federal government go to the expense of entombing these most forgettable remarks in *The Public Papers of the President?* Why would the Washington Redskins, after the excitement of the moment had passed, probably not pause to reflect again on the momentous events of November 23, 1971? And why have speaking occasions of this sort become standard for certain Americans during the past 35 years: Harry Truman on the back of his train in Pocatello, Idaho; Lyndon Johnson speaking in front of a one-room schoolhouse in Johnson City, Texas; Jimmy Carter sweating through a town meeting in Yazoo City, Mississippi?

Some of the answers come readily: Nixon, Truman, Johnson, and Carter spoke a great deal because that was their job—they gave the nation's speeches for a living. The press and the football players were able to contain their excitement because their cultural experience as American citizens had taught them that hearing a president speak was not a particularly unique thing—it had been done many times before; it would be done many times again. But it is interesting that the president, the football players, and the American citizenry nevertheless require the federal archivists to scurry around behind modern chief executives and record their remarks for posterity, sparing no expense or tree for the sake of Presidents' speeches perhaps because they have become convinced in a media-saturated age that a president is earning his keep only when he stands in public and talks.

Why would they believe such a thing? Prior to this century, presidents rarely spoke at all. When they did, their speeches were usually regarded with curiosity by the people. But all of that has changed, as we see in Figure 1.1.[2] Comparing 1945 to 1975, for example, public speeches by America's chief executives increased almost 500% in just 35 years. Several of the presidents upped the rhetorical ante dramatically, culminating in Gerald Ford's herculean suasion of 1976 during which he personally delivered *682* public addresses—seven times the number of speeches it took to get fellow Republican Dwight Eisenhower reelected in 1956. Apparently to little avail, Jimmy Carter averaged one speech a day during *each* of his 4 years in the White House only to be ousted from his swivel chair by a man people later called "The Great Communicator." As political scientist James Ceaser and

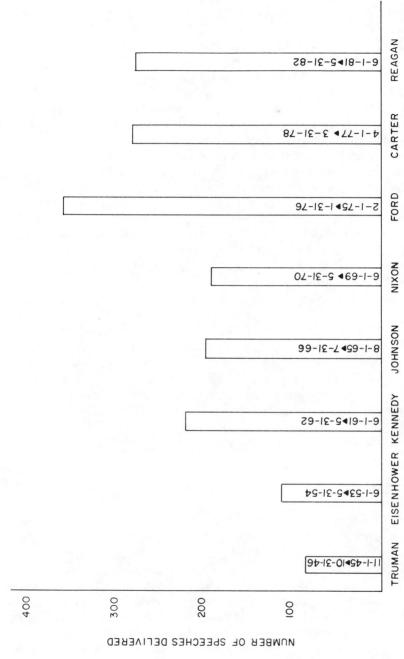

Figure 1.1 Speech productivity of modern presidents (first year only). Calculation begun after initial "adjustment period" had lapsed.

his colleagues recently observed, "more important even than the quantity of popular rhetoric is the fact that presidential speech and action increasingly reflect the opinion that speaking *is* governing."[3] In recent years, it has become possible to conceive of a corrupt president or an inept president or a truculent president, but it is not now possible to imagine a quiet president.

If it is true that a president's success is becoming increasingly dependent upon his speechmaking, and if it is true that the nation's citizens (prodded, no doubt, by the nation's press) are increasingly using rhetorical criteria when evaluating the merits of their chief executives, it behooves us to learn something of this presidential art. Here, I take presidential rhetoric seriously, more seriously perhaps than presidents would advise were their advice requested. I shall report the results of 6 years of study based on a computerized examination of over 800 speech texts.

When examining much of the presidential discourse delivered between 1945 and 1981, I tried not to think like a philosophical historian and assume that only a chief executive's "ideas" are worth studying. Instead, I looked carefully at certain microscopic features of presidential language, at *how* those ideas were expressed. I also tried not to think like a president, and hence paid attention to aspects of language not normally considered important by presidents or their speechwriters. In part, I did try to think like a Washington Redskin when examining presidential speeches, exercising care not to smirk as often as these football players probably did when listening, but still attempting to understand the statement behind the presidential statement. Throughout the project, I assumed that to understand presidential language in detail was to understand both presidents and the presidency. In this chapter, I try to demonstrate the worth of examining presidential persuasion and then explain how I conducted my examination.

An Attitude toward Presidential Speech

Traditional models of the presidency, of course, would not pay much attention to Richard Nixon and the Washington Redskins. Since grade school, for example, we have been taught by political scientists that the presidency is one of several institutions making up a thing called government and that another thing called checks and balances keeps the whole entity intact.[4] In such a model, a president becomes a psychological presence only to the extent that the pages of a youngster's civics book emphasize such features. Professional historians, on the other hand, have often abandoned the civics model for a psychological or philosophical understanding of the president as a person. Here, the presidency becomes personality writ large and biography is often emphasized over cultural commentary.[5] The third model of the presidency might be termed the journalist's model, a model in which the president is necessarily a functionary of certain "backstage" forces—political parties, economic cartels, pressure groups, and personal advisors—that secretly run the person who runs the country.[6] In such a model, the tasks of journalism become those of ferreting out such byzantine operations and exposing the president as a puppet.

But Figure 1.1 shows us that another model of the presidency is needed as well. In an era in which a president can, virtually at will, "go to the people," a new presidency has been born. The nation's media and the presidency have, especially since 1945, developed an intensively symbiotic relationship: The media need their presidential fix on a daily basis and presidents themselves now worry less about how they are being heard by the citizenry than about how they are being overheard by the press. Thus, a model of the presidency that attempts to explain (1) the communicative peculiarities of the various presidents, (2) their sensitivities to the demands of conscience, situation, and opportunity, and (3) those characteristics of speech endemic to the office and those native to the officeholder, seems very much in order. No such collection of information yet exists. But if Teddy Roosevelt was right when describing the presidency as a bully pulpit,[7] and if Richard Neustadt was correct in isolating the power of the presidency as the power to persuade its various rival constituencies,[8] then a communication-based history of the presidency seems very much in order, especially a history that begins when television itself began.[9]

How does one look at the presidency "rhetorically"? Above all else, a rhetorical model of the presidency is a *people's model.* It recognizes that a presidency is but an abstraction to the general public and that what the citizen most remembers about a president is how emotionally resilient that president was during the Korean conflict or the Bay of Pigs, how convincingly that president excused himself for Vietnam or Watergate, how clear that president was when explaining the nation's economy or its supply of natural resources. While political scientists often view the presidency as a political system operating within other systems, and while a historian might become interested in tracking the intellectual lineage of a presidential decision, the rhetorical model views the presidency as a string of public conversations. It argues that to dismiss presidential speechmaking as mere puffery and to concentrate exclusively on the machinations transpiring behind closed doors in the White House is to deny the essentially public nature of the presidency. After all, recent presidential history has surely told us that plots hatched behind closed doors must be ultimately carried off on the most public stage the nation possesses. A president is first and foremost a talker. He may do other things, too, but he does few of them well unless he does them persuasively. Thus, if we are to understand what a given presidency meant to the nation's citizens, we must reckon carefully with what that presidency said.

Rhetorical thought calls for a particular kind of discernment, a way of discovering how the human mind conceives of and then adjusts to a social situation. A rhetorical model of the presidency is, to use an unsettling phrase, a *strategic model*.[10] Such a model holds (1) that the most important decision a modern president makes is not that of deciding policy but that of articulating policy in ways that will make the Congress and the people want to adopt that policy; (2) that anything that a modern president says in public becomes important—both wheat and chaff, both foolish and serious—and that foolish and serious remarks alike affect policy; (3) that presidential messages "do" as well as "say," that the making of a speech in Topeka—regardless of what is said—constitutes powerful social action because the president has been there; (4) that even the most authoritatively worded presidential directive is impotent unless the president can convince the people that he has the power to carry out that directive and unless he can convince the press that he can convince the people; (5) that even the most existential event (say, the bombing of Pearl Harbor) is denied essential meaning in a president-dependent culture until the chief executive delivers a speech about that event so as to make it meaningful (and thereafter call his people to action); and (6) that the voters' evaluations of presidents are often rhetorically based. We warm to the gentle pleadings of a Ronald Reagan despite the uncertain course of Reaganomics; we relax our guards in the presence of a Dwight Eisenhower despite his Sherman Adams; we think uncommonly large thoughts when seated in the audience of a Lyndon Johnson despite what those thoughts will do to our taxes. When we find a Richard Nixon too slick, or a Jerry Ford too inelegant, or a Jimmy Carter too indirect, we are making almost metarhetorical judgments by castigating them for being strategically inept. There is thus a certain amount of cynicism in the rhetorical model. It acknowledges that the American people can turn out of office an admittedly pleasant fellow like Jimmy Carter because he could not persuade them that he could continue to persuade them.

The rhetorical model of the presidency is also a *creative model* for it judges a president not by his ability to use what exists (like nuclear armaments) but by his ability to conceive of possibilities (like detente) and to effect social agreements that never before existed. Thus, the space program was John Kennedy's rhetorical triumph and the war on poverty Lyndon Johnson's rhetorical victory because they and their writers found levels of discourse sufficient to foster imaginings that were wholly new and awesome to their listeners. While an economic model of the presidency may attribute Kennedy's and Johnson's victories solely to a then-healthy gross national product, the rhetorical model would inquire why these and other grand imaginings remained inert during the economically robust 1950s. From such a perspective, the presidency is a vast thesaurus, and the president is first and foremost a user of human symbols, not a disembodied functionary of some sort of abstract governmental structure. Moreover, this perspective regards political events as often being the products of overt, symbolic choices made by active human beings and not those of a deterministic set of historical, economic, or even militaristic realities.

A rhetorical model of the presidency is also a *projective model* in that it is concerned less with the president as a person than with the images of that president generated in the public consciousness by his words and by others' words about him.[11] In this sense, the rhetorical model departs radically from the historian's and the political psychologist's models of the presidency, for these latter models take pains to understand in detail the emotional stability, intellectual habits, family upbringing, and interpersonal attractions of the person–president being studied.

From a communicative standpoint, such intimate factors are interesting only when they become part of the public consciousness (as they did, e.g., in the case of Lyndon Johnson's brother Sam). An examination of Jimmy Carter's public speeches can therefore tell us a good deal about the "Jimmy Carter" that flittered about in the public mind, and it may even tell us why voters mentally constructed the particular "Jimmy Carters" they did. But no analysis of presidential discourse is likely to uncover the dark secrets of the peanut farmer–nuclear scientist known as Jimmy Carter of Plains, Georgia. Thus, examining Jimmy Carter's speeches better helps to gauge the effects of his remarks than to penetrate the psychological or philosophical causes of his public statements.

The rhetorical model is also a *corporate model* in that it treats a presidential message as the product of a "persuasive factory" and not as the simple outpourings of one man good and true. With a gaggle of wordsmiths to help him stoke the fires of invention, and with political advisors to help him assess each drafted word for its presumed impact, A president hardly presents his lone, essential self to us when he speaks. Rather, a president is an emanation of staff, party, and the electorate. A president's speech is a sociopsychological composite: of circumstance, of supporters and detractors, of diverse motivations. The rhetorical model encourages us to forsake the polite fiction that person and message are wed in presidential discourse and to think about such speech in suitably complex ways. To listen to a presidential speech, then, is to listen to a group discussion.

The rhetorical model recommends that we conceive of the president as a person who uses public words. Public words are calculated words, words whose heft and thrust are known to their user. They do not trip off the tongue spontaneously, although an experienced president will find ways to detract attention from their artifice. Thus, during an informal chat with Barbara Walters, during a tour of the rose garden with the Girl Scouts, or conceivably even when speaking to their own teenage children, presidents speak a language meant for the tabloids. (One is reminded that even Jerry and Betty Ford's "pillow talk" made news.) Over time, a president becomes adept at generating whole strings of these flowing, connected, public words, most of which have been chosen for their capacity to nestle impressively (and harmlessly) in the circuitry of some electronic recording device.

Presidents speak public words because they are public persons. In that sense they are not people as you and I are people. Unlike us, they eat with élan and sleep strategically. When angry they do not scream, they grimace. When happy they do not guffaw, they grin carefully. From the perspective of the home viewer, a president stands no taller than 15 inches high—exactly the vertical dimensions of the average television screen. In the life of the average citizen, the president exists only during the news at 6:00 P.M. and 11:00 P.M. and, on special occasions, at 8:00 P.M. (eastern standard time). Presidents thus occupy less space and time than do private persons, and they permit us as spectators to see less of their emotional range than do our everyday associates. Journalists, of course, attempt to go behind the scenes and find the "real" president amidst his spray of public words, and columnists regularly charm us with such reconstructions as President Reagan's napping habits. But in so doing, the journalists are only providing more public words about public words, while Ronald Reagan of California lives out his personal life privately.

In short, the rhetorical model encourages us to study presidencies rather than presidents. It urges that when we use a phrase like "Jimmy Carter" that we not confuse it with what Ms. Lillian Carter was thinking when she used that phrase. Rather, we should treat "Jimmy Carter" as shorthand for the political projection occupying the Oval Office between 1977 and 1981. By keeping such distinctions in mind, we shall then not be tempted to regard presidential messages as Rorschach inkblots, hiding flesh-and-blood persons in their ambiguity.

The rhetorical model also reminds us that presidents use human speech in strange ways. In contrast to ordinary speakers of the language, presidents (1) speak in public more often, (2) frequently do not see their hearers, (3) are forced to address a much wider range of topics, (4) are required to comment in public about their personal lives, and, most frustratingly of all in an era of audio and video tape, (5) rarely have the luxury of watching their words drift away forever. Sensing these differences between private and public persons, presidents develop certain attitudes toward speaking that sometimes affect their presidencies.

Presidential Attitudes
toward Presidential Speech

The bulk of this book presents and interprets an array of facts about presidential discourse. There have been few such facts available heretofore. But there have been more than enough opinions. Columnist Hugh Sidey's opinion is that "Presidents quite naturally like to hear themselves prattle on. Regular news conferences are important, but [Jimmy] Carter may have done considerable damage by his flow of words. . . . Language ultimately was cheapened and meaning diminished. The Carter White House echoed with so much talk that it finally became a bore."[12] Former presidential speechwriter Theodore Sorenson complains that such increased quantity has done little for rhetorical quality: "Stirring phrases have given way to 'applause lines.' Witty passages have been replaced by opening jokes. Majestic understatement has lost out to hyperbole. Precise command of language as a quality of leadership has been dismissed in favor of 'charisma.'"[13] The most acidic opinion is that of *Harper's* Lewis Lapham, who castigates presidents for resembling "characters in the soap opera of television news, their slogans and phrases worn so smooth by repeated use that they resemble ancient coins to which nobody can assign either a value or a city of origin."[14]

Presidents also have opinions about their speech activities, and it is worthwhile to consider such "soft" data before confronting the facts gathered here. A president's attitudes toward talk can sometimes tell us a good deal about his presidency—what sort of refuge he seeks during troubled times, how he celebrates when the world favors him, how ambitious and daring he is, how much of himself he is willing to share with the American people. After all, speech is both a mental and a physical activity; even the president of the United States submits himself to the lash of sweaty palms, accelerated heart rate, increased visceral activity, and muscular contractions endemic to speaking in public. Such physical realities are accompanied by emotional ones since to speak in public is to admit to a relationship with one's hearers. No matter how cynical a veteran speaker may become, the Other constrains during communicative contact. By soliciting the approbation of others, a president admits to being unable to solve certain problems on his own and thereby acknowledges the ultimately submissive role that any celebrity—rock star, actress, preacher, politician—plays relative to an audience. In short, public speaking disciplines.

Evidence about the various presidents' attitudes toward their speaking performances is largely anecdotal but it appears that such attitudes have consequences. For example, if one believed, as Richard Nixon appeared to believe, that one could argue oneself out of even the tightest spots, one might fail to destroy certain incriminating audio tapes, safe in the knowledge that a dramatic public performance at the eleventh hour, another Checkers speech, would befuddle or cower his detractors.[15] Speech had never let him down before, he seemed to reason. Even John Kennedy probably would have admitted that Nixon had won the 1960 debates "on points" (if not in people's hearts). And Nixon's presidential press conferences were often virtuoso performances—no notes, hands behind the back, facts at the ready. For Richard Nixon, argument was an old friend. But it may have been his misplaced faith in public debate that caused him to wait too long relative to Watergate. An early admission of ineptness—not even an admission of partial complicity—might have saved his presidency, but that would have meant his revising a long-standing custom of playing the man in the arena.

For Richard Nixon, public speaking was not communication—it was first and foremost a performance. It was to be planned for, practiced, monitored, and then evaluated. Lyndon Johnson's attitudes were less mechanistic than Nixon's, and he clearly preferred the corridor to the coliseum. Like Nixon, however, Johnson placed his faith in rhetoric—not in its quality, but in its sheer, massive presence. If one speech would not turn the trick for him, five surely would bind listeners to him. The "Johnson treatment," his famed working over of the poor souls who had the bad taste to disagree with him, began during his congressional days and became the model for his subsequent public performances: "Johnson tried to treat crowds the way he treated individuals in the Oval Office, by dazzling them with a storm of scattered talk"[16] (from the book, *The Presidential Character,* 2nd Edition, by James David Barber. © 1977, 1972 by James David Barber. Published by Prentice-Hall, Inc., Englewood Cliffs NJ 07632). He used a saturnalia of arguments to overwhelm his listeners. When he became mired in Vietnam, Johnson's natural impulse was to increase the talk, not the listening, and therein lies the story of his latter presidency.

Johnson and Nixon give evidence of what might be called a super-rhetorical attitude toward presidential speaking, which held that no exigence could withstand an onslaught of persuasion. John Kennedy and Ronald Reagan would not have gone that far. Their attitude was simply rhetorical, acknowledging that public speech was but one of many options available to them and that excessive dependence upon such performances would ultimately leave their private flanks unprotected. Therefore, we found Ronald Reagan simultaneously working the congressional byways and the lobbyists' encampments even as he prepared a national address (just in case). John Kennedy also knew that public presentations counted a good deal and his presidency was the first to exploit the mass media on a regular basis. But John Kennedy was ever the practical politician and, like his rhetorical forefather, Franklin Delano Roosevelt, he treated public speaking as an important ally but one that could entrap a president too filled up with himself.

Although Harry Truman, Dwight Eisenhower, and Gerald Ford had little in common, ideologically or personally, they agreed on one thing: Public speaking was best thought of as overheard conversation. This nonrhetorical attitude surely does not mean that they were unconcerned with their public images. Harry Truman doggedly read his speeches, Dwight Eisenhower hired a professional actor for private speech lessons, and Jerry Ford employed an professional joke writer from time to time. But each seemed unconcerned with inventing a special, public self. For Truman, public speaking was an instrument of power, useful for telling you what he was thinking and useful for launching an attack on the nation's ingrates. If his public performances were persnickety, it was because Harry Truman was, well, persnickety. Harry Truman did not like Dwight Eisenhower and Dwight Eisenhower, in turn, did not like public speaking. It was intrusive, he felt, a formal barrier between himself and his listeners. Press conferences were better in this regard for Ike because they at least retained some of the conversational amenities he prized. "His remarkable rhetorical success," said James David Barber, "seems to have happened without either great skill or great energy on his part."[17]

Jerry Ford was Dwight Eisenhower's rhetorical legatee. Neither developed a particularly "literary" style as public speakers, perhaps because neither had ridden the coattails of public performance into the White House. Eisenhower, with the aid of his military staff, and Ford, with the aid of his congressional colleagues, had, by the time they arrived in the Oval Office, become skilled conversants. In that way, they were similar to Lyndon Johnson. But, unlike Johnson, neither Eisenhower nor Ford had the gumption (or ego) necessary to try to master public speaking (which is surely not to say that Johnson succeeded in his quest). Jerry Ford put in his time on the public platform, but there is scant evidence that he enjoyed it or was good at it. On this latter point, most commentators would especially agree.

Jimmy Carter, of the speech-a-day fame, probably had less regard for the suasory arts than any of our recent chief executives. His attitude might well be called antirhetorical despite his excessive speechmaking (or perhaps because of it). During his 4 years in the White House, Carter never missed a banquet, an award ceremony, a state political convention, a press conference, or a trip to the hinterlands. Carter was a rhetorical iron man, but he appeared to have little personal taste for this side of his job and probably had little respect for listeners who could be swayed by rhetoric.

For the moment, one anecdote will suffice to enforce this point. Achsha Nesmith, a long-time Carter speechwriter, reported that upon receiving the first draft of a speech from one of his writers, Mr. Carter would immediately scan the message, looking for purple passages and phrases that smelled of the lamp. These he would habitually strike, thus ensuring that "mere words" would not obtrude upon the spare but honest message he wanted to share with his audience.[18] Businessman and scientist that he was, Carter disdained the easy, suasory grace of a Teddy Kennedy. With such attitudes, one wonders why Carter accepted a job as fulsomely rhetorical as that of the presidency of the United States. Indeed, Ronald Reagan's economic policies may have been superior to those of Jimmy Carter only in the sense that Reagan enjoyed talking about them more than Carter.

Studying Presidential Persuasion

If one were in doubt about the rhetorical nature of the American presidency, one need only consult popular works written about it during the past 20 years. A biographer like Fawn Brodie documents her claims about Richard Nixon's curious personality by quoting his speeches.[19] A historian like Arthur Schlesinger, Jr., justifies heralding an "imperial presidency" by requiring us to listen again to Lyndon Johnson.[20] Journalist Theodore White marks the changes in the presidential elections of 1960, 1964, and 1968 by comparing the public statements made during those Octobers.[21] Many of political scientist James David Barber's psychobiographies in *The Presidential Character* are based on his evaluations of what the men in the White House have said during their unguarded moments on the job.[22] Popular magazines, television news shows, newspaper editorials, public symposia, and governmental conferences are devoting more and more of their space or time to asking communication-based questions of the presidency: Should Richard Nixon have been allowed to curtail his press conferences during the darkest days of Watergate? Were FDR's fireside chats, and his resultant popularity, tantamount to a rhetorical monarchy? Is Ronald Reagan circumventing constitutional separation of powers when he slyly requests that the electorate bash in the heads of recalcitrant congresspersons?

Heretofore, scholarly examinations of presidential communication have generally fallen into one of four categories:

1. *Campaign studies*   The majority of the literature explains how politicians talked their ways into the Oval Office. The roles played by the mass media and the professional political consultant have been given special scrutiny of late.[23]

2. *Historical studies*   This category includes examinations of great speeches (e.g., "Ich Bin Ein Berliner") or the activities of the chief executives during major public controversies (e.g., the League of Nations and civil rights). Examinations of this sort have largely been case studies of single events or single issues.[24]

3. *Generic studies*   This category includes inquiries into those speak-

ing situations that recur frequently in the life of a modern president and explanations of how different chief executives have reacted to equivalent communicative events. Political ceremonies, nominating speeches, war-time oratory, state of the Union messages, inaugural addresses, and other classic speech forms have been examined;[25]

4. *Personality studies* This has been a popular area of investigation in which researchers have tracked down the remarks of a given chief executive and then related their findings (unwisely, in my opinion) to the presumed mental habits and emotional predispositions of the president studied.[26]

Specific Goals

This book is an attempt to survey the rhetorical scope of the modern presidency in a comprehensive and precise fashion and in a manner not previously attempted. I am interested here in individual personalities as well as in the institutional forces affecting the modern presidency, because it is with the institution of the presidency that most of us will live our lives. I shall examine great speeches and major controversies but shall comment on more humble rhetorical instances as well. My focus will not be on presidential campaigns but on the day-to-day business of running the nation. When making my observations I shall, to the extent possible, base my commentaries on fact.

To many, a scientific study of something as mellifluous as presidential talk may seem absurd. To others, it may seem simply unnecessary. Alistair Cooke, for example, hardly operated systematically or comprehensively when remarking about presidential prose in the *New York Times Magazine,* yet proved himself a succinct student of rhetoric:

> Truman, indeed, had a declared ambition to leave behind a set of state papers so plain and straightforward as "to do for English what Cicero did for Latin." He damn near made it.
> Eisenhower's . . . preference for bureaucratic euphemisms and his evident distaste for such simple nouns as "men" and "women" doomed him. . . .
> Lyndon Johnson suffered from the Southern Exposure Affliction . . . his talk was juicy, droll, vivid, and earthily idiomatic. But in public he feared he would betray his natural Southern gift for melding the language of the Old Testament with the language of animal biology.[27]

Cooke goes on to claim that there was nothing wrong with Nixon's prose except that he could not be believed, that Gerald Ford's prose was "comatose," and that Jimmy Carter was "the dullest presidential speaker since Woodrow Wilson."[28]

Surely it would be hard to improve upon such epigrammatic logic. Cooke's pithy summaries seem so authoritative as to both begin and end discussion. One feels like a pedant for asking such questions as: In what percentage of the cases was Harry Truman clear? Was he never, ever, circumlocutory? How did Cooke arrive at his estimate? What, precisely, is an "egregious monument of rhetoric"? What specific remarks of Johnson's revealed his multimindedness? Was not Richard Nixon's talk believed by many persons, and is not *that* important data, too? Might not Jerry Ford's comatose rhetoric have endeared him to an equally comatose, which is to say plain-speaking, body politic? "Academic quibbles," Cooke would undoubtedly respond.

The story to be told here will be more complicated than that fashioned by Cooke in his five-column article in the *Times.* This is not to say that my story will be a better story, but it will be (1) *precise,* for I clearly defined the language features that interested me before looking at the presidents' remarks; (2) *comprehensive,* for I have studied a great number of presidential speeches and hence shall not be thrown off the track by an idiosyncratic instance or two; (3) *comparative,* and so I will be able to say things like, "Compared with Jimmy Carter, Harry Truman was plainspoken but compared with Richard Nixon he was a bit on the windy side;" (4) *quantitative,* hence I shall not be able to resort to flashy, stylistic adjectives when commenting on Gerald Ford's speeches; and, unfortunately, (5) *cautious,* for even a quantitative and reasonably comprehensive examination of presidential language is only as good as the quality of the search tools, the representativeness of the sample, and the willingness of a writer to be honest about the research assumptions made and watchful of those assumptions he or she knows not.

The DICTION Program

The method of study employed here was computerized language analysis, a procedure by which the text of a message (a poem, a letter, an editorial, a presidential speech) is converted into machine-readable characters (often by keypunching) and the computer then asked to "pass over it" and to "look" for certain features of language. The computer can perform such operations because it is guided by a software program, in this case a program named DICTION, which was expressly developed by me for this examination.[29] Using similar computerized techniques, scholars have studied the imagery in Shakespeare's plays,[30] determined the authorship of the disputed *Federalist Papers* (by comparing the long-standing verbal habits of the rival authors to those in the unattributed papers),[31] produced concordances to the Bible,[32] judged the psychological patterns of suicide notes,[33] and, with a surprisingly high rate of success, distinguished the remarks of liars and nonliars in controlled laboratory sessions.[34] One value of such a research tool is that it can perform its analyses with incredible speed; the more than 800 messages examined here were each analyzed from 30 different vantage points and yet required only a few minutes of computer time. Moreover, with the aid of the computer, the researcher can examine *combinations* of words that he or she could hardly conceive of, never mind calculate without machine assistance.

When using such a tool, the scholar has to be wary of what Theodore Nelson has called cybercurd, which means "putting things over on people by using computers."[35] With only minimal training, after all, even the least gifted college student can be trained to keypunch a parent's letter from home and then subject it to the indignity of someone's computer program. Robert Wachal correctly notes that "in too many projects, a text passes through the brain of the computer without ever engaging the brain of the scholar."[36] To many people, Wachal says elsewhere, the "computer-using literary researcher is a poacher in the scholarly game preserve. The benevolent view is that his traps mangle what they hope to capture, or that they are set for deer and only catch gnats. A more pessimistic view is that his traps have no springs in them."[37]

In computerized language analysis, the "traps" become lists of words (or dictionaries) built into the program. These dictionaries must be carefully constructed so that they accurately measure what they are designed to measure. A dictionary called Household Pets, for example, might contain such words as dog, cat, goldfish, and parakeet. Employing this dictionary as a sorting tool, we would expect to find greater usage of such words in a child's letter to a friend than, say, in a speech by Governor Jerry Brown. Herein lies both the greatest danger and greatest advantage of computerized language study: Computer-based investigation is no better than the dictionaries it employs. If the dictionaries are silly, the study itself will be foolish. Reporting that Jerry Brown rarely mentions household pets in his public remarks will surely say more about the reporter than about the intellectual habits of the former governor of California.

The main dictionaries used in this study were compiled keeping in mind four questions that have often been asked of American presidents: (1) How does the president use *power,* when and why does he do so, and does he cope well when power is denied him? (2) How *practical* is the president, how clear and well documented is his political vision, and how capable is he of translating that dream into concrete reality? (3) How *dynamic* is the presidency in question, how much momentum does the president generate, and how quickly can he select alternative courses of action? (4) What sort of emotional *resilience* is evident in the White House, is that resiliency imparted to the president's followers, and does the president show that he can withstand the rigors of everyday political life?

Using these stimulus questions, I developed four major dictionaries and seven minor dictionaries. In each case, certain words were seen as contributing to and others as detracting from the concept measured.[38] The four major dictionaries were labeled Activity, Optimism, Certainty, and Realism. A given speech could range from a low of 0 to a high of 300 on each of these dimensions. The four variables turned out to be quite statistically independent of one another. This indicates, for example, that knowing a president's Realism score for a particular speech does *not* enable one to guess at his Activity score for that same address. The dictionaries used in this study are discussed in the following:

MAJOR DICTIONARIES

Activity   Statements referring to motion, change, or the implementation of ideas. Subcategories contributing to Activity include aggressiveness (fight, attack), accomplishment (march, push, start), etc., while passive words (quiet, hesitate) and words referring to mental functions (decide, believe) were seen as detracting from Activity.

Optimism   Statements endorsing someone or something, offering positive descriptions, or predicting favorable occurrences. Words indicating praise (good, loyal, sweet), enjoyment (exciting, cheerful), or inspiration (courage, trust) contributed to Optimism, while negations (won't, cannot) and terms of adversity (conflict, despair) detracted from the Optimism scores.

Certainty   Statements indicating resoluteness, inflexibility, and completeness. Leveling terms (all, everyone), collective nouns (bureau, department), and rigid verbs (will, shall) make for assured statements, while qualifying terms (almost, might), specificity (e.g., numerical citations), and first-person pronouns signalled an individual's refusal to speak ex cathedra.[39]

Realism   Expressions referring to tangible, immediate, and practical issues. Factors contributing to Realism included concreteness (building, family), present-tense verbs, spatial and temporal references (now, day, city, south) and person-centered remarks (child, us). Realism scores decreased as past-tense verbs and complicated linguistic constructions (e.g., polysyllabic words) increased.

MINOR DICTIONARIES

Embellishment   A selective ratio of adjectives-to-verbs based on the idea that heavy use of adjectival constructions makes for a "literary" style that "slows down" a verbal passage.[40]

Self-Reference   Signals a willingness to invest oneself in one's message directly and immediately. Included all first-person pronouns.

Variety   Also known as the type-token ratio. Variety was calculated by dividing the number of different words by the total number of words. A high score indicates a speaker's unwillingness to be repetitious, a decision that produces a "wordy" style.[41]

Familiarity   Consists of C. K. Ogden's "operation" and "direction" words, which he calculated to be among the 750 terms most frequently encountered in everyday speech. A high score thus becomes a measure of colloquialness.[42]

Human Interest   An adaptation of Rudolph Flesch's notion that multiple reference to human beings gives discourse a lively, down-home quality. Includes such words as you, me, father, themselves.[43]

Complexity   A simple measure of the average number of characters-per-word in a given passage. Borrows Flesch's notion that big words confuse more than they clarify.[44]

Symbolism   A list of the nation's "sacred" terms which have long been a part of public discourse in the United States. This category contains both "designative" terms (America, national, people) as well as "ideological" terms (democracy, freedom, law).[45]

In essence, the computer was asked to indicate how often and where the various presidents used the types of words just described. Such a procedure is obviously not without its problems. For example, the computer cannot analyze the context within which a given word is used but can only report its frequency.[46] In addition, these computerized counts do not take into consideration such important, albeit subtle, features of language as syntax, imagery, rhythm, and arrangement. Also, by scrutinizing just the middlemost 500 words of each speech text, no comment could be made about the introductions and conclusions of the presidents' speeches, which are, on occasion, miniature forms of rhetorical art (but which also make cross-comparisons problematic).[47]

Many of these limitations become less troublesome when we remember the computer's greatest strength: It deals capably with tremendous *amounts* of verbal information. It can help us track a given president across a great many speaking situations and through several years in the White House. It can therefore aid us in assessing his overall rhetorical style, his universe of discourse—the very sorts of things that the average citizen is likely to find important.

Perhaps the main value of the DICTION program is that it searches a speech for words that most speechwriters and politicians treat as unimportant. Although a president may choose his words deliberately, he will still find it all but impossible to monitor the complex of verbs and adverbs that connotes resoluteness, or to match the enthusiasm of today's speech to that of last week's. Because DICTION operates at the micro-stylistic level of language use, its discriminatory powers are considerable. Naturally, most political speakers scrutinize (and often sanitize) their main ideas when preparing their remarks. The DICTION program, however, is interested only in how those remarks are eventually presented. Such a methodology sets up the intriguing possibility of beating the professional wordsmith at a game he or she did not know was being played.[48]

Having said all of this, though, one cannot help but feel that computerized studies have a special burden when dealing with speechmaking. There is an important instinct within us that senses that a computer is too cumbersome to deal creatively with verbalization and that human intuition is a far better guide to the texture of discourse. Consider, for example, the text presented in the exerpt below.[49] This was a speech given by John Kennedy, then newly inaugurated, who had been asked to speak to the Democratic National Committee in Washington, D.C.

This is hardly a remarkable one. It is a straightforward, back-slapping piece of political celebration. It is brief, convivial, and seemingly spontaneous. We do not need a computer to tell us these things. We "know" them to be true because we have heard politicians talk before. We can apprehend the tone of the speech by drawing on a lifetime of communicative experience.

But how well can we cope with more complicated questions? Does our experience tell us how straightforward this speech was compared to others made by Kennedy? If the speech had been televised, would JFK have made any major changes in his approach? Is Kennedy as folksy here as, say, Lyndon Johnson or Jimmy Carter would have been in similar circumstances? What particular language cues tell us that Kennedy is being spontaneous? Is the speech twice as clear, or half as clear, as the inaugural address he had made the day before? Was it typical of Kennedy to name so many names when speaking? How frequently did he employ on other occasions the glib generalizations found in the penultimate paragraph? Did he normally make direct contact with his listeners, referring to himself and his activities, or was he being uncharacteristically personal here? Can this be called a "typical" presidential speech? Indeed, can it even be said to be a good example of the fabled "Kennedy style"? Finally, can we trust intuition to instruct us wisely and at the level of detail demanded by the foregoing questions?

Table 1.1 shows that intuitionism has its limitations as well as its strengths. It indicates that, yes, John Kennedy's language was especially simple here (see Variety data), that he was folksy both absolutely and relatively (see Human Interest), and that he was about as colloquial as a public speaker can be (see Familiarity). In these cases, the computer documents common sense (i.e., common sensitivities).

TABLE 1.1

COMPARISON OF KENNEDY SPEECH OF 1/21/61 TO KENNEDY AND PRESIDENTIAL AVERAGES[a]

DICTION category	1/21/61 Speech	Kennedy average	Other presidents' average
Activity	192.0	204.0	200.5
Realism	241.0	198.0	191.0
Certainty	196.0	190.0	185.3
Optimism	238.0	213.0	220.0
Complexity	4.70	4.58	5.20
Variety	.410	.493	.488
Self-Reference	18.00	4.68	8.57
Famimliarity	135.0	102.0	102.1
Human Interest	32.0	26.0	27.8
Embellishment	.042	.070	.066
Symbolism	6.00	2.21	5.45

[a]See Table B.1 for additional normative data.

But the computer tells us more. In general, it tells us that the press misled us when depicting the off-handed Kennedy as the typical Kennedy (viz., his press-conference self.) That is, the January 21, 1961 speech was massively uncharacteristic. Table 1.1 shows that Kennedy was much more pragmatic on this occasion than he normally was (see Realism), that such public buoyancy was almost never seen again during his presidential years (see Optimism), and that his extensive use of Symbolism and Self-Reference belied his usual diffidence. Table 1.1 also shows that Kennedy's style was not, in the main, appreciably different from that of the other presidents (at least from the standpoint of language).

More generally, Table 1.1 points out how difficult it is to be precise about language usage without recourse to *comparative measures* (i.e., other speeches, other presidents, other situations). The cross-checking techniques used in this study thus prevent one from being misled by a single, unrepresentative passage. They give specific hints as to why a particular verbal effect was produced; they permit us to say why, specifically, Kennedy seemed especially disclosive here; and they help to distinguish conventional wisdom about presidential speech from the facts of language themselves. Computerized language analysis is therefore not a generous ally to the researcher interested in premature confirmation of unfounded hunches. Computer studies all too often fail to document lay perceptions, and they make the irritating demand that a researcher specify what language means and why people react to its permutations as they do. Computerized language analysis is no haven for the solipsist.

Figure 1.2 presents the Kennedy speech as analyzed by the DICTION

I WANT to express my appreciation to all of you for your kind welcome, and also to take this occasion to express my great appreciation—and I think the appreciation of us all—to Senator Jackson who assumed the chairmanship of the Democratic Party at the Convention, who was greatly responsible for our success in November and has been an invaluable aid during the transition. Whatever has been done that is useful in the party in the last 5 or 6 months he has played a great part in it. And I feel that the party has served a most useful national purpose—and while Senator Jackson is obligated to serve the people of Washington in the Senate, I know that we can continue to count on him in the days to come for counsel and advice and support. So I hope we will all stand and give a good cheer to Scoop Jackson.

Scoop atuomatically loses his share of the $4-million debt—we are not going to let him in on it. John Bailey has become the proprietor, along with Mac, of this enterprise. I think we are particularly fortunate to have John Bailey. I heard Governor Lawrence in his seconding speech say the trouble with everything is that they don't know enough of what is going on here in Washington; they ought to get out in the field. I agree with him completely. We have got a man from the field who knows what's wrong here in Washington, and I am delighted that John Bailey is going to take over this job. He is more popular today than he will be any time again in his life. I will feel that he is doing a good job when you all say, "Well, Kennedy is all right, but Bailey is the one who is really making the mistakes." That's the way it was in Connecticut. Ribicoff was never wrong, it was always Bailey's fault. So that is what he is going to do down here.

Up beat introduction results from Kennedy's Optimism score of 238, which was one of the highest in the sample.

Heavy use of prepositional phrases and passive voice constructions decrease Kennedy's Activity score.

JFK's Realism score of 241 is exceptionally high and derives from a combination of personal, temporal, concrete, and spatial references.

Semantically, humor is often the product of overly assured language devoid of qualification, all of which results in a high Certainty score.

But/I/am/delighted/that/he/is/going/to/do/it./It/is/a/sacrifice/for/him./But/I/think/we are/getting/the/services/of/someone/who/works/in/the/party/year/in/and/year/out,/understands/what/the/party/can/do,/understands/what/the/role/of/the/Chairman/is—and/I must/say/that/I/am/delighted/to/see/him/assuming/the/position/vacated/by/Senator/Jackson.

Lastly, I want to thank all of you for being with us at the inaugural. The party is not an [end] in itself—it is a means to an [end.] And you are the people who, in victory and defeat, have [maintained] the Democratic Party, [maintained] its traditions and will continue to do so in the future. I hope the relationship between all of us can continue to be as cordial as possible. I believe in [strong] political organizations in our country. The Republican Party is [strong] and vigorous today after the election of 1960. [I think] we are, also. And when we do that, [I think] we serve great national purposes.

The party is the means by which programs can be put into action—the means by which people of talent can come to the service of the country. And in this great free society of ours, both of our parties—the Republican and the Democratic Parties—serve the interests of the people. And I am hopeful that the Democratic party will continue to do so in the days to come. It will be in the interest of us all, and I can assure you that I will cooperate in every way possible to make sure that we do [serve the public interest.] (You) have done so well in the past (We) couldn't possibly have won without (you) help. (I) look forward to working with (you) in the future, and (I) want (you) to know that here in Washington, (we) may not know always what is going on as well as (you) do, but at least (we) are trying.

Thank (you).

Colloquial phrases produce a very high Familiarity score; monosyllabic words result in a low Complexity score; and a paragraph devoid of adjectival constructions accounts for the low Embellishment score.

Parallel constructions linked in sequence produce a Kennedyesque flourish as well as a very low Variety score.

Kennedy uses hallowed, albeit stock, phrases to generate an uncharacteristically high Symbolism score.

This is a traditional political peroration consisting of high Self-Reference and Human Interest scores which, together, build speaker–audience bonds.

Figure 1.2 Kennedy's speech as analyzed by DICTION program.

program. The purpose here is to show why the numerical data turned out as they did. (Naturally, I have taken pains to isolate the most distinctive examples of the phenomena identified.) Figure 1.2 is every bit as important as Table 1.1 since the former tears us away from the magic of numbers and forces us to deal, microscopically, with the structure of language. Such procedures return us to the lived reality of symbol-using and demand that we document for ourselves the facts unearthed by the computer. Throughout this book, therefore, examples of presidential persuasion will be used extensively. In almost all cases, I have confined the numerical data to the Appendixes so that words—not numbers—receive the attention due them. The numbers, of course, are indispensible, for they add the level of detail necessary to make sharp discriminations and valid comparisons. But every attempt will be made here to tell the *rhetorical* story of the modern presidency; to appreciate that story, we must listen, critically, to what our presidents have said.

Speeches Analyzed

Given my purposes here—to discover features of language unique to individual presidents and to learn something about the presidency in general—a number of different (stratified) samples were constructed. The presidential sample consisted of 38 speeches each for Presidents Truman through Ford. For each president, 19 addresses were chosen from the first half of the administration and 19 from the second half. In all cases, domestic audiences were being addressed. Also, roughly half of the speeches were delivered to national audiences via the electronic media, with the remainder being presented to local listeners only. Finally, a wide range of speaking situations was included: ceremonies, conferences, political gatherings, briefings, etc.

The Carter sample was larger so I was able to gain a developmental glimpse of presidential language during a single administration. From each of Carter's 4 years 38 speeches were selected for analysis. The Reagan sample, in contrast, was much less comprehensive, and consisted of 24 speeches delivered during his first year in the presidency. (The bulk of the Reagan analysis was completed well after that of his seven predecessors in office.)[50]

In preparing these samples, care was taken to achieve equivalence among three speech topics because what is said can obviously affect how it is said. The topics include (1) *pragmatics*—speeches focusing on such tangible problems as the economy, energy, labor, and party politics; (2) *values*—speeches detailing the overriding principles and goals of the American people (e.g., freedom, civil rights, justice, national destiny); and (3) *strife*—speeches describing domestic and international conflicts such as Vietnam, the Middle East, and nuclear disarmament.[51]

To discover what might characterize presidential discourse as a whole, the remarks of the presidents were examined in light of a comparison sample. This included speeches by:

1. *Corporation executives* This sample included 50 speeches delivered at industrial conferences by the heads of major American industries. Topics varied here but normally dealt with such broad-based matters as governmental regulation, social responsibility, and economic fluctuations.
2. *Social activists* In this category were 50 speeches by prominent leaders of both liberal and conservative minority causes. Speakers such as Jesse Jackson, Kate Millett, William Kunstler, Robert Welch, and Ralph Nader were featured in this sample and the topics they addressed were diverse.
3. *Political candidates* Those persons who ran for, but failed to reach, the White House since 1948 comprised this subsample. The 129 speeches examined were almost exclusively campaign speeches and they addressed the broad range of topics found in a presidential campaign.
4. *Religious leaders* This was a sample of 160 sermons delivered by both nationally respected and rather obscure prelates. Eight different denominations, ranging from Mormonism to Judaism and from Roman Catholicism to Unitarianism, were equally represented. The subjects they discussed dealt largely with the social and political responsibilities of the contemporary church.[52]

This comparison sample made it possible to answer certain important questions about presidential leadership: Is a president little more than the head of America's biggest corporation or must he play some other role as well? Do modern conditions permit a president to be as truculent as a social activist or as sermonic as a religious leader? Does a president labor under any special constraints imposed by the office he holds or is he just a political candidate who has found permanent work? The 389 speeches comprising the comparison sample were all delivered between 1945 and 1975 and collectively represent the universe of issues which concern contemporary Americans. By examining the presidents vis-à-vis this sample, I was afforded a unique understanding of the institutional forces affecting the nation's leaders.

One final sample, a developmental sample, was constructed. This grouping included 29 speeches delivered by Richard Nixon when serving as vice-president and 30 speeches presented by Lyndon Johnson during his congressional days. My purpose was to discover changes brought about in their speech as they moved from positions of limited responsibility to the very highest office in the land. If "the man makes the office," we probably should not expect major changes in rhetorical behavior. But if the reverse is true, we can learn much about the special problems a president faces and what allows him to play well, or not so well, in all of those Peorias he must govern.[53]

Conclusion

The role of speech in the life of a modern president is not yet well known, but it seems amply true that when presidents are thought of at all, they are thought of on their feet and talking. Although the public speeches of an American president are oftentimes embarrassingly prosaic and even though their artifice may seem transparent at times, such talk has locked within it important clues about the people who produce it as well as those who listen to it. After all, if the bicentennial speeches of Jerry Ford are found to be mawkishly patriotic, it must be remembered that they are that way because American listeners are a rather sentimental lot. If Harry Truman's speech seems a bit crude by modern standards, they may be because people's verbal tastes have become more elegant during the last 35 years. Someday, undoubtedly, our children will wonder why the sophisticates of the 1980s were so attracted by the soothing imprecations of a former movie actor. In answering that question, they will learn a good deal about their parents (as well as about Ronald Reagan). Thus, to study presidential speech is to study the American people themselves.

The approach used here will surely not answer all questions about the presidency. Computerized language analysis cannot ensure insight nor eliminate the facile generalization. No mere technique can produce ideas; only its user can do that. Indeed, throughout this volume it will be useful to remember the words of novelist John Barth, who opines in *Giles Goat-Boy* that "the computer could not act on a hunch or brilliant impulse; it had no intuitions or exaltations; it could request but not yearn; indicate, but not insinuate or exhort; command but not care. It had no sense of style or grasp of the ineffable; its correlations were exact, but its metaphors wretched; it could play chess, but not poker."[54] Barth has indeed cut out our work for us, for we shall here try to understand the exhortations and styles of some of the greatest political poker players of our times. My hope is that this volume will stand as a refutation of Barth's claims.

In Chapter Two we shall examine presidential discourse generally and then move on to consider the individual presidents, searching for those habits of locution which best explain popular reactions to their respective presidencies. By examining both the personal and institutional aspects of the presidency across a considerable period of time, we shall discover how integral a president's communicative skills are to his success as a leader and, presumably, to our clarity of vision as a people.[55]

Notes

1. "Remarks to Members of the Washington Redskins Professional Football Team," November 23, 1971, *Public Papers of the Presidents, 1971* (Washington, D.C.: U.S. Government Printing Office, 1972), pp. 1134, 1137.

2. The facts presented here are part of a data-base collected by me but unpublished as yet. The study involves a day-by-day recounting of the speechmaking engaged in by Presidents Truman through Reagan. The basic facts surrounding each of the more than 8000 presidential speeches made since 1945 have been introduced into a computerized data bank. Partial results are available from the author upon request.

3. James Ceasar *et al.,* "The Rise of the Rhetorical Presidency," *Presidential Studies Quarterly,* 11 (1981), p. 159.

4. One fairly recent exponent of this approach is Steven A. Shull and Lance T. LeLoup's, *The Presidency: Studies in Policy Making* (Columbus, OH: King's Court, 1979).

5. There are countless examples of this approach to the presidency. One of the best is the distinguished "American Presidency Series" now being published by the Regents Press of Kansas (1973–present).

6. Obviously, a large number of such analyses have been written, especially in the past 20 years. The tremendous success of such best-sellers as Bob Woodward and Carl Bernstein's *All the President's Men* (New York: Simon and Shuster, 1974) attest to the popularity of this approach.

7. Roosevelt's use of the phrase obviously pre-dated television, but an interesting extrapolation of that concept has been authored by Newton Minow, John Martin, and Lee Mitchell, *Presidential Television* (New York: Basic Books, 1973), pp. 17–69.

8. This is a theme Neustadt develops throughout his *Presidential Power: The Politics of Leadership, with Reflections on Johnson and Nixon* (New York: Wiley, 1960, 1976).

9. The rhetorical perspective upon which this book is based is as old as humanism itself. The perspective prizes, above all, the human being's capacity to generate symbols and to use them for practical effect. The perspective has been used by students of literature (cf. Wayne Booth, *The Rhetoric of Fiction,* Chicago: University of Chicago Press, 1961); philosophy (Don M. Burks, ed., *Rhetoric, Philosophy, and Literature: An Exploration,* West Lafayette, IN: Purdue University Press, 1978); political behavior (Roderick P. Hart, *The Political Pulpit,* Layfayette, IN: Purdue University Press, 1977); anthropology (Maurice Bloch, ed., *Political Language and Oratory in Traditional Society,* London: Academic Press, 1975); sociology (Richard Merritt, *Symbols of American Community, 1735-1775,* New Haven: Yale University Press, 1966); urban affairs (Murray Edelman, *Political Language: Words that Succeed and Policies that Fail,* New York: Academic Press, 1977); American history (Steven Lucas, *Portents of Rebellion: Rhetoric and Revolution in Philadelphia, 1765-76,* Philadelphia: Temple University Press, 1976); and modern technology (Michael Hyde, ed., *Communication, Philosophy, and the Technological Age,* University, AL: University of Alabama Press, 1982).

10. An expanded version of this discussion can be found in my "The Functions of Human Communication in the Maintenance of Public Values," in Carroll Arnold and John Bowers, eds., *Handbook of Rhetorical and Communication Theory* (Boston: Allyn and Bacon, 1984).

11. Much of this discussion has been borrowed from my "A Commentary on Popular Assumptions about Political Communication," *Human Communication Research,* 8 (1982), pp. 366–389.

12. Hugh Sidey "On the Need to Relax, Stay Home and Meditate," *Time,* January 5, 1981, p. 37.

13. Theodore Sorenson, "Presidents and the King's English," *New York Times Magazine,* August 19, 1979, p. 8.

14. Lewis Lapham, "Political Discourse," *Harper's,* August, 1980, p. 9.

15. Richard Nixon, "The Expense Fund Speech," September 12, 1952, *U.S. News and World Report*, October 3, 1952, pp. 60–70.

16. James David Barber, *The Presidential Character: Predicting Performance in the White House* (Englewood Cliffs, NJ: Prentice-Hall, 1972), pp. 85–86.

17. Barber (1972), p. 161.

18. Ms. Nesmith's remarks were presented at the University of Maryland on November 6–7, 1980, in conjunction with the special seminar on campaign communication sponsored by the Department of Communication Arts.

19. Fawn Brodie, *Richard Nixon: The Shaping of his Character* (New York: Norton, 1981).

20. Arthur Schlesinger, *The Imperial Presidency* (New York: Popular Library, 1973).

21. See Theodore White's series, *The Making of the President,* published by Atheneum Press quadrennially between 1960 and 1972.

22. Barber (1972).

23. For a fairly helpful discussion of this type of research see Dan Nimmo and Keith Sanders, eds., *Handbook of Political Communication* (Beverly Hills, CA: Sage, 1981).

24. Representative studies of this sort include Carol Jablonski, "Richard Nixon's Irish Wake: A Case Study of Generic Transference," *Central States Speech Journal,* 30 (1979), pp. 164–173: Richard Gregg and Gerard Hauser, "Richard Nixon's April 30, 1970 Address on Cambodia: The 'Ceremony of Confrontation,'" *Communication Monographs,* 40 (1973), pp. 167–181; Andrew King, "The Rhetoric of Power Maintenance: Elites at the Precipice," *Quarterly Journal of Speech,* 62 (1976), pp. 127–134; and John Patton, "A Government as Good as its People: The Restoration of Transcendence to Politics," *Quarterly Journal of Speech,* 63 (1977), pp. 249–257.

25. See, for example, Donald Wolfarth, "John F. Kennedy in the Tradition of Inaugural Speeches," *Quarterly Journal of Speech,* 46 (1961), pp. 124–132; Robert Ivie, "Presidential Motives for War," *Quarterly Journal of Speech,* 60 (1974), pp. 337–345; James Prothro, "Verbal Shifts in the American Presidency: A Content Analysis," *American Political Science Review,* 50 (1965), pp. 726–739; and Marshal Smith *et al.,* "A Content Analysis of Twenty Presidential Nomination Acceptance Speeches," in Philip Stone *et al.,* eds., *The General Inquirer: A Computer Approach to Content Analysis* (Cambridge: MIT Press, 1966).

26. Sample studies include those by Richard Donley and David Winter, "Measuring the Motives of Public Officials at a Distance: An Exploratory Study of American Presidents," *Behavioral Science,* 15 (1970), pp. 227–236; Karen Dovring, *Frontiers of Communication: The Americas in Search of Political Culture,* (Boston: Christopher Publishers, 1975); John Kessel, "The Parameters of Presidential Politics," *Social Science Quarterly,* 55 (1974), pp. 8–24; and Robert Frank, *Linguistic Analysis of Political Elites: A Theory of Verbal Kinesics* (Beverly Hills, CA: Sage, 1973).

27. Alistair Cooke, "Presidential Prose," *New York Times Magazine,* July 19, 1981, pp. 6, 7.

28. Cooke (1981), p. 7

29. DICTION is a binary search program written in COBOL and implemented on a Cyber machine manufactured by Control Data Corporation. In processing a single 500-word passage, the program requires approximately 35.0 CP seconds. Printout provided by the program includes character statistics, dictionary totals, and a list of high-frequency words. Further information about the technical aspects of the program can be found in my "Systematic Analysis of Political Discourse: The Development of DICTION," in Keith Sanders, Dan Nimmo, and Lynda Kaid, eds., *Political Communication Yearbook: 1984* (Carbondale, IL: Southern Illinois University Press, forthcoming).

DICTION was constructed for the express purpose of analyzing consecutive public discourse produced by contemporary Americans; its dictionaries reflect those biases. There are a number of other computerized language analysis programs available. Another general program of this sort is H. Wayland Cumings and Steven L. Renshaw's *SLCA–II: A Computerized Technique for the Analysis of Syntactic Language Behavior* (Minneapolis: Burgess Publishing Co., 1976).

30. Dolores M. Burton, *Shakespeare's Grammatical Style: A Computer-Assisted Analysis of* Richard II and Antony and Cleopatra (Austin: University of Texas Press, 1973).

31. Frederick Mosteller and David L. Wallace, *Inference and Disputed Authorship:* The Federalist (Reading, MA: Addison-Wesley, 1964).

32. For a general commentary on the uses of the computer in "literary" matters, see George Gerbner *et al.*, eds., *The Analysis of Communication Content: Developments in Scientific Theories and Computer Techniques* (New York: Wiley, 1969).

33. Philip Stone and Earl Hunt, "A Computer Approach to Content Analysis: Studies Using the General Inquirer System," *Proceedings of the Spring Joint Computer Conference* (Washington, D.C.: Spartan Books, 1963).

34. Mark Knapp, Roderick Hart, and Harry Dennis, "Deception as a Communication Construct," *Human Communication Research,* 1 (1974), pp. 15–29.

35. Quoted in Robert Wachal, "Humanities and Computers: A Personal View," *North American Review,* 8:1 (1971), p. 30.

36. Robert Wachal, "The Machine in the Garden: Computers and Literary Scholarship, 1970," *Computers and the Humanities,* 5:1 (1970), p. 27.

37. Wachal (1971), p. 30

38. In all, there are 28 different word lists used in the DICTION program. The dictionary counts provided by the program are mathematically standardized and then combined, using a series of simple equations, to form the major variables. Naturally, because some of the minor variables are already included in the major variables, correlations among them are not reported in Tables B.5 and B.10 of Appendix B. Correlations intentionally omitted are Activity/Embellishment, Certainty/Self-Reference, Certainty/Variety, Realism/Familiarity, Realism/Human Interest, and Realism/Complexity.

The dictionaries used in DICTION harbor some redundancy. That is, some of its search words were intentionally assigned to more than one category, precisely because words are multi-meaningful. Thus, a word like *country* contributes to both the Symbolism score (because of its patriotic implications) as well as to the Realism score (because it identifies a specific geographical/sociological unit). While such an accommodation slightly (and artificially) raised some of the intervariable correlations in isolated instances, it had no general effect on the data; in any event, it was seen as a necessary accommodation, given the nature of the English language.

One interesting feature of DICTION is that it is capable of treating homographic meanings differentially. That is, by employing certain statistical weighting procedures, DICTION distinguishes, on a mathematical basis, between the word *state* as it is used in the phrase "please state your opinion" versus "the state of the nation." Naturally, such statistical weights are assigned automatically and without regard to actual contextual facts. Still, such a technique is seen as a modest improvement over many context-blind computer programs because roughly 12% of the more than 3000 words contained in the DICTION dictionaries were homographs. The sourcebook used to generate the statistical weightings was Helen Easton, ed., *Word Frequency Dictionary* (New York: Dover, 1940), pp. 217–259. For a complete presentation of the DICTION program, see Appendix D of this volume.

39. This variable has been used, in slightly modified form, in previous research. See my "Absolutism and Situation: *Prolegomena* to a Rhetorical Biography of Richard M. Nixon," *Communication Monographs,* 43 (1976), pp. 204–228.

40. The concept, but not the measuring technique, has been borrowed from David Boder,

"The Adjective-Verb Quotient: A Contribution to the Psychology of Language," *Psychological Record,* 3 (1940), pp. 310–343.

41. Variety, or the type-token ratio, has been a popular tool in previous language analyses. For a recent example of its use see Ronald Carpenter and William Jordan, "Style in Discourse as a Predictor of Political Personality for Mr. Carter and Other Twentieth Century Presidents: Testing the Barber Paradigm," *Presidential Studies Quarterly,* 3 (1978), pp. 67–78.

42. C. K. Ogden, *Basic English: International Second Language* (New York: Harcourt, 1968).

43. Rudolph Flesch, *The Art of Plain Talk* (New York: Collier, 1951).

44. Flesch (1951).

45. This construct is similar to the notion of "God terms" discussed by Richard Weaver in his *The Ethics of Rhetoric* (Chicago: Regnery, 1951), pp. 211–232.

46. Some computer programs can, in primitive fashion, account for contextual meanings. Unfortunately, these programs are often so cumbersome as to be of negligible practical value. For an example see Philip Stone (1963).

47. The main reason for eliminating the beginning and ending portions of the presidents' speeches from analysis was, of course, that such speech segments typically contained localized and personalized cues unique to the speaking occasion, thus making cross-comparisons meaningless. Typically, the middle-most 500 words of a public speech are not heavily affected by such contextual factors.

48. Additional theoretical defense of systematic language analysis can be found in Louis T. Milic, "Rhetorical Choice and Stylistic Option: The Conscious and Unconscious Poles," in Seymour Chatman, ed., *Literary Style: A Symposium,* (London: Oxford University Press, 1971), pp. 77–94; Richard M. Ohmann, "Prolegomena to the Analysis of Prose Style," in Harold C. Martin, ed., *Style in Prose Fiction,* (New York: Columbia University Press, 1959), pp. 9–10, and Sally Yeats Sedelow and Walter A. Sedelow, Jr., "A Preface to Computational Stylistics," in Jacob Leed, ed., *The Computer and Literary Style* (Kent, OH: Kent State University Press, 1976), pp. 6–7.

49. John F. Kennedy, "Remarks at a Meeting of the Democratic National Committee," January 21, 1961, *Public Papers of the Presidents, 1961* (Washington, D.C.: U.S. Government Printing Office, 1962), pp. 4–5.

50. Because the Reagan data were collected quite late in the project, his speeches have not been included in the "institutional" portion of the study reported in Chapter Two.

51. A general breakdown of the speech-by-speech data is provided in Appendix A. To make the data useful for others, only the most distinctive rhetorical features have been indicated for the presidential speeches analyzed.

52. Space prohibits a complete presentation of bibliographical information for the comparison sample. A listing of the 389 speeches can be obtained from the author upon request.

53. For the presidential sample, 171 speeches were nationally televised (65 on values, 62 on pragmatics, and 44 on strife) and 209 were delivered to local audiences (102 on values, 83 on pragmatics, and 24 on strife). One hundred and ninety speeches from both the first half and second half of the presidents' respective administrations were included, with the topical distribution by time being virtually identical.

54. John Barth, *Giles Goat-Boy,* (New York: Doubleday, 1966), p. 61.

55. Whenever results are reported in this book, they will constitute statistically significant differences (except in those few cases where noted). The statistical tests run on the data were the traditional ones: analyses of variance, *t* tests, Pearson correlations, etc. There has long been some dispute in the area of language analysis concerning the intervality of language data. Although parametric statistics were applied exclusively to the data gathered here, nonpara-

metric analyses were also run in roughly one-quarter of the cases as a checking device. The resulting statistical profiles were identical.

All of the main statistical effects discovered are reported in Appendix B. Throughout the book, every attempt has been made to comment upon the most important findings. Because of the great amount of data uncovered, however, it was not possible to detail every statistical effect noted. Thus, although I often comment here on important "interaction effects" among two or more language variables, I do not discuss them all. When such effects related directly to overall trends, of course, they have been duly noted in the text.

THE PRESIDENCY SPEAKS

Political scientist William Spracher has commented that we know a good deal about our presidents but precious little about our presidency.[1] Popular magazines with articles focusing on the president are inevitably person-centered, dutifully chronicling the political waxings and wanings in the White House, the lurching of polls measuring presidential popularity, the state visits of little-known potentates, the president's appearance on opening day in Baltimore, and the colorful activities of the first family. These things and more we are told, and the telling itself becomes almost artful—as witnessed by the predictable sales of the presidential exposés that have haunted each of our recent heads of state.

We seem to understand presidents. But the presidency itself remains an enigma, an abstraction used to designate those ineffable linkages that tie together a Texas cattle rancher, a World War II hero, a Georgia peanut farmer, and a Hollywood matinee idol. We know comparatively little about those features native to the office, the "first principles" of the executive branch of government that transcend the Oval Office's temporary occupant.

Those few observers who have discussed institutional aspects of the presidency have focused upon a variety of matters. Some of them have treated the presidency as an organizational system, trying to explain the constraints faced by the chief executive when confronted by recalcitrant bureaucrats, truculent governors, or ego-maniacal aides.[2] Others have examined presidential roles—military commander, mediator of special-interest groups, legislative champion, ceremonial head of state—and tracked what happened to the presidency when such roles became increasingly conflictual (as they have in recent times).[3] Numerous authors have concerned themselves with how the presidency relates to other branches of government such as the judiciary, the military establishment, and the Congress, to see who wields what power under which circumstances. Especially in recent times, commentators have examined the interface between the presidency and the fourth estate, shedding light on a labyrinthine relationship marked by mutual exploitation.[4] Thus, although some institutional analyses of the presidency have appeared, virtually none of them has been animated by rhetorical concerns.

The purpose of this chapter is to outline aspects of presidential speech that a newly elected chief executive may not have yet developed upon assuming office. The task is a somewhat curious one for we shall here concentrate on rhetorical data—data that are typically regarded as idiosyncratic. An individual's speech, after all, is thought to be his or her most unique possession, a primordial method of asserting one's distinctiveness. "Know my words, know me" is the folk wisdom that usually guides us on such matters. Thus, to conceive of how an *institution* "speaks" is to risk committing some variety of anthropomorphic sin.

But it is worth asking what is left in presidential speech after we have subtracted Harry Truman's feistiness, Lyndon Johnson's garrulousness, and Dwight Eisenhower's malapropisms. In what common ways did such different persuaders as John Kennedy and Richard Nixon speak to their respective constituencies? When Gerald Ford relinquished the White House to Jimmy Carter, what rhetorical legacy also changed hands and was later bequeathed to Ronald Reagan? In short, what generalizations can be made about presidential discourse sans personality?[5]

From these general queries, several more specific questions emerge:

1. *Role* What unique rhetorical tasks do our presidents have when compared to themselves as nonpresidents or when compared to a variety of other speakers?
2. *Style* In contrast to other public persuaders, what sorts of special persuasive habits do presidents form?
3. *Time* Can any major changes be noted in recent presidential discourse? Also, as an individual president matures in office, does he typically alter his speechmaking to account for changing institutional forces?
4. *Circumstance* Do presidents deal with certain topics in distinctive ways? Do particular types of speaking situations make them talk in a predictable manner? Have the electronic media made them speak differently?

While these questions appear primitive, answers to them might well be worth having. If it is true that respect for the presidency, national esprit de corps, domestic vision, party platforms, and international attitudes are affected by presidential speechmaking, then carefully examining what a president says, and hence where the presidency stands, may be worthwhile indeed.

Presidential Role

Several writers have claimed that the expectations we as citizens have of any president are excessive, confusing, contradictory, often arbitrary, and ultimately harmful to him as a person and to the institution he serves. Clinton Rossiter tells us, for example, that a president is a chief of state, chief executive, commander in chief, chief diplomat, chief legislator, chief of party, voice of the people, protector of the peace, manager of prosperity, and world leader.[6] Being all of these things constantly, and yet being no one of them for very many days at a time, obviously complicates presidential life. Indeed, political scientists have seriously considered the effects of a "plural presidency" because the position's various manifestations are so prodigious and inconsistent and because of the psychological danger for the person wearing so many different presidential top hats for so long.[7]

Before wringing our hands, however, we are wise to ask exactly how these multiple roles are manifested. To answer this question, two sorts of comparisons were made: (1) presidential language was compared with the language of the corporation executives, religious leaders, social activists, and political campaigners mentioned earlier and (2) Lyndon Johnson's congressional speeches and Richard Nixon's vice-presidential speeches were compared with mesages they delivered while serving in the Oval Office. Both comparisons provide anchor points—standards against which individual stylistic deviations could be gauged—and thus a cross-checking device for assessing institutional effects on the presidency. These tests indicate that the modern president speaks a unique language. Let us consider its main features.

Humanity

Numerous commentators, especially those critical of the modern television extravaganza centered in the White House, have warned that Americans have become a nation of hero worshippers, that a "cult of the presidency" has emerged.[8] The language analyses performed here add fuel to that fire, as we see in Figure 2.1. Compared to all other speakers considered, presidents mention themselves and their actions with special frequency. Averaging more than eight Self-References per passage, the presidents' totals were double the number of times the corporation execu-

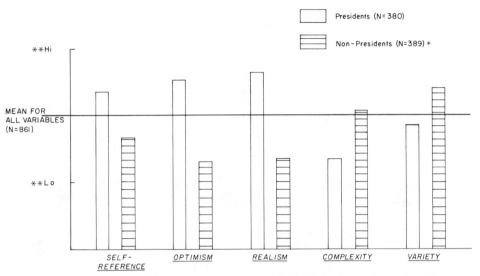

Figure 2.1 Institutional features of presidential style. All differences significant. See Table B.9. ** ± ½ sd from mean. See Table B.1 for exact values. *Comparison sample speeches. See Chapter One.

tives spoke of their personal experiences and convictions. Even on such a prosaic occasion as delivery of a State of the Union Message, for example, Gerald Ford found it natural and fitting to thrust himself into 8 of the 10 paragraphs comprising the sample: "I propose tax changes to encourage people to invest. . . . I propose catastrophic health insurance. . . . I do envision the day when. . . . I am recommending. . . . I am concerned."[9] In presidential government, it appears that a chief executive's job is to personify issues, to link self with policy in such a way that human flesh is added to the bare bones of political decision.

When speaking as president, Lyndon Johnson referred to himself much more often than when he addressed political matters as congressman. The same proved true of Richard Nixon's presidency versus his vice-presidency. (See Figure 2.2.) Consider, for example, Johnson's remarks at a Virginia political rally in August of 1960: "The Democratic Party does not believe that we can hold back and go forward at the same time. We do not believe that we can get ahead by standing still. We do not believe that we can be strong abroad and weak at home."[10] Far less distanced in tone were Johnson's ruminations as president at an off-year election rally in Chicago of 1966: "I have tried to base my decisions and my thinking and my actions on what I think is really best for this country. I believe that is what my country expects me to do."[11]

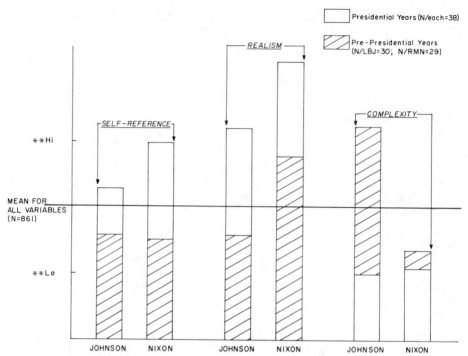

Figure 2.2 Institutional effects on Lyndon Johnson and Richard Nixon. All differences significant. See Tables B.3 and B.4 ** ± ½ sd from mean. See table B.1 for exact values.

None of the other groups of speakers examined here were as self-centered as the presidents, perhaps revealing that the presidency is a political pedestal upon which the president—as person—resides and from which he—as person—may topple. The fact that personal references are so ubiquitous may also indicate that the presidency is a breeding ground for rampant megalomania, as some of the institution's more acerbic critics have already suggested.

But the presidency is more than that. One rather dramatic finding was that the presidents' Optimism scores were significantly higher than those of all other speakers examined. Combining these findings with those just mentioned, we gain an impression of the president as the country's first cheerleader, personally leading the national chant of hope and perseverance. As Winston Churchill and Franklin Delano Roosevelt demonstrated during World War II, a leader's rhetoric can perform wondrous acts for citizens by keeping angst at bay. Indeed, the presidents examined here scored much higher on Optimism than even the religious leaders sampled. More priest than priest must a president be.

Even a practical person like Richard Nixon larded his speeches with positivity. In his second inaugural address, for example, he told the American people that "We have the chance today to do more than ever before in our history to make life better in America, to ensure better education, better health, better housing, better transportation, a cleaner environment, to restore respect for law, to make our communities more livable and to ensure the God-given right of every American to full and equal opportunity."[12] This is heady stuff especially for a person habitually given to contemplating expediencies of the moment (as the Watergate tapes later revealed with shocking, sometimes amusing, clarity).

The mantle of the presidency is not meant for the shoulders of the nation's naysayers. The social activists, in contrast, were the least optimistic of the speakers sampled, as we see in Figure 2.3. Compare the following remarks of Paul Erlich with those above by Richard Nixon (both of whom were dealing with kindred issues): "There are some threats to our existence which are fundamentally environmental. . . . The urbanization problem is so severe over the world today. . . . Here is a single example from outside the United States of how we can make very silly mistakes. . . . These are the people who are looting and polluting the world."[13] Such candid appraisals of our woes are not the material out of which presidential speeches are fashioned. As Jimmy Carter discovered after his ill-fated "crisis of confidence" speech in July of 1979, presidents are not meant to be professors. Instead, they must sound the upbeat. As religious leaders have charge over

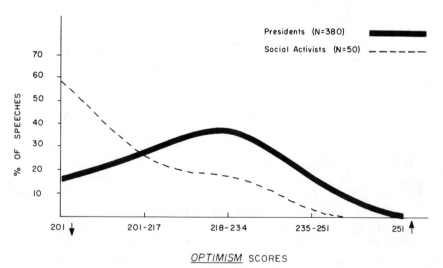

Figure 2.3 Distribution of presidents' (N = 380) and social activists' (N = 50) optimism scores. Mean for optimism for all samples was 214.2 (N = 861).

the nation's souls, so the presidents are given charge over the nation's souls as well as its bodies, or so their rhetoric would have us believe.

Presidents scored significantly higher on Human Interest ("people" words) than did the corporation executives examined. Also reflecting this institutional mandate was Lyndon Johnson, who significantly increased his use of Human Interest terms when he became president. For example, when speaking at a banquet in May of 1954, Johnson clung to the hypostatizations popular at the time: "The struggle between Communism and freedom is a many-sided struggle. It is between atheism and religion; between tyranny and justice; between disregard for the individual and regard for the individual; between a free economy and a controlled economy.[14] Nine years later, soon after the weight of the presidency had been placed upon him, Johnson evidenced the human touch expected of a leader of the American people: "So in these days the fate of this office is the fate of all of us. I would ask all Americans in reverence to think on these things. Let all who speak . . . reflect upon their responsibilities to bind our wounds, to heal our sores, to make our society well and whole for the tests ahead of us."[15] People and their needs function in presidential discourse as impersonal abstractions do in other kinds of talk. As Ronald Reagan has amply demonstrated, it is even possible for a skilled president to infuse a speech on economic matters with Human Interest, thereby reducing to human scale issues that remain gray and ethereal when discussed by other speakers in other situations.

Practicality

The presidents' high Optimism scores bespeak the presidential image commanded by American folklore—a man of the people, close to his roots, ever a panegyrist. As Carroll Arnold and Irving Kristol have observed, an American politician can hardly afford to be some affable European dandy.[16] The people of the United States are an eminently practical people, searchers after life's bottom line, a people impatient with schemes that fail or policies that frustrate. Our presidents seem to have realized these things about the persons who pay their salaries.

The single most striking institutional feature of presidential discourse was the great amount of Realism found there. (See Figure 2.1.) Even compared with such practical persons as political campaigners, social activists, and corporation executives, the presidents spoke concretely. Religious leaders, as might be expected, were far less pedestrian than the presidents.

The comparison with the political campaigners on this score is particularly interesting. Although one might reason that presidents and political campaigners are children of the same loins, the voter apparently has different psychological expectations and different rhetorical tolerances for them. Thus, when speaking about the excesses of the Nixon administration, George McGovern effortlessly climbed the ladder of abstraction: "It will take more than a new administration to restore that faith. We will need new rules, new standards and new tools. Toward that end, I am today proposing an Ethics in Government program designed to prevent abuses, and to restore the integrity of our government in the eyes of the people."[17]

Perhaps during the best of times, citizens permit such philosophizing from their presidents as well. But their chief executives rarely seem to depend upon it. If they do use abstractions, presidents typically do so in utilitarian ways. Harry Truman demonstrates that, even in ceremonial settings, the *existenz* presses upon a president: "The women of the United States have a great opportunity and a great responsibility to play the decisive part [in striving for greatness]. Women in this country won the right to vote only after a long, hard struggle. . . . And yet when the time comes to register and the opportunity comes to vote, many of our women neglect this responsibility of citizenship."[18]

But it is not just an old pragmatist like Harry Truman who speaks practically about issues that might have been treated theoretically by a George McGovern. Like Truman, Lyndon Johnson and Richard Nixon adapted their styles to the practical concerns of the White House. Nixon's Realism levels were significantly higher in his presidential speeches than in his earlier public messages; this pattern was even more pronounced for Johnson. As vice-president Richard Nixon could declaim mightily that "to secure real peace we must be strong enough to deter aggression, yet always willing to seek a world that is governed by law and moral principles."[19] As president he planted his feet securely in the world of economic opportunity: "This is a country where a young person knows that there is a peaceful way he can change what he doesn't like. . . . We have the ability to clean up the air and clean up the water and provide better jobs and better opportunity and all of these things for our people. And this is because we are so fortunate to be so rich in those things that are material."[20]

Other data (shown in Figure 2.4) reveal the presidents' respect for the nation's grass roots. Of all five classes of speech analyzed, presidential messages used the least Complexity; moreover, the presidents' speeches and those delivered by religious leaders were lowest on Variety. In other words, presidents did not speak in convoluted ways. Although there are surely many exceptions to this general rule (one is reminded of Gerald Ford's and Dwight Eisenhower's speeches), presidential language is hardly prolix.

Even a patrician like John Kennedy was able to master the required presidential vocabulary. While he was—as a former author, sometimes journalist, and Harvard graduate—more than able to turn a telling phrase, his

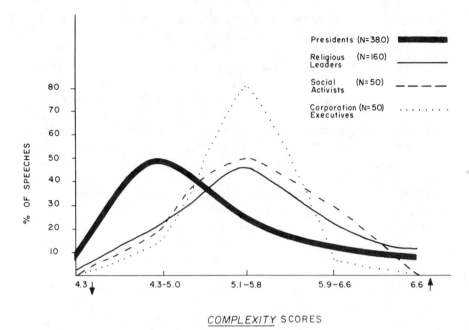

COMPLEXITY SCORES

Figure 2.4   Distribution of complexity scores for presidents and others. Mean for complexity for all samples was 5.39 (N = 861).

presidential style was highly direct and unaffected. When speaking on wages and prices, for example, he said: "These [economic] exhortations have not had a very great effect but with your help I intend to get a look at the situation before there is a crisis. I do not want the White House to have to come in at the last minute. Since we are breaking new ground, I am not sure how much we can accomplish but I do think it is extremely important that we move ahead."[21] Even Kennedy's skillful inaugural address had much less Complexity and Variety and more Familiarity than the average address made by the comparison speakers. When presidents strive for eloquence, they apparently seek a patois fit for the history books but fit, too, for their practical, contemporary hearers.

Although some might find it difficult to conceive of a florid speech by Richard Nixon being given at any time during his life, he also changed when assuming the presidency by employing less Complexity, less Variety, and more Familiarity after taking office. (See Figure 2.5.) For example, when speaking as vice-president about international commerce, Nixon remarked: "To remedy this situation [i.e., lack of agreement among nations about the international court] the administration will shortly submit to the Congress recommendations for modifying this reservation. It is our hope that by tak-

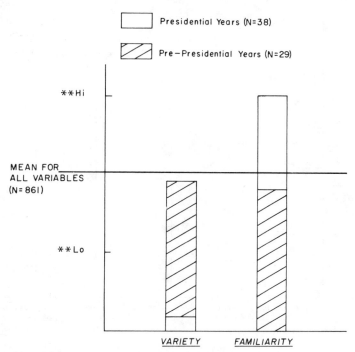

Figure 2.5 Other institutional effects on Richard Nixon. All differences significant. See Table B.3. ** ± ½ sd from mean. See Table B.1 for exact values.

ing the initiative in this way, other countries may be persuaded to accept and agree to wider jurisdiction of the international court."[22] Later, when serving as president, Nixon eschewed the involved syntax, the passive voice, and the polysyllabic words to talk about economic matters in terms understandable by the least discerning of his listeners: "This nation must dedicate itself to the ideal of helping every man who is looking for a job find a job. Today, about 96 percent of the work force is employed. We want it to be more."[23] In short, the pundits' stereotype of the presidential speech as an artless assemblage of swollen prose really misses the mark. While presidential talk can hardly be called elegant, it is, for the most part, simple and practical.

Caution

As mentioned earlier, presidential talk is quite high on Realism. Such a finding means two things—presidents are practical (which has just been discussed) and presidents are typically not ideological, as revealed in Figure

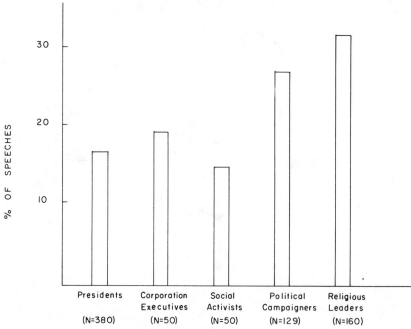

Figure 2.6   Presidential use of high certainty scores (≥ 203).

2.6. While presidents occasionally used abstractions to remove themselves from the political thicket, they seemed to know instinctively that abstractions (e.g., equality, honor) border dangerously on intense partisanship. Presidents appear to reason that issues low on Realism (like human rights) are equally as likely to stir up society's ideologues as they are to capture a favorable headline or two. Some presidents, like Harry Truman, grasped this point more quickly than did other presidents, like Jimmy Carter.

Politician and preacher alike used significantly more Certainty than did the naturally cautious presidents, as revealed in Figure 2.6. While a Lutheran pastor like Joseph Ellwanger could isolate his parishioners' basic problems with assuredness, a president must be more careful when specifying the causes of natural hubris. Thus, Ellwanger could argue definitively that "it is in Christ that we get a glimpse of what God's great plan of unity really means. It is not just a resolution about unity broadcast from heaven. It is a unity lived out here on earth by Jesus Christ."[24] Jimmy Carter, on the other hand, had to be exceedingly more circumspect when detailing (for the nation's governors) his conception of political grace: "It was particularly beneficial, I think, to the members of the Cabinet yesterday to get to know you and for you to get to know them. This is a time, I think, of restoration in our country. . . . I think this gives us all a sense of assurance about the future. I've got an awful lot to learn. And I think that you can help me with it and, perhaps, we can learn together.''[25]

While Jimmy Carter may have had a special penchant for tentativeness, his remarks point up the most attractive rhetorical option presented to the nation's chief executive: say it with as much strength as your epistemological system permits. Because presidents cannot normally claim the benefits of divine revelation, their speech reflects a caution borne of the knowledge that they deal with issues that other agencies in society were unable to resolve previously. Such is the nature of presidential politics.

Nonpresidents, on the other hand, may opt for a stronger rhetoric primarily because their audience is usually narrower and more partisan than that which listens to a sitting president. Thus, it is not surprising that Barry Goldwater's words often connoted the surety associated with hot-blooded religion. Goldwater's flaying of communism demonstrates this: ''Mark these words well. This is what the Communists really mean by 'peaceful coexistence.' They do not mean 'peace.' 'Peaceful coexistence' is simply the Communist strategy for world conquest.''[26]

A president's world, in contrast to the world of a Barry Goldwater, is more likely to be replete with uneasy military victories and elusive political solutions. Dwight Eisenhower, when announcing the Korean armistice, shows how carefully a president must tread even during moments of exultation: ''Now we strive to bring about [peaceful] wisdom, there is, in this moment of sober satisfactions, one thought that must discipline our emotions and steady our resolutions. It is this: we have won an armistice on a single battleground, not peace in the world.''[27] While such ''sober satisfactions'' hardly cause a listener's eyes to widen as Barry Goldwater's rhetorical pyrotechnics do, it was Eisenhower, not Goldwater, who would have had to answer for the excessive zeal and overweening expectations such rhetoric engenders.

Humanity, practicality, and caution are the very special sound of presidential discourse. Those who employ such speech may scheme grand schemes but they cannot remove themselves completely from the marketplace of political values. They may fulminate and exhort but they dare not become hortatory lest they, like Barry Goldwater, appear as sounding brass or, like George McGovern, appear as tinkling cymbal. They may be formal, to a point, but they are unwise to forget that the president is the nation's first citizen and, as such, generates in us expectations for direct, if not folksy, communication. From a rhetorical point of view, then, Michael Novak has somewhat misdirected us when describing America's chief executive as a combination of priest, prophet, and king,[28] for a president is more acolyte than priest, more interpreter than prophet, more prime minister than king. Buoyancy with pragmatism, clarity with prudence, simplicity with personality, these are the things out of which presidential speech is fashioned.

Presidential Style

Style might best be thought of as the complex of language habits that makes a speaker unique. To inquire into presidential style is to ask if presidents use words in such ways that interesting and repetitive patterns emerge. They do. By examining how the 11 language variables group within presidential speechmaking, and by then comparing these patterns to those produced by other spokespersons, we get a rough sense of the habits of mind that make presidential speaking distinctive. In this section, then, we are not concerned with how often a president used a particular semantic category, but with when he did so relative to other words. We shall be more concerned with the structural aspects of presidential discourse rather than with its content per se.

Presidents

For the presidential speakers, two styles emerged: (1) *a motivational style,* which used Optimism and Embellishment without Activity and (2) *a pedagogical style,* in which Symbolism was typically accompanied by Realism, Certainty, and Human Interest (but not Variety). In the first instance, presidents embroider things (as we see in Figure 2.7). They look for the sanguine interpretation whenever they can but they are careful not to link their enthusiasms to specific policies (perhaps because they have none to offer or because they fear being accused of dealing with the nation's business in a facile manner). In the second instance, it is interesting to note that absolute and concrete language is more typically used with Symbolism than with Activity. When Symbolism is used, it is apparently used to point up essential truths (hence, the low amount of Variety) and to relate such truths to human concerns. It is fine to be Realistic and Certain, our presidents appear to reason, as long as such prose enforces venerated abstractions (like "progress"). However, more concrete matters like the MX missile systems or voting rights laws demand a defter presidential touch.

Harry Truman and John Kennedy, hardly a natural duet, exemplify the *motivational style* in action. On December 24, 1949, for example, Truman provided the obligatory amount of yuletide cheer when he said, "Love has clung to this day down all the centuries from the first Christmas. There has

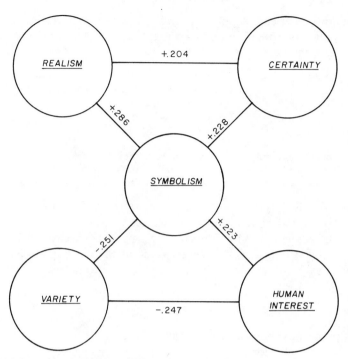

Figure 2.7 A schematic of presidents' pedagogical style (Pearson correlations for assorted variables, N = 380). For additional information, see Table B.5.

clustered around Christmas day the feeling of warmth . . . of kindness, of innocence, of love—the love of little children. . . ."[29] Fourteen years later, JFK adopted a more cerebral but complementary approach when he reflected at a college commencement: "Our national tradition of variety in higher education shows no sign of weakening. . . . We are learning to talk the language of progress and peace across the barriers of sect and creed. It seems reasonable to hope that a similar process may be taking place across the quite different barriers of higher learning."[30] Such talk was not characteristic of Kennedy's rhetoric, of course, but in employing it on this occasion Kennedy used a style that his gushier successors would have gladly adopted.

Lyndon Johnson, more than most presidents, seems to have had an instinctive feel for the *pedagogical style* (which is fitting, one supposes, for a former school-teacher). The pedagogical style requires its user to frame the nation's values in human terms and to drive home its practical implications with assurance. Johnson's salesmanship of Great Society programs typified how American Symbolism can act as a natural bridge between theory and policy (via Realism and Certainty). Johnson lectured his contemporaries as follows:

> [The Democratic] party, and the programs it has inspired and legislated and turned into action, has set a standard in the 1960's by which every administration that follows must be judged.
>   For it was we who said poverty must be abolished
> —a good education must be the birthright of every child
> —our cities must be made fit for a free people
> —the environment must be cleansed and protected for every family
> —our streets must be made safe for law-abiding citizens, and
> —basic human rights must be made real for every man and woman among us.[31]

Presidents, then, serve as sources of inspiration and wisdom, translating life's options for their fellow citizens and, at the same time, keeping their spirits from plunging. While the statistical patterns discovered here were not especially strong, they do suggest some of the duties imposed on our presidents, impositions that many of them appear to have welcomed.

Nonpresidents

The special possibilities of presidential speech are better realized when we inspect the behavior of other public speakers. The political candidates, for instance, were "optimistically passive" like their colleagues in the White House but added a great deal more Human Interest to their remarks when doing so, perhaps because they sought to prove that the rosy pictures they painted represented the will of the people incarnate. Adlai Stevenson demonstrated this when he accepted the Democratic nomination in 1952 by saying:

> You have summoned me to the highest mission within the gift of any people. I could not be more proud. Better men than I were at hand for this mighty task, and I owe to you and to them every resource of mind and of strength that I possess to make your deed today a good one for our country and our party. I am confident, too, that your selection of a candidate for vice president will strengthen me and our party immeasurably. . . .[32]

Later in that same speech, Stevenson also exemplified the forceful simplicity (demonstrated by the negative relationship between Certainty and Complexity) found in the political candidates' speech. This particular blending makes for a somewhat facile style, a style that Adlai Stevenson may not have been proud of, but a style that convention audiences clearly demand: "[I am not] afraid that the Democratic Party is old and fat and indolent. After 150 years it has been old for a long time; and it will never be indolent as long as it looks forward and not back, as long as it commands the allegiance of the young and the hopeful who dream the dreams and see the visions of a better America and a better world."[33] Unlike presidents, then, political candidates are often histrionic. They are more likely than presidents to opt for the simple, unvarnished statement and for the folksy overstatement, perhaps because the buck has obligingly stopped on another's desk.

Even more histrionic were the social activists. Their style was either assaulting (high Realism and Certainty, low Optimism) or, depending on the speaker or circumstances, ideological (high Embellishment, low Realism, Self-Reference, and Human Interest). Few social activists launched an assault with more energy than did 1960s' spokesman Stokely Carmichael: "I don't think that we should follow what many people say, that we should fight to be leaders of tomorrow. Frederick Douglass said that the youth should fight to be leaders today. God knows we need leaders today, because the men who run this country are sick."[34] When using the ideological style, the social activists spoke ex cathedra, referring neither to their personal viewpoints nor to their audiences' experiences, but confidently assuming that their listeners would tolerate the simple re-presentation of basic doctrine. Sally Gerhart, a radical feminist, provides an example of the ideological style in her attack on the established church: "The structure of the church (God over man, man over woman, father over family, clergy over laity, power over powerlessness) is vertical, hierarchical. The church's basic identity depends on that hierarchy. This identity is dependent upon standards of success and failure, on authority, on competition. It is dependent upon who has power over whom."[35]

How differently presidents speak, with their embellished optimism and their attempts to humanize the fragile understandings they share with their very heterogeneous listeners. Unlike social activism, the presidency allows few retreats to safe, internally consistent dogma. It rarely permits use of the activist's predictable belligerence or the political candidate's easy assurance. Moreover, it cannot tolerate for long a world of pure abstraction like that of religion (where Complexity and Embellishment normally prevailed over Realism, Familiarity, and Activity). Instead, the presidential pattern is more akin to the glad-handing of the corporation executive (Self-Reference, Optimism, Realism, Human Interest). Like the corporation executive, a president must peddle a product to a constituency and simultaneously make that constituency feel it received its money's worth. But unlike corporation executives, presidents can also use basic American symbols to provide the strength of conviction and goal-directedness that an accelerating sales curve provides for the corporate audience. The president, then, is the nation's first chauvinist as well as its most dependable teacher. The Constitution may not have intended for this to be so, but the chief executives since 1945 have taken on these jobs nonetheless.

Presidential Time

So far, we have considered how presidents behaved as a group. We have seen that presidents play three special roles when addressing their contemporaries and that their language choices cluster in two distinctive ways. This is not to say, of course, that there exists some sort of uniform presidential style that each chief executive adopts when moving into the White House. While our presidents have shared some communicative priorities, they have also differed from one another and they have not always been personally consistent from day to day either. These alterations help to explain how the presidency has evolved since 1945. They also tell us about the pressures brought to bear daily on our chief executives and about the prospects we might reasonably envision for the presidency during the 1980s and beyond. The presidency is no static thing. This is as true rhetorically as it has been true politically and culturally.

Changes across the Years

Consider the following unremarkable, but typical, flourish of election-year rhetoric: "Just a word about my own administration. . . . When I came into the White House about 21 months ago, we had 10 million Americans who couldn't find a full-time job. . . . [Today] we've given better services to our people, stronger defense, better highways, better education. We've tried to give what people need, because I spent two years learning what our nation hungered for."[36] Consider, secondly, a set of remarks made in similar circumstances some thirty years earlier: "And remember, if the Republicans were to come into power for the next four years, the future of American housing would be in the hands of the same men who killed the housing bill—the men who obey the lobbyists of the selfish interests."[37]

Jimmy Carter's warm braggadocio in the first passage typifies some of the major differences in presidential rhetoric occuring over the past 35 years. Carter's use of Human Interest (we, our, Americans, people), his Self-References, and his Optimism contrast sharply with the removed, negative approach used by Harry Truman, author of the second campaign speech. And the differences in these two passages are not merely attributable to the very different political personalities involved. The early modern presidents—Truman, Eisenhower, and Kennedy—used significantly less Optimism, Hu-

man Interest, and Self-Reference than did the later modern presidents—
Johnson, Nixon, Ford, and Carter. (See Figure 2.8.)

The increasing number of Self-References is particularly striking. Whether
these changes result from galloping egotism on the parts of our chief executives, or whether they reflect certain stylistic tastes we as a nation of

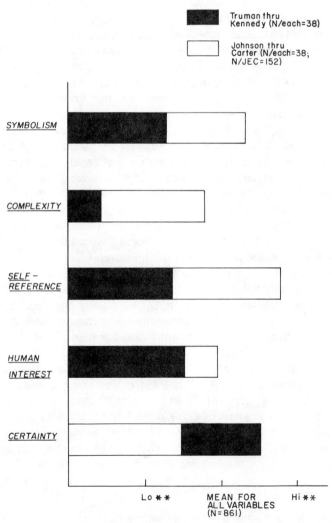

Figure 2.8 Stylistic differences between early modern and later modern presidents. All
differences significant. See Table B.6. ** ± ½ sd from mean. See Table B.1 for exact values.

listeners have developed, is hard to determine. In the absence of hard evidence on the matter, it seems most probable that the American people now have rather exact expectations for the personal performances of their presidents and that the voters now hold their leaders personally accountable for the nation's failures and successes. This interpretation is rendered more plausible when we consider the great amount of publicity Presidents Johnson through Carter have received from a voracious press corps. (One is reminded, serially, of brandished appendix scars, flabby jowls, poorly coordinated feet, and flashing teeth.) Moreover, the opinion polls now remind us, on a monthly basis at minimum, "how *he's* doing," and we are increasingly finding our presidents baring their souls and "going to the people" via the media whenever Congress is too reluctant or too impetuous for their tastes. All such developments caused our recent presidents to give special attention to the several aspects of "humanity" mentioned in the first section of this chapter.

"Caution," too, is on the rise. Our most recent presidents have employed more Complexity, less Certainty, and more Symbolism than their predecessors. In other words, Harry Truman's assertiveness has given way to Jimmy Carter's tidy moralisms. Our recent presidents have substituted equivocation for expostulation, bravado for brevity.

Such changes may have been occasioned by any number of forces including personality differences in the presidents themselves, changing rhetorical fancies of the American voters, random chance (although that seems especially unlikely), the replacement of the stump speech by the cool, televised message, or the growing complexity of domestic and international affairs (which more easily permits use of the nation's symbols than the bald-faced assertion). Whatever the reason, the presidency has been changed in rhetorical temper. The statistical magnitude of the changes is not impressive in all cases, but a general drift toward "cautious humanity" on the parts of our chief executives is clear.

In a sense, then, the rise to power of Jimmy Carter was very much in step with the presidential times. While Harry Truman may have blanched visibly had he had the opportunity to hear Jimmy Carter make the following statement in November of 1977, a statement replete with tentativeness, personalism, and optimism, the events of 1978 alone might have vindicated Carter's use of what appears to have become the new presidential approach to persuasion—a wary, wordy concoction of what is possible:

> I had a chance today to listen to the Shah explain to me the perspective of the region and the rest of the world as viewed from the great country of Iran. [Our conversation] helped me greatly to understand the special challenges that face us as a great nation and the importance of the partnership that we have with the people of Iran. . . . Iran seeks no dominion over other people. They seek no territorial gains. They just want peace,

and they have spread their influence, because of the great leadership of the Shah, very rapidly.[38]

Changes within the Administrations

If one thought about the turbulent administrations of Harry Truman, Lyndon Johnson, and Richard Nixon and then contrasted them to the comparatively placid reigns of Dwight Eisenhower, John Kennedy, and Gerald Ford, one would not expect to find consistent changes in speaking within presidential administrations. But changes there have been, and some of them have not been inconsiderable, as we see in Figure 2.9.

A major effect was observed when language usage in the first half of the seven presidents' administrations was contrasted with remarks each of them made in the second half of their administrations. Over time, Certainty increased significantly as did Complexity, but Self-Reference dropped off dramatically. Although each of these effects did not hold true for each president, each president shared some portion of the overall effect. In other words, the chief executives spoke in an increasingly forward manner as their

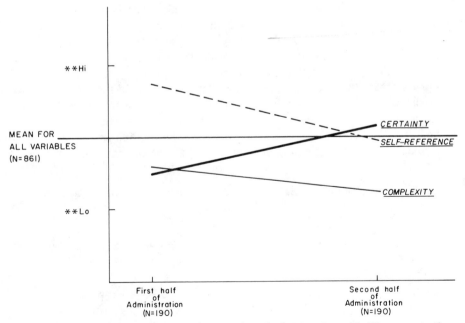

Figure 2.9 Rhetorical changes within presidential administrations. All differences significant. See Table B.6 ** ± ½ sd from mean. See Table B.1 for exact values.

presidencies unfolded; moreover, they developed an inability or an unwillingness to speak with the simplicity of their earlier days in office.

As Bruce Buchanan remarks in *The Presidential Experience,* every president undergoes stress during a tenure in office.[39] This stress, Buchanan argues, is a natural function of the deference, dissonance, and frustration that increasingly besiege the chief executive over time: the press becomes testy, if not hostile; legislation is lost in the congressional maze; voters tire of their own workaday problems and look for a convenient national scapegoat; the president's staff becomes less effective and, often, increasingly untrustworthy. As these problems mount, they affect the way a president speaks. As political life becomes complex, so the president's words must reflect that complexity. The formulation of a clear, elegant retort is now beyond the president's grasp because of the multitude of perspectives he has gathered on the problems he has faced during his days in office. The strong statement, even the overly strong statement, also develops an attraction for the president as he tires of the timorous phrase and takes pride (or seeks refuge) in his personal resolve.

Examples of such rhetorical modifications abound in the samples analyzed here. When announcing his intention to run for a second term, for example, Dwight Eisenhower exercised great care when discussing his fitness for continuing with the job: "[My medical advisors] believe that adverse effects on my health will be less in the Presidency than in any other position I might hold. They believe that because of the watchful care that doctors can and do exercise over a president, he normally runs less risk of physical difficulty than do other citizens."[40] When addressing the 1960 Republican National Convention $4\frac{1}{2}$ years later, Ike purged the tentativeness from his voice. He no longer sought to curry favor with the voters but simply to explain the state of the nation he was leaving them. Below, we hear a president speak, not a would-be candidate. Gone is the borrowed testimony and the qualified attestations. Ike knew quite well what he wanted to say:

> When this administration took office, continental United States defense was almost nonexistent. . . . In 1953, our Navy had yet to launch its first nuclear-powered ship. . . . The American space satellites, now providing answers to great scientific problems, were ignored during the previous administration.
>
> Fellow Americans: the United States today possesses a military establishment of incalculable power . . . the free world is prepared to meet any threat, and, by its retaliatory strength, to face any potential aggressor with a mighty deterrent.[41]

The changes in Eisenhower's rhetoric (changes repeated in one form or another in most of the other chief executives' remarks) suggest a persistent—maybe even necessary—institutionalization of the presidency. Such institutionalization is not surprising. Over time, the president spends more and more of his working hours with his cadre of experts than with the voters themselves—hence the growing Complexity. The president naturally sees himself as the presidency personified—hence the attractions of the "papal we" and the corresponding disuse of Self-Reference. The increasing Certainty seems irresistible, too, since to act with authority naturally leads one to talk with authority. If presidential rhetoric thereby becomes rigidified, it might well be attributed to forces native to the office, to a process of institutionalization that becomes virtually inevitable when role and person are fused over time by the white heat of politics, pressure, and publicity.

Presidential Circumstance

Common sense suggests that presidents, like all public speakers, adjust their remarks to suit the particular situations they face. Common sense does not suggest, however, the pattern of such adaptations nor does it say whether these patterns should hold true for all presidents. Moreover, common sense remains reticent about such complicating matters as the effects of television on presidents' remarks. Common sense also fails to predict how chief executives would speak during rituals and ceremonies, as opposed to legislative or crisis situations, or how speeches dealing with economic issues would differ from those focusing on international accord or domestic human rights. In short, common sense fails us just where common sense usually fails us—at the level of detail. And common sense becomes an especially unlikely ally when we try to imagine what consistent adaptations might be made by personalities as different as Harry Truman and Gerald Ford. Thus, we shall here consider the very heart of persuasion—how presidents adjust their symbols to suit their circumstances.

Topic

By examining how modern presidents addressed the three general topics discussed in Chapter One—values, pragmatics, and strife—we examine, once again, some of the distinctive "rhetorical roles" forced upon the chief executive. When discussing the value-charged subject of women's rights, for example, Gerald Ford once said: "Every American mother bears, as we all know, a great, great responsibility. . . . It is up to you to see your children take joy in living and develop strength and self-confidence. It is up to you to see that the next generation of all Americans will carry with them throughout their lives the values that has made America a great, free nation."[42] Ford here typifies the approach most presidents took when discussing values: they used a great deal of Optimism. Before dismissing such a finding as mere common sense, it is worth considering that the presidents were not significantly pessimistic when discussing strife. Moreover, it is not hard to imagine that such values as equality, freedom, justice, and honor could have been discussed in very negative ways if left in nonpresidential hands (say, for example, in the hands of a social activist).

Presidents, however, characteristically seek the silver lining, exhorting the nation to follow through on its basic mission. (See Figure 2.10.) An interesting thing about the value-based speeches is that only 1 of the 11 variables (Optimism) produced a significant effect for all presidents. America being America, it perhaps could not have been otherwise. While it is not hard to imagine all presidents lionizing the nation's values, it becomes more difficult to imagine them taking a universally forceful stand on such values, or being consistently specific and personal when discussing them. Values are a varied and a volatile commodity, especially in contemporary times and especially in the United States of America, and thus seem to dictate no single rhetorical approach.

The presidents were equally individualistic when speaking on pragmatic topics. While a major effect was found for Self-Reference and Embellishment, none of the other variables behaved consistently. This is somewhat

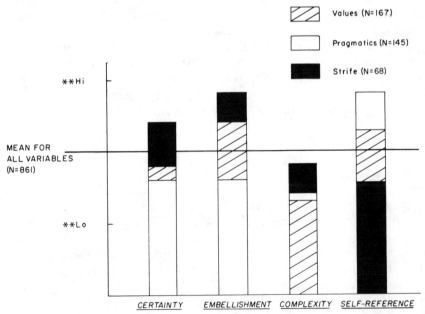

Figure 2.10 Topical differences in presidential speechmaking. Several differences significant. See Table B.9 ** ± ½ sd from mean. See Table B.1 for exact values.

explained by the very different issues these very different presidents addressed—Truman on MacArthur, Eisenhower on labor crime, Kennedy on Southern integration, Ford on inflation, Carter on energy. The only approach the presidents agreed upon was to keep embroidery to a minimum and to highlight their own experiences in their discussions. The presidents seemed to reason that they were their own best allies on legislative issues and that a personal but direct style would best predict success in the congressional go-rounds. Thus, even in his lame-duck State of the Union speech delivered in 1969, Lyndon Johnson followed the personal, unembellished tradition: "In 1967 I recommended to Congress a fair and impartial random selection system for the draft. I submit it again tonight for your most respectful consideration. I know that all of these commitments I talk about will cost money. And if we retain the strong rate of growth that we have had in this country in the past eight years, I think we shall generate the resources that we need to meet these commitments."[43]

On matters of strife, the presidents seemed of one mind: be firm, be formal, be florid. Here, the chief executives were high on Certainty, Embellishment, and Complexity, but low on Self-Reference. The infrequent use of Self-Reference may mean that stressful situations encourage presidents to hearken to constitutionally determined mandates. They stand with the office in such circumstances, lest the nation's enemies look for a chink in their personal armor or lest their domestic critics accuse them of personal derring-do. In short, the *president* speaks when the chips are down. An example: when articulating his Pacific Doctrine, Gerald Ford, after a typically warm (and personal) introduction to his University of Hawaii audience, launched into the meat of his remarks by replacing "I's" with "We's." "But we did find a common ground. We reaffirmed that we share very important areas of concern and agreement. They say and we say that the countries of Asia should be free to develop in a world where there is mutual respect for the sovereignty and territorial integrity of all states. . . . We share opposition to any form of hegemony in Asia or in any other part of the world."[44]

That strife produces Certainty in presidential speech is to be expected. Even John Kennedy sensed the need for meeting force with force, and he minced few words when discussing his arms quarantine of Cuba in October of 1962: "Aggressive conduct, if allowed to go unchecked and unchallenged, ultimately leads to war. This nation is opposed to war. We are also true to our word. Our unswerving objective, therefore, must be to prevent the use of these missiles against this or any other country; and to secure withdrawal or elimination from the Western Hemisphere."[45]

Presumably, Kennedy and the other presidents added Embellishment to their remarks during stressful circumstances in order to heighten the gravity of the situations they described. In addition, since strife-generated speeches often serve as the nation's formal reply to some major exigence, the presidents dotted every "i" and crossed every "t" when framing their responses. Thus, Harry Truman's "warning to Japan" of August 1945 was especially high on Complexity, as he took pains to detail the then-emerging plans for dividing Europe after World War II.[46] While Truman justifiably prided himself on his spare, efficient vocabulary, redrawing the world's map placed special demands even on him. Truman, like the other presidents, often followed his own course when speaking but he, like them, was aware of the institutional, temporal, and topical realities of presidential discourse as well.

Medium

Radio and television have changed how our presidents talk. The president in our living rooms bears only partial resemblance to the president speaking in the courthouse square. This may seem natural. A "live" audience places on-going demands upon a speaker whereas the studio-bound orator must follow his script, fervently hoping that his distant listeners' feelings correspond to those predicted by his speechwriters prior to air-time. Local audiences permit targeted appeals and spontaneous adaptations. When a president speaks on television, however, and even when a president speaks on television in the presence of a live audience (as in a State of the Union situation), the president must invent a self befitting the added formality of his electronic circumstances. Because presidents now request national air time so frequently and because those requests are so generously granted, the televised speech may best tell us where our presidency is tending and why it is going there.

Television gives us a one-dimensional presidency. It presents our presidents to us in their Sunday best but without their souls or feelings. Consider, for example, the following Richard Nixon—a Richard Nixon who was seen and heard by only a few hundred elderly citizens on Thanksgiving Day in the White House, a spontaneous Richard Nixon, even an awkwardly fulsome Richard Nixon, but one that few of us would recognize as a presidential Richard Nixon:

> We were trying to think on this Thanksgiving Day what group we could invite to be with us. In our family we always had Thanksgiving as a family day. We have in the past, and we do now.
>
> Our parents cannot be here now, but we wanted people who have been with this nation for so many years, who have lived good lives, to be here as our guests today. . . . Incidentally, right now I invite you back to the White House on your 100th birthday, right here. You are going to be here.[47]

There is little reason for most citizens to recognize this Richard Nixon; he rarely visited them at home. The at-home Nixon was a controlled, detached, ever-precise person, didactic or argumentative depending upon his political circumstances: "The time has come to lay the record of our secret negotiations [with the North Vietnamese] on the table. Just as secret negotiations can sometimes break a public deadlock, public disclosure may help to break a secret deadlock. Some Americans, who believed what the North Vietnamese led them to believe, have charged that the United States has not pursued negotiations intensively. As the record that I now disclose will show, just the opposite is true."[48]

Nixon's adaptations to the mass media are representative of presidents generally. Even though the televised speeches in the presidential sample embraced the same topics as the "live" speeches, several major differences were noted, as can be seen in Figure 2.11. When their remarks were being broadcast, the presidents used less Self-Reference, Familiarity, Human Interest, and Optimism than in live settings. In other words, the presidents spoke in a direct, personal manner to their *live* audiences, being careful to use common parlance and to inject enthusiasm. Television, on the other hand, demanded a "cooler" image (according to the late Marshall McLuhan).[49] Television intrudes upon presidential speech, just as it intrudes upon the youngster in the Sears' store who becomes suddenly, and comically, serious when performing in front of the videotape demonstration camera. Television sucks in the presidential gut, causing him to stand unnaturally tall and firm so that his words are not treated casually or regarded in haste by listeners. Television tolerates none of the gaucheries to which a president can fall victim on the hustings. Televised talk must be fit for all comers, clever domestic reporters and foreign heads of state alike.

In addition, because televised speech is the presidential form we contemporaries know best, it sets our expectations for presidential performances in general. When a president speaks on camera in a personal, familiar, and humane way, as Jimmy Carter did when discussing Bert Lance's resignation, the television audience is tempted to balk at such sentimentality. Thus, some of the American people became suspicious of Jimmy Carter early in his administration. A president who says under the klieg lights that "Bert Lance is my friend. I know him personally, as well as if he was my own brother. I know him without any doubt in my mind or heart to be a good and honorable man,"[50] can also cause us to fidget on our sofas at home in the presence of a chief executive turned chief confrere. In contrast, local audiences, whether they be Detroit Republicans listening to Richard Nixon, broadcasting executives convening with Lyndon Johnson, or the citizens of Acton, Massachusetts, in a town meeting with Jimmy Carter, expect as much communicative directness from their president as they would from

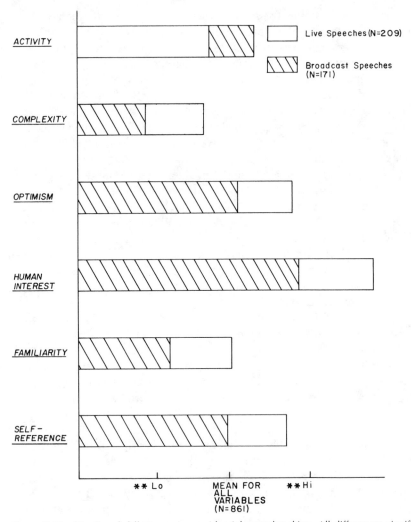

Figure 2.11 Situational differences in presidential speechmaking. All differences significant. See Table B.9. **±½ sd from mean. See Table B.1 for exact values.

any local resident. The findings here also suggest that television is often thought of as a medium ideally suited to presenting a dynamic message in the simplest manner possible. Television, in short, is a sales medium. When used by Presidents Truman through Carter, it caused them to increase their verbal Activity and to markedly decrease their Complexity. Television is a perfect showcase for an energetic story well told. Because even a John Kennedy is little more than a "talking head" when performing on a thoroughly visual medium, the media direct a president to invest his speech with suitably grand schemes of progress, persistence, and accomplishment. On television, action words predominate. Lyndon Johnson demonstrates: "We shall *continue* on a sensible course of fiscal and budgetary policy that we believe will keep our economy *growing* without new inflationary *spirals;* that will finance responsibly the needs of our men in Vietnam and the *progress* of our people at home; that will support a significant *movement* in our export surplus, and will *press forward* toward easier credit and toward lower interest rates" (emphasis added).[51] To make a balance sheet come alive in this manner is no small feat, but it is a constant challenge for a president in an electronic age.

Television tells a simpler story, too. Richard Nixon had a special ability to fit his remarks to the vernacular of television. One can choose almost any of Nixon's televised addresses and find the same simple syntax, the avoidance of imbedded phrases, the artless (but communicative) chaining together of short clauses, the uncomplicated vocabulary. Although his first speech in office was less personal than his last, both speeches were pellucid:

> With these [efforts], we can build a great cathedral of the spirit, each of us raising it one stone at a time, as he reaches out to his neighbor. Helping, caring, doing. I do not offer a life of uninspiring ease. I do not call for a life of grim sacrifice. I ask you to join in a high adventure, one as rich as humanity itself, and exciting as the times we live in.[52]

And somewhat later:

> These [five and a half] years have been a momentous time in the history of our nation and the world. They have been a time of achievement, of which we can all be proud. Achievements that represent the shared efforts of the administration, the congress, and the people. But the challenges ahead are equally great.[53]

The electronic media have multiple effects on presidential discourse. They simplify the message, invigorate it, but make it less uplifting and less personal than do local circumstances. It is somewhat difficult to tell which of these two styles—the mediated or the nonmediated—is the more natural language of the presidency. "Local talk" is quite clearly political talk—glib, folksy, happy. But as we have seen earlier, presidential politics is a special kind of politics. Because this is true, television and radio become a kind of rhetorical launching pad from which legislation and human hopes are sent aloft. But it is worth wondering whether the verbal energy demanded in televised messages sends policies aloft too quickly or whether the president misses something important, as person and as leader, by spending so much time speaking to red lights, teleprompters, and hushed, admiring aides.

Setting

So far, we have been talking about presidential speeches as if they were all of a type. Clearly, they are variegated, ranging from formal to casual and from politicized to pedagogical. As numerous authors have suggested, the generic "rules" surrounding certain public speeches make them somewhat standardized, regardless of the speakers' idiosyncracies.[54] Naturally, speakers are sometimes ignorant of such rules. At other times, they may ignore these rules intentionally, choosing to be guided only by the inspiration of the moment or by their own sense of appropriateness. Being cautious by nature, however, presidents are more likely to produce speech-by-formula than to risk appearing unseemly.

Five classic presidential speaking situations were selected for special examination: (1) political rallies, (2) inaugural festivities, (3) States of the Union presentations, (4) college commencements, and (5) award ceremonies. These speech situations account for roughly 20% of the speeches collected here and they were fairly evenly distributed across the seven presidents examined.

The statistical differences were modest but suggestive. (See Figure 2.12.) When speaking during political rallies, presidents made an unusually high number of Self-References and employed less Variety than in any other speaking situation. Such rallies also produced the most Realism and least Embellishment found, but these effects were not as pronounced. Political rallies provide a welcome respite from the pressures of the job, allow a president to relax in the presence of friends and admirers, and enable him to speak in a candid manner. Such situations normally place the president— as person—on center stage and often permit more levity than do the presidents' more staid (and more numerous) public encounters. John Kennedy's speech on the day after his inauguration is a good case in point: "I am delighted that John Bailey is going to take over this job [as Democratic National Committee Chairperson]. He is more popular today than he will be at any time in his life. I will feel that he is doing a good job when you all say, 'Well, Kennedy is all right, but Bailey is the one who is really making the mistakes.' "[55]

Inaugural situations enticed greater Certainty and Human Interest from the presidents but caused them to use few Self-References and relatively little Familiarity. A president's first speech appears to be his most predictable in many ways. It presents him with an opportunity to pound his fist on the national podium. Also, the modern inaugural has attached to it certain rhetorical encrustations. The president speaks not for himself but for his people; he uses cadences reserved for majestic moments; he borrows his lexicon from his predecessors. Even the plain-spoken Richard Nixon

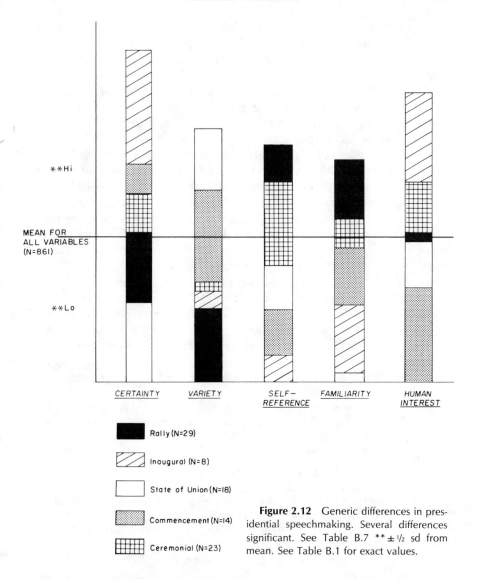

Figure 2.12 Generic differences in presidential speechmaking. Several differences significant. See Table B.7 ** ± ½ sd from mean. See Table B.1 for exact values.

sought to wax eloquent in his first inaugural address. While preparing for this long-awaited occasion, he assembled and read many previous inaugurals. Although his resulting speech was surely not grand, it did have its moments: "The American dream does not come to those who fall asleep. But we are approaching the limits of what government alone can do. Our greatest need now is to reach beyond government, to enlist the legions of the concerned and the committed. What has to be done, has to be done by government and people together or it will not be done at all."[56]

If the inaugural address constitutes the president's major chance to operate in the grand style, the State of the Union brings the president back to earth. Such speeches have much less Certainty and Familiarity than any other speech type and employ the greatest amount of Variety as well. In the State of the Union, the president is no longer afforded the easy cordiality of his political cronies nor can he promise all things to all people (as when taking his oath of office). Gone also is the possibility of speaking vox populi, for he now must address the intricacies of price support systems, super-hardened missile silos, and federal entitlement programs. The State of the Union produces few flights of rhetorical fancy. It is technical, wordy, and very often displays options instead of wholeheartedly advocating them.

This all becomes necessary because the political process initiated by the State of the Union address will be fraught with compromise and mind-numbing debates between expert witnesses of all stripes. The president knows that the states of his union are no more unified today than they were at the time of the founding fathers. Thus, he can only gently beseech and patiently explain and thus try to create the bargaining room necessary during the months ahead. In the following passage, Dwight Eisenhower gives evidence of all these rhetorical constraints as he describes the formation of a committee which will study the nation's economic health. In his remarks, Eisenhower's *coulds* and *shoulds* signal his constrained circumstances:

> The new committee would be concerned, among other things, with the better living standards of our people, their health and education, their better assurance of life and liberty and their greater opportunities. It would also be concerned with methods to meet such goals and what levels of government—Local, State, or Federal, might or should be particularly concerned. . . .
> Such studies would be helpful, I believe, to government at all levels and to all individuals. The goals so established could help us see our current problems in perspective. . . . Prices have displayed a welcome stability in recent months and, if we are wise and resolute, we will not tolerate inflation in the years to come. But history makes clear the risks inherent in any failure to deal firmly with the basic causes of inflation. Two of the most important of these causes are the wage-price spiral and continued deficit spending.[57]

The State of the Union addresses display the workaday president; like the rally speeches and inaugural orations, they have a fair number of built-in rhetorical procedures. Such is not the case with college commencements and award ceremonies. Individual presidents handle these speaking situations in their own ways. No consistent persuasive features characterized them. Instead, commencements and ceremonials give the presidents rhetorical license and the presidents often seek out these occasions because of that. Thus, we found Lyndon Johnson making news at Johns Hopkins University in search of his silent majority, and Jimmy Carter trying to regain his grip on the presidency before the midshipmen of the U.S. Naval Academy. On each occasion, political news was made because rhetorical permissiveness was allowed. American University and Ohio State allowed John Kennedy and Gerald Ford, respectively, to make politically important statements also. Because speech type, topic, and medium of presentation often create complex institutional demands for our presidents, such special moments of rhetorical freedom must be jealously guarded indeed.

Conclusion

How does our presidency look now that we have listened to it? What statements can be made about the institution based on the rhetorical descriptions just presented? For one thing, it appears that the presidency is more than the president himself. The office changes the person; Richard Nixon and Lyndon Johnson are but two examples. Presidents' long-standing rhetorical habits are reshaped by the duties of office as they grapple with the intricacies of governing the American people. In some ways, the average president resembled corporation executives, but he resembled the clergymen, too, the amalgation being not quite gray flanneled but not quite roman collared either. Rather, upon assuming the presidency the president submits to a special kind of rhetorical discipline not imposed upon those merely running for office. The differences between the presidents and the political candidates were striking, suggesting that the presidency is a sobering institution. Although they were not uniform on this matter, the presidents were significantly more cautious than their (unsuccessful) political rivals. The presidents resorted to abstractions less frequently also. Thus, while the presidency does have its rhetorical liberties, it apparently does not allow the easy generalities found on the campaign trail.

The rhetorical patterns also indicate that the presidency reflects the character of the American people. Despite its occasional pomp and circumstance, the presidency is still a damned informal monarchy. The American people have consistently demanded a "folksy" president who can keep their indomitable spirits indomitable. In addition, the American people have never been fond of standoffish politicians like Adlai Stevenson or doomsayers like Barry Goldwater. The American people have also retained from their history some antiintellectualism and hence demand a full measure of practical talk from their presidents. The presidents have obliged the American people in these ways and more, fashioning for themselves a role constructed of equal parts education and inspiration.

Other facts gathered here suggest that the presidency is changing. The three early presidents spoke somewhat differently than their successors in office. Presidential talk has become less simple of late and less authoritative as well. Clear-cut verities have been sacrificed for people-centered chatter replete with basic American symbolism. Evermore, presidential talk looks like some sort of rhetorical sideshow rather than the political center ring itself. Whether this is good or bad depends upon what one wants from the presidency. Jimmy Carter may have sounded less like a leader than an altar boy but at least his rhetoric did not retain the jingoism that propelled the United States into international conflict so frequently during its history. "That may well be," a conservative might reply, "but a president who doesn't sound like a leader places the nation in jeopardy." Perhaps only time will sort out these political, and rhetorical, priorities.

Clearly, the presidency is potentially seductive. The rhetorical modifications made by the presidents during their administrations were often striking. Most of them became more sure of themselves and more technical as time went on; this was true even of the comparatively short-lived presidencies of Gerald Ford and Jimmy Carter. Institutions, even presidential institutions, rigidify. The pressures of the job being what they are, it becomes increasingly easy to justify the simplistic overstatement. A parallel finding was the decline in Self-Reference during the average presidency. Depending upon one's perspective, this finding is either heartening or ominous. It could mean that presidents become less self-centered as their jobs unfold by addressing themselves more and more to genuinely national mandates. Less optimistically, it may mean that an experienced president begins to feel that his will and the nation's are isomorphic, that he has become America incarnate. Such an interpretation gives new meaning to the anecdote often told about Lyndon Johnson who, upon being corrected for heading to the wrong military transport by an erstwhile young aide, turned and said, "Son, they're all my planes."

It has become a truism that television changes everything it touches—it causes fans to bemoan the lack of instant replays at live football contests, it provides work for actors who fail to find work in the legitimate theatre, and it modifies the products we buy, the faces we recognize, and perhaps even the goals to which we aspire. It seems clear that the presidency has been changed by television as well. By and large, the president's televised addresses were much more formal than their local remarks (a finding that cannot be attributed to differences in topic). The personal stamp, the uncomplicated vocabulary, and the human touch are removed from presidential speech by television, the rolled-up sleeves replaced by the regimental tie. This, too, may be a good sign, for it may suggest that the presidency has finally come of age and that it no longer constitutes the bumptious frenzy it did during, say, Ulysses S. Grant's administration.

Television may also have changed the type of president we are likely to get in the future. The political spellbinder of years past seems an albatross in a mediated age. The great convention halls with their bad acoustics, places that only an old pol like Hubert Humphrey could fill with emotion, are being replaced by television studios with mauve carpeting. The contrast between Teddy Kennedy and Jimmy Carter during the 1980 Democratic race was particularly striking in this regard. Kennedy personified the old oratorical tradition in politics and Carter the new, mediated one. Kennedy moved the conventioneers to tears in New York while Carter entoned the careful words of a professional conversationalist. Kennedy, on the other hand, badly botched an innocent enough interview with television commentator Roger Mudd while Carter thrived in such controlled rhetorical settings. In some ways, it may have been television, rather than Democrats, that selected their candidate in 1980.

Despite television, or perhaps because of it, we will continue to have presidents. These presidents will continue to talk to us and we will continue to judge their matter and manner, embracing some, disdaining others. As we judge, we will consult certain feelings we have about the institution of the presidency itself, trying to decide how we know a good president when we see one. My guess is that we will be remembering rhetorical instances when so doing, using as an electoral template things we have learned from experience about "presidential" talk.

Institutionally based features of the presidency do exist; they are observable, and they affect what a president does and how he thinks. Yet, significant though they are, institutional forces are always played off against personal forces. Presidents are people, after all, and until we study them as people we can understand them neither as people nor as keepers of their institution. The remainder of this book, consequently, is devoted to precisely such inquiries.

Notes

1. William Spracher, "Some Reflections on Improving the Study of the Presidency," *Presidential Studies Quarterly,* 9 (1979), pp. 71–80.

2. See, for example, Erwin C. Hargrove, *The Power of the Modern Presidency* (New York: Knopf, 1974) and the more recent book by Godfrey Hodgson, *All Things to All Men: The False Promise of the Modern American Presidency* (New York: Simon and Schuster, 1980).

3. A brief, but classic, statement on these matters is that by Thomas Cronin, "The Text-

book Presidency and Political Science," in Stanley Bach and George T. Sulzner, eds., *Perspectives on the Presidency* (Lexington, MA: Heath, 1974).

4. See, for example, Michael Grossman and Francis Rourke, "The Media and the Presidency: An exchange Analysis," *Political Science Quarterly*, 91 (1976), pp. 455–470, and the more global consideration contained in Michael Grossman and Martha Kumar, *Portraying the President: The White House and the News Media* (Baltimore: Johns Hopkins University Press, 1981).

5. One limited, but interesting, attempt to answer questions of this order is the essay by Sonja K. Foss, "Abandonment of Genus: The Evolution of Political Rhetoric," *Central States Speech Journal*, 33 (1982), pp. 367–378.

6. Clinton Rossiter, *The American Presidency* (New York: Harcourt, 1960).

7. Some of the more interesting perspectives on this matter are surveyed in Bruce Buchanan, *The Presidential Experience: What the Office Does to the Man* (Englewood Cliffs, NJ: Prentice-Hall, 1975).

8. See Thomas Cronin, *The State of the Presidency* (Boston: Little-Brown, 1975).

9. "The State of the Union," January 19, 1976, *Weekly Compilations of Presidential Documents*, 12:4 (1976), pp. 47, 48.

10. "Address at the 10th District Rally," August 24, 1960, Special files, Box #4, Lyndon Baines Johnson Presidential Library, Austin, Texas, p. 4.

11. "Remarks at Party Rally in Chicago," May 17, 1966, *Weekly Compilations of Presidential Documents*, 2:20 (1966), p. 659.

12. "Second Inaugural Address," January 20, 1973, *Public Papers of the Presidents, 1973* (Washington, D.C.: U.S. Government Printing Office, 1974), p. 14.

13. Paul Erlich, "Eco-Catastrophe!" June 9, 1970, reprinted in Karlyn K. Campbell, ed., *Critiques of Contemporary Rhetoric* (Belmont, CA: Wadsworth, 1972), pp. 342–343.

14. "Address at Senior Banquet, Texas A & M University," May 15, 1954, Special files, Box #2, Lyndon Baines Johnson Presidential Library, Austin, Texas, p. 2.

15. "Our System of Government," November 28, 1963, *Vital Speeches of the Day*, 30:5 (1963), p. 132.

16. Carroll C. Arnold, "Reflections on American Public Discourse," *Central States Speech Journal*, 28 (1977), pp. 73–85 and Irving Kristol, *On the Democratic Idea in America* (New York: Harper, 1972).

17. "Government Corruption," October 13, 1972, in *An American Journey: The Presidential Campaign Speeches of George McGovern* (New York: Random House, 1974), p. 71.

18. "The Moral Force of Women," October 8, 1947, *Vital Speeches of the Day*, 14:1 (1947), p. 24.

19. "A Blunt Challenge to our Free World," November 24, 1957, *Vital Speeches of the Day*, 24 (1957), p. 131.

20. "Remarks at Billy Graham's Crusade," May 28, 1970, *Public Papers of the Presidents, 1970*, p. 468.

21. "Address to Labor-Management Committee," March 21, 1961, *Public Papers of the Presidents, 1961*, p. 201.

22. "The Rule of Law for Nations," April 13, 1959, *Vital Speeches of the Day*, 25:14 (1959), p. 422.

23. "Address on the Cost of Living," October 17, 1969, *Public Papers of the Presidents, 1969*, p. 810.

24. Joseph Ellwanger, "God's Plan," 1963, in Alfred T. Davies, ed., *The Pulpit Speaks on Race* (New York: Abingdon, 1965), p. 46.

25. "Remarks to National Governor's Conference," March 1, 1977, *Weekly Compilations of Presidential Documents*, 13:10 (1977), p. 279.

26. "Foreign Policy," October 21, 1964, *Vital Speeches of the Day,* 31:2 (1964), p. 37.

27. "The Korean Armistice," July 26, 1973, *Vital Speeches of the Day,* 19:21 (1953), p. 642.

28. Michael Novak, *Choosing our King: Powerful Symbols in Presidential Politics* (New York: Macmillan, 1974).

29. "The Love of our Fellow Man," December 24, 1949, *Vital Speeches of the Day,* 16:6 (1949), p. 162.

30. "Address at Boston College," April 20, 1963, *Public Papers of the Presidents, 1963,* p. 336.

31. "Remarks to Democratic Fundraising Dinner," October 7, 1967, *Weekly Compilations of Presidential Documents,* 3:41 (1967), p. 1417.

32. "Nomination Acceptance," July 26, 1952, *Vital Speeches of the Day,* 8:21 (1952), p. 645.

33. "Nomination Acceptance," (1952), p. 646.

34. Stokely Carmichael, "Black Power," November 1966, in Charles W. Lomas, ed., *The Agitator in American Society* (Englewood Cliffs, NJ: Prentice-Hall, 1968), p. 142.

35. Sally Gerhart, "The Lesbian and God-the-Father," February, 1972, in Herbert Simons, *Persuasion: Understanding, Practice, and Analysis* (Reading, MA: Addison-Wesley, 1976), p. 341.

36. "Remarks at Greater Buffalo Airport," October 28, 1978, *Weekly Compilations of Presidential Documents,* 14:44 (1978), p. 1885.

37. "The Democratic Record," September 20, 1948, *Vital Speeches of the Day,* 14:24 (1948), p. 739.

38. "Remarks During the Shah's Visit," November 15, 1977, *Weekly Compilations of Presidential Documents,* 13:47 (1977), pp. 1784-5.

39. Buchanan (1975).

40. "Candidacy Announcement," February 29, 1956, *Vital Speeches of the Day,* 22:11 (1956), p. 323.

41. "America's Goal," July 26, 1960, *Vital Speeches of the Day,* 26:21 (1960), p. 653.

42. "Remarks to American Mothers Committee," May 5, 1976, *Weekly Compilations of Presidential Documents,* 12:19 (1976), p. 825.

43. "The State of the Union," January 14, 1969, *Vital Speeches of the Day,* 35:8 (1969), p. 229.

44. "Pacific Doctrine," December 7, 1975, *Weekly Compilations of Presidential Documents,* 11:50 (1975), p. 1356.

45. "Arms Quarantine of Cuba," October 22, 1962, *Vital Speeches of the Day,* 29:3 (1962), p. 67.

46. "Warning to Japan," August 9, 1945, *Vital Speeches of the Day,* 11:21 (1945), pp. 642-645.

47. "Remarks at a Thanksgiving Day Dinner," November 27, 1969, *Public Papers of the Presidents, 1969,* pp. 971-2.

48. "Peace in Vietnam," January 25, 1972, *Public Papers of the Presidents, 1972,* p. 102.

49. See, for example, Marshall McLuhan, *Understanding Media: The Extensions of Man* (New York: Signet, 1964).

50. "President's News Conference," September 21, 1977, *Weekly Compilations of Presidential Documents,* 13:39 (1977), p. 1390.

51. "State of the Union," January 10, 1967, *Vital Speeches of the Day,* 33:8 (1967), p. 230.

52. "First Inaugural Address," January 20, 1969, *Public Papers of the Presidents, 1969,* p. 3.

53. "Speech of Resignation," August 8, 1974, *Public Papers of the Presidents, 1974*, p. 628.

54. For a more complete discussion of such matters, see Karlyn Campbell and Kathleen Jamieson, eds., *Form and Genre: Shaping Rhetorical Action* (Falls Church, VA: Speech Communication Association, 1978).

55. "Remarks to Democratic National Committee," January 21, 1961, *Public Papers of the Presidents, 1961*, p. 4.

56. "First Inaugural Address" (1969), January 20, 1969, *Public Papers of the Presidents, 1969*, p. 2.

57. "State of the Union," January 9, 1959, *Vital Speeches of the Day*, 25:8 (1959), p. 233.

SPEECH UNDER PROTEST: THE CASE OF TRUMAN AND EISENHOWER

Hermes, the god of eloquence, smiled neither on Harry S Truman nor Dwight David Eisenhower, yet both managed to sustain enviable political careers. Truman worshipped at the shrine of Hephaestus—the god of the forge—with his sense of public duty, hard work, and plebeian virtue. Ares, the fearsome god of war, watched over the career of General "Ike" Eisenhower—West Point graduate, Chief of Staff of the United States Army, protégé of George Marshall, and a man whose political strength lay in his being the most recognizable GI in the United States. Thomas S. Dewey and Adlai Stevenson, devotees of Hermes, were not able to translate the siren song into political advantage. Although Harry Truman's style was bumptious, and Dwight Eisenhower's clumsy, they managed to talk their ways to success and thereby revealed the practical limits of eloquence in American politics.

In analyzing the oratory of Truman and Eisenhower, we are therefore analyzing the art form in its most primitive incarnation. Harry Truman's first public speech was delivered in Lee's Summit, Missouri. The prospect of public performance substantially unnerved this voluble conversationalist: "I was so scared I couldn't say a word. So I just got off the platform."[1] The very same person who later gave some 300 speeches as he criss-crossed the American countryside at the rear of a Pullman train was able to say, upon leaving the presidency, that "I have never had any talent for public speaking. Whatever I have learned about speechmaking I have learned the hard way. My first speech was a complete failure. It took a lot of appearances after that before I felt at home on the platform and could put my ideas across the way I wanted."[2]

Unlike his predecessor in the presidency, Truman showed little interest in the speech preparation process. According to Samuel Rosenman, an aide to both FDR and Truman, the latter "did not contribute twenty percent of what Roosevelt did to speeches. I'm talking now about language only rather than thought . . . his participation in the actual phraseology was slight."[3] Although he was a voracious reader (especially of American history), and although he possessed a remarkably good vocabulary for one who had no higher education, Truman's interest in the purely verbal aspects of speech-making was slight. As one commentator observed, and as we shall see later, Truman's "goal in choosing words was accuracy, not ornateness. Short speeches, short sentences, and short words"[4] were his trademarks. This same president who believed that "a leader is one who can persuade people to do what they don't want to do and like it"[5] and who "seized every opportunity he could to get out into the country to make speeches, attend conventions, cut ribbons,"[6] apparently did so out of an iron-willed sense of duty, not because of the pleasures accompanying speechmaking.

Dwight Eisenhower, in contrast, was a literary craftsman, or, at least, a literary journeyman. Unlike Truman, he read comparatively little, but found much pleasure in writing (typically, in a sprightly, journalistic style). He was perhaps the White House's only resident grammarian, a person who would sometimes puzzle longer over the advisability of splitting an infinitive than over the ideas to which his infinitives were subordinate. Critics sneered superciliously at Eisenhower's "West Point English . . . . His style was sometimes stilted, but his grammar was nearly impeccable."[7] Upon leaving the presidency, Eisenhower wrote a great deal (for a former president), authoring both substantive memoirs as well as several light remembrances.

While the solitude of the writing process brought him much pleasure, the emotional and physical immediacy of speechmaking left Eisenhower cold. Pressed to give a televised address, Ike would bellow, "I keep telling you fellows I don't like to do this sort of thing. I can think of nothing more boring, for the American public, than to have to sit in their living rooms for a whole half hour looking at my face on their television screens."[8] Paradoxically, although Eisenhower had an instinct for public relations, he passionately resisted the public platform. James David Barber expands on this point:

> Furthermore, he did not want to get into traditional political speechmaking: "I don't think the people *want* to be listening to a Roosevelt, sounding as if he were one of the Apostles, or the partisan yipping of a Truman." Asked to make a speech, he would respond with irritation: "What is it that needs to be said? I am not going out there to

listen to my tongue clatter!" Sometimes he would agree reluctantly: "Well all right, but not over twenty minutes."[9]

Despite a natural disinclination toward public speaking, both Truman and Eisenhower succeeded where more talented speakers failed. Despite his public infelicities, perhaps even because of them, Truman's political jawjutting earned him the respect of his contemporaries. Eisenhower's malapropisms made him seem especially warm and avuncular. As this chapter will reveal, Truman's speaking style was rough and unmistakable, coarse by many people's standards, and yet his basic appreciation for the human contact afforded by speechmaking allowed him to maximize his modest talents. A 5-year evaluation of the Truman presidency presented by *U.S. News and World Report* found that "Mr. Truman's mind approaches problems as do the minds of many politicians who think in terms of people rather than in terms of administration. It is a mind that remembers like an elephant's when people are at stake."[10] Similarly, Dwight Eisenhower, a man who was once called "a sort of Roosevelt in reverse,"[11] seemed incapable of talking himself out of the hearts of the American people. "This man," said Barber, "who had little use for inspirational blather, whose speeches would not be long remembered for their eloquence, and who continually resisted demands that he lecture his fellow citizens, revitalized national confidence almost in spite of himself. He is a puzzling case. *His* political habits never stressed rhetoric, yet that is where he excelled."[12]

Despite their kindred attitudes toward public speaking, Truman and Eisenhower differed considerably in behavior. Whereas Truman gave 'em hell, Eisenhower gave 'em heaven.[13] Whereas Truman was "the backwoods Baptist laying down a personal treatment of God and Mammon," Ike was "the high priest, whose utterances contain less fire and more theology."[14] Whereas Eisenhower was "smooth in human relationships, able to say the right thing in an innocuous way," Truman could become "scrappy and irritable and pointed."[15]

This chapter will, by and large, document empirically these oft-observed features. In so doing it will perhaps shed light on the mutual antagonism harbored by Truman and Eisenhower. Although they pursued very different careers, Truman and Eisenhower confronted each other more often than either would have preferred. And they nettled one another on quite a few occasions: when Eisenhower refused to run on the Democratic ticket in 1948, when Truman fired MacArthur, when Eisenhower declared in 1952 that he would never ride down Pennsylvania Avenue with his predecessor, when Truman proclaimed his Fair Deal, and when Eisenhower ostensibly refused to take a phone call from ex-President Truman in October of 1953.[16] In these ways and more they jousted. But their contrasting public styles may have been more alienating than any single personal slight. As we examine these contrasting styles in detail, we will be reminded once again how personal relationships—between presidents, and between presidents and their constitutents—are molded by the talk they share and appreciate or share and fail to appreciatre.

The Truman Style

If the DICTION program failed to find Harry Truman's speech to be (1) pragmatic, (2) absolute, and (3) slightly sentimental, it would be a sorry research tool indeed. Everyone, it seems, knew these things about the Truman Style. Certainly Winston Churchill knew them when describing Truman's "simple and direct methods of speech"[17] and elsewhere when declaring that Truman "takes no notice of delicate ground, he just plants his foot firmly on it."[18] But it did not take an early twentieth-century Prime Minister or a later twentieth-century computer to discover these features in Truman. The American people found them too. And because they were Americans they liked what they heard. They still do. Merle Miller's oral biography of Truman, *Plain Speaking,* was a resounding publishing success. Gerald Ford, Jimmy Carter, and even Ronald Reagan have expressed admiration for Harry Truman's candor and have compared themselves to him. The Trumanesque style, because it springs directly from the populist tradition, reads as refreshingly in the 1980s as it was listened to in the 1940s. If the nation's citizens ever see fit to erect a national Rhetorical Museum, Harry Truman will be the prime exhibit in the American Gothic wing and the turnstiles there will whir.

Pragmatism

On April 25, 1945, just 13 days after taking the oath of office in the presence of Eleanor Roosevelt, Harry Truman broadcast a speech to the United Nations Conference on International Organization, then meeting in San Francisco. Perhaps because he was such a newly minted chief executive, or perhaps because a war-ravaged world needed an especially inspiring address, Truman waxed almost eloquent as he spoke of "the bitter wrath of generations yet unborn" who would hold his listeners in contempt if they continued "to sacrifice the flower of youth merely to check madmen, those who in every age plan world domination." Truman rhapsodized about proceeding "with humility and determination," of "harmonious cooperation" among the member nations of United Nations, of "Divine Guidance," of a "mighty united effort," of a "powerful mandate from our people."[19]

The style here is closer to hortatory discourse, and was not typical of Harry Truman. While he and his speechwriters could rise to meet such occasions, he (and presumably they) did so reluctantly.

Compared to his successors in office, Harry Truman was exceptionally high on Familiarity, not disposed to using Variety, and he reduced the Complexity of his remarks significantly as his tenure in office unfolded. (See Figure 3.1.) In other words, his U.N. speech was uncharacteristically strained for the occasion. With precious few exceptions, Truman used the plainest of plain-speaking. His Familiarity and Variety scores held remarkably constant across the many different topics he addressed, across the range of audiences he faced, and from the beginning to the end of his administration. Harry Truman, whose style was marked by stout verbs and slender adjectives, spoke as he was taught to speak.

One of Truman's aides, Charles G. Ross, a classmate of Truman's at Independence High, Phi Beta Kappa at the University of Missouri, journalist for the *St. Louis Post-Dispatch,* and later press secretary to President Truman, was also the author of *The Writing of News,* a textbook for students in college reporting and editing courses. In that book, Ross provided

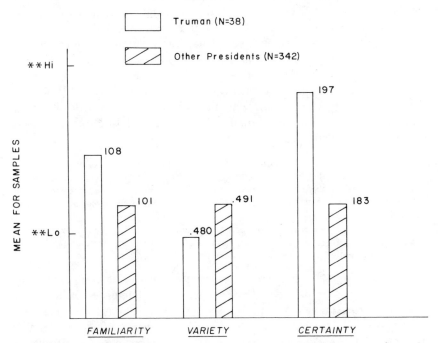

Figure 3.1 Dominant features of Harry Truman's style. All differences significant. See Table B.8. ** ± ½ sd from mean. See Table B.1 for exact values.

the sort of syntactical advice which made him ideally suited to be Truman's assistant. In his primer, Ross advised, "Don't overwork 'very.' Through abuse the word has lost much, if not all, of its force. 'He's a very good man,' as spoken, usually gives the idea that he is only passably good. 'He's a good man,' is stronger. Be sparing in the use of superlatives."[20] Truman was an unashamed devotee of Ross's imperative, and his speeches were remarkably neat and clean as a consequence. According to Robert Underhill in *The Truman Persuasions,* Truman's writers were instructed to "depolish" the President's speeches, to excise "flowery language that was not in keeping with Truman's everyday oral practices."[21] The result was that Harry Truman did for hearing what Norman Rockwell did for seeing:

> Now, do you know how Congress has broadened the base of Social Security? They've just taken 750,000 people off Social Security and sent me a bill to that effect and tied a rider onto it increasing the old-age assistance, hoping I'd take that bait and let them get away with tearing up Social Security. I didn't do it. I vetoed the bill this morning. I've told Congress that if they would pass the bill in the proper form I'd be happy to sign it, and they have plenty of time to pass it in the proper form—don't think they haven't.[22]

One interesting finding was that Complexity and Variety were not highly correlated for Truman, even though they were highly correlated for *all* of his successors in office. (See Table B.10 in Appendix B.) In other words, even on those occasions when a somewhat "grander" (i.e., more diversified) style was customary, Truman refused to alter his basic vocabulary. To his way of thinking, gracefulness could be achieved by simply taking familiar words and arranging them in more stately cadences. By playing with the structure rather than with the substance of his style, Truman achieved eloquence of an ideational rather than a linguistic sort. A speech on human rights delivered in June of 1947 exemplifies:

> Many of our people still suffer the indignity of insult, the harrowing fear of intimidation, and, I regret to say, the threat of physical injury and mob violence. The prejudice and intolerance in which these evils are rooted still exist. The conscience of our nation, and the legal machinery which enforces it, have not yet secured to each citizen full freedom from fear.
>   We cannot wait another decade or another generation to remedy these evils. We must work, as never before, to cure them now. The aftermath of war and the desire to keep faith with our nation's historic principles makes the need a pressing one.[23]

Truman's pragmatic style emanates from an interesting communication theory. It seems to hold that: (1) ideas enlighten, language confuses; (2) education is the equivalent of persuasion; (3) a politician is not a preacher. Truman himself testified on behalf of such notions: "[When speaking] I just stood there, and I didn't have to make any fancy speeches or put on any powder or paint. I just told people the facts, and the people believed me."[24] On another occasion, Truman opined:

> The thing I could never understand about the fella that ran on the Democratic ticket in 1952 [Stevenson], he always spent a lot more time worrying about *how* he was going to say something than he did on *what* he was going to say. I told him once, I said, "Adlai, if you're telling people the truth, you don't have to worry about your prose. People will get the idea."
>
> He never did learn that, though. He was a very smart fellow, but there were some things he just never got through his head, and one of them was how to talk to people.[25]

"Listeners have to feel a bond with the speaker," said Truman many years after his presidency, "they aren't likely to if they feel he is a 'high-hat' or 'show-off.' "[26] Many people felt that Adlai Stevenson was a show-off. Linguistically they were right. Fully 85% of the speeches in the Stevenson subsample exceeded the Truman average for Variety. Stevenson searched hard for effect and his labors were more often rewarded with applause than with votes. Truman, in contrast, suffered from a kind of verbophobia, the sense that artistic expression was the by-product of confused thinking.[27] Truman's Spartan communication theory refused to acknowledge rhetoric's validity as an agent for quickening a listener's pulse. As one columnist observed, the people could understand Truman's speeches but there was "no lift of the spirit in them."[28] "Truman lacked the wheedling appeal," commented historian Victor Albjerg, and he also lacked "the flattering witchery, the insinuating threat and the commanding voice of his immediate predecessor."[29] Athenians like Franklin Roosevelt and Adlai Stevenson, on the other hand, conceived of persuasion as an affair of the heart as well as the mind. At times, almost despite themselves, audiences wish to hear the merest of nothings said well. When their backs are to the wall, they will often opt for a fanciful myth or a challenging vision. Truman understood these things about listeners, but he did not respect such feelings nor think it proper to placate listeners in these ways.

In his book, *The Truman Presidency,* Cabell Phillips seizes upon just this point when trying to explain why Truman lost popular support toward the end of his presidency. Phillips writes:

> Why did President Truman lose the confidence of the country in the closing months of his term? . . . There were several reasons. In perspective, two stand out.
>
> One was that Harry Truman did not have the capacity—the magnetism, charm, charisma, or whatever that ineluctable quality is—for strong personal leadership. He was liked, he was admired, he evoked steadfast loyalty in many, but he could not inspire. People gave him their hands but not their hearts. He could make them laugh, but he could not make them cry. He was a plain man with honesty and guts ("Give-'em-hell-

Harry"), but you couldn't picture him in gleaming armor astride a white horse. The public is a fickle lover at best, and in Truman's case that love was never more than skin deep. When the jealous tongue-waggers got busy on him, there was not much reserve to hold the romance together.[30]

Were he confronted with Phillips's claim, Truman would presumably inform Phillips that if a country needed prettier speech as its guide or a play-actor in the White House to look up to and admire, it was a sorry country indeed and it should find another boy.

Absolutism

It is equally plausible that Mr. Truman would tell Mr. Phillips to go straight to hell. Harry Truman's speeches were the most rigid speeches delivered from 1600 Pennsylvania Avenue in the last 36 years. Truman's Certainty scores were significantly higher than all other presidents. (See, again, Figure 3.1.) Twenty-eight of his 38 speeches were above the presidential average for that variable; 12 of Truman's speeches were virtually off the scale on Certainty. In addition, Truman almost never varied his style on the 10 other language dimensions, suggesting that he took pride in being the same sort of speaker from one moment to the next. Over time, only one variable (Complexity) changed significantly and that change only served to heighten his sense of assuredness (i.e., he became plainer). There were negligible changes in his style from topic to topic and from audience to audience. In short, Harry Truman bespoke himself in precisely the way his self decided it should be bespoken and did not alter to fit the circumstances. When reading Truman's most rigid remarks, then, one senses that one is reading the essential Truman:

When Relieving MacArthur

We have taught the enemy a lesson. He has found out that aggression is not cheap or easy. Moreover, men all over the world who want to remain free have been given new courage and new hope. They know that the champions of freedom can stand up and fight and that they will stand up and fight.[31]

Repealing the Taft-Hartley Act

All the oratory in the world won't change a bad law into a good law. . . . When the Taft-Hartley Act was before the Congress, a Republican Senator called it "a device for making unions so weak they cannot carry on effective collective bargaining." That was true then, and it is true now. . . . The Taft-Hartley Act is an insult to the working men and women of this country and they will not rest until it is destroyed.[32]

On the Korean Conflict

If I understand this country correctly, there is no desire to backtrack on the path we have taken toward peace. There is no intention of running out on the obligation we undertook to support the principles of the Charter. We made our decision, it was the right decision, we are going to follow it out—and that is that.[33]

The Pleasures of Capitalism

Business was never so productive, vital, and energetic as it is today. All this talk about weakening private enterprise is sheer political bunk.[34]

Anecdotal evidence suggests that Truman's impromptu remarks were even firmer than his formal speechmaking. Truman's controversial secretary of state, Dean Acheson, commented that during press conferences "President Truman's mind is not so quick as his tongue. He could not wait for the end of a question before answering it. Not seeing where he was being led, he fell into traps."[35] Unlike some speakers who save their resoluteness for gratuitous pieties or for uncontestable abstractions, Truman simply put down his head and came charging on all fronts. No other president's Realism and Certainty scores were as highly correlated as Truman's. (See Table B.10.) He was not just firm. He was firm and clear about what he was being firm about. Realism, a concentration on the practical realities of the moment, becomes hyper-realism when conjoined with Certainty. Apparently, "Truman seemed convinced that he could prove a case if only he had enough facts"[36] and this simple rhetorical credo guided him throughout his political career.

Reflecting some years later on this aspect of Truman's style, George Elsey, a Truman speechwriter, felt guilty "that there is little or nothing that may be termed eloquence in many of the most important pronouncements of the Truman administration."[37] In addition to the pedestrian language he helped to write, Elsey was also bothered retrospectively by Truman's absolutism: "Language that is too terse or too direct and unequivocal may close the door to negotiation or accommodation of conflicting views. A little ambiguity in political matters, domestic and foreign alike, can be useful."[38] Another observer suggests that Truman's assured style contributed to the political losses he suffered during his second term in office.[39] In many ways, it is even questionable whether Truman can rightfully be called a *political* speaker. James David Barber offers what would surely constitute a strange epitaph for a machine-bred leader: "He never mastered the politician's rhetorical talent for dissembling."[40]

Had he been given the choice, Truman might have offered his own epitaph in contradistinction to Barber's: "I was either for something or against it and you always knew which it was." At times, nonetheless, this tendency got the better of Truman as when he single-handedly prepared the text of a speech (a later version of which was delivered on May 24, 1946) that castigated the railway unions for pre-emptive strikes. Sensing a national emergency, Truman penned a sulfurous draft that rocked his advisors,

Charles Ross and Clark Clifford. With relatively little time to spare, Clifford managed to take the sting out of Truman's message. The sanitized speech rated only 188 on Certainty, 9 points lower than the Truman average. While on this one occasion Truman was saved from himself, he typically called them as he saw them. In 1960 he once addressed an audience in San Antonio and ventured the opinion that any Texan who voted for Richard Nixon "ought to go to hell." Although his advisors were unable to check Truman's straightforwardness in this instance, he was chagrined to report later that "the madam . . . had heard his speech on television and said flatly to him, 'If you can't talk politer than that in public, you come right home!'"[41]

Naturally, every downside has an upside. It is arguable that Truman's brand of absolutism won him reelection in 1948. It is also arguable that his unequivocal public posture permitted him to compromise in the private arena from a position of strength. In Phillip Dolce's terms, it is possible that "giving 'em hell" described the form rather than the substance of the Truman presidency.[42]

Sentimentality

There was a kind of emotional transparency to Harry Truman. As we see in Figure 3.2, Truman's Optimism scores ranged widely, suggesting that his public remarks were a kind of emotional barometer of his presidency. His "Warning to Japan" of August 9, 1945, his speech on wartime wages and prices that was given 2 months later, and his September 1, 1950, remarks on the Korean conflict all bespeak a president pressed by the sober realities of his day. But Figure 3.2 reveals the sharp upswings in temperament, too. His inaugural address, for example, was decidedly upbeat: "We have beaten back despair and defeatism. We have saved a number of countries from losing their liberty. Hundreds of millions of people all over the world now agree with us, that we need not have war—that we can have peace. The initiative is ours."[43]

While many other presidents (most of those studied here) were able to make strategic use of Optimism, Truman's timing was especially good. Between October 8, 1947, and March 8, 1949, Truman was unusually enthusiastic. Seven of the nine speeches from this time period were exceptionally high on Optimism, most of them rating 20 points above the Truman average for that variable. Other findings indicate that Truman's speeches were significantly higher on Optimism and significantly lower on Complexity than those of his political rival, Governor Thomas Dewey of New York. These data may shed new light on Truman's famed reelection campaign in which he castigated the "do-nothing Eightieth Congress" from Somerset to Sioux

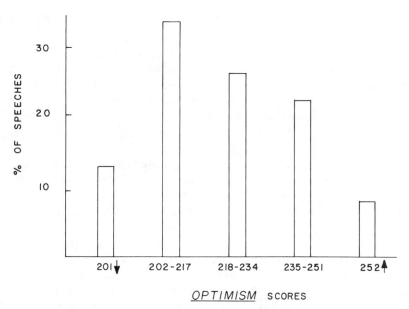

OPTIMISM SCORES

Figure 3.2 Range of optimism scores for Harry Truman (N = 38).

City to Sausalito. It may not have been Truman's feistiness alone that wooed the voters. He also painted a picture of a better tomorrow. It may have been *this* Harry Truman that the citizens of Denver voted for on election day. When speaking to them a few weeks earlier, Truman combined three of his surest touches—his practicality, his assuredness, and his vibrancy:

> The Democratic Administration won its fight for conservation and for Western development against the bitter opposition of Wall Street. You of the West see the results in bigger and better crops; in new industries; in the growing national parks and forests and the tourists who visit them; in the rising standards of living in the peoples of the West, and in the stronger economy of the whole nation.[44]

Tom Dewey was no Cassandra, but his comparative inability to tell a simple, up-beat story may have given the edge to the incumbent. Speaking of Truman's optimism, Howard Gosnell observes, "[Truman] always hoped for the best. In running for renomination as U.S. Senator from Missouri in 1940, the press, his friends, and the opposition counted him out in advance. But Truman refused to think negatively and put together a winning combination. The same thing happened in 1948 when he ran for president in his own right. Some psychologists claim that such optimism is formed at a very early stage in the individual's development. It is called *oral optimism* since it develops as a fixation at the infant sucking age."[45] One can only imagine how Truman would have responded to such an elaborate explanation of himself.

Several other findings get to the core of what has been labeled "sentimentality" here. Figure 3.3 shows an unusually strong set of relationships among certain language variables. Taken collectively, they point up the most attractive features of the Truman style: humanity, positivity, clarity, patriotism. It was his combination of these traits that allowed him to succeed. He was able to link human concerns to a better future and thereby escape the image of a glad-hander. When using Symbolism, he was somehow able to avoid the tiresome negativity of, say, a Joe McCarthy. Another statistical test (see Table B.9) indicated that Truman used especially heavy doses of Symbolism and Optimism when speaking about Values, a natural finding, one would suppose, but a finding which does not apply to any of the other presidents.

Somehow, Truman engaged in puffery without appearing unctuous. Johnathan Daniels describes Truman well when he asserts, "He is both the product and the embodiment of the American faith which is set up more clearly now than ever as a faith for the world. He speaks that faith in the language of his countrymen."[46] Not to mention his countrywomen. When addressing the women of America in October of 1947, Truman presented a straightforward homily on the nation's essential goodness:

> As a nation we stand now on the threshold of a wonderful opportunity, unique in history. We are a thriving country. The facts of our high employment and our great farm and industrial production speak for themselves. We are a strong and peace-loving nation.
>
> The United States, more than any other nation, is in a position to give reality to the four freedoms. The United States should and can be the first nation in which the people—all the people—are free from want and free from fear, free to speak and to write as their hearts dictate, and free to worship as they will.

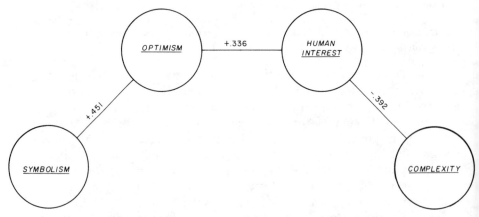

Figure 3.3 Harry Truman's sentimental style (Pearson correlations for selected variables, N = 38). For additional information, see Table B.10.

This is no idle dream. It is a goal well within the power of this mighty nation of ours to achieve.[47]

In many senses, Harry Truman was an old-fashioned orator. Table 3.1 indicates that he typically used a much higher proportion of "axiological symbols" (e.g., peace, freedom, democracy) than did his presidential successors. These latter individuals were much more heavily dependent upon "designative symbols" (e.g., America, country, government) than was Mr. Truman. In this way, Truman seems more closely connected to the ideational fabric of the American creed than to its institutional manifestations. That is, Truman wore his and his nation's emotions on his sleeve. Thus, Barber labels Truman correctly when he calls him an "active-positive" president, a person who "did not become embittered and morally exhausted," who understood that "decisiveness meant . . . a way of making up his mind how he felt about a matter, a way of confronting it directly and choosing what he wanted," who could use Symbolism, Optimism, Certainty, and Familiarity with a "free-will and an open heart."[48]

The computerized probes made here have not discovered an essentially new Harry Truman. Rather, they have provided the fine brush strokes necessary to bring into sharper relief the self-portrait his words etched in the minds of his contemporaries. When Truman's speeches are regarded panoramically, as they have been here, they summarize both his rhetorical and his political approach to the presidency. Jimmy Carter may have envied Harry Truman, but because he could not talk like Truman, he could not govern like him either (as we shall see in Chapters Six and Seven).

The Eisenhower Style

Some commentators might well object to use of a phrase like "the Eisenhower style" by charging that Eisenhower had none. The charge seems fair, for one is hard pressed to recite a single ringing phrase from the Ei-

TABLE 3.1

HARRY TRUMAN'S USE OF AMERICAN SYMBOLOGY

Type of symbol	% Used in speechmaking	
	Truman[a]	Other presidents[b]
Designative	46.2	71.4
Axiological	53.8	28.6

[a]Total symbols used = 171 ($\bar{x}$ = 4.5).
[b]Total symbols used = 1034 ($\bar{x}$ = 4.5).

senhower rhetorical corpus or to isolate a single speech that changed the tide. Eisenhower, good soldier that he was, valiantly manned the nation's public platforms when required to do so, but it was always his presence and style, rather than the words themselves, that made his audience crane their necks. The people liked Ike. Ike's words did little for them.

The Style

The findings gathered here amply support the popular, usually negative, evaluations of the Eisenhower style. He generated the highest Variety score of any of the presidents from Truman to Carter. He also had the lowest Realism score, indicating a strong preference for abstraction. His Familiarity score was the second lowest in the presidential sample. (See Figure 3.4.) Eisenhower was a wordy, fuzzy, somewhat arcane speaker who inspired people despite his best efforts not to do so.

It was probably Eisenhower's high Variety scores that caused him to suffer at the hands of the nation's pundits. One of these pundits once composed a parody of the typical Eisenhower speech, imagining him delivering the Gettysburg Address. Examining the parody carefully, one notes that the humor derives from the cornucopia of words that became standard in an Eisenhower speech:

> I haven't checked these figures but 87 years ago, I think it was, a number of individuals organized a governmental set-up here in this country, I believe it covered certain Eastern areas, with this idea they were following up based on a sort of national independence arrangement and the program that every individual is just as good as every other individual. Well, now, of course, we are dealing with this big difference of opinion, you might almost call it a civil disturbance, although I don't like to appear to take sides or name any individuals, and the point is naturally to check up, by actual experience in the field, to see whether any governmental set-up with a basis like the one I was mentioning has any validity and find out whether that dedication by those early individuals will pay off in lasting values and things of that kind.[49]

This parody, and the many others that appeared during the Eisenhower years, naturally irked a president who thought of himself as something of a stylist. But the greatest share of umbrage was taken by his speechwriters, particularly, by Arthur Larson: "Before anyone makes fun of the alleged garbled syntax of Eisenhower's answers [during press conferences] as liberally reported syllable by syllable in the papers, let him just once read an equally literal stenographic transcript of something he himself has said. . . . Let him watch in utter astonishment the unfinished sentences, the dangling clauses, the unattached phrases that fill the page."[50]

Larson's defense is, of course, a sound one, especially when one thinks of the awkwardness likely to beset a speaker during a heated and extem-

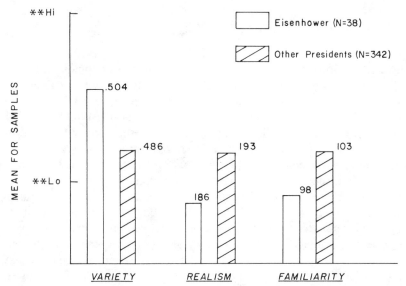

Figure 3.4   Dominant features of Dwight Eisenhower's style. All differences significant. See Table B.8. ** ± ½ sd from mean. See Table B.1 for exact values.

poraneous exchange like a press conference. But the Eisenhower sample used here consisted solely of his prepared remarks, remarks over which Larson, Bryce Harlow, Kevin McCann, and the other White House writers labored carefully on behalf of Mr. Eisenhower. He, they, or some unidentified muse conspired to make the digression and the imbedded clause standard stylistic procedures. It was not an impromptu Dwight Eisenhower who extolled the virtues of public service to the graduates of Notre Dame in June of 1960, but a man equipped with a script (and his reading glasses). Despite these conveniences, Ike combined Variety with Realism and precious little Familiarity to produce the following mélange:

> We ought not to make it inordinately difficult for a man to undertake a public post and then to return to his own vocation. In the government, one must obviously have no special end to serve, but citizens should not, invariably, be required to divest themselves of investments accumulated over a lifetime in order to qualify for public service.
>
> The basic question is this—is such divestment necessary to remove any likelihood that the probity and objectivity of his governmental decisions will be affected? And that question is proper and ethical whether the individual holds either elective or appointive office. We need to review carefully the conflict-of-interest restrictions which have often prohibited the entry into government of men and women who had much to offer their country.
>
> But let me return to the more broadly based consideration; that thinking Americans in all walks of life must constantly add to their own knowledge and help build a more

enlightened electorate and public opinion. For herein lies the success of all government policy and action in a free society.[51]

Of the 10 paragraphs analyzed for this particular speech, 4 consist of only one (obviously long) sentence. Of the 20 sentences contained in these 10 paragraphs, only 2 are simple and only a handful use the active voice. And the speech is not unrepresentative of Mr. Eisenhower's usual practice. Although it is the second highest speech on Variety (his 1960 State of the Union address was both Ike's highest as well as the highest for all presidents), Eisenhower produced four even more abstract addresses and a full dozen containing even less Familiarity. Sonorous is the word that most aptly captures the Eisenhower approach to speechmaking.

Eisenhower's penchant for abstraction can be dramatized by contrasting him to other political speakers. Adlai Stevenson, for example, was always considered the better speaker. Stevenson was a genuine stylist whose voice was a beguiling invitation to listen and learn. For a writer like John Steinbeck, there was no contest between the two: "Eisenhower seems to have lost the ability to take any kind of stand on any subject. . . . Eisenhower's speeches have become more formless and mixed up and uncertain. We have seen in a pitiful few months the Eisenhower mind crumble into uncertainty, retire into generalities, fumble into friendships and juggle alliances."[52] Stevenson, in contrast, was thought to be a model of clarity by Steinbeck: "[He] has touched no political, economic, or moral subject on which he has not taken a clear and open stand even to the point of bearding selfish groups to their faces."[53]

Steinbeck was quite right: Ike used significantly less Realism than Stevenson and significantly more Complexity (see Table B.11). One could choose almost at random from among Stevenson's speeches and find ample supplies of lucidity on any topic, before any audience:

While our cars have grown longer, our television screens broader, our washing machines grander, our kitchens brighter, at the same time our schools have grown more dilapidated, our roads more crowded, our cities more stagnant, our suburbs more messy, our air more fetid, our water more scarce, and the whole public framework on which our private living depends more shabby and worn out.[54]

Our efforts [toward peace] will be erratic, and the world will remain a dangerous place to live. But we have our wits and our resources; we have the United Nations in which to pool them for peace-keeping and nation-building; we have the beginnings of a habit of cooperation on a good many kinds of problems.[55]

Despite such genuine eloquence, the American voters cast their ballots on two separate occasions for Mr. Stevenson's verbally unrealistic and complex opponent. That, of course, has always been one of the greater mysteries of modern politics. How could a silk purse consistently lose to a sow's ear? Perhaps it is because silk purses have a faintly European aura to them, a wordiness bordering (in many American's eyes) on affectation. Sows are domesticated, and, although they are ugly, they are dependable and not at all stupid. "Ike's very bumbling appears to have made him more 'sincere,' to use one of the favorite qualities of the 1950's,"[56] said one political scientist. Such an ability carried over to the new medium of television as well, even though Ike's mediated speeches contained even less Realism than those he delivered to live audiences. Nothing, it seems, could stop him: "President Eisenhower has what counted on television. As often as he was exposed to this medium, he never failed to convey an impression of honesty, sincerity, and reliability. Indeed, the fact that his delivery was not very facile, and his style not much endowed with the devices relied on by orators, added to this wholesome impression."[57]

Judged by the dictates of English composition or public speaking textbooks, Ike did almost nothing right. In his *Rhetoric,* Aristotle isolated three virtues to be prized by the public speaker, virtues that modern researchers have since designated competence (knowledge of one's subject), similarity (between speaker and audience), and dynamism (a sense of energy). Aristotle suggested that these qualities can be built into a speech by a speaker, given proper training and sufficient skill, but Aristotle was wise enough also to mention that listeners themselves sometimes permit a speaker to forego such labors because of their good feelings about the speaker. Ike depended upon his listeners a great deal.

The amount of this dependence can be seen (in Table B.10) in three totally singular statistical relationships. For Eisenhower, (1) Variety and Activity were negatively correlated (when he became wordy, his prose slowed to a crawl); (2) Familiarity and Embellishment were also negatively correlated (when searching for special linguistic effect, Eisenhower forgot about his listeners' native vocabularies); and (3) except when employing Symbolism, Mr. Eisenhower tended to find little use for either Realism or Certainty. By making such semantic choices, Ike ran the risk of violating all three of Aristotle's dicta, thereby throwing himself on the mercy of the people's rhetorical court. Generally, the people obliged Ike, or at least enough of them did to ensure his continuity in the White House. They did so despite his speeches' inspecific images, their stultifying lack of momentum, their technical vocabulary, and their lack of well-wrought examples. To put it unkindly, Dwight Eisenhower talked like a Republican:

Still, the world has moved on from the Nineteen Thirties: good times have supplanted depression; new techniques for checking serious recession have been learned and tested and a whole array of problems has sprung up. But their obsession with the depression still blinds many of our opponents to the insistent demands of today. . . .

The party of the young and all ages says: Let us quit fighting those battles of the past and let us turn our attention to these problems of the present and future, on which the long-term well-being of our people so urgently depends. . . .

Republicans have proved that it is possible for a government to have a warm, sensitive concern for the everyday needs of people, while steering clear of the paternalistic "big-brother-is-watching-you" kind of interference. The individual—and especially the idealistic young person—has no faith in a tight Federal monopoly on problem-solving. He seeks and deserves opportunity for himself and every other person who is burning to participate in putting right the wrongs of the world.[58]

One wonders what "good times" are being referred to here, what "new techniques" will solve our problems, or what "battles of the past" must not be refought. More importantly, one wonders how the "everyday needs of people" will be met, or whose ox will be gored when the "insistent demands of today" are made less insistent. While these things may cause contemporary Americans to wonder, Mr. Eisenhower's listeners at the 1956 Republican National Convention were probably more than willing to fill in the requisite blanks and to allow his voice and physical presence to excite them, rather than his trite phraseology.

Mr. Eisenhower never changed. No statistically significant differences were observed for any of the language variables over time. Curious though Ike's speech formula may have seemed, it was a formula, it did work, and it was not materially altered. Not only did he remain constant during his 8 years in the White House, but it is also possible that he never talked much differently. Columnist Merriam Smith reports, for example, that while Eisenhower "made numerous public addresses during his army career and as president of Columbia University . . . his style tended to be somewhat formal and wooden. His sentence structure frequently was complicated and hard to follow."[59] It may well be the case that Eisenhower's writers wrote doggedly for the slightly reticent, "aw-shucks" fellow the American people lionized during the Second World War. Although it would be slightly reductionistic to claim that the American people received rhetorically what they had asked for politically—a general, not a statesman, a political general, not a warrior—it is true that Americans of the 1950s were a fairly sober lot themselves and that their president seemed to match them stride for emotional stride.

The Reasons

Dwight Eisenhower's public speaking style is one of the best remembered aspects of his presidency. It has been explained with scorn and it has been explained with fondness. The explanations themselves become part of the Eisenhower record for, as is so often the case, it seems that how one reacted to Ike's speaking was intimately related to what one wanted from a president and a presidency. These explanations run the gamut from the psychological to the philosophical and thus constitute an interesting cultural footnote to American political history.

THE INTELLECTUAL EXPLANATION

According to some of Mr. Eisenhower's most ardent supporters, his opaque style has been seriously misunderstood. He did not have a confused mind, such commentators say; in fact, he had a first-rate intellect: "The President nevertheless took great care not to reply impulsively. Precision, not style, was his concern. A perfectionist with the written word, he also tried to edit as he spoke."[60] According to one of Ike's head speechwriters, the president's Variety scores resulted from a quick, not a slow mind: "When President Eisenhower would set out to answer a question fraught with possible explosive consequences, he might in his answer start down one verbal path and then, no doubt reminding himself of some possible impact on this or that interest or country, he would backtrack and take a somewhat different turning."[61] This explanation may shed light on some underappreciated features of our thirty-fourth president, but it does not explain why a John Kennedy, for example, used few such disfluencies when speaking to the press or why Eisenhower's prepared remarks were just as obtuse as his spontaneous ones.

THE MACHIAVELLIAN EXPLANATION

This explanation takes respect for Eisenhower's mind a step further and holds that his characteristic abstractness was a deliberate attempt to confuse his listeners. One of Ike's speechwriters, Kevin McCann, is said to have affirmed "the necessity of generalities in speeches: details change from day to day, even minute to minute; a writer must rise to assertions that the passage of time will not invalidate."[62] Another observer contends that Eisenhower resorted to circumlocutions especially when sensitive matters of foreign policy were being discussed.[63] According to still another source, Ike was actually adept at press conferences and that "one time when a tricky question was anticipated, his press secretary, Hagerty, was concerned. Ike told him not to worry—that he, the president, would just confuse the reporters."[64] Indeed he did—frequently, persistently. It strains credulity, however, to think that a man of unquestionably modest intellect could have expected to out-shrewd the sharpies in the press corps in this way.

THE SITUATIONAL EXPLANATION

Mr. Eisenhower's more objective defenders admit that he had trouble communicating in public settings. Robert Donovan, who wrote the first "inside story" of the Eisenhower White House, argued that there was "nothing taciturn about the President in company. He loves to talk and laugh. Once he gets started he can talk for hours. He prefers the concrete to the abstract."[65] Such an explanation implies that only when Ike ascended a public platform did he ascend the ladder of abstraction. Merriam Smith reports that some of Ike's better speeches were delivered from outline, not from text, and thereby took advantage of his natural, direct sense of communication. When Ike used an outline on one occasion, says Smith, "the net effect was a sort of compelling informality far to be preferred by speaker and listener alike than the dull spectacle of an alleged orator grinding his way through a fully prepared text."[66] Ike's address of April 5, 1954, on the topic of national destiny is said to have been prepared and delivered in precisely this way.[67] My results indicate that the speech was remarkably high on Realism and Human Interest and low on Complexity. Thus, the situational explanation may have some validity, although it is probably not sufficiently powerful to account for the myriad unclear things Dwight Eisenhower said from time to time. As Robert Sickels notes, even Eisenhower's "unrehearsed language was an inimitable mixture of moral fervor and plain confusion."[68]

THE THEORETICAL EXPLANATION

Whether they know it or not, most presidents (and most people for that matter) have theories of communication, notions about how listeners are best persuaded. Eisenhower's theory of communication was word-centered. That is, he believed that effective speech preparation lay in the editing, not in the creating. Typically, he would not involve himself in the early stages of speechwriting but would wait until it was time for line-by-line changes. "I'm afraid to look at my speech after it's gone to the President,"[69] confessed one writer. "He [Eisenhower] could never have a ghostwriter," said another, "the experience would be too upsetting for any ghost who had a pride of authorship."[70] Ike said boastfully: "I have never yet had a speech prepared for me that I did not change."[71]

A word-centered speaker is more likely to become tedious than one who is idea-centered or audience-centered. A stickler for grammatical niceties is not likely to have his mind oriented toward the people who react—sometimes passionately—to misplaced but heartfelt modifiers. Eisenhower attended to his speeches only after the hard intellectual work had been done and thus often succeeded in confusing the author's intentions. Because a president's corrections must be reckoned with, Eisenhower's public remarks often read like those of the last speaker in the party game of Whisper, who pronounces the final, thoroughly garbled message that has passed from party-goer to party-goer (which is to say, from editor to editor). In tinkering with style rather than with ideas, Ike made public communication a linguistic rather than a philosophical enterprise. He also helped to ensure that

when one thinks of the phrase, "an Eisenhower speech," one does so with
a wrinkled brow and a faint smile.

THE ANTI-POLITICAL EXPLANATION

Perhaps the most plausible understanding of Eisenhower's speaking style
holds that he saw himself as a Phoenix rising above the political ashes and
hence used ambiguity to avoid intense partisanship. "Nobody," he may
have reasoned, "can accuse me of political gouging if they can't understand
me." This explanation is not so frivolous as it may appear at first.

Some of the facts in the case are these: (1) Eisenhower routinely refused
to make avowedly political addresses; (2) his Gallup Poll ratings continually
showed that most Americans thought him to be "above politics"; and (3)
when patently political controversies did arise (McCarthyism, Sherman Adams, a second term for Nixon, etc.), Eisenhower vigorously resisted becoming party to them. Indeed, the only public remark he made that might
be seen as a rebuke of Joe McCarthy was made at the Dartmouth College
Commencement on June 14, 1953, in which he told his listeners: "Don't
join the book burners."[72] Although this statement was a "genuinely spontaneous talk, off the cuff,"[73] it was no more specific than his usual public
fare (scripted or otherwise) nor was it likely to send the District of Columbia
into paroxysms of vicious gossip. Another anecdote reinforces this point.
Once, when delivering a ceremonial address, Eisenhower was approached
by a reporter who congratulated him for his talk. "His face lighted with
the kind of spontaneous glow that is so much a part of his natural charm.
That, he said with genuine feeling, was the kind of speech he liked to make
because you didn't have to get into any political stuff."[74]

The Formal Style

Although they had relatively little in common, Dwight Eisenhower and
Harry Truman did use substantially fewer Self-References than those who
followed them in office. As a result, their speeches have a somewhat antique
flavor, as if they were destined to be deposited in some federal museum
devoid of their makers' imprints. As we saw in Chapter Two, the super-
personalization of presidential speech did not take hold until Lyndon Johnson's administration and even he could be considered modest when compared to Richard Nixon and Gerald Ford. Truman and Eisenhower, in
contrast, spoke as if they thought it presumptuous or dangerous to attach
themselves to the policies they endorsed. The statistical effect is so pronounced that it deserves more than passing consideration. (See Figure 3.5.)

Harry Truman averaged fewer than 4 Self-References in the 500-word

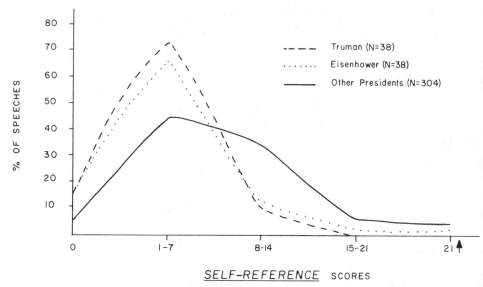

SELF-REFERENCE SCORES

Figure 3.5   Distribution of Self-Reference scores for Truman, Eisenhower, and other presidents. Mean for Self-Reference for the presidential sample was 8.01 (N = 380).

passages analyzed. Although he used a few more Self-References in his first 4 years in office when dealing with pragmatic topics (perhaps thereby attempting to distinguish his political platform from Roosevelt's), he never used very many. This was true of his national addresses, his rally speeches, and his state of the Union presentations. Typically, he used the first person plural when addressing his listeners as, for example, when he spoke at the World War Memorial Park in Little Rock in June of 1949:

> To maintain . . . prosperity, it is not sufficient to drift with the tide. We must take advantage of the new opportunities, the increased demands which result from the natural growth of our population. We must develop our natural resources and restore those we have depleted or wasted. We must establish a fair distribution of business opportunity; we must have a free labor movement able to hold its own at the bargaining table; we must protect the purchasing power of Americans against the hazards and misfortunes of life.[75]

In the sample of Truman speeches analyzed, there were only rare exceptions to this pattern. One of the few times he did use an unusually large number of Self-References (and he only used 14 of them) was during his valedictory address of January 15, 1953, a permissable breach of modesty, he may have reasoned.

Truman's unwillingness to refer to himself may seem curious, for he was certainly not loath to hold an opinion nor was he unwilling to stand in the center ring and take on all challengers. In private, Truman was as personal and direct with language as one could wish (and a good deal more personal and more direct than his wife and his advisors often wished). Why, then, did he maintain a low public profile?

One explanation relates to simple rhetorical fashion. The 1940s and 1950s may have been particularly unreceptive to overly personal public talk (although there is not, to the best of my knowledge, reliable evidence on this matter). As far as Harry Truman is concerned, there exists yet another explanation: he had a genuine sort of institutional humility, a heightened need to separate his pet priorities and favored platforms from the duties and obligations residing in the presidency itself. Although the following statement was made to Merle Miller many years after Truman sat in the Oval Office, and even though it is somewhat natural for an aging leader to say grand things in grand ways, Truman's remarks ring true. In any event, there is no doubt that they dovetail with his presidential behavior:

> You see the thing you have to remember. When you get to be president, there are all those things, the honors, the twenty-one gun salutes, all those things, you have to remember it isn't for you. It's for the Presidency, and you've got to keep yourself separate from that in your mind.
>
> If you can't keep the two separate, yourself and the Presidency, you're in all kinds of trouble.[76]

During his years in the White House, Harry Truman got into all kinds of trouble, but this was one area in which he was safe. (Even Truman's political enemies rarely accused him of personal aggrandizement.) Richard Neustadt even goes so far as to claim that Truman only ran for the presidency in 1948 because of his ideological, not his personal ambitions. Neustadt argues that Truman sought a second term to vindicate his and his party's political commitments. "Never in his tenure," says Neustadt, "does he [Truman] seem to have conceived that he fulfilled the presidency by being Harry Truman. He saw himself not as a man for whom the job was made, but as a man who had the job to do. He drew his confidence from seeing himself do it."[77] Naturally, Richard Neustadt was an aide and admirer of Truman's, but given what we now know about Harry Truman, one would have to be an arch cynic to find essential fault with Neustadt's analysis.

Dwight Eisenhower was equally formal in his public remarks. He used less Human Interest than any other president and was second only to Truman in avoidance of Self-References. Several explanations for this can be offered and they range from the partisan to the scholarly. One of Ike's revisionist admirers, Elmo Richardson, says, "He [Eisenhower] preferred to restrain and even conceal his personality, while displaying his strength of character."[78] Other of Ike's supporters viewed his personal reserve as a device for keeping emotion out of politics and they mention, for example, that he never attacked his political enemies by name as a result. Ike's refusal to use Human Interest and Self-References thereby removed the emotional dialectic from politics—the "I" versus "you" or "them"—and replaced it with a third-person attitude toward life. Said one commentator: " 'The President feels—' and 'It seems to the President—' have become standard marks of his speech, supplanting the widespread and overworked 'I.' The impression he gives is of standing aside, as employer, and viewing himself as employee."[79]

The anti-political intepretation of Ike may also be relevant here. "The politics of self-aggrandizement as Roosevelt practiced it affronted Eisenhower's sense of personal propriety," says Richard Neustadt, "Besides, the General seems to have had mental reservations about politicians as a class, mistrusting not alone their business but their characters. . . . Roosevelt was a hero seeking personal power; Eisenhower was a hero seeking national unity. He came to crown a reputation not to make one. He wanted to be an arbiter, not master. His love was not for power but for duty—and for status."[80] Naturally, when the self is removed from speech, the human interdependence of communication is made less obvious. Research has shown that Self-References are rarely found in the remarks of "true believers" (doctrinal preachers, political ideologues, institutional spokespersons, etc.) for precisely this reason.[81] In Gestalt terms, when the self is made ground, doctrine, ideology, and institution become figure. Reared in the military with its Manichean separation of person and rank, Ike rather naturally used his speech to emphasize systemic priorities. Even so sharp a critic of Eisenhower's as Marquis Childs acknowledges that he had a "persistent belief, originating long before his nomination to the presidency with the friends who were working on him to say yes, that he would be president of all the people standing above the battle, unifying the country."[82]

Conclusion

As one rereads the speeches of Harry Truman and Dwight Eisenhower 30 years after they were delivered, one cannot help but discern a certain quaintness about them. Truman's rhetoric seems too clear for a generation taught to distrust simple things. His rigidity bumps up against our modern relativism and his cheery use of chauvinistic symbols seems downright corny. We do not find in Eisenhower's remarks the snappy Madison Avenue patter we have become accustomed to hearing. When viewed through modern eyes, Ike's distended prose and self-interruptions render him an almost pitiable character, an aging uncle who has long since passed into the valley of senility.

Eisenhower and Truman's third-person sentences grind on modern ears. We have been taught by television personalities in the early 1960s, and by sensitivity trainers in the late 1960s, that self-expression is to be preferred to communication, that emotional distance in discourse is to be eschewed, and that listeners should be dazzled by our personalities or touched by our serial disclosures (or by both, if one is on a television talk show). We have also been taught by our Marxist cultural critics that impersonal speech is the stuff out of which suppression of the masses is fashioned.

It is hard to imagine that either Harry Truman or Dwight Eisenhower would fare well in the televised extravaganza of contemporary politics. Truman would be too "hot" for a medium that feeds upon controlled, rather than genuine, emotion. His several verbal indiscretions would be detected early by a news-hungry populace and he would go the way of Earl (Have you heard the latest one?) Butz. Ike would never get to first base with the modern media, for war heroes do not sell as well these days and wordy abstractions are now reserved for the college lecture hall. At root, neither Truman nor Eisenhower seems sophisticated enough for the times in which we live, and we take our sophistication seriously. The presidency changed after Truman and Eisenhower left. It changed politically and rhetorically, and therefore culturally. To say that is has *progressed* by so doing, Harry and Ike would be pleased to learn, is considerably less clear.

Notes

1. Quoted in Merle Miller, *Plain Speaking: An Oral Biography of Harry S. Truman* (New York: Berkley Medallion, 1973), p. 126. © by Berkley Publishing Corporation.
2. Quoted in Eugene E. White and Clair R. Henderlider, "What Harry S. Truman Told us about His Speaking," *Quarterly Journal of Speech,"* 40 (1954), p. 38.
3. Quoted in Samuel and Dorothy Rosenman, *Presidential Style: Some Giants and a Pygmy in the White House* (New York: Harper, 1976), p. 473.
4. Robert Underhill, *The Truman Persuasions* (Ames, IA: Iowa State University Press, 1981), pp. 322-323.
5. Quoted in Lester Marke, "After Four Years: Portrait of Harry Truman," *New York Times Magazine,* April 10, 1949, p. 57.
6. Cabell Phillips, *The Truman Presidency: The History of a Triumphant Succession* (New York: Macmillan, 1966), p. 140.
7. Quoted in William Bragg Ewald, Jr., *Eisenhower the President: Crucial Days, 1951-1960* (Englewood Cliffs, NJ: Prentice Hall, 1981), p. 170.
8. Quoted in James David Barber, *The Presidential Character: Predicting Performance in the White House* (Englewood Cliffs, NJ: Prentice Hall, 1972), p. 157.
9. Barber (1972), p. 157.
10. "Mr Truman after Five Years: Sizing up His Faults and Merits," *U.S. News and World Reports,* April 14, 1950, p. 13.
11. Richard Neustadt, *Presidential Power: The Politics of Leadership, with Reflections on Johnson and Nixon* (New York: Wiley, 1960, 1976), p. 231.

12. Barber (1972), p. 162.
13. "How Ike and His Aides Work Out a Speech," *U.S. News and World Report,* October 5, 1956, p. 84.
14. "The President and the Press," *Reporter,* April 18, 1953, p. 27.
15. Robert H. Ferrell, *The Eisenhower Diaries* (New York: Norton, 1981), p. xiii.
16. For further insight on this matter, see Ewald (1981), pp. 31–32.
17. Quoted in Phillips (1966), p. 88.
18. Quoted in Rosenman and Rosenman (1976), p. 429.
19. "Justice of the Greatest Power," April 15, 1945, *Vital Speeches of the Day,* 11:15 (1945), pp. 454–455.
20. Quoted in Robert Underhill (1981), p. 124.
21. Underhill (1981), p. 196.
22. "The Eightieth Congress," June 14, 1948, *Vital Speeches of the Day,* 14:18 (1948), p. 551.
23. "Human Rights," June 19, 1947, *Vital Speeches of the Day,* 12:19 (1947), pp. 584–585.
24. Quoted in Miller (1973), p. 145. © by Berkley Publishing Corporation.
25. Quoted in Miller (1973), p. 271. © by Berkley Publishing Corporation.
26. Quoted in White and Henderlider (1954), p. 39.
27. An intimate commentary on this aspect of Mr. Truman's personality is provided by Charles Murphy in Francis H. Heller, ed., *The Truman White House: The Administration of the Presidency, 1945–1953* (Lawrence, KS: Regents Press of Kansas, 1980).
28. Gerald W. Johnson, "Mr. Truman Makes Sense," *Saturday Review,* September 7, 1946, p. 10.
29. Victor Albjerg, "Truman and Eisenhower: Their Administrations and Campaigns," *Current History,* October, 1964, p. 224.
30. Phillips (1966), pp. 402–403.
31. "Far Eastern Policy," April 11, 1951, *Vital Speeches of the Day,* 17:14 (1951), p. 419.
32. "Taft-Hartley Act Repeal," February 24, 1949, *Vital Speeches of the Day,* 15:10 (1949), p. 291.
33. "Peace Comes High," October 15, 1951, *Vital Speeches of the Day,* 18:2 (1951), p. 35.
34. "Democratic Aims and Achievements," May 15, 1950, *Vital Speeches of the Day,* 16:16 (1950), p. 497.
35. Quoted in Bert Cochran, *Harry Truman and the Crisis Presidency* (New York: Funk and Wagnalls, 1973), p. 135.
36. George Elsey, "Foreward," in Underhill (1981), p. vii.
37. Underhill (1981), p. vii.
38. Underhill (1981).
39. Cochran (1973), pp. 225–226.
40. Barber (1972), p. 273.
41. Quoted in Cochran (1973), p. 226.
42. See "Harry S. Truman and the Postwar World," in Phillip Dolce and Leo Skau, eds., *Power and the Presidency* (New York: Scribners, 1976), p. 125.
43. "The Faith by which We Live," January 20, 1949, *Vital Speeches of the Day,* 15:8 (1949), p. 227.
44. "The Democratic Record," September 20, 1948, *Vital Speeches of the Day,* 14:24 (1948), p. 739.
45. Howard Gosnell, *Truman's Crises: A Political Biography of Harry S. Truman* (Westport, CT: Greenwood, 1980), p. 542.

46. Quoted in Phillips (1966), p. 131.
47. "The Moral Force of Women," October 8, 1947, *Vital Speeches of the Day,* 14:1 (1947), pp. 23–24.
48. Barber (1972), p. 285.
49. Anonymous, presented in *New Republic,* June 17, 1957, p. 7.
50. Arthur Larson, *Eisenhower: The President Nobody Knew* (New York: Scribners, 1968), p. 169.
51. "Public Service," June 5, 1960, *Vital Speeches of the Day,* 26:19 (1960), p. 579.
52. "Foreward," *Speeches of Adlai Stevenson* (New York: Random House, 1952), p. 7.
53. Steinbeck (1952).
54. "Turning Point in History," December 9, 1957 *Vital Speeches of the Day,* 24 (1957), p. 133.
55. "The United Nations: Past and Present," October 24, 1963, in George W. Hibbitt, ed., *The Dolphin Book of Speeches* (Garden City, NY: Dolphin, 1965), p. 241.
56. Barber (1972), p. 161.
57. Larson (1968), p. 165.
58. "The Republican National Convention," August 23, 1956, *Vital Speeches of the Day,* 32:22 (1956), p. 687.
59. Merriam Smith, "Evolution of Eisenhower as Speaker," *New York Times Magazine,* August 7, 1955, p. 18.
60. Elmo Richardson, *The Presidency of Dwight D. Eisenhower* (Lawrence: Regents Press of Kansas, 1979), p. 29.
61. Larson (1968), p. 168.
62. Paraphrased in Ewald (1981), p. 147.
63. Richardson (1979), p. 29.
64. Ferrell (1981), p. 298.
65. Robert Donovan, *Eisenhower: The Inside Story* (New York: Harper, 1956), p. 197.
66. Smith (1955), p. 18.
67. *U.S. News and World Reports,* April 16, 1954, p. 52.
68. Robert Sickels, *Presidential Transactions* (Englewood Cliffs, NJ: Prentice Hall), p. 151.
69. Unnamed writer, quoted in "How Ike and His Aides Work Out a Speech," *U.S. News and World Report,* October 5, 1956, p. 87.
70. Unnamed writer, quoted in Smith (1955), p. 66.
71. Quoted by Sherman Adams, "At Work in the White House," in Dean Albertson, ed., *Eisenhower as President* (New York: Hill and Wang, 1963), p. 12.
72. Quoted in Ewald (1981), p. 122.
73. Ewald (1981).
74. Marquis Childs, *Eisenhower, Captive Hero* (New York: Harcourt, 1958), p. 139.
75. "Address Delivered at World War Memorial Park in Little Rock, Arkansas," June 11, 1949, *Public Papers of the Presidents, 1949* (Washington: U.S. Government Printing Office, 1964), p. 288.
76. Quoted in Miller (1973), p. 288. © by Berkley Publishing Corporation.
77. Neustadt (1976), p. 243.
78. Richardson (1979), p. 195.
79. Unnamed aide, quoted in Barber (1972), p. 160.
80. Neustadt (1976), pp. 232, 233.
81. See, for example, my article, "The Rhetoric of the True Believer," *Speech Monographs,* 38 (1971), pp. 249–261.
82. Childs (1958), p. 271.

JFK, LBJ, AND THE POLITICS OF DISCOURSE

Throughout the history of American politics, it would be difficult to find persons more political than John Kennedy and Lyndon Johnson. From the standpoint of this study, Kennedy was a transitional president. Many of the changes mentioned in Chapter Two were accelerated during his short tenure in office. Kennedy gave birth to the televised presidency, an inheritance that his immediate successor in office, Johnson, would decry frequently with a brand of profanity native to his beloved Hill Country. The televised press conference became a fairly standard procedure during the Kennedy and Johnson administrations and "going to the people" via a special presidential address became a tool of lightning-like immediacy and powerful effect. Between 1960 and 1968, television commentators began to supplant print reporters as the nation's primary gatekeepers and gadflies. The advent of regular television coverage of the presidency superheated the political environment, an environment already suffused with the towering personalities of JFK and LBJ. The 1960s introduced into the presidential lexicon such now-standard terms as image, audience share, teleprompter, packaging, and targeting. The Truman and Eisenhower presidencies appear, in contrast, as primitive political *objets d'art*. Institutionally, politically, and especially communicatively, the Kennedy and Johnson presidencies are still very much with us.

The entire concept of presidential rhetoric broadened considerably during the 1960s, and presidents began to view their persuasive possibilities to be linked to those of the mass communication industry itself. Manipulation of the media became a much discussed topic as the chief executive sought to control both what he said and what others said about his speeches. To suggest that JFK and LBJ were image conscious is to suggest far too little. Kennedy's much heralded cancellation of the White House's 22 subscriptions to the *New York Herald Tribune* was a metaphor for the times, a symbolic swipe at the professional symbolists who had offended him. In his less splenetic moments, Kennedy liked to suggest stories about his administration to newsmen: "Once he held up a photograph of himself and General Douglas MacArthur and said: 'How about that for a magazine cover.'"[1] A former journalist himself, Kennedy sought to stretch his impact by sometimes suggesting certain language he would like to see in a news story about his White House, or by phoning scribes with a detailed critique of their recent efforts.[2]

Although he was never a journalist, Lyndon Johnson was also concerned with the rhetoric surrounding his rhetoric. "You-all say I've got no charisma—that the crowds don't respond to me like they did to Kennedy," he once said to a group of reporters, "You fellows stay right here beside me and I'll show you that you're wrong! . . . Watch this!"[3] With that, Johnson plunged into a crowd, pumping hands and slapping backs in his inimitable manner, working his fellow Americans to fever pitch. Although he never cancelled newspaper subscriptions, Johnson did watch three television sets simultaneously, thus revealing a concern for image that a Harry Truman would have considered downright obscene.

It is also interesting to note that when Jack Kennedy and Lyndon Johnson are compared, two things are true: (1) the comparisons are image-based, not issue-based, and (2) Johnson always fall short. As the revisionists are now amply demonstrating, precious little of substance from the Kennedy presidency made its way into the 1980s. In contrast, Ronald Reagan is still waging a Sisyphean struggle to tear down just a portion of Lyndon Johnson's Great Society legislation, which fundamentally changed the lives of every American citizen. Yet John Kennedy still casts a shadow ample enough to eclipse, in many people's eyes, every inch of the six-foot plus Texan. As we shall see in this chapter, there were many differences between Kennedy's and Johnson's styles. But why these stylistic differences should be singled out for contrast so often and so insistently is less clear.

Whether they are friend, foe, or neutral, however, most commentators take the rhetorical measure of Kennedy and Johnson. Richard Neustadt complains that an essential difference between the two men lay in their wit. Johnson resorted to ridicule and Kennedy watched "himself with wry detachment; his sense of humor was a sign of his perspective."[4] Kennedy's felicity of expression obviously pleased those in the wordy establishment that is the American press. Jack Valenti, himself a media person (and LBJ aide), observed that Johnson "recoiled from being compared with John F. Kennedy, as superb a television performer as ever inhabited the White

House. Somewhere deep in LBJ there lingered some messy doubts about his TV image being measured against JFK's."[5] Alfred Steinberg, an unkind Johnson biographer, singles out Johnson's failure "in the necessary Presidential act of leading the American people and communicating with them" as his fatal flaw and says that his inability "to establish a warm relationship with the citizens of the nation" contrasted sharply with the Kennedy style.[6] For David Culbert it was Johnson's "accent and garbled syntax" that caused LBJ to lose out to Kennedy's youthful good looks," "playful banter," and "image of heroic leadership."[7] Even France's Charles de Gaulle got in his licks with a dramaturgical metaphor: "Kennedy was a mask on the face of America while Lyndon Johnson *was* America."[8]

It is instructive, and for some it will be disconcerting, to know how pervasively rhetorical criteria have been used to assess the modern presidency. Humor, banter, accent, mask—these constitute the essential vocabulary of the New Politics, which is to say televised politics, which is also to say Kennedy politics. Naturally, not all observers of the presidency focus on these matters. For many commentators, issues like civil rights, the Bay of Pigs, Vietnam, space exploration, and equality of educational opportunity must figure into any meaningful assessment of Kennedy and Johnson. But it is also true that until recently John Kennedy's style had considerable positive impact on the commentaries written about his presidency. Only now are authors reacting with understandable discomfort when they recognize the interventionist political undertone ("we shall pay any price, bear any burden, meet any hardship") of his eloquent inaugural address. Only recently have commentators bravely asserted that "Kennedy looked fine, made nice speeches, but he didn't get much done."[9] Only in the last few years have some observers begun to probe this matter of presidential image in suitably complex ways: "If you read the dictionary about style the fact is that Johnson had more style than Kennedy. If style is individuality—that individuality by which one distinguishes a person—he was just a goddamn bank vault of style."[10]

In drawing communication-based portraits of Kennedy and Johnson, I shall therefore capture what many see as the essence of the modern American presidency. But if these two administrations are best distinguished rhetorically—a supposition that leaves me nonplussed—and if presidential assessment *should be* substantially rhetorical in nature—a supposition with which I vehemently disagree—it is best that we have the most accurate and comprehensive data possible about the presidential discourse in question. The communicative facts to be presented here are sometimes predictable and sometimes surprising. In most cases, however, the subtlety of these facts warrants caution when talking about the essential JFK and LBJ. Each of them was more than they appeared to be and yet not as much as they appeared to be. In the space between these two realms of appearance, the political presidency dwells.

Kennedy Cool

There is little doubt that John Kennedy's speechmaking was his presidential legacy. Through it, and through his various media events, Kennedy's administration fattened up three key subsections of the index to the *Reader's Guide to Periodical Literature*—Presidency: Press Relations, Public Relations, Messages, and Speeches. Kennedy's inaugural address, his "Ich Bin Ein Berliner" speech in Germany, and his talk on racial integration at American University became classics in American political literature. School children and even foreign intellectuals memorized parts and entire texts of his speeches.[11] During his administration, everyone became a rhetorical critic. At times, commentaries on his discourse were themselves inspirational:

John Emmet Hughes: "[John Kennedy] detested cant but delighted in eloquence. He could appeal for conciliation without foreswearing power. And he could respect ideas without confusing them with deeds, exhort action without unharnessing it from reason, and esteem words without becoming infatuated with his own."[12]

Tom Wicker: "Before he leaves the White House, in fact, John F. Kennedy may well become the best known speaker in American history, not excluding such storied orators as Daniel Webster [and] William Jennings Bryan."[13]

The New Yorker: "Whatever the impact of the Inaugural Address on contemporary New Frontiersman, we find it hard to believe that an Athenian or Roman citizen could have listened to it unmoved, or that Cicero, however jealous of his own reputation, would have found reason to object to it."[14]

Strong stuff, this, but there is little doubt that John Kennedy and Ted Sorensen could write a helluva speech. What is even more impressive is that they did so without using the traditional flourishes. Looking closely at Kennedy's speechmaking, one senses an unmistakable emotional reserve, an authorial distance from the subject matter, an unwillingness to gut-spill. His infrequent use of Symbolism (patriotic language) is a case in point. Table 4.1 is instructive in each of its parts. Not only did Kennedy depend upon images of nationhood less than any other chief executive but he also failed to use any Symbolism at all in a full 60% of his formal remarks (a good number of which were ceremonial). Moreover, his most extensive use of Symbolism (9 references during a West Virginia Political rally) pales in

TABLE 4.1

JOHN KENNEDY'S VERSUS OTHER PRESIDENTS' USES OF AMERICAN SYMBOLISM

President	Average references per speech	Speeches containing symbolism (%)	Maximum references in single speech
Truman	4.50	57.9	16
Eisenhower	2.97	57.9	15
Kennedy	*2.21*	*39.5*	*9*
Johnson	5.08	76.3	16
Nixon	6.79	68.4	23
Ford	4.02	63.2	16
Carter	6.15	76.3	25

comparison to Jimmy Carter's whopping use of 25 patriotic allusions during a speech in the cynical 1970s.

According to Ted Sorensen, Kennedy habitually refused to be "folksy or to include any phrase or image he considered corny, tasteless, or trite."[15] Arthur Schlesinger, Jr., declared that Kennedy was detached from even "the pieties of American liberalism."[16] The slightly (but only slightly) more dispassionate Douglass Cater remarks that Kennedy's "public record is singularly free of the posturing and phony piety" to which most other politicians succumb and he quotes Kennedy as having said, "No politician really likes to be a whore, but I must say some are less reluctant about it than others."[17] Assuming the presidency in the early 1960s, Kennedy's cerebral style caught the fancy of the "hip" reporters of his day. Kennedy was, in their eyes, a thinking man's president, not given to the tiresome litany of the McCarthy years.

Unlike most of the other presidents, Kennedy's Symbolism scores correlated negatively with Variety and Complexity (see Table B.10); not only did he avoid the "heart on the sleeve," but in Schlesinger's happy phrase, he also disdained "the tongue on the cliché."[18] The portion of his famed inaugural address analyzed in this study contains no instances of Symbolism, nor did he use Symbolism in his speech on the Berlin crisis. He used no Symbolism to advance his space program at Rice University in 1962, and he used none during the last speech he made (in Dallas, which would have responded appreciatively to clarion calls.) Eschewing symbology "with the contempt of a man for whom words are precise instruments,"[19] Kennedy ended his life talking about national defense in quantitative terms:

In the past three years we have increased the defense budget of the United States by over 20 percent, increased the program of acquisition of Polaris submarines from 24 to 41, increased our Minuteman missile-purchase program by more than 75 percent, doubled the number of strategic bombers and missiles on alert, doubled the number of nuclear weapons available in the strategic alert forces, increased the tactical nuclear forces deployed in Western Europe by over 60 percent, added five combat-ready divisions to the Armies of the United States, and five tactical fighter wings to the Air Force of the United States, increased our strategic airlift capability by 75 percent and increased our special counterinsurgency forces which are engaged now in South Vietnam, by 600 percent.[20]

A cold warrior, yes, but a cool warrior as well. While there may have been bombs bursting in air, there were no purple mountains or purple prose in Dallas that day.

Arthur Schlesinger, Jr., Kennedy's most gifted interpreter, has argued with some passion that the meaning of the Kennedy administration lay in its implicit social criticism. During the Eisenhower decade, reasons Schlesinger, "it was almost deemed treasonous to raise doubts about the perfection of the American way of life. But the message of Kennedy's 1960 campaign had been that the American way of life was in terrible shape, that our economy was slowing down, that we were neglectful of our young and old, callous toward our poor and our minorities, that our cities and schools and landscapes were a terrible mess, that our motives were materialistic and ignoble."[21] As if in support of Schlesinger's claim, John Kennedy's use of Optimism was the lowest in the presidential sample. Although the magnitude of the statistical difference is not pronounced—as we saw in Chapter Two, all presidents are obliged to be relatively cheery—Kennedy avoided the expected glad-handing whenever possible.

JFK had an habitual distaste for what columnist Doris Fleeson calls "sophomoric buoyancy."[22] To read his speeches is to gain perspective on the issues he treats. It would have been easy, for instance, to gush about the grand adventure of space exploration. But Kennedy did not do so on September 13, 1962. Instead, he urged that we try, "without repeating the mistakes that man has made in extending his writ around this globe of ours," mindful that the hazards of space "are hostile to us all," and mindful also that the "opportunity for peaceful cooperation may never come again."[23] Such academic balance made Kennedy attractive to the detached, intellectual set that inhabited the Kennedy White House. His social criticism also endeared him to a press corps schooled in the tradition of muckraking. In the 1960s reporters were glad to cover a president who liked little of what he saw around him:

On education: "We have in this country 8 million who have been to school less than 5 years. As a result they can't read or write or do simple arithmetic. They are illiterate in this rich country of ours, and they constitute the hard core of our unemployed. They can't write a letter to get a job, and they can't read, in many cases, a help-wanted sign."[24]

On communism: "Today no war has been declared—however fierce the struggle may be, it may never be declared in the traditional fashion. Our way of life is under attack. Those who make themselves our enemy are advancing around the globe. The survival of our friends is in danger. And yet no war has been declared, no borders have been crossed by marching troops, no missiles have been fired."[25]

On civil rights: "Are we to say to the world—and much more importantly to each other—that this is the land of the free, except for the Negroes; that we have no second class citizens, except for Negroes; that we have no class or caste system, no ghettos, no master race, except with respect to Negroes."[26]

This last set of remarks, Kennedy's June 11, 1963, speech on integration, was popular with the left-leaning newspapers of the time. Of the 380 presidential speeches analyzed in this study, only 3 contained less Optimism than did this speech of Kennedy's. Paeans rang forth in connection with this speech—for his "burning language,"[27] for his appraisal of "the risks of social alienation,"[28] for his courage in "illuminating America's moral crisis."[29]

Why JFK avoided the rhetoric of hope is unclear. Some, like Schlesinger, argue that Kennedy's political platform left him no choice but to attack the institutions of his day. "He voiced the disquietude of the postwar generation," says Schlesinger, "the mistrust of rhetoric, the disdain for pomposity, the impatience with the postures and pieties of other days, the resignation to disappointment."[30] Other observers give philosophical explanations (he was "skeptical by nature and inclined toward a personal fatalism"),[31] list psychodynamic reasons ("He seems temperamentally unable to develop an emotional theme. He addresses a rally gestureless, inflectionless."),[32] mention cultural forces ("the Irishness remained a vital element in his constitution [with its] view of life as comedy and tragedy")[33], or chalk it up to personal coldness ("If my dear old mother were to fall and break her leg, Hubert Humphrey would cry, but I'm not so sure about Jack.")[34]

Whatever the reason, Kennedy was not a sentimentalist. Even on ceremonial occasions he was restrained. During remarks at a civic reception in New Orleans, for example, he talked about "great technological changes" that would benefit the South, the "strength and vigor of the United States," and about "moving this country forward in this decade," but he also reminded his listeners—presumably so that they would keep all things in perspective—that their sons and brothers, serving at the time in Berlin or in Vietnam, were "the Americans who are bearing the great burden."[35] His New Orleans speech was the most positive in my sample. Rarely was Kennedy accused of Rooseveltian excess.

Kennedy's coolness emerged from what he did not do when speaking. He was not chauvinistic, he did not offer glib affirmations, and, like Truman and Eisenhower, he used far fewer Self-References than the other presidents (see Table B.8). This latter tendency began at the beginning. When preparing his inaugural address, Kennedy suggested that they "eliminate all the I's. Just say what 'we' will do. You'll have to leave it in about the oath and the responsibility, let's cut it everywhere else.''[36] If it had been possible, JFK might well have eliminated Self-References from the oath of office as well, for he kept his public and private persons distinct. After hours, we are also told, Kennedy retreated to the company of his old cronies; his presidential associates, in contrast, were left to find their own evening meal. Whether this personal detachment was a function of Kennedy's New England reserve[37] or of the formality of the traditional presidency is hard to determine. There is evidence for either interpretation.

For example, popular writer Bill Adler indicates that even before Kennedy became president he showed an "ironic mental detachment" by speaking of himself in the third person. When a little girl shrank back from Kennedy's attempt to bestow upon her the candidate's traditional kiss, Kennedy commented: "I don't think she quite caught that strong quality of love of children so much a part of the candidate's makeup which has made him so dear to the hearts of all mothers."[38] According to Henry Fairlie, the impersonal quality of Kennedy's remarks resulted from his awareness "at all times that he stood on a conspicuous stage, the world marking his demeanor, he always took to it apparelled; even his attractive qualities were those of an attractive public figure; one gazed on the compleat politician, accepted him as such, and did not much consider the man."[39] Fairlie's analysis is astute. My findings indicate that Self-References by Kennedy were even harder to find in "businesslike" situations—on television or in nonceremonial settings (see Table B.9). These situations caused Kennedy to fade farther and farther into the background until, like Alice's Cheshire, only his smile remained. For many, the Kennedy smile was enough: "[Kennedy] has gained rapport with the people less because he is one of them and more because he is above them—approachable, humble, sincere, with his roots clearly recognizable as emergent from them but nonetheless above them."[40]

Others were not impressed by the Kennedy Cool. Fairlie feels that Kennedy's emotional distance from his remarks left a rhetorical void. If one tries to walk around oneself when talking, after all, one is tempted to say grand things. Fairlie accuses Kennedy's speeches of being grandiloquent ("John Kennedy spoke in public as Byzantine emperors appeared on state occasions: sheathed in gold, suspended between heaven and earth").[41] Fairlie senses that it was Ted Sorensen's lust for magnificence that all too frequently produced the banal, rich, and pompous phrasings and that if Sorensen had been asked to write about sugar subsidies for JFK, he would have been likely to exult, "Let the word go forth from this time and place that the American people will not permit the growers of sugar. . . . ''[42]

Kennedy's "high style" produced an interesting and unique correlational profile as can be seen in Figure 4.1: infrequent use of Self-Reference led to

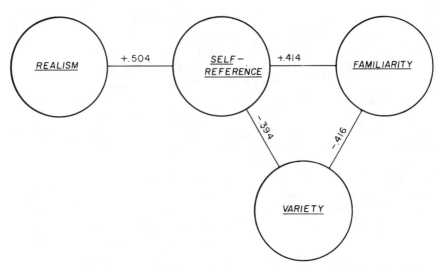

Figure 4.1   John Kennedy's sophisticated style (Pearson correlations for selected variables, N = 38). For additional information, see Table B.10.

less use of Realism and Familiarity and to greater use of Variety. In other words, his style can be described as striving for effect. Such a style placed a premium on turns of phrase and semantic bravado. Kennedy's speech on July 4, 1962, delivered at Independence Hall in Philadelphia, could serve as a primer for the student of classical tropes: "the theory of independence is as old as man himself," "it was in this hall that the theory became a practice," "this Nation—conceived in revolution, nurtured in liberty, maturing in independence. . . . ," "a great new effort—for interdependence— is transforming the world about us," "our forefathers sought to find freedom in diversity and in unity, strength."[43]

What some people miss in a linguistically clever style is genuine emotion. Hans J. Morgenthau complains that Kennedy failed to move people in the way Roosevelt and Churchill had, despite the literary qualities of his speeches. Morgenthau claims that only once when listening to Kennedy speak did he sense "a suggestion of emotion" akin to that he typically felt when listening to Roosevelt and Churchill.[44] The speech Morgenthau referred to was Kennedy's address on old-age benefits to the National Council of Senior Citizens given on May 20, 1962. In the passage analyzed here, Kennedy refers to himself 18 times (more than four times his normal rate and more than twice what was typical for presidents in general). In his speech, Kennedy spoke movingly of the elderly's plight, of his personal disdain for those who would penalize the old for being old, and he even spoke of his concern for his father's health.[45] This was not a Kennedy often seen in public.

There is little doubt that John Kennedy's most impressive public performances came during his press conferences. The results in the preceding paragraph suggest why. A speaker given neither to self-revelation nor to
sentimentality makes an ideal Daniel for the electronic lions. A controlled,
verbally adept president can give as good as he gets and probably better:
"He [Kennedy] was absolutely true in his instinct, he used reporters as
pawns to make himself look smarter, shrewder, better informed and more
capable than he really was."[46] A president who sees his job as political
theatre can trade quips and even jibes without becoming ruffled. Richard
Nixon could not do so and that is probably because he saw his role less as
performance than as confrontation. But John Kennedy rose above that, as
he had in his 1960 debates with Nixon and as he later did with Cuba, Laos,
Berlin, and Tuscaloosa. Kennedy took to his media circumstances as if he
had invented them. In some measure, he had.

It is interesting to think in this context of what is meant by the fabled
Kennedy wit. His verbal dance was as skilled as had ever been seen in Washington, "the product of a quick, agile, penetrating mind, coupled with an
innate sense of irony."[47] He was the District of Columbia's Johnny Carson.
People knew no more about Johnny Carson than they did about John Kennedy, but both Carson and Kennedy knew that the language of the mass
media was a cool one long before Marshall McLuhan knew it was.

Kennedy Careful

Immediately after John Kennedy died, the mythmakers took over, inventing Camelot and The Kennedy Legacy. Many of JFK's oldest friends
resented such deification and vowed to write a history of him as a fellow
politician. "The real man is being swept away by legend," they declared,
"and there's danger that soon there'll be only a demigod, instead of the
man we knew. Jack Kennedy was first and last a pol."[48] Kennedy's closest
advisor concurs. Ted Sorensen claims that all of Kennedy's White House
decisions were guided by JFK's "unusually acute political antennae" and
he suggests that Kennedy's rhetorical sensors were equally perceptive: "He
liked to be exact. But if the situation required a certain vagueness, he would
deliberately choose a word of varying interpretations rather than bury his
imprecision in ponderous prose."[49] Perhaps only Ted Sorensen could bestow moral sanctity upon circumlocution.

Kennedy confidante, Dave Powers, argues that Kennedy's sensors had
worked well from his earliest days on the stump (or stoop): "You know
those three-decker houses around Bunker Hill? The ones where the Kellys
live on the first floor, the O'Malleys on the second and the Donovans on
the third? The President used to have to walk up those stairs and knock on

all those doors and talk and joke with all those families in their own kind of language and about their own special problems. He never has lost that old three-decker sense of what to say."[50] As we see in Table 4.2, John Kennedy varied his remarks to suit the topics he addressed more than any other modern president. Interestingly, his adaptations were not as much audience-centered or time-based as they were intellectual. He tailored his remarks to suit the gravity, formality, or concreteness of his subject matter. Kennedy had a practical self, an honorific self, and warrior self. A Kennedy speech was thus a performance in the truest sense of the word, for he re-created himself each time he spoke. As Table 4.2 reports, Kennedy's tendency to do so was, on the average, thrice that of the other chief executives.[51]

Some of these topical adaptations have been chalked up to the Kennedy-Sorensen relationship. After all, JFK often ad-libbed his remarks in certain settings while Sorensen crafted Kennedy's prose for other situations. But authorship differences would be presumably revealed in the Audience column in Table 4.2; as we see, Kennedy sensed no special need for inventing a televised versus a nontelevised self. Moreover, most all the presidents spoke from manuscript at times and impromptu at other times, so we will have to look elsewhere for a unique explanation of Kennedy's adjustments.

The simplest explanation may be the most parsimonious: John Kennedy was a deft politician, a deft stylist, and a deft thinker who saw no special virtue in selecting and doggedly adhering to a single presidential script. Because the topics he addressed differed considerably—communism, labor-management relations, medical care, the Democratic party—his remarks reflected those differences. While other presidents were also politicians, stylists, and thinkers, they were not, one might presume, as deft as John

TABLE 4.2

ADAPTABILITY OF JOHN KENNEDY VERSUS OTHER PRESIDENTS:
NUMBER OF STATISTICALLY SIGNIFICANT DIFFERENCES[a]

President	Audience effects	Topical effects	Temporal effects	Total effects
Truman	1.00	2.50	1.50	5
Eisenhower	3.00	1.50	2.50	7
Kennedy	*2.50*	*11.00*	*1.50*	*15*
Johnson	7.00	6.00	5.00	18
Nixon	6.50	1.50	0.00	8
Ford	2.67	2.67	4.67	10
Carter	1.50	3.50	4.00	9

[a]For further information, see Table B.9.

Kennedy. Few presidents, for example, would attempt to give an unprecedented speech on racial integration 24 hours after an unprecedented speech on detente. But John Kennedy did just that on June 10 and 11, 1963. Few presidents would speak threateningly of Cuban–Soviet expansionism to newspaper editors one week and then berate another group of editors for journalistic expansionism the next week. But John Kennedy did that, too, on April 20 and 27, 1961. And few presidents could move as easily as John Kennedy did from an emotional treatise on human freedom on January 20, 1961, to a sharply expedient analysis of political power blocks on January 21.

John Kennedy could do and did do these things and more, largely because he had the confidence and savvy to adjust to the matter at hand. A reader of JFK's public papers looking for his essential self is pushed headlong toward frustration. Ever appropriate, John Kennedy was each of his speeches, but more than each of them as well. He was a verbal technician, a person who found comfort in the texture and suppleness of words. He confessed to no rhetorical orthodoxy, was as likely to find irony in a political dispute as perfidy, more able than most to say old things in new ways. In essence, he was a political version of actor Peter Sellers, substituting rhetoric for makeup but still able to become a whirling dirvish of talent and mystery.

As is so often the case, rhetorical behavior has political counterparts. Students of the Kennedy administration are just now beginning to ask exactly what he stood for politically. Early interpreters of his presidency were content to wax about his charm, his charisma, his youthful excitement. But such qualities fade with the fading of newsreels, and scholars 20 years hence are eager to know where Kennedy stood and why he stood there. The search will be an interesting one and it seems unlikely that Kennedy's public remarks will unravel his mystery. We find in his speeches a resistance to ideological pronouncement and a caution borne of political loins. It is for these reasons that some of Kennedy's critics claimed that he talked like Churchill and acted like Chamberlain,[52] that he was the thinking man's Cal Coolidge,[53] and that the Kennedy rocking chair was the symbol of the New Frontier: "You get the feeling of moving but you don't go anywhere."[54]

What Kennedy's critics so often found missing in his speeches was his political *weltanschauung*. The communicative facts largely bear them out: (1) only Richard Nixon surpassed Kennedy's use of Realism and (2) when speaking on matters of practical policy, John Kennedy used very little Certainty and very little Embellishment (see Table B.9). In other words, Kennedy did not typically trade in abstractions; he stayed with specifics rather than outline overall policy options. Also, he was cautious when addressing the political nitty gritty. Depending upon what one thinks a president should do or what presidential rhetoric should sound like, one could respond in any number of ways to JFK's timidity. Many have:

> And when he played the leading conversational role himself, he invariably dealt in facts, not theories, in salty human realities, nor moral generalities.[55]

> [Kennedy's mind is more analytical than creative, more curious and penetrating than wide-ranging or philosophically speculative, more skeptical than confident, more catalytic than original or imaginative. He shuns doctrinaire solutions and dogmatic talk. He is uneasy with slogans—and sometimes with statements of principle.[56]

> Kennedy was simply not all that interested in being a public educator—and to understand this lack of interest is to begin to understand the essence of his conception of leadership.[57]

> He was pragmatic in the sense that he tested the meaning of a proposition by its consequences; he was also pragmatic in the sense of being free from metaphysics. . . . Kennedy was bored by abstractions. He never took ideology very seriously.[58]

> Kennedy's attitude [toward pragmatism] compromised his promise to be an assertive executive who would be willing to serve the people even at the risk of incurring their momentary displeasure. Too often—particularly when an important issue was controversial—Kennedy was very reluctant to address the issue in a major speech.[59]

It is noteworthy that when Kennedy spoke about economic matters he was particularly loath to offer broad philosophical statements or to present far-reaching solutions. Among his most cautious and concrete speeches were the following: his speech to the Labor-Management Advisory Committee on March 21, 1961, his speech to the U.S. Chamber of Commerce on April 3, 1962, his national address of August 13, 1962, on the economic future, and his televised speech of September 18, 1963, on tax reductions. In these speeches, which are liberally larded with facts and figures Kennedy always had at the ready, we find an emphasis on the practical, the doable, not on economic theory per se. In the words of Bruce Miroff, Kennedy had no "inclination to dabble in economics"; rather, his economic rhetoric was "cautious, adhering rather closely to the dictum of balanced budgets. The Keynesian vocabulary favored by his economic advisors seldom intruded into Kennedy's public discourses."[60]

According to Henry Pachter, it is ironical that Kennedy became the idol of the Left since Kennedy never laid out his political axiology brazenly.[61] According to Kennedy himself, little was certain in the world of economic fluctuations. Thus, he once said that his legislation should be passed because "according to some predictions," young people "may have trouble finding jobs." In support of this hazy claim, Kennedy used the most tentative constructions possible: "I think that this bill should be carried out before this Congress goes home. . . . I think the National Government should play its fair part in higher education. . . . I think it is better to stimulate employment than having them standing on a street corner without hope."[62]

Kennedy's State of the Union messages were usually cautious as were some of his most famous addresses: his Berlin crisis speech, his address on space exploration, his speech on medicare. Perhaps Kennedy reasoned that it was best to use tempered language when introducing radically new proposals. If that is what he thought, he was reasoning in a classically political way: to do what was possible within the ambit of his control. Kennedy considered himself a "practical liberal," a politician rather than a preacher.[63] In this connection, it is interesting to note that his Roman Catholicism failed to permeate his rhetoric. At least when addressing practical matters, Kennedy avoided what Arthur Schlesinger, Jr., has called "the black-and-white moralism" of his Irish Catholic heritage.[64] Alfred Kazin is also unable to find much Roman Catholicism in America's first Catholic president. As Kazin puts it, "John F. Kennedy seems to have been more aware of Catholics as a source of political support than of the Church as a source of intellectual inspiration."[65] Henry Fairlie believes that John Kennedy's administration makes no sense unless we view him as an American positivist who felt that "the city of man can be built in the image of the City of God *on this earth.*"[66]

There is one important exception to John Kennedy's general caution. Like many of the presidents studied here, and more so than any one of them, Kennedy increased his use of Certainty and Embellishment when speaking on matters of Value (also seen in Table B.9). It is this John Kennedy that most of us remember—the ceremonial orator, the ask-not-what-your-country-can-do-for-you orator, the champion of civil-rights-in-Birmingham orator. But there is another John Kennedy here as well—a rhetorical legacy. This is the John Kennedy who makes his liberal admirers squeamish. Consider the list of his most strident presentations: his speech on foreign policy at the University of California in March, 1962, his address at West Point in June of the same year, his speech on Cuban armaments in October, 1962, and his speech on relations with the Soviet Union 2 months before he was assassinated. When speaking on communistic matters, John Kennedy often became heated:

> Our way of life is under attack. Those who make themselves our enemy are advancing around the globe. The survival of our friends is in danger. . . . If the press is awaiting a declaration of war before it imposes the self-discipline of combat conditions, then I can only say that no war ever posed a greater threat to our security. If you are awaiting a finding of "clear and present danger," then I can only say that the danger has never been more clear and its presence has never been more imminent.[67]

This speech was given to the American Newspaper Publishers Association on April 27, 1961, at the suggestion of Kennedy's press secretary, Pierre

Salinger (a suggestion that he later regretted). As Salinger tells it, the re-action to Kennedy's attempt to muzzle the press was "violent."[68] The pub-lishers reasoned that, coming as it did 11 days after the Bay of Pigs fiasco, Kennedy's speech was both ill-timed and ill-tempered. In his highly critical book, *Pragmatic Illusions: The Presidential Politics of John F. Kennedy*, Bruce Miroff declares that "Kennedy was seldom again to present his Cold War theory in such a complete (and extreme) form as in these post–Bay of Pigs speeches, but their themes remained a constant feature of his rhetoric. These speeches are difficult to reconcile with the claim of Kennedy's ad-mirers that he was notably free of the stale dogmas of the Cold War. Even a cursory examination of them turns up a host of such dogmas."[69]

My findings corroborate Miroff's claims and they also add support to the remark made by Henry Fairlie, who asserts that John Kennedy was even willing to use the dedication of the Robert Frost Library as a beachhead for the Cold War. His speech on this occasion was the second highest on Certainty and second highest on Embellishment in the Kennedy sample. In his remarks, Kennedy develops the theme of power, equating the poet's strength of expression with the nation's strength of purpose. He talks of "the fibre of our national life," of a country which matches "its military strength" with its "moral restraint."[70] Naturally, Kennedy was essentially lionizing Frost here, but the imagery of power is unmistakable and more than a bit reflective of Kennedy's approach to intentional politics. As Fair-lie puts it, "Even the poets on the New Frontier had to be tough."[71]

My data hardly establish John Kennedy as an ideologue, even though he often used ceremonial settings for political salesmanship. On most occa-sions, Kennedy was detached, eminently cautious. Often he was extraor-dinarily eloquent. Always he was a politician. Stewart Udall tells another story about John Kennedy and Robert Frost in which Udall suggested to the newly elected president that he ask the famed poet to speak at the in-augural ceremonies. Kennedy is said to have replied with a grin "We'll do it. But with Frost's skill with words, people would remember his speech instead of mine. I think we'd better have him read a poem."[72] History records that Frost read and that Kennedy spoke on that cold day in Jan-uary. While Kennedy's speech had a poetic lilt to it, it was rhetoric through and through because its maker was a political animal through and through.

Johnson the Populist

No graceful transition can be made between a discussion of John Ken-nedy's magisterial rhetoric and the plainer fare served up by his replace-ment. Lyndon Johnson was all too aware of this problem of transition. His inauguration had no poets and he had no poetic flair. Throughout his first year in office and from time to time throughout his entire administration, Johnson labored under the semantic (and psychological) burden of being John Fitzgerald Kennedy's successor in office. Although Johnson's speechwriter, Richard Goodwin, was every bit the writer that Ted Sorensen was, Johnson himself revealed little talent for editing what was written for him and even less talent for speaking those words. If public presentations constituted the essence of the presidency for JFK, they were nothing but a colossal nuisance for a man who was an habitué of the Senate cloakroom. Naturally, Lyndon Johnson spoke in public—a good deal in fact—but he did so with little relish and almost never with significant effect. Lyndon Johnson speaking was not a pretty sight.

Of Johnson's public remarks, one thing is clear: they were clear. Johnson is said to have told his writers: "I want four-letter words, and I want four sentences to the paragraph. Now that's what I want and I want you to give it to me."[73] Although no statistics were gathered here about sentences, Johnson's writers delivered as ordered. Of his 38 speeches 36 averaged less than five characters per word. Johnson's statements used less Complexity (see Figure 4.2) than any other president and were second lowest on Em-

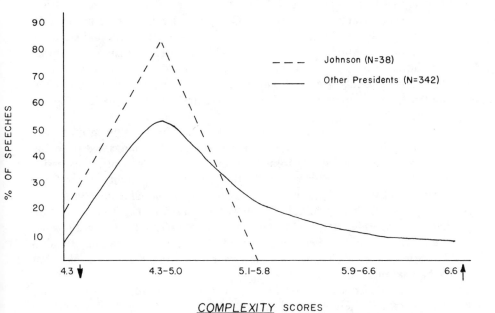

Figure 4.2 Distribution of Complexity scores for Lyndon Johnson and other presidents. Mean for Complexity for the presidential sample was 5.11 ($N = 380$).

bellishment. Almost without exception, Johnson spoke the language of the people he served, not the language of John Kennedy's Harvard advisors. Although he was accused of many things during his years in office, few responsible reporters accused Johnson of dilating (like Dwight Eisenhower), equivocating (like Jimmy Carter), or misspeaking (like Richard Nixon). There may have been a credibility gap during the Johnson years, but there was never a clarity gap. The first words he spoke as president of the United States were as pellucid as his last:

> For 32 years, Capitol Hill has been my home, I have shared many moments of pride with you—pride in the ability of the Congress of the United States to act, to meet any crisis, to distill from our differences strong programs of national action.
> An assassin's bullet has thrust upon me the awesome burden of the Presidency. I am here today to say I need your help. I cannot bear this burden alone. I need the help of all Americans in all America.[74]

> And now it is time to leave.
> I hope it may be said, a hundred years from now, that by working together we helped to make our country more just, more just for all of its people—as well as to insure and guarantee the blessings of liberty for all of our posterity. That is what I hope, but I believe that it will be said that we tried. Thank you.[75]

Although domestic riots and political scandal rocked his administration, they never garbled his prose. During the second half of his term in office, he was even clearer (i.e., used less Complexity) than during his first 30 months on the job. Although he may have become truculent, and certainly he was irascible, during his time in the White House, confusion never beset him. Some of his critics saw this as one of Johnson's greatest weaknesses— that he never really grappled with the genuine remedies available to him, but trusted too surely in what Teddy White has called "a quality of grand simplicity."[76]

In contrast to his immediate predecessors in office, Johnson used considerably more Self-References in his speeches. Two things are probably true about this finding: (1) Johnson rejected some aspects of the excessive formality that John Kennedy and other presidents thought proper for a chief executive and (2) he intended to place his personal stamp on a presidency that was his by default. There was also a strong negative correlation between Self-References and Complexity for Johnson—the simpler his style, the more personal he became (see Table B.10). When speaking, Lyndon Johnson wanted his listeners to know what he had said and know also that *he* had said it.

Johnson was not as excessive on this matter as were some of the later presidents. But there is little doubt that he saw a very personal connection between himself as president and the issues facing the nation. "He took a proprietary interest in everything and everyone," said UPI correspondent

Frank Cormier, "He would not think twice, for instance, about saying, in a state dinner receiving line, 'Mr Prime Minister, I want you to meet a member of *my* Supreme Court,' He even talked in one speech about the 'State of *My* Union Address,' which we recorded as a Freudian slip."[77] The speeches containing an unusually high number of Self-References (and little Complexity) are a measure of the issues closest to Johnson's heart: his voting rights speech of March 1965, his speech on higher education presented at his alma mater in November of that year, his defense of Medicare in April 1966, and his remarks on the death of Martin Luther King in April of 1968. These speeches contain personal markers as if to suggest to his biographers: "take note of this; it was important to me."

Nothing was more important to Lyndon Johnson than his war in Vietnam. Most of his speeches on this topic were presented on television, and for reasons to be detailed shortly, he rarely referred to himself in such settings. But one speech on the war was delivered to a Democratic party rally in Chicago on May 17, 1966. Throughout Johnson's speech he showed how central the Vietnam conflict was to him and to the goals he had set on behalf of the American people: "I have tried as best I could to lead this country to peace and lead this country to prosperity. . . . I have tried to be the President of all the people. . . . As much as I love my Democratic party, I love America more. . . . I ask you and I ask every American to put our country first if we want to keep it first. . . . I have tried to base my decisions and my thinking and my actions on what I think is really best for this country."[78] LBJ's apologia was the most self-centered set of remarks in the Johnson sample; 31 of his 500 words were Self-References. Here was a man released from the television coverage that plagued him and finally given a chance to show how important this war was to him (and how important it should be to people vying for his favor). It is little wonder that his speech was labeled petulant by *The Christian Century,* which editorialized as follows: "When the most powerful man in the United States includes such condemnations of anti-war critics in a prepared manuscript carefully edited by his advisers, his charges have to be viewed as a calculated attempt to disgrace and intimidate American critics of United States intervention in Vietnam."[79]

Johnson's war in Vietnam did not endear him to the American intelligentsia but his unaffected speaking style may have prompted even greater disdain on their parts. His comparatively low Variety and Embellishment scores suggest a man uninterested in stylistic effect. Doris Kearns argues that Johnson "expressed a lasting distrust and fear of ideas, intellectuals, debates, books, and eloquence,"[80] which may be why he was once termed a "peasant intellectual"[81] (by a person whose motivations are not evident from the epithet). Interestingly, Johnson's speaking style became no more florid in ceremonial settings than it did in wordaday political forums. And his stylistic preferences seem quite intentional (he once omitted the word "podiatrist" from a speech because he did not know how to pronounce it).[82] All of this was to no avail in the eyes of the intellectuals of his day, for even in an era of "communication" they wanted rhetoric. One of them once said, "I don't hate Johnson. I just hate the fact that all the grace and wit has gone from what the American President says."[83] Waging war like a Philistine was bad enough, but talking like one was decidedly worse.

Perhaps Lyndon Johnson's most grievous offense in the eyes of his media detractors was that he forced them to take their citified selves to his "speak-in's" on the road. In such settings, Johnson was magnificent (if one were being fair in one's judgment, which most were not). Raised in what Frank Cormier called "the Southern and rural tradition of long-winded political oratory," Johnson understood that, for listeners (as opposed to newspaper reporters), public speaking should offer "prime opportunities for entertainment, conviviality and, perhaps, some measure of enlightenment."[84] One of the most vivid depictions of Johnson on the stump has been supplied by Richard Harwood and Haynes Johnson:

> Our first impression remains indelible. It was a political rally in Washington, some-time in the 1950s, dreary in its way, as they all are. All the war horses of the Democrats had turned out: Harry Truman; "Mister Sam" Rayburn, the tough, balding, flinty, somewhat inscrutable Speaker of the House; Averell Harriman, an ambassador who wanted to become President. There were others who wanted to become President, senators all of them—Hubert Humphrey of Minnesota, Stuart Symington of Missouri, John Kennedy of Massachusetts. Then there was LBJ. He took the podium, leaned forward, and launched into a loud, stemwinding stump speech. He flailed his arms. He pounded the lectern. He shouted until he was hoarse. He leaned forward to watch the crowd. You could see the veins bulging out in his neck. No one was surprised; that was the way the rangy majority leader regaled the faithful in Texas.[85]

Johnson's rhetorical tradition specified that a government that could not be brought to the people face-to-face was a government to be scorned. In this connection, he admitted to being entranced by Huey Long. Said Johnson: "I made a special deal with the doorkeeper to let me know when Long was about to speak on the Senate floor. For leading the masses and illustrating your point humanly, Huey Long couldn't be beat."[86] With each passing year in politics, however, Johnson found himself being drawn farther and farther away from "the people." Each new governmental obligation precipitated dozens of speaking invitations, invitations for prepared remarks. Faced with reading from manuscript, Johnson became oblivious to the human dynamics of his situation and operated as if formal speech-making were not a fundamentally communicative enterprise. With a manuscript in his hands, says Robert Caro, "Johnson could not seem to stop reading it—his phrasing was awkward and stilted as his gestures; he shouted the speech, without inflection. Although he was continually urged by his advisors to look at his audience, he did so infrequently, as if he were afraid to lose his place in the text."[87]

The presidency brought increased invitations for the very sort of speaking Johnson detested. But the presidency brought a still more insidious factor: television. Although they say it in different ways, Johnson's friends and foes alike indict television for many of the president's difficulties:

Liz Carpenter: "With a live audience, he became as eloquent as an Adlai Stevenson and as persuasive as a Billy Graham. He was never at ease under the soulless eye of a television camera."[88]

Jim Heath: "Although in small groups he could mesmerize listeners with his commanding presence and endless string of anecdotes and political fables, when he spoke to large gatherings or on radio and television he was dull, uninspiring, and—to some flatly unpleasant."[89]

Harry McPherson: "He was a poor performer on television, and for a generation raised on it, that was inexcusable."[90]

When Johnson's live speeches were compared with his broadcast remarks, the differences were far more dramatic than they were for any other president except Richard Nixon. (See Figure 4.3.) In particular, television caused Johnson to appear both unnatural (less Self-Reference and Human Interest) and overly cautious (more Complexity, less Certainty, and less Symbolism). Television removed from Johnson's character precisely those elements that had gotten him to the White House—his folksiness, his emotional simplicity, his directness of speech. With television, Johnson became classically self-conscious, and his natural garrulousness was replaced by what he felt was Kennedyesque dignity. Standing before the camera, Johnson forsook the cornpone formulas used when pressing flesh. The speechwriting advice he once gave to Douglass Cater was not, Johnson seemed to feel, appropriate for television. Handing back a draft to Cater on one occasion, Johnson had said, "Pretty good, Doug. You've got the idea. But you've got to get more PAY-thos into it, hear? We gotta have more people livin' in wretched hovels and things like that. Doug, you've gotta get your hand *up* under the dress!"[91]

On television, Johnson was all business. It was not difficult to tell that his Medicare speech (first speech below) was presented to an audience of hospital leaders while his more legalistic remarks on this subject (second speech below) were heard by a national audience. Perhaps it was this rhetorical disjunction the young people sensed in the mid-1960s when they declared that a generation gap existed between themselves and their president. Perhaps the Lyndon Johnson they heard on television was too antiseptic and system-centered for them:

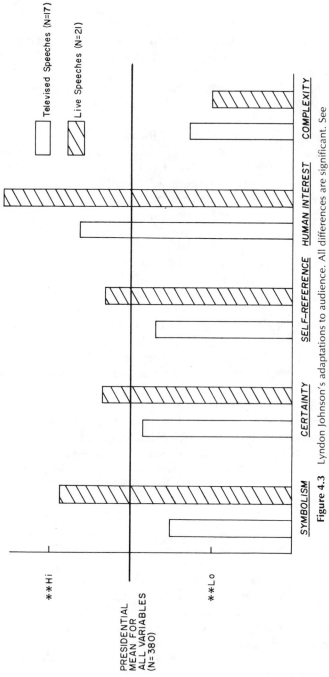

Figure 4.3 Lyndon Johnson's adaptations to audience. All differences are significant. See Table B.9. ** ± ½ sd from mean. See Table B.1 for exact values.

Live

I am not 65 yet, but I have known many people in my lifetime who were 65. Some have been mighty close to me. I have seen their eyes when they wondered whether they would be welcome in their old age in their sister-in-law's home, or whether their brother-in-law would be happy when they are all there using the one bath. I have seen them worry about how they were going to pay the doctors or the medical services. I have seen them grateful for the considerations that the preacher and the women of the church had extended to them in times of illness—how they loved the doctor who would come anytime in the night, who gave his whole life, away from his family most of the time, and who waited for his bills to be paid year after year, whether there was drought or too much rain.[92]

Televised

We must provide hospital insurance for our older citizens, financed by every worker and his employer under Social Security by contributing no more than $1 a month during the employee's working career to protect him in his old age in a dignified manner, without cost to the Treasury, against the devastating hardship of prolonged or repeated illness. We must, as part of a revised housing and urban renewal program, give more help to those displaced by slum clearance; provide more housing for our poor and our elderly, and seek as our ultimate goal in our free enterprise system a decent home for every American family.[93]

As we saw in Chapter Two, radio and television present special problems to all presidents because of the formalization these media encourage. The only points being made here are that (1) Johnson succumbed to such pressures more than most presidents and (2) his natural speaking style was particularly informal to begin with, thus causing his television style to be singled out for special parody. The parodies were fueled by the White House correspondents who constantly saw both the folksy and the formal Johnson. The LBJ who entertained informally at his ranch, who picked up his hounds by the ears, and who swapped earthy stories with reporters seemed unacceptably different from the wooden creature who spoke on television. The perception of Johnson as a wheeler-dealer was thus nurtured by his own labored adaptations to unseen listeners whose faces he could not see and whose applause he could not hear.

Johnson's national address of January 10, 1967, is a case in point. According to my data, it was a typical television speech for Johnson—tentative, emotionally restrained, distant. The press fell all over itself trying to describe this "new" Johnson. *Time* marveled that the speech was "restrained in tone," "judicious," "pragmatic," and "surprisingly modest."[94] The *New Republic* recounted that "reporters pinched themselves" when they discovered that Johnson "was sober, muted, and quiet. None of the old bombast. . . . Oldtimers blanched and trembled when they heard Mr. Johnson admit that he didn't know all the answers."[95] One can hardly blame the reporters for their surprise, because just 3 months earlier they had heard a swaggering LBJ boast to a live audience that he was turning

Washington, D.C., upside down. Fragments from his speech on that occasion capture the braggadocio: "I am proud of all the laws that the 89th Congress gave us. . . . I didn't come out here to see you this afternoon because I was running for anything this year. . . . I want to take a moment to make sure that all of you know a number of fine Congressmen who stand beside me in Washington." Johnson goes on to tell his listeners how certain unfair immigration laws had been "wiped out" by him, how he intended to "remake the cities," and how he would remove "freedom from fear for about 20 million Americans" through Medicare.[96] This walking, talking personification of the Great Society bore only faint resemblance to the stern, pale figure who had loomed out at the American people from their television sets 90 days previously.

In *Lyndon Johnson and the American Dream,* Doris Kearns offers a number of useful explanations for Johnson's radical change in behavior from live to mediated settings. Kearns proposes that Johnson suffered from a kind of cultural self-consciousness that caused him to be "terrified of making slips, swearing or using ungrammatical constructions." As a result, says Kearns, he stuck closely to his text, projecting "an image of feigned propriety, dullness, and dishonesty."[97] Kearns also emphasizes that Johnson was an essentially social creature who needed the physical presence of people before he could communicate with them. She reports that he even proved unable to tape-record his memoirs: "Whenever Johnson sat down to "remake the cities," and and how he would remove "freedom from and he insisted on having sheaves of memos on his lap before he'd say a word."[98] Finally, Kearns comments that Johnson possessed an old-fashioned sense of formality about affairs of state (as opposed, presumably, to affairs of politics) and felt that his office "was a stately institution demanding decorous appearance at all times."[99]

All of Kearn's explanations are intuitively attractive and it is probably not necessary to get to the ontological root of the matter. Whatever his reasons, the informal Johnson was rarely seen by most Americans, with one notable exception. On December 19, 1967, LBJ staged a virtuoso television performance. Chatting with three network correspondents in the Oval Office, he ranged far and wide—in substance and in style—confronting his accusers with a directness, a firmness, an unrelentingness, which ineluctably established who was the shrewdest, and in many senses the most articulate, of the four interlocutors. This rare appearance by the Cloakroom Johnson was impressive to all who had eyes to see (which, in late 1967, may not have been very many). Despite his success in this format, Johnson never repeated it. The rhetoric of the people was a rhetoric Johnson reserved for the people.

Johnson the Politician

While J. Alfred Prufrock may have measured out his life in coffee spoons, L. Baines Johnson measured his in coffee klatches. There has not been a president more political than LBJ. His father was a professional politician; with minor exceptions during his life, Lyndon's own paycheck was almost always drawn on a governmental account. Like John Kennedy, he saw little advantage in premature philosophical commitments and no moral virtue in doctrinaire preachment. In fact, much of Johnson's trouble with public speaking was that it was public. Johnson sensed, and his congressional experience reinforced the notion, that the most stable political deals were cut in back rooms. For Johnson, the public platform was a forum for celebrating deals well cut and for creating a psychological backdrop suitable for cutting the next one.

If rhetoric were war, then Lyndon Johnson would have been a guerrilla. Barry Goldwater, in contrast, would have stood erect and in full view on Breed's Hill, red coat brushed and bayonet gleaming. The contrast between Johnson and Goldwater could not have been more stark. They differed significantly on 6 of the 11 language variables tested. And the profiles produced (see Figure 4.4) are precisely those one might expect: (1) Johnson used less Certainty and more Realism than Goldwater, thus trading exhortation for expediency; (2) Johnson's speeches employed considerably less Complexity and Variety than did Goldwater's; Johnson sought efficiency while Goldwater developed his arguments intricately; (3) Johnson was people-centered, Goldwater idea-centered, with LBJ using more Optimism and Human Interest than his rival. Theodore White, author of *The Making of the President, 1964,* has probably given more considered judgment to the Johnson–Goldwater interface than anyone else. His thumbnail sketches of the two men eerily presaged the linguistic findings just reported.

[*On Johnson*] He was, first, no man of words, not given to verbalizations or abstractions. When he thought of his America, he thought of it either in primitive terms of Fourth-of-July patriotism or else as groups of people, forces, individuals, leaders, bosses, lobbies, pressures that he had spent his life intermeshing. He was ill at ease with the broad phraseologies, purposes and meanings of civilization. Problems had to be brought to him in the concrete, to deal with and to solve.[100]

[*On Goldwater*] For Goldwater, on examination, was indeed a frustrated intellectual come late in life to the wonder of books and ideas. Thus, ideas, for him, seem to have a vigor and validity and virulence strange to those inoculated by learning later in life. His outrage was that of a man who could perceive all things with the brittle certainty of the frustrated intellectual—with mechanical precision and fixes entirely unreal, as if he were a Trotsky of the far right. Where his conqueror, Lyndon B. Johnson, knows

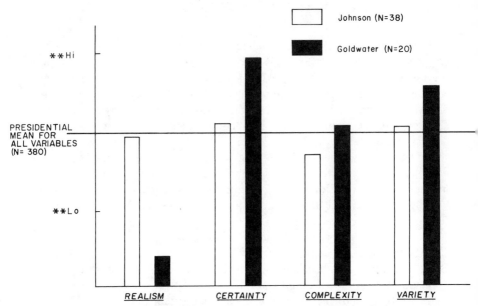

Figure 4.4 Stylistic differences between Lyndon Johnson and Barry Goldwater. All differences significant. See Table B.12. ** ± ½ sd from mean. See Table B.1 for exact values.

there are only pressures and directions, Goldwater is a man who believes there are certainties.[101]

Speaking the language of compromise, Lyndon Johnson embodied what is both best and worst about presidential politics. Speaking the language of contentiousness, Barry Goldwater embodied what is both best and worst about political oblivion. Even when read during an age that has produced the Moral Majority, Goldwater's rhetoric sounds shockingly forthright. Heavy doses of Certainty and precious little Realism produce apologetics:

> History shows us, demonstrates that nothing, nothing prepares the way for tyranny more than the failure of public officials to keep the streets safe from bullies and marauders.
> Now we Republicans see all this as more—much more than the result of mere political differences, or mere political mistakes. We see this as a result of a fundamentally and absolutely wrong view of man, his nature and his destiny.[102]

Addiction to Complexity and Variety produces prolixity:

> It is urgent at this moment that we revitalize our constitutional principles in all branches of government, that we reconstitute a system of federated governments and separated powers. We are directly challenged to reverse the accelerating drift into arbitrary and distant power, by reclaiming our legacy of checks and balances.[103]

Failure to use Optimism and Human Interest produces boredom:

We must, at the same time, accept the necessity of helping some of the less-developed nations. Proper ways to accomplish this are available, as through the International Development Association. But this way requires constant sharing of the burden, lest any of the well-developed economies, our own in particular, be crippled by an excessive lead. Other nations are able to and should contribute substantially to this course of action.[104]

If Lyndon Johnson's goal in discourse was to get his hand up under the audience's dress, Barry Goldwater's wish was to get them home chaste and at an hour permitting a good night's sleep. Teddy White claims that Goldewater wanted the triumph more and the presidency less than anyone before him in American politics.[105] It was not just that his sulfurous blasts were too hot for his listeners (political sectarianism has always found a modestly comfortable haven in these United States). Rather, he almost never seemed to have a plan that others could understand, that could be discussed with one's neighbors, that could be summarized in a single newspaper headline, that could be legislated. (When asked what he would do about Vietnam, Goldwater replied bouncily, "I would turn to my Joint Chiefs of Staff and say, 'Fellows, we made the decision to win. Now it's your problem'").[106]

Barry Goldwater will remain both a political and a rhetorical classic. Even the man who eventually brought a portion of Goldwaterism to the White House, Ronald Reagan, would have had the good sense to quit the campaign trail the day after the campaign had ended. But not Barry Goldwater. His telegram of concession was as belligerent as his nomination acceptance speech: "Congratulations on your victory. There is much to be done with Viet Nam, Cuba, the problem of law and order in this country, and a productive economy. Communism remains our No. 1 obstacle to peace, and I know that all Americans will join you in honest solutions to these problems."[107]

In similar circumstances, Lyndon Johnson would never have sent such a telegram. He would have reasoned, aptly, that there would be yet more fish to fry and more days on which to fry them. According to Doris Kearns, Johnson deeply felt that "public expressions tended to freeze men into positions, making it more difficult for them to accept later compromises of modifications, and thus reducing or limiting the capacity for bargaining that was the source of effective legislative action."[108] Johnson himself once said that "the biggest danger to American stability is the politics of principle, which brings out the masses in irrational fights for unlimited goals."[109] Although he felt deeply about certain matters, he rarely confessed them in public. Barry Goldwater's rhetoric was high church—doctrinally constrained, unyielding. Johnson's style was grass-roots preaching, animated not by eschatological hope of political sanctity but by a concern to at least keep the parlor tidy lest the pastor drop by unexpectedly. Johnson's inaugural address was called "preachy" by one news organ,[110] "prayerful and paternal"[111] by another, "Biblical"[112] by a third. The religious metaphors were appropriate, not because Johnson's text was drawn from Goldwater's Old Testament, but because it developed themes of brotherhood and sisterhood. This speech had the distinction of being the fourth highest in the sample on Human Interest.

At least when compared with Barry Goldwater, LBJ was quite measured in his public remarks. There is little doubt that the private Lyndon Johnson was often irascible, nor can it be gainsaid that he vigorously prosecuted a war that many Americans did not want. But a close inspection of his speeches, even those on Vietnam, fails to discover the stridency found in the remarks of other presidents or in Johnson's own private statements. It is at least an interesting historical footnote that the Johnson speech containing the least Certainty in the sample was his Vietnam speech of October 31, 1968. The speech with the greatest Certainty was one he delivered a few months earlier at Glassboro State College in which he argued for defente with the Soviet Union. In other words, the popular image of Johnson as a militaristic ideologue may have some credence in theoretical terms (I leave that for others to judge), but his public remarks reveal a much more political beast.

If one were to select a single speech to serve as an exemplar of the Johnson era (i.e., a speech that fits the overall statistical profile for Johnson), it might well be his voting rights address of March 15, 1965. Because his remarks were designed to initiate legislation, the speech lay midway in the Activity and Certainty rankings (thereby leaving room for compromise). Because the speech was vintage Johnson, it was suitably low on Complexity, Variety, and Embellishment. And because the speech dealt with the very heart of his Great Society program, it was high on both Realism and Self-Reference. The blending of these rhetorical humours produced what Rowland Evans and Robert Novak rated "by all odds the best, most genuinely moving speech Johnson had made as President."[113] In his remarks, Johnson reveals sensitivity to the great sacrifice he was asking of southern legislators; he also admitted that change could not occur overnight and yet he assumed the politician's classic burden of pointing out what was possible. The result is not literature but merely political eloquence and thus deserves to be quoted at length:

> We ought not, and we cannot, and we must not wait another eight months before we get a bill.
> We have already waited 10 years and more and the time for waiting is gone.
> So I ask you to join me in working long hours and nights and weekends, if necessary, to pass this bill. And I don't make that request lightly, for from the window where I sit with the problems of our country I recognize that from outside this chamber is the en-

raged conscience of a nation, the grave concern of many nations and the harsh judgment of history on our acts. . . .

The Black cause must be our cause too. Because it's not just Negroes, but really it's all of us, who must overcome the crippling legacy of bigotry and injustice. And we shall overcome.

As a man whose roots go deeply into Southern soil, I know how agonizing racial feelings are. I know how difficult it is to reshape the attitudes and the structure of our society. But a century has passed—more than 100 years—since the Negro was freed. And he is not fully free tonight. . . .

And so I say to all of you here and to all in the nation tonight that those who appeal to you to hold on to the past do so at the cost of denying you your future. This great rich, restless country can offer opportunity and education and hope to all—all, black and white, all, North and South, sharecropper and city dweller.

These are the enemies: poverty, ignorance, disease. They are our enemies, not our fellow man, not our neighbor. And these enemies too—poverty, disease and ignorance— we shall overcome.[114]

It is now cliché that our sharpest memory of the Johnson administration is of its private orders to increase troop strengths in South Vietnam rather than its public proclamations on human rights. Even though Johnson's rhetorical talents were meager, they were certainly the equal of Harry Truman's, Dwight Eisenhower's, and Jerry Ford's, but LBJ chose to fight an unpopular war and his words will evermore be given special scrutiny because of that fact. Other presidents may have been equally afflicted by a poor television presence, an overly folksy vocabulary, and the unsavory image of being a pol's pol, but at least during his lifetime (and perhaps during the lifetime of his daughters), only Southeast Asia will be remembered with universal fidelity when people think of Johnson and his times. As if to acknowledge this, Johnson wrote a fittingly rhetorical epitaph for himself when he said, "Look, I know my biggest problem is communication. If I could just communicate with the people so they'd understand the problems we face in the world and in the country. . . . "[115]

Conclusion

Both John Kennedy and Lyndon Johnson were political presidents, the former because of how he played the game, the latter because he usually won. John Kennedy was a political speaker to be reckoned with as well, Lyndon Johnson one to be forgotten. Johnson's erstwhile vice-president, Hubert Humphrey, once said that Johnson was a "muscular, glandular, political man. Not an intellectual, but bright. Not a talker, a doer. Kennedy was more a talker."[116] Indeed he was. When most modern Americans think of John Kennedy, they think of him behind the podium. Many still appreciate what he said despite the fact that his "tangible accomplishments were less than spectacular."[117] What is important to remember, says Jim Heath, is Kennedy's ability to "motivate, to inspire, and to give Americans a sense of national direction."[118] Kennedy was liked so well that, when motivating and inspiring, he was seen as performing an essentially presidential task.

The founding fathers would have thought all of this quite strange—this president as cheerleader business. Their instinct would be to measure Kennedy's presidency with a more traditional yardstick. They would be surprised to find that JFK was only the first of the modern presidential motivators (Ronald Reagan being the most recent, surely not the last). For the founding fathers to truly appreciate Kennedy and his Camelot, they would have to be taught how hard it is in modern times for a president to actually do something. They would have to be instructed in the intricate rules of modern political contesting. They would have to be taught about lobbyists, international money supplies, and party caucuses. Most of all, they would have to be schooled in the criteria for presidential assessment as set forth by the mass media and told how tangible a thing charm has become in the last hundred years.

Ted Sorensen has said that Kennedy was no orator, that others could be more forceful in voice, gestures, emphasis, and pauses. Still, says Sorensen, one must remember that "as Lord Rosebery said of the impassioned oratory of Pitt, it was 'the character which breathes through the sentence' that was impressive. Kennedy's character could be felt in every word."[119] Sorenson, of course, was deeply biased, but his statement adequately captures the sentiment of his times. The people liked John Kennedy, and because they did, they forgave much. If presidents danced instead of talked, they would have called Kennedy a good dancer.

With noted exception, the people did not like Lyndon Johnson, or, at least, they could not manage to do so in a sustained manner. Compared with Kennedy, and he was always compared with Kennedy, Johnson was coarse, bordering on vulgar. Despite his landslide election in 1964, Johnson never generated the popularity JFK did when he squeaked past Richard Nixon 4 years earlier. The people seemed more than willing to accept Johnson's munificence—his Model Cities Program, Medicare, War on Poverty, aid to higher education, Job Corps, support of Housing and Urban Development, anti-crime legislation, etc. But the people did not like his method, his back-room compacts and arm-twisting. One of them made the crack that the shortest distance between two political points in Johnson's administration was a tunnel.

Despite the differences in style and impact, the speechmaking of John Fitzgerald Kennedy and Lyndon Baines Johnson was thoroughly political because the men themselves were model politicians. The successes and failures of their presidencies were political successes and failures, not moral ones, as it seemed with Richard Nixon, or circumstantial ones, as it seemed with Jimmy Carter. The Kennedy and Johnson presidencies deserve scrutiny because they provide grounding for Hans Morgenthau's haunting question of whether statesmanship can ever be in vogue on political soil. In contrasting the politician with the statesman, Morgenthau points up how carefully we must watch a presidency preoccupied with rhetorical matters:

> The politician can take words for deeds, and insofar as his words seek to influence people to vote for him or his measures, his words actually are deeds. He can make promises without keeping them, and his promises may not even be expected to be kept. He can run on a platform every two or four years and take his stand on quite different ground in between. He can equivocate between different courses of action and bridge the chasm between incompatible positions by embracing them both. He can vote one way today and another way tomorrow, and, if he can't make up his mind, he can abstain from voting. He can try to reduce to a minimum the uncertainties of the future by preparing his action with proper attention to the facts, organization and planning. . . .
>
> The statesman must commit himself to a particular course of action to the exclusion of all others. He must cross the Rubicon or refrain from crossing it, but he cannot have it both ways. If he goes forward he takes certain risks, and if he stands still he takes other risks. There is no riskless middle ground. Nor can he, recoiling before the risks of one course of action, retrace his steps and try some other tack, promising risks different and fewer. He has crossed the Rubicon and cannot undo that crossing.[120]

Notes

1. "Care and Feeding of the Kennedy Image," *U.S. News and World Report,* September 9, 1963, p. 20.

2. "The Kennedy 'Image'—How it's Built," *U.S. News and World Report,* April 9, 1962, p. 58.

3. Frank Cormier, *LBJ the Way He Was* (New York: Doubleday, 1977), p. 114.

4. Richard Neustadt, *Presidential Power: The Politics of Leadership, with Reflections on Johnson and Nixon* (New York: Wiley, 1960, 1976), pp. 32–33.

5. Jack Valenti, *A Very Human President* (New York: Norton, 1975), p. 275.

6. Alfred Steinberg, *Sam Johnson's Boy: A Close-up of the President from Texas* (New York: Macmillan, 1968), p. 838.

7. David Culbert, "Johnson and the Media," in Robert A. Divine, ed., *Exploring the Johnson Years* (Austin: University of Texas Press, 1981), p. 215.

8. Quoted by Erv S. Duggan in Merle Miller, *Lyndon: An Oral Biography* (New York: Putnam's, 1980), p. 344.

9. James H. Rowe as quoted in Miller (1980), p. 342.

10. Benjamin C. Bradlee, quoted in Miller (1980), p. 343.

11. Cecil Osbaine, "Kennedy: The Making of a Myth," in Earl Latham, ed., *J. F. Kennedy and Presidential Power* (Lexington, MA: Heath, 1972), p. 284.

12. John Emmet Hughes, "An Echo in the Silence," *Newsweek,* December 2, 1963, p. 52.

13. Tom Wicker, "Kennedy as a Public Speaker," *New York Times Magazine,* February 25, 1962, p. 14.

14. "The Talk of the Town," February 4, 1961, p. 5.

15. Ted Sorensen, *Kennedy* (New York: Harper, 1965), p. 62.

16. Arthur Schlesinger, Jr., *A Thousand Days: John F. Kennedy in the White House* (Greenwich, CT: Fawcett, 1965), p. 91.

17. Douglass Cater, "The Cool Eye of John F. Kennedy," *Reporter,* December 19, 1959, p. 29.

18. Schlesinger (1965), p. 113.

19. Cater (1959), p. 27.

20. "Strength of the United States," November 22, 1963, *Vital Speeches of the Day,* 30:4 (1963), p. 102.

21. Schlesinger (1965), p. 666.

22. Quoted in "From all Directions," *Time,* January 25, 1963, p. 50.

23. "The Space Challenge," September 13, 1962, *Vital Speeches of the Day,* 27:24 (1962), p. 739.

24. "Commencement Address at San Diego State College," June 6, 1963, *Public Papers of the President, 1963* (Washington, D.C.: U.S. Government Printing Office, 1964), p. 447.

25. "The President and the Press," April 27, 1961, *Vital Speeches of the Day,* 27:15 (1961), p. 451.

26. "A Moral Imperative," June 11, 1963, *Vital Speeches of the Day,* 29:18 (1963), p. 547.

27. Schlesinger (1965), p. 880.

28. Neustadt (1976), p. 269.

29. Bruce Miroff, *Pragmatic Illusions: The Presidential Politics of John F. Kennedy* (New York: McKay, 1976), p. 257.

30. Schlesinger (1965), p. 112.

31. Jim F. Heath, *Decline of Disillusionment: The Kennedy-Johnson Years* (Bloomington: Indiana University Press, 1975), p. 25.

32. Harvey Wheeler, quoted in Lester Thonssen, A. Craig Baird, and Waldo Braden, *Speech Criticism,* 2nd ed., (New York: Ronald Press, 1970), p. 532.

33. Schlesinger (1965), p. 80.

34. Unnamed Democratic senator quoted in Cater (1959), p. 32.

35. "Remarks in New Orleans at a Civic Reception," May 4, 1962, *Public Papers of the Presidents, 1962,* p. 362.

36. Sorensen (1965), p. 243.

37. Joseph Green, "The Public Image of President Kennedy," *Catholic World,* May, 1961, p. 110.

38. Bill Adler, *The Complete Kennedy Wit* (New York: Citadel Press, 1967), p. 13.

39. Henry Fairlie, *The Kennedy Promise* (New York: Doubleday, 1972), pp. 350–351.

40. Green (1961), p. 110.

41. Fairlie (1972), pp. 85–86.

42. Fairlie (1972), p. 87.

43. "Address at Independence Hall, Philadelphia," July 4, 1962, *Public Papers of the Presidents, 1962,* p. 538.

44. Hans J. Morgenthau, *Truth and Power: Essays of a Decade, 1960–1970* (New York: Praeger, 1970), pp. 159–160.

45. See "Medical Care through Social Security," May 20, 1962, *Vital Speeches of the Day,* 28:17 (1962), p. 515.

46. David Halberstam, "Forward," in George Johnson, ed., *The Kennedy Presidential Press Conference* (New York: Coleman Enterprises, 1978), p. iii.

47. Adler (1967), p. 11.

48. Quoted in Fletcher Knebel, "The Unknown JFK," in Latham (1972), p. 23.

49. Sorensen (1965), pp. 61, 332.

50. Quoted in Wicker (1962), p. 70.

51. This table indicated the number of statistically significant effects ($p < .05$) observed for the independent variables listed. Main effects were weighted fully and interaction effects were weighted proportionally (e.g., an audience/topic interaction effect was accorded ½ under both "audience effects" and "topical effects"). For more information see Table B-9 in Appendix B.

52. "JFK and his Critics," *Newsweek*, July 16, 1962, p. 16.

53. *Newsweek*, July 16, 1962.

54. *Newsweek*, July 16, 1962, p. 17.

55. Joseph Alsop, "The Legacy of John F. Kennedy: Memories of an Uncommon Man," in Latham (1972), p. 263.

56. James McGregor Burns, *John Kennedy: A Political Profile* (New York: Harcourt, 1959), pp. 262–263.

57. Miroff (1976), p. 23.

58. Schlesinger (1965), pp. 109, 110.

59. Lewis Paper, *The Promise and the Performance: The Leadership of John F. Kennedy* (New York: Crown, 1975), p. 242.

60. Miroff (1976), pp. 2, 170.

61. Henry Pachter, "JFK as an Equestrian Statue: On Myth and Mythmakers," in Latham (1972), p. 40.

62. "The Nation's Economy," August 13, 1962, *Vital Speeches of the Day,* 28:22 (1962), pp. 675–676.

63. This is Henry Fairlie's understanding. See Fairlie (1972), pp. 78–79.

64. Schlesinger (1965), p. 106.

65. Alfred Kazin, "The President and Other Intellectuals," in Latham (1972), p. 251.

66. Fairlie (1972), p. 362.

67. "The President and the Press" (1961), p. 451.

68. Pierre Salinger, *With Kennedy* (New York: Doubleday, 1966), p. 157.

69. Miroff (1976), p. 54.

70. "Remarks at Amherst College upon Receiving an Honorary Degree," October 26, 1963, *Public Papers of the Presidents, 1963,* p. 817.

71. Fairlie (1972), p. 222.

72. Quoted in Knebel in Latham (1972), p. 27.

73. Robert Sherrill, *The Accidental President* (New York: Grossman, 1967), p. 174.

74. "The Forward Thrust of America," November 27, 1963, *Vital Speeches of the Day,* 30:5 (1963), p. 130.

75. "The State of the Union," January 14, 1969, *Vital Speeches of the Day,* 35:8 (1969), p. 231.

76. Theodore White, *The Making of the President, 1964* (New York: Atheneum, 1965), p. 264.

77. Cormier (1977), p. 137.

78. "Democratic Party Dinner in Chicago," May 17, 1966, *Weekly Compilations of Presidential Documents,* 2:20 (1966), pp. 658–659.

79. "Is Dissent Traitorous?," *The Christian Century,* June 1, 1966, p. 703.

80. Doris Kearns, *Lyndon Johnson and the American Dream* (New York: New American Library, 1976), p. 44.

81. Unnamed White House aide quoted in "Communication Gap: LBJ's Monologue with the Intellectuals," *Science,* July 14, 1967, p. 175.

82. Cormier (1977), p. 157.
83. Unnamed reporter quoted in Harry McPherson, *A Political Education* (Boston: Little, Brown, 1972), p. 248.
84. Cormier (1977), p. 113.
85. Richard Harwood and Haynes Johnson, *Lyndon* (New York: Praeger, 1973), p. 14.
86. Quoted in Kearns (1976), p. 97.
87. Robert Caro, "The Years of Lyndon Johnson," *The Atlantic Monthly,* April, 1982, p. 77.
88. Liz Carpenter, *Ruffles and Flourishes* (New York: Doubleday, 1969), p. 258.
89. Heath (1975), pp. 37-8.
90. McPherson (1972), p. 445.
91. Quoted in Sherrill (1967), pp. 174-5.
92. "Medicare Program," June 15, 1966, *Weekly Compilations of Presidential Documents,* 2:24 (1966), pp. 777-8.
93. "State of the Union," January 8, 1964, *Vital speeches of the Day,* 30:7 (1964), p. 195.
94. "The Presidency," *Time,* January 20, 1967, p. 13.
95. "New Image," *New Republic,* February 18, 1967, p. 6.
96. "Columbus Day in New York," October 12, 1966, *Weekly Compilations of Presidential Documents,* 2:41 (1966), p. 1462.
97. Kearns (1976), p. 318.
98. Kearns (1976), p. 370.
99. Kearns (1976), p. 370.
100. White (1965), p. 60-61.
101. White (1965), p. 219.
102. "Extremism in Defense of Liberty," July 16, 1964, in George W. Hibbitt, ed., *The Dolphin Book of Speeches* (New York: Dolphin, 1965), p. 295.
103. "Remarks to the Republican Platform Committee," July 10, 1964, press release by the Republican National Committee, p. 2.
104. "Economic Realities," January 15, 1964, *Vital Speeches of the Day,* 30:8 (1964), p. 235.
105. White (1965), p. 218.
106. Quoted in Harwood and Johnson (1973), pp. 77-78.
107. Presented in Steinberg (1968), p. 696.
108. Kearns (1976), p. 143.
109. Quoted in Kearns (1976), p. 161.
110. "Lyndon Johnson's Pledge," *Newsweek,* February 1, 1965, p. 11.
111. "The Presidency," *Time,* January 29, 1965, p. 9.
112. Kenneth Crawford, "Hope and Reality," *Newsweek,* February 1, 1965, p. 24.
113. Rowland Evans and Robert Novak, *Lyndon B. Johnson: The Exercise of Power* (New York: New American Library, 1966), p. 521.
114. "The Right to Vote," March 15, 1965, *Vital Speeches of the Day,* 31:12 (1965), p. 355-356.
115. Quoted in "Life with Lyndon," *Newsweek,* January 1, 1968, p. 11.
116. Quoted in Miller (1980), p. 346.
117. Heath (1975), p. 163.
118. Heath (1975), p. 163.
119. Sorensen (1965), p. 331.
120. Morgenthau (1970), p. 146.

RICHARD NIXON:
PRISONER OF RHETORIC[1]

"He taught me everything I know about speechwriting. Writing for the printed word and the spoken word is different entirely. He's like a tutor: he'll tell you how to reorganize a draft, what to put in and leave out and how to use highlights."[2] The quote is from Raymond K. Price, Jr., a former presidential speechwriter, author, and journalist. Price's tutor had also assisted Eliot Richardson some 16 years previously: "He opened up to give me a short and unforgettable lesson in speechwriting. He showed me how to put myself in the shoes of the speaker, standing in front of a live audience of thousands. . . . It was a far better speech for his editing, but it would not have been unless he had been invited to edit."[3] The tutelage provided Price and Richardson was not offered by some Georgetown English professor nor by some fugitive journalist afflicted with Potomac fever. The pedagogue so admired by Price and Richardson was a college debater turned political gutfighter turned president of the United States, a man of such sagacity that he made rhetorical surrogates out of Spiro Agnew and Henry Kissinger, and rhetorical sacrifices out of Alger Hiss and Helen Gahagan Douglas, a man so profoundly and consistently canny that he even fashioned persuasive manipulanda out of his dog and his wife's cloth coat.

Richard Milhous Nixon was more aware of practical communication than was any other president, even though he surely was not among our most literary or perhaps even among our most persuasive chief executives. It was Richard Nixon's awareness of how human influence works that set him apart from his presidential peers. It was Richard Nixon's fascination with strategizing, camera angles, applause lines, Tele-Prompters, and parallel sentence structure that made him a metarhetorical president, a president as much concerned with *why* a given speech worked or did not work as with its absolute success or failure. Indeed, Nixon's consciousness of the communication process afforded much of the humor fashioned at his expense: "Let me be perfectly clear," "I want to speak with candor there," "You're probably asking why I said that," etc. Whether such strategy-consciousness is indicative of deep-seated repressions, as psychiatrist Eli Chesen would have us believe,[4] or whether they merely constitute political preening, as author Jules Witcover argues,[5] they do suggest a special turn of mind, a person who, when he "addresses the nation over television, the immediate audience is always himself."[6]

Throughout his career, Richard Nixon personally labored over each of his major public speeches. Modern political history will retain as one of its storied images that of Richard Nixon sitting with pen in hand, scratching upon yellow legal pads, searching for that special turn of phrase or unappreciated fact that would mark the difference between victory and defeat. Nixon's world was a world of words. He rose to prominence because of his savage rhetoric in 1948 (the Hiss affair) and avoided political limbo because of his homespun rhetoric in 1952 (Checkers). He first tasted political defeat because of his mediated rhetoric in 1960 (the Kennedy debate), nearly buried himself because of his spontaneous rhetoric in 1962 (after his loss to Pat Brown), regained momentum because of his tireless rhetoric in 1966 (the off-season elections), and then gathered in the garlands by virtue of his managed rhetoric in 1968 (the presidential campaign). Until the summer of 1974, his was a career that spun dizzyingly on the fulcrum of public discourse. Ironically, his was also a career undone by talk, talk witnessed only by his most trusted lieutenants and a silent, hidden, mechanical auditor.

According to many, Richard Nixon's essential self "is not to be found in some private sanctuary of his subconscious, but rather in the accidental markings of the public record."[7] Nixon's fondness for public revelation helped to make psychohistory a popular commodity on publishers' row. Bruce Mazlish, Gary Wills, Fawn Brodie, and countless lesser writers have, when preparing their commentaries on Nixon, dutifully listened to the oral histories, conducted the requisite interviews with Nixon intimates, and pored over correspondence and report cards from his youth.[8] Yet when searching for anecdotes suitable for telling the essential Nixon tale, the best and the worst of Nixon's biographers inevitably returned to his public remarks to validate their claims about his intellectual habits and, as many of them would have it, his sundry weaknesses of the spirit. As David Halberstam correctly notes, "We are told about Nixon that we do not know the real man, that the real man in small private conversation is intelligent, forceful, even brilliant, but I think the judgment is finally that we poor uninitiates on the outside know more about him than those so privileged as to be on the inside. He is what we always thought he was."[9]

Richard Nixon depended upon persuasion. Not surprisingly, he was aware of that dependence. As he pondered his concession speech of 1960, he was beset by memories of the uniquely rhetorical crises upon which his then-short career already seemed to turn:

> I thought back over other crises which had confronted me as I prepared for speeches or press conferences: the fund speech in 1952; my White House press conference after the President's stroke in 1957; trying to hold my temper as I met the press in Lima and Caracas after the riots there in 1958; those tense moments when Kruschev had verbally assaulted me at the American Exhibition in Moscow and I had a split-second to decide to remain silent, to retreat, or to fight back.[10]

Had he been extraordinarily prescient, Nixon could have completed the listing by adding certain presidential turning points: his Kennedyesque inaugural, his galvanizing speech on Cambodia, his legalistic Watergate explanations, his rhetorical coronation of Gerald Ford, his dignified resignation speech, and his bizarre farewell to his staff.

It may be that the only suitably powerful way to probing Nixon's speechmaking is to use a computer. Deft though he was, even Richard Nixon could not possibly monitor or control the microstylistic patterns that contributed to his public self. By looking for continuities across speaking situations, for exceptions to the persuasive patterns established early in his public life, and for the adaptations he made to the various crowds he engaged, we can perhaps explain why people reacted to Richard Nixon as they did. Failing that, we may at least be able to understand why people report having seen so many different Richard Nixons on the American scene during the 30 years he captured political attention.

Nixon the Pragmatist

"He'll be known as 'the practical president,' earnest but flexible, unspectacular but highly competent," predicted an unnamed Washington politico in the pages of *U.S. News and World Report* in August in 1969.[11] Although one cannot be sure of the basis for this prediction, Richard Nixon's previous service as a fact-gathering congressman, his lawyerly fascination with fully documented cases, and his admitted intolerance of pure abstraction were all well-known aspects of the Nixon personality. That Nixon's presidency was, in fact, a bit more spectacular than our unnamed observer had anticipated was due to changing political circumstances, not to Richard Nixon's natural wont.

Always the master of the cliché, Nixon once advised, "When the action is hot, keep the rhetoric cool."[12] Nixon followed his own advice. No president even approached the amount of Realism to be found in Nixon's speeches. Of his 38 speeches 26 surpass the presidential average on this dimension. In addition, Nixon's Activity score is highest by far, with 26 of his speeches scoring 200 or higher (see Figure 5.1). These stylistic features reveal a man immersed in the problems of this world, a dynamic leader in the American rather than the European mode—one who gets things done, who finds (and honors) the bottom line, who does not flinch at being termed a modern Horatio Alger, who runs the presidency as the good Republican corporation the forefathers intended it to be. He was not a flashy president, but a president you could count on, and certainly not a president to get mired down in a philosophical discussion nor, for that matter, a president to invite Pablo Casals to play at the White House.

Clear-headed American pragmatism resounded throughout his speeches. This was particularly true when he attempted to justify policy decisions. For example:

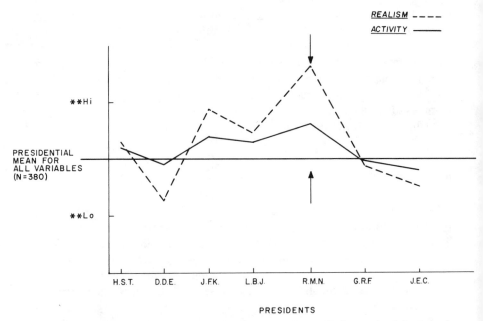

Figure 5.1   Richard Nixon compared with other presidents on realism and activity. In each case, N = 38, except Carter (N = 152). ** ± ½ sd from mean. See Table B.1 for exact values.

Why are we in Vietnam?

We Americans are a do-it-yourself people, an impatient people. Instead of teaching someone else to do a job, we like to do it ourselves. This trait has been carried over into our foreign policy.[13]

How is revenue sharing justified philosophically?

Revenue sharing. What does that really mean? I will tell you what it means. For 190 years we have seen power in this great country of ours flow from the people and from the cities and from the state to Washington D.C. and now I say it's time for power to flow back from Washington to the states and to the cities and to the people of this country.[14]

What is the importance of American agriculture?

But there is one area where America is by all odds number one, and that is Agriculture. And looking to the future, the fact that America is so productive in Agriculture, that we produce enough to feed all of the American people, to clothe the American people, and to provide billions of dollars in aid as well as in sales to countries abroad, that is a great instrument for peace in the world, and we are using it for peace as well as for humanity.[15]

The war in Vietnam as a cultural mandate, revenue sharing as a political balancing act, food production as international leverage—these are the realities, Nixon would say, and they have to be addressed as such. Nixon's speeches are thus punctuated with names, dates, concrete terms, an emphasis on the present, expediency. In his presidential speeches, we do not find the ideological breast-thumping of his Communist-hunting days. Realpolitik reigns supreme.

Richard Nixon also knew how to quicken a listener's pulse by speaking in a brisk manner. As evidenced by his Activity scores, Nixon's rhetoric marched along smartly, the transitive verbs crackling as he pushed forward his anti-inflation program: "The time has come for decisive action. . . . I am today ordering a freeze. . . . We will break the back of inflation. . . . I have directed the Secretary of the Treasury to take the action necessary. . . . I have [suspended] temporarily the convertibility of the dollar. . . ."[16] Nixon was able to generate a sense of momentum in his listeners when talking about guns as well as butter: "Tonight, American and South Vietnamese units will attack the headquarters for the entire Communist military operation in South Vietnam. . . . The areas in which these attacks will be launched are completely occupied. . . . Once enemy forces are driven out of these sanctuaries and once their military supplies are destroyed, we will withdraw. . . . The action I take tonight is essential. . . ."[17] Perhaps because his own delivery was decidedly lackluster when compared, say, to Harry

Truman's or John Kennedy's, Nixon depended upon verbal energy to give his ideas the requisite force. His use of Activity also served to breathe life into the fact-laden constructions that were stored in his capacious mind. The combination allowed him to appear suitably presidential.

Nixon's Realism built the image of substance that his rivals for the presidency failed to generate in many voters' minds. Both Hubert Humphrey and George McGovern scored significantly lower on Realism than did Richard Nixon, and they used more Complexity and Variety and less Familiarity as well (see Figure 5.2). At least in the samples at hand, neither candidate was able to match Nixon's uncomplicated presentations of how things were. Nixon's unwillingness to pursue issues to their philosophical cores earmarked him as a pedant in the eyes of many, especially in the eyes of those inhabiting academe. For academics, George McGovern's understanding of racial prejudice was more like their own and they could empathize with both the substance and the style of his expositions: "Many Americans hoped that this single act [the Civil Rights Act of 1964] would set us on a rapid course toward the extinction of racial prejudice. But the real crisis is still ahead of us—and it is still unresolved. In the last decade we have learned that discrimination is rooted in attitudes and frustrations, and fears that cannot be dispelled by law, but in our hearts."[18]

Probing his or others' hearts was not Richard Nixon's style. In his speech of August 8, 1969, for example, Nixon also dealt with racial discrimination, but did so in his characteristically pragmatic way:

America prides itself on being the "land of opportunity." I deeply believe in this ideal, as I am sure everyone listening to me also believes in this ideal.

Full opportunity means the chance for upward mobility on every rung of the economic ladder and for every American, no matter what the handicaps of birth. The cold, hard truth is that a child born to a poor family has far less chance to make a good living than a child born to a middle income family.[19]

Hardly a sublime passage, and hardly an emotionally compassionate statement, but a passage that demonstrates Nixon's understanding of America's sociopolitical routines. Dispassionate philosophy aside, Nixon's capacity to size up an issue and reduce it to its pragmatic understructure impressed the American people in the early 1970s. McGovern also impressed some of them, but he impressed the majority of the voters as being too high-minded or too ideological or too impractical to guide an essentially pragmatic people. Richard Nixon seemed a man in charge of things. Even the cruelest of his detractors granted him that.

Hubert Humphrey was no pointy-headed intellectual but he, too, could not rival Richard Nixon's stolid use of language. Humphrey, too, would claim that "human rights is not basically a social issue, an economic issue, a political issue, or even a legislative issue. It is primarily a moral issue."[20]

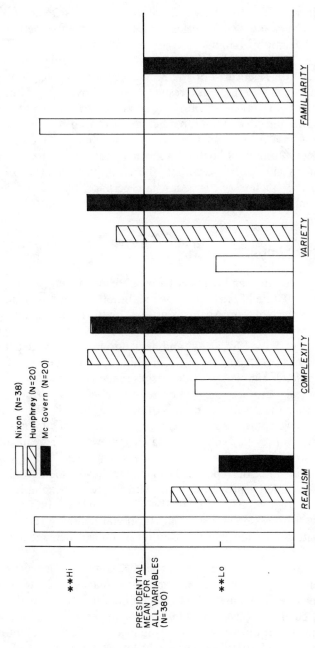

Figure 5.2 Comparison of Nixon, McGovern, and Humphrey styles. Several differences significant. See Table B.12. ** ± ½ sd from mean. See Table B.1 for exact values.

Perhaps it may seem that all we are observing here is Democratic cant vis-à-vis civil rights and that on other issues the differences between Richard Nixon and Humphrey–McGovern are not so pronounced. This is not the case. Of the 20 Humphrey speeches sampled, only 4 surpassed Richard Nixon's average on Realism. For the McGovern sample, only one surpassed the Nixon average. Perhaps as a result, both McGovern and Humphrey had difficulty in being taken seriously by some voters. For many, Humphrey was too shrill and McGovern too ethereal. Nixon, in contrast, was a workaday fellow in a brown suit who counted his change. One of his speechwriters, Rev. John McLaughlin, reported that "He [Nixon] believes in persuasion by citing facts: assemble the facts and the facts will speak for themselves."[21] Such a style is pedestrian, perhaps, but a familiar style to a nation founded by shopkeepers and tinkers.

Nixon the Demagogue

While not among the highest art forms, demagoguery has had a special history in the United States. In large measure the nation was christened by the demagoguery of Sam Adams, nurtured by the demagoguery of Andrew Jackson, entertained by the demagoguery of Huey Long, challenged by the demagoguery of Joe McCarthy, and helped to mature by the demagoguery of Richard Nixon. Demagoguery is a technique of speech whereby complex matters are made simple, two-sided issues rendered one-sided, neutral ideas colored purple, and persistence elevated to a rhetorical virtue.

Considering the desultory features of demagoguery, it may seem odd that America has welcomed so many demagogues and often purchased the questionable wares they hawked. But in a curious way, our demagogues have served us well by calling attention to ideas that cooler heads would eventually translate into social policy. Demagogues have also allowed journalists to ply their trade by providing them with impressive examples of perfidy in our times. In addition, demagogues offer a rallying point for the nation's politically dispossessed and serve as emotional lightning rods for those of the opposite persuasion. Seen in a cultural context, demagogues provide a useful service.

By all conventional standards, Richard Nixon was a demagogue. To put the matter more precisely, he was the most demagogic of our modern presidents, as we see in Figure 5.3: (1) His Familiarity score was the highest of the seven chief executives; all but nine of his speeches scored above the presidential mean on use of plain language; (2) he habitually effected a staccato style, his Variety score being the lowest among the chief executives; (3) his language was also the least Embellished; he did not mince his words

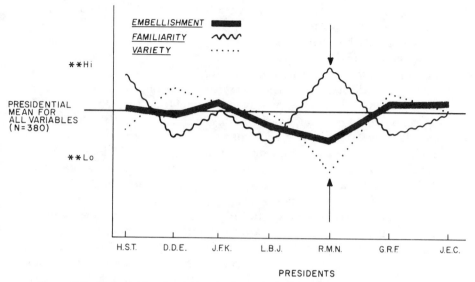

Figure 5.3   Richard Nixon's plain style. In each case, $N = 38$, except Carter ($N = 152$). ** ± ½ sd from mean. See Table B.1 for exact values.

but called things as they were; (4) Nixon's use of Human Interest was also the highest in the presidential sample, providing him with the homespun quality necessary for an American demagogue; and, finally, (5) Symbolism was used with much greater frequency by Nixon than by any other chief executive; he felt no compunction about dipping into the well of sacred American values when the need arose. Apparently, the need arose regularly for him.

To call Richard Nixon a demagogue in this context is to make a rhetorical, not a political, statement. However, it was the political implications of this style that caused Nixon to be pilloried by the press throughout his career and vilified by every college professor worth his AAUP card. Both groups, rightly enough as it turns out, discerned in Nixon an overly facile use of language, a willingness to make things clearer than the facts would permit, and a certain waywardness with ideas. Jerry Voorhis and, later, Archibald Cox also came to understand the Nixon rhetorical style. And, as we saw in Chapter Two, most of the demagogic aspects of this style actually increased when he became president, causing the press (during "the early, good years") to search their thesauruses feverishly for appropriately dignified adjectives to describe this new-but-old style. But even the press was often at a loss to explain why this style appealed to so many of the American people for so many years. To examine his speechmaking carefully is to begin to answer that question.

There are many reasons why Richard Nixon was envious of John Kennedy. Kennedy was born into wealth; Nixon worked in his father's grocery store. Kennedy had natural good looks; Nixon was not especially handsome. But perhaps the main source of his envy was John Kennedy's obvious comfort amidst intellectuals, which is to say poets, professors, journalists, and lawyers, which is also to say literary men and women. Nixon, of course, was highly intelligent; in some ways more intelligent than John Kennedy. But Nixon could not banter comfortably in the literary salons or toss off *bon mots* with the wordy grace expected on the eastern seaboard. Interpreting Mr. Nixon's attitudes on such matters, David Halberstam says: "Young men who want to get ahead are not likely to value language. Indeed, a sense of language might be interpreted as a weakness. Adlai Stevenson, after all, cared about language, and look where it got him."[22]

For Nixon, there was probably something faintly effeminate about excessive concern for verbal elegance. As one of his speechwriters complained, "After he goes through eight or ten drafts, he's drained the life out of it; it's bloodless."[23] Nixon's real passion during speech preparation was strategy, assembling the ideational knockout punches that would overwhelm his several enemies. Language for him was a decided afterthought, the sort of thing that one employed former journalists to handle. According to one of these former journalists (Raymond Price), Mr. Nixon was more concerned with the number of words he used in his speeches than their evocative power. As a matter of course, Price furnished a precise word count for Nixon when drafting his presidential speeches.[24]

We thus see a fairly predictable relationship between world view and behavior in Nixon's speeches. They were unembellished, colloquial, and repetitious—especially repetitious. Apparently he thought that a thing well said once ought to be said again. Nixon also had a fondness for parallel constructions. His announcement of Gerald Ford as vice-president designate had the lowest Variety scores of the speeches sampled:

We need strong and effective leadership, for the hope of the world for peace lies with the leadership. . . .
. . . Our ability to build a prosperity in this country, a prosperity without war. . . .
This is a time for a new beginning in America, a new beginning in which. . . .
And I'm confident we can meet those dangers. . . . I am confident that we shall do so.[25]

Richard Nixon was a man without a thesaurus. Thesauruses, after all, were the refuge of the bookish scoundrels who hounded him over the years. Moreover, Nixon would argue, the people are not looking for literary craftsmanship in their presidents. The American people, especially, want language that has the appearance of Abraham Lincoln—plain, gaunt, and modest.

To some extent, Richard Nixon was right about the American people.

As Ralph Lane noted many years ago when interviewing dock workers, bartenders, and bus drivers about their political world views, the American voter is sharply ambivalent about public figures who use language well.[26] Because of this wariness of eloquence, a portion of the American nature embraced the patrician-sounding Adlai Stevenson while another portion rejected him as too continental for the craggy face of American discourse. Thus, if his spare style caused Richard Nixon to be labeled a demagogue, it was a risk he ran willingly.

Nixon's second inaugural address was one of the most colloquial speeches he delivered as president. The formal trappings of the inaugural ceremony notwithstanding, Nixon's Familiarity score for the second inaugural was 123. Roughly one out of every four words he used was drawn from a list of the simplest English words, which caused his speech to be reductionistic, a pastiche of two-syllable words and cloying aphorisms:

> A person can be expected to act responsibly only if he has responsibility. . . .
> Let us measure what we will do for others by what they will do for themselves. . . .
> In trusting too much in government, we have asked more than it can deliver. . . .
> Government must learn to take less from people so that people can do more for themselves.[27]

Demagoguery involves more than excessive simplicity. As a columnist in the *Nation* once commented (when, incidentally, discussing Richard Nixon's speeches), "The marks of a demagogue are many, but the principal ones are an appeal to the emotions, the lower the better."[28] Richard Nixon was always ready for this challenge—as communist baiter, as expense-fund supplicant, as denouncer of media bias. All of these Richard Nixons understood the nature of emotion and how it could be used to excoriate. When one is president of the United States, however, one cannot always keep emotion at the ready. As president, Richard Nixon needed another tactic, isolate-and-attack now being a bit unseemly. Moreover, his own natural diffidence ruled out using himself to transmit the requisite emotion. The solution he happened upon was to lard his speeches with a good deal of Human Interest, references to "the little people" who populated Nixon's America.

It was probably his use of Human Interest that caused so many people to feel so uncomfortable when listening to Richard Nixon speak. The words seemed homey enough but the communicative package of rigid body, forced smile, and practiced gestures often belied such folksiness. Many voters would not buy a used car from Nixon because of this awkwardness, and others had difficulty accepting détente or revenue sharing for the same reasons. The more Richard Nixon tried to mingle among the hoi polloi, the less successful he was. Three of his speeches suggest why.

Nixon's first inaugural contained the third heaviest usage of Human In-

terest in the sample. In one portion of that speech, he borrowed traditionally Democratic language but used it for decidedly Republican ends:

> The lesson of past agony is that without the people we can do nothing; with the people
> we can do everything. To match the magnitude of our tasks, we need the energies of
> our people enlisted not only in grand enterprises, but more importantly in those small,
> splendid efforts that make headlines in the neighborhood newspaper instead of the na-
> tional Journal.
>   With these, we can build a great cathedral of the spirit, each of us raising it one stone
> at a time as he reaches out to his neighbor, helping, caring, doing.[29]

For some listeners, Nixon's deployment of Human Interest on such occasions probably seemed like an all too transparent set-up in which "the
people" would ultimately be sacrificed for the nameless, faceless entities of
corporate America. If some had political misgivings about Nixon's proletarian instincts, others found them to be unsettling psychologically. One
such group must have been senior citizens (mentioned in Chapter Two) who
were invited to the White House for Thanksgiving dinner in 1969 and confronted by a gushing chief executive turned master of ceremonies:

> We were trying to think on this Thanksgiving Day what group we could invite to be with
> us. In our family we always had Thanksgiving as a family day. We have in the past and
> we do now. Our parents cannot be here now, but we wanted people who have been with
> this nation for so many years, who have lived good lives, to be here as our guests today.
> We feel that you are part of our family and we invite you here and we hope you enjoy
> this house as part of our family, the White House family, the American family.[30]

Discomforted though Mr. Nixon's elderly guests may have been, they
must have been even more baffled by his performance on August 9, 1974,
during his last speech in the White House, the speech containing the greatest
amount of Human Interest found in the sample. Commenting on this address, one observer remarked that "Richard Nixon could never rise above
piety to insight, he remains fixed in our memories as a pathetic object, not
fully human, striving always to portray a soap opera version of what it
means to be steadfast and heroic in the face of domestic adversity."[31] Perhaps our observer has understated the case. When one looks at Nixon's last
speech, one can almost imagine that his speechwriters consisted of Russell
Conwell, Vince Lombardi, and Dickens's Tiny Tim:

> I remember my old man. I think that they would have called him sort of a little man,
> a common man. He didn't consider himself that way. You know what he was? He was
> a streetcar motorman first, and then he was a farmer, and then he had a lemon ranch.
> It was the poorest lemon ranch in California, I can assure you.[32]

That such personal remarks could have issued from a president who had
just been deposed may seem understandable, given the emotion of the moment. But Richard Nixon made a habit of using sentimentality to achieve
his rhetorical ends. His famed Checker's speech set him on that course, and

on that course he persevered in his contrived way, trying to reach people's hearts, their guts, or whatever else of themselves they were willing to share.

Such expediency marks the demagogue and so does the use of the nation's pantheon of basic values. Nixon's Symbolism scores are consistently higher than those of other presidents (see Table B.8). *America, people,* and (ironically) *peace* were his favored words, but he used most of them from time to time—during a Republican rally in May of 1969, during his Vietnamization speech of that November, during J. Edgar Hoover's eulogy, during an address on agriculture at Oklahoma State University, during his resignation speech. His excessive use of Boy Scout imagery was variously described as "sloganeering,"[33] "something redolent of the rubber-chicken circuit,"[34] an "exercise in rhetoric and histrionics,"[35] "blustering, impotent fury,"[36] and, cruelest of all, "Kennedy in rhinestones."[37] Criticisms aside, such symbology can be effective. When traveling to meet Billy Graham at the University of Tennessee in May of 1970, for example, Richard Nixon reasoned that a college campus that would permit him to speak during those turbulent times was also a college campus that would permit tear-stained observations like the following:

> I know there are things about America that are wrong. But I also know that this is a country where a young person. . . .
> I also know that of all the nations in the world, this is the one country where. . . .
> As one who works in the field of government, I can tell you my life is dedicated to. . . .
> There is one thing that government cannot do. We may still have a sterile life because we lack the spirit, a spirit that cannot come from a man in government, a spirit that. . . .[38]

All politicians are schooled from their earliest days on the stump to use bromides of this sort. But Richard Nixon was less ashamed than most to provide them over and over again. It is also not surprising that Nixon's use of Symbolism and Certainty were very highly correlated, something that was not true for most of the other presidents. Unfortunately, rhetorical havens permitting this mixture of Symbolism and Certainty were not close at hand during the Nixon presidency. He had to seek them out in Knoxville, Tennessee; Manhattan, Kansas; and Stillwater, Oklahoma. In more urban locations the cry of "demagogue!" was likely to be heard.

Nixon the Automaton

Computer science has generated a new vocabulary (feedback, input, loop, bug, etc.) for describing ordinary reality. Practitioners of the art distinguish between "dumb" and "smart" machines, the former having only the capacity to perform a limited number of routine chores and the latter able to adjust to changing circumstances by taking the creative leap necessary to solve complex problems.

If Richard Nixon was an automaton, he was certainly an intelligent machine. He planned his strategies with numbing precision but also retained flexibility for meeting changing political circumstance. Therefore, while Stewart Alsop was correct in describing Nixon as "the most reserved, the most totally self-controlled, politician of this generation,"[39] and while William Lee Miller wisely observed that when "Mr. Nixon gets the most effective phrases and themes worked out and polished, he then repeats them at each town. By the end of the campaign his speech has become a veritable masterpiece of planned spontaneity and deliberate loss of temper,"[40] we should not conclude that Nixon's manner was rote. Rather, he carefully matched his remarks to the complex social geometry of the presidency. For many observers, the gaucherie came in Nixon's consciousness of these adaptions, the precision with which this well-oiled machine hummed along. Edwin Black commented:

> One can see the willfulness in his walk. The legs are stiff; the arms are rigid; the stride is not a single motion but a sequence of discrete motions; the body is slightly crouched, like a wary boxer's. We can find the same characteristics in people who wear leg or back braces, and whose conscious minds must instruct each step.
>
> Most conspicuously, it is in his discourse. "Let me make one thing perfectly clear . . ." "Let me say this . . ." The discourses are full of statements about the discourses themselves. The compositional machinery—things like transitions and internal summaries—are just a bit clumsy, just a bit conspicuous.
>
> *The man is not inventing a speech. He is inventing a man inventing a speech.*[41]

At first glance, Nixon's control over his style may seem preposterous. Not 1 of the 11 language variables produced a statistically significant difference over time; in general, Nixon ended his presidency just as he began it. Not 1 of the 11 variables was altered significantly in light of the topics to which Mr. Nixon addressed himself; he generally spoke about the nation's historic values as he did about its farm subsidies (see Table B.9). On the basis of these simple variables alone, it appears that Nixon found a rhetorical formula and stuck to it.

Perhaps even more surprising were the results of a follow-up investigation. To test the fabled "Nixon control," 24 of Nixon's foreign policy speeches were selected for special analysis; 12 had been delivered from text and the remainder were impromptu. One of the findings (see Table B.3) was probably inevitable: The speeches presented without notes showed less Variety than did the prepared remarks, probably reflecting inherent modality differences (i.e., we tend to repeat ourselves more often when speaking than when writing). The other finding was that Nixon employed greater Activity when speaking from a prepared text about foreign policy, indicating that Nixon's speechwriters were more able than he to find the requisite verbal energy.

The most important findings, though, were the nonfindings: Not one of the other nine factors changed from condition to condition. Whether Nixon habitually spoke as his speechwriters wrote, or whether his ghosted speeches were designed to suit his "natural voice" (whatever that may have been), the results attest impressively to the inordinate control over self and circumstance possessed by Nixon. His language remained equally uncomplicated in both conditions; he made no greater use of familiar or realistic language in the impromptu situation (which one would have expected) nor significantly less Human Interest or Symbolism when using a prepared text (which one also might have anticipated). Most surprising of all is that Nixon did not significantly increase his use of Self-References when speaking extemporaneously. All of these results stand in stark contrast to long-standing and consistent research findings showing clear-cut differences between formal and informal prose.[42] Obviously, the researchers had not met Richard Nixon.

It seems highly unlikely that the remarks of any other contemporary politician would have produced similar findings. The self-monitoring required to speak written words is prodigious indeed. To use the passive voice when speaking without notes (as Nixon does consistently in these speeches), to refer to oneself in the first person plural (as he also does), and to be able to name names and cite specific statistical information easily in such circumstances are capacities possessed by few. What we are probably seeing here is the language of diplomacy, a curious language requiring excessive self-scrutiny for fear of hoisting one's constituency on one's verbal petard. Richard Nixon was more than up to this task. As James David Barber says, Nixon is "a man on the run, watching himself run, criticizing his form as he runs. He *tends* himself."[43]

Stories of Mr. Nixon's difficulties with the mass media are legion. From his facial makeup problems in the 1960 debates with John Kennedy, through the televised debacle after he lost to Pat Brown for the California governorship in 1962, to his oftentimes testy press conferences when serving as president, Nixon approached the media with a steely eye and a special rhetorical style as well. Nixon's vaunted self-control became especially apparent when his mediated speeches were compared with those presented to live audiences. The differences are the following: the televised speeches were more complex and varied than his local addresses, but he used fewer Self-References and less Realism (see Figure 5.4) when his remarks were carried by the media (his five most abstract speeches were televised addresses). Depending upon one's preferences for imagery, television caused Mr. Nixon to become up-tight, cool, wooden, or distanced. Television audiences saw

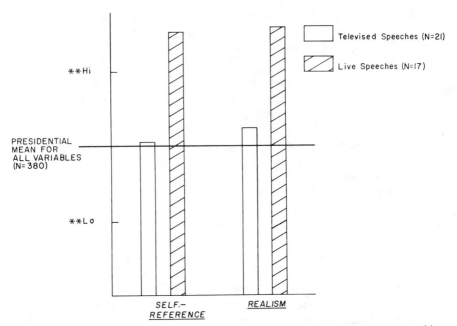

Figure 5.4   Richard Nixon's adaptations to audience. All differences significant. See Table B.9. **½ sd from mean. See Table B.1 for exact values.

a wordier and less personal Nixon, a Nixon prone to abstractions. He possessed none of the easy grace of a Walter Cronkite or the winsomeness of a Johnny Carson or even the practiced humility of a Ronald Reagan. As Michael Murray has reported, "No president has been more conscious of the media. . . . Mr. Nixon approaches the media as he does everything else, with wary hostility; these are barriers to be overcome rather than tools to use."[44]

Naturally, Richard Nixon had ample reason to monitor his words carefully when speaking on television. He had never been the darling of the media and his self-consciousness had made him an ample target for satire. As his alter ego on media relations (Spiro Agnew) correctly noted, Mr. Nixon's speeches were typically savaged during the networks' instant commentaries. Well before he became president, however, Nixon tried to counter his foes by perfecting his television style. As his media adviser, Roger Ailes, once reported, "Mr. Nixon took time when he was out of politics to learn about television. He listened to people. He watched. And audiences grew up, television grew up, and Mr. Nixon examined his mistakes. The next time he walked into a studio, he approached it very confidently. He knew what he had to do."[45]

Mr. Nixon's televised speeches were largely tutorials. He achieved professorial distance from his subject matter (via his low Self-References) and even burdened his typically unbloated syntax with complexification and abstraction. During his presidential years he lectured the American people in their homes on Vietnamization, welfare reform, wages and prices, energy, and inevitably, Watergate. At time he employed visual aids to untangle the syntax he had deliberately tangled and family portraits to humanize the discourse he had made impersonal. The rhetorical composite was meant to ensure us that he was indeed our president and not the political sniper of old. The formal Nixon was thus a safe Nixon, a supremely pedagogical Nixon:

> Until the day comes when science finds a way of installing a conscience in every computer, we must develop human, personal safeguards that prevent computers from becoming huge, mechanical, impersonal robots that deprive us of our essential liberties.
>
> Here is the heart of the matter. What a person earns, what he owes, what he gives to his church or to his charity is his own personal business and should not be spread around without his consent. When personal information is given or obtained for one purpose, such as a loan or credit at a store, it should not be secretly used by anyone for any purpose. To use James Madison's terms, in pursuing the overall public good, we must make sure that we also protect the individual's private rights.[46]

In unprecedented numbers we watched this televised Nixon, sonorous moralizer that he was, perhaps secretly hoping that he would somehow lose his cool and let a more interesting self show through. He never did. On television, at least, he was ever the Bache-Halsey senior executive.

The off-camera Nixon was different: more human, not abstract, less the persuader and more the debater. Wrapped in the arms of a friendly audience, he exulted in the comfortable, partisan way that was his natural style:

> Four years ago crime was rising all over America at an unprecedented rate. Even our nation's capital was called the crime capital of the world. I pledged to stop the rise in crime. . . . I have kept that promise. I am proud of the appointments I have made to the courts, and particularly proud of those I have made to the Supreme Court of the United States. . . . I want the peace officers across America to know that they have the total backing of their president in their fight against crime.[47]

Except during his press conferences (which have not been examined here), Mr. Nixon did not allow Nixon-the-battler to show through on television. Even in his valedictory address, Nixon achieved the same stilted style he reserved for television. Control, iron control, was the key, even as the locks were being changed on the front door of the White House. He did not curse those who did him in. That would have been unthinkable for a man who even then had his eye on the history books of two decades hence.

To suggest that Richard Nixon was highly controlled is not to suggest that he was inflexible. In some ways, Edwin Black was right in describing

Nixon as an "*ad hoc*" personality.[48] Consummate politician that he was, Nixon knew how to bob and weave in the public arena. But he carefully prepared his footwork ahead of time, following the fight plan, so that he effected a new pugilist's style—controlled expedience. Black aptly describes his footwork:

> One does not find in [his] discourses any accretion of experience, any decisive formations of character, any distinctive individuation. He is a man without a patina, perenially new and chronically shallow. This makes possible his extraordinary adaptiveness. He can be the bellicose Cold Warrior one year, and go to China and Russia the next. He can be the darling of the conservative wing of his party, and yet propose a major reform of welfare. He can proliferate into a "new Nixon" and an "old Nixon." He can, in sum, commit deeds that in another politician would be regarded as outrageous contradictions; but in Nixon we perceive them as, at worst, mere paradoxes.[49]

If Nixon was a hard man to pin down politically, he was even slipperier rhetorically. It is well known that his two chief-speechwriters—Patrick Buchanan and Raymond Price—were chosen for their respectively conservative and liberal political instincts. According to Johnathan Schell, Buchanan was known as Mr. Inside because he knew how to appeal to Nixon's hard-core supporters while Mr. Outside, Price, concentrated his firepower on the aliens in the Nixon camp.[50] This is not to say that Nixon absolutely needed his Boswells in order to fashion telling adaptations. As Fawn Brodie relates in her *Richard Nixon: The Shaping of his Character,* just after Mr. Nixon's father died, he resumed his campaign for reelection as vice-president. Flying first to Buffalo,

> he began his speech with the words, "My father"—then paused, as if to contain his emotions, gripping the sides of the podium, and went on—"I remember my father telling me a long time ago, 'Dick, Dick,' he said, 'Buffalo is a beautiful town.' It may have been his *favorite* town." Nixon flew on to Rochester where he began his speech in exactly the same fashion changing only the name of the city. He repeated the performance in Ithaca. One efficient reporter kept notes.[51]

A glance at the data reveals just how clever Nixon's adjustments were and how dominant a part control played in his overall strategy. During just 1 year (1969), for example, young people were treated to highly familiar, simple language (February 7) while older folks heard an especially heavy dose of Optimism and Human Interest (November 27). Eulogies called for Symbolism (March 30), commencements for the papal "we" (May 3). Problematic audiences—such as women—required indirection and low Activity (April 16) while truculent audiences, such as welfare advocates, were met with the lowest level of Certainty Mr. Nixon could muster (August 8). For an old political hand, such adjustments came readily. Nixon trusted rhetoric and what it could do for him. During his career it did much.

The way in which Mr. Nixon handled the two most important issues of his presidency—Vietnam and Watergate—is especially instructive. For Nixon, the variable of Certainty was an especially important one. As Garry Wills once put it, Nixon's speechmaking reflected a "Heepish combination of the assertive and the mealymouthed."[52] His legal training probably convinced Nixon that strong language used at the wrong time could undo the cleverest of defenses. On the other hand, his conservative religious background documented the moral fervor one could generate via a resolute declaration of first principles or a denunciation of political sin. Vietnam and Watergate gave Richard Nixon vast experience with both the judicial and apocalyptic styles, as we see in Table 5.1.

Clearly, Nixon prosecuted the war in Vietnam with rhetorical, as well as military, vigor. Watergate was handled with kid gloves. Consider, for example, the tenacity of his Cambodian announcements:

> Tonight, American and South Vietnamese units *will attack* the headquarters for the *entire* Communist military operation in South Vietnam. This key control center has been occupied by the North Vietnamese and Vietcong for five years in blatant violation of Cambodia's neutrality.
>
> This *is not* an invasion of Cambodia. The areas in which these attacks *will be launched* are *completely occupied* and controlled by North Vietnamese forces.
>
> Our purpose *is not* to occupy the areas. Once enemy forces are driven out of these sanctuaries and once their military supplies are destroyed, we *will withdraw*.
>
> These actions *are in no way* directed to security interests of any nation. Any government that chooses to use these actions as a pretext for harming relations with the United States *will be doing so* on its own responsibility and *we will draw* the appropriate conclusions.[53]

These are strong words, fully presidential words, even a bit reminiscent of FDR himself, the sorts of words that separated the men from the boys (or the college kids from their parents.)

TABLE 5.1

RICHARD NIXON ON VIETNAM AND WATERGATE
VIS-A-VIS CERTAINTY

Certainty level[a]	Topic	Date of speech
210.7	Vietnam	5/14/69
189.7	Vietnam	11/3/69
204.5	Vietnam	4/30/70
184.1	Vietnam	4/7/71
202.4	Vietnam	1/25/72
174.7	Watergate	4/30/73
176.7	Watergate	8/15/73
145.4	Watergate	4/29/74

[a] Nixon's overall mean for Certainty = 190.1 ($N = 38$).

Watergate was a different story. No time for incautious remarks now. Time to tread lightly, or to do a little softshoe, or to find some other metaphor for being careful. The *wills* of Vietnam were transmuted into the *woulds* of Watergate:

> *If* I were to make public these tapes, containing as they do blunt and candid remarks on many different subjects, the confidentiality of the Office of the President *would always be suspect* from now on. It *would* make no difference whether it was to serve the interests of a court, of a Senate committee, or the President himself—the same damage *would be done* to the principle, and that damage *would be* irreparable. . . .
>
> No one *would want* to advance tentative ideas that *might* later *seem* unsound. No diplomat *would want* to speak candidly in those sensitive negotiations which *could bring* peace or avoid war. No Senator or Congressman *would want* to talk frankly about the Congressional horsetrading that *might* get a vital bill passed. No one *would want* to speak bluntly about public figures, here and abroad.[54]

As one set of scholars has commented, this Watergate apologia was "delivered from a 'back-to-the-wall' position. . . . [Nixon] was unable to turn the situation around to create an impression that he was generating the action of the moment."[55]

Another finding revealing much about the Nixon style is that Activity and Realism were inversely correlated, indicating (1) that when Nixon dealt specifically with an issue he typically chose not to detail its programmatic implications, and (2) that when he set forth his preferred policy options he did so in as obscure a manner as possible. What Nixon gave his audiences with the right hand, he snatched from them with his left. Thus, in his April 30, 1973, speech on Watergate,[56] he manfully claimed that he would "not place the blame on subordinates, on people whose zeal exceeded his judgment," but he did not accept the blame either. He vowed that "I will do everything in my power to ensure that the guilty are brought to justice," but he conveniently forgot to explain just how Madam Justice would be avenged. He placed his faith in a "determined grand jury," "honest prosecutors," and a "vigorous free press," but he did not mention his plans for circumventing those grand jurors, frustrating those honest prosecutors, and punishing those erstwhile journalists.

Richard Nixon's long-standing control never really lapsed. Stories are told about Hubert Humphrey's campaign advisors who searched feverishly (in 1968) through the videotape of Nixon's ill-fated press conference after his defeat by Pat Brown. Try as they did, Humphrey's lieutenants could not find a usable segment for showing Nixon unbalanced, so careful was he to choose his language well, even as intense emotion welled up within him. As Garry Wills put it, "Tricky had evaded the trap after all. He does not know how to break down."[57] He did not completely break down on August 9, 1974, either. While he gushed fulsomely about his parents and nervously searched for grace amidst the gloom, his rhetorical dam never broke; his last speech in office was among the most cautious speeches delivered in the White House between 1945 and the present.

Conclusion

Surely no president in modern times has seemed so clearly understandable as Richard Nixon, so ripe for parody even by amateur parodists. In the early 1970s, what sixth-grader in the nation's schoolyards could fail to provide a good impersonation of a Nixon speech—neck firmly ensconsed in his collar, two fingers on each hand forming the victory sign, "perfectly clear" being uttered *sotto voce.* Two things are important about this: (1) Mr. Nixon seemed transparent and (2) the parodies centered on his rhetorical personality. Even among his biographers and chroniclers, it was always communicative gaffes that came under scrutiny: his unguarded moment of prayer with Henry Kissinger in the White House passageways, Dan Rather's stinging challenge of his authority during a turbulent press conference, Nixon's scatalogical tutorials in the privacy of the Oval Office. Biographers and schoolchildren alike sensed intuitively that the real Nixon lay among the words, the legal pads, the blue suits, and the words again.

But the picture is not quite as simple as some would have us believe. Yes, Richard Nixon was a demagogue by conventional standards, but he must have been something more than that as well to inspire Rabbi Korff and his fellow loyalists to rally 'round as they did. He was a pragmatist, but he managed to articulate certain heady visions—détente and a new China policy—that may ultimately stand his presidency in better stead than his oil deletion allowances and his revenue sharings. Controlled he most certainly was, but he was not a feckless captain of rhetoric, unwilling or unable to sense the winds of change and adjust his rudder accordingly. The sense we get here about Richard Nixon's discourse is that almost all of the parodists were right about his simplistic pieties, his shocking insensitivities, and his slippery syntax. The computer documents these charges, but it also reveals a complexity that renders schoolyard parodies insufficiently edifying. Indeed, even the rigor of computerized language analysis is not sufficient to tell the complete rhetorical story of Richard Nixon's manifold complexities.

Notes

1. The title of this chapter was suggested by Stewart Alsop's article in *Newsweek,* March 26, 1973, p. 116.

2. Quoted in Dom Bonafede, "Speechwriters Play Strategic Role in Conveying, Shaping Nixon's Policies," *National Journal,* February 19, 1972, pp. 311–320.

3. "State of the Union," *Newsweek,* February 1, 1971, p. 17.

4. Eli Chesen, *President Nixon's Psychiatric Profile* (New York: Wyden, 1973), p. 207.

5. Jules Witcover, *The Resurrection of Richard Nixon* (New York: Putnam's 1970), p. 23.

6. James David Barber, *The Presidential Character: Predicting Performance in the White House* (Englewood Cliffs, NJ: Prentice-Hall, 1977), p. 385.

7. Charles P. Henderson, Jr., *The Nixon Theology* (New York: Harper, 1972), pp. 126–127.

8. Bruce Mazlish, *In Search of Nixon* (New York: Basic Books, 1972); Gary Wills, *Nixon Agonistes: The Crisis of the Self-Made Man* (Boston: Houghton-Mifflin, 1969); Fawn Brodie, *Richard Nixon: The Shaping of His Character* (New York: Norton, 1981).

9. David Halberstam, "Mr. Nixon Meets the Language," *Harpers,* July, 1970, pp. 30–31.

10. *Six Crises* (New York: Doubleday, 1962), p. 387.

11. *U.S. News and World Report,* August 11, 1969, p. 25.

12. Quoted in Rowland Evans, Jr., and Robert D. Novak, *Nixon in the White House* (New York: Random House, 1971), p. 288.

13. "Address to the Nation on the War in Vietnam," November 3, 1969, *Public Papers of the Presidents, 1969* (Washington: U.S. Government Printing Office, 1971), p. 905.

14. "Remarks in Kansas City, Missouri," October 19, 1970, *Public Papers of the Presidents, 1970,* p. 895.

15. "Remarks at Commencement Exercises at Oklahoma State University, May 11, 1974, *Public Papers of the Presidents, 1974,* p. 430.

16. "Address to the Nation on Outlining a New Economic Policy," August 15, 1971, *Public Papers of the Presidents, 1971,* p. 888.

17. "Address to the Nation on the Situation in Southeast Asia," April 30, 1970, *Public Papers of the Presidents, 1970,* p. 407.

18. "Presidents' Day Address," in Alton Motler, ed., *Preaching on National Holidays* (Philadelphia Fortress, 1976), p. 21.

19. "Address to the Nation on Domestic Programs," August 8, 1969, *Public Papers of the Presidents, 1969,* p. 641.

20. "Civil Rights Award," March 3, 1958, *Congressional Record,* 104:3 (1958), p. 3373.

21. Quoted in Bonafede (1972), p. 313.

22. Halberstam (1970), p. 30.

23. Quoted in Bonafede (1972), p. 313.

24. Raymond Price, *With Nixon* (New York: Viking, 1977), p. 344.

25. "Remarks Announcing Nomination of Gerald R. Ford as Vice-President," October 12, 1973, *Public Papers of the Presidents, 1973,* p. 868.

26. See Ralph Lane, *Political Ideology: Why the American Common Man Believes as He Does* (New York: Free Press, 1962).

27. "Second Inaugural Address," January 20, 1973, *Public Papers of the Presidents, 1973,* p. 14.

28. "The Complete Demagogue," *Nation,* March 25, 1968, p. 296.

29. "Inaugural Address," January 20, 1969, *Public Papers of the Presidents, 1969,* pp. 2–3.

30. "Remarks at a Thanksgiving Day Dinner," November 27, 1969, *Public Papers of the Presidents, 1969,* pp. 972–972.

31. Lawrence W. Rosenfield, "August 9, 1974: The Victimage of Richard Nixon," *Communication Quarterly,* 24:4 (1976), p. 23.

32. "Remarks on Departure from the White House," August 9, 1974, *Public Papers of the Presidents, 1974,* p. 631.

33. Lynn Hinds and Carolyn Smith, "Rhetoric of Opposites," *Nation,* February 16, 1970, p. 174.

34. "Counterrevolution," *National Review,* February 16, 1973, p. 192.

35. "Answering Mr. Nixon," *Nation,* November 17, 1969, p. 524.

36. Robert L. Scott, "Rhetoric that Postures: An Intrinsic Reading of Richard Nixon's Inaugural Address," *Western Speech,* 34 (1970), p. 47.

37. "Shades of the Past Haunt an Inaugural," *Commonweal,* February 7, 1969, p. 577.

38. "Remarks at Dr. Billy Graham's East Tennessee Crusade," May 28, 1970, *Public Papers of the Presidents, 1970,* p. 468.

39. Stewart Alsop, "Living with Two Nixons," *Newsweek,* August 19, 1968, p. 92.

40. Lee Miller, "The Debating Career of Richard M. Nixon," *The Reporter,* April 19, 1956, p. 15.

41. Edwin Black, "Electing Time," *Quarterly Journal of Speech,* 59 (1973), p. 128.

42. For a summary of this literature, see Joseph DeVito, *The Psychology of Speech and Language: an Introduction to Psycholinguistics* (New York: Random House, 1970).

43. Barber (1977), p. 361.

44. Michael Murray, "The President on Television," *Commonweal,* March 22, 1974, p. 62.

45. Roger Ailes, "How Nixon Changed his TV Image," *U.S. News and World Report,* February 2, 1970, p. 68.

46. "Radio Address about the American Right of Privacy," February 23, 1974, *Public Papers of the Presidents, 1974,* pp. 196–197.

47. "Remarks on Accepting the Presidential Nomination," August 23, 1972, *Public Papers of the Presidents, 1972,* p. 791.

48. Black (1973), p. 129.

49. Black (1973), pp. 128–129.

50. Jonathan Schell, *The Time of Illusion* (New York: Vintage, 1975), p. 22.

51. Brodie (1981), p. 52.

52. Wills (1969), p. 145.

53. "Cambodia," April 30, 1970, *Contemporary American Speeches,* Wil A. Linkugel, R. R. Allen, and Richard L. Johannesen, eds., 3rd. edition (Belmont, CA: Wadsworth, 1972), p. 240. Italics mine.

54. "Address to the Nation about the Watergate Investigations," April 30, 1973, *Public Papers of the Presidents, 1973,* pp. 330–331. Italics mine.

55. J. Harrell, B. L. Ware, and W. A. Linkugel, "Failure of Apology in American Politics: Nixon on Watergate," *Speech Monographs,* 42 (1975), pp. 259–260.

56. "Address to the Nation about the Watergate Investigation," April 30, 1973, *Public Papers of the Presidents, 1973,* pp. 330–331.

57. Wills (1969), p. 416.

THE SOFT-SPOKEN PRESIDENCY: FORD AND CARTER

In 1973, historian Arthur Schlesinger, Jr., authored a book entitled *The Imperial Presidency*. Seven years later, journalist Haynes Johnson wrote *In the Absence of Power*. The difference in titles is suggestive. The books describe fundamentally different presidential experiences. In 1973, Schlesinger warned that "the Nixon Presidency was not an abberation but a culmination. It carried to reckless extremes a compulsion toward presidential power rising out of deep-running changes in the foundations of society."[1] When Johnson described the Carter presidency, on the other hand, he found little of the overweening pride and lust for influence depicted by Schlesinger. In contrast to Carter's imperial forebears in office, says Johnson, Jimmy·Carter gave the impression "that he found politics ignoble and the practice of it faintly distasteful."[2]

Commenting upon the Ford and Carter administrations, columnist William Raspberry opined that "perhaps there was a need, after Nixon and Watergate, for a period of R & R, a passionless period in our history and our government. What we wanted, perhaps, was an Eisenhower-like period when people could take a respite and feel that maybe we wouldn't do anything great, but at least we won't be doing anything greatly wrong either."[3] Following this line of cyclical thinking, then, it is possible to conceive of Ronald Reagan emerging in 1980 to reimperialize the presidency, to beat America's drum louder in the world community, to serve as Jimmy Carter's symbolic foil in the way that John Kennedy had served as Dwight Eisenhower's.

Historical determinism aside, what else could account for the differences in the presidency seen in the 1970s? Several alternatives present themselves: a

150

gradual deterioration in American influence abroad, a worsening economic situation domestically, wildly fluctuating changes in Americans' perceptions of the decent use of power, growing belligerence on the part of the nation's news media, sharpened cleavages between traditional political entities (Jews and blacks, clergymen and government officials, men and women), the emergence of a new kind of social conservatism. Any one of these individually, or all of them in riotous collectivity, could have produced the effects described by Raspberry in 1979.

Yet another possibility exists. My research suggests that Gerald Ford and Jimmy Carter brought to the White House a new attitude toward speechmaking as well as a new set of communicative habits. The result was a different-sounding presidency, a presidency bereft of Trumanesque assertiveness and Nixonian Realpolitik. Gerald Ford—dependable, unexceptional, professional politician—and Jimmy Carter, who was more at home in a television studio than in a Senate antechamber, presented a new voice to the American people. As we shall see, both men adopted roughly similar rhetorical styles, styles that may have been nicely suited to their prepresidential years but that probably cost both of them reelection. Although it is risky to posit a kind of rhetorical determinism, the data gathered here suggest that Ford and Carter may have talked themselves out of office.

Presidential behaviors, unsurprisingly, result from presidential attitudes. According to Richard Reeves, by the time Gerald Ford became president, he was accustomed to not being listened to and "clearly did not understand the power of his presidential words."[4] Instead of rousing the citizenry out of its economic doldrums with the imperial touch of a Franklin Roosevelt, Ford urged American industry to batten down the hatches and told the American people to plant "radishes in the back yard."[5] "Conditioned not to offend," says Reeves, Gerald Ford "did not know how to inspire, persuade, or force people to go anyplace . . . all he could offer was a parody of leadership."[6] Like many journalists, Reeves is more that a bit reductionistic here, but it does seem clear that Jerry Ford never fully trusted his own suasory abilities and unwisely placed his faith in his old friend and head speechwriter, Robert Hartmann. According to John Casserly, a former underling to Hartmann, Hartmann's "unwillingness to project a more intelligent, sophisticated President cost Mr. Ford the election. . . . the point is, I believe very few individuals, if any, more affected the presidency of Gerald R. Ford than did Hartmann."[7]

Even in his first year in the presidency, Jimmy Carter came under stinging attack. The interesting thing about the charges made against him is that they often contained imperial wistfulness. Carter was described as symbolizing "the ineptitude of innocence,"[8] of being the "most ineffectual postwar President,"[9] and of establishing a presidency that, "had [it] been a play, it would have closed in New Haven."[10] Again, one must be careful not to ascribe all of Carter's problems to his rhetorical misdeeds. But his distaste for political talk probably cost him a good bit. Arthur Link, the noted historian of Woodrow Wilson, amplifies:

> Carter is unable to communicate great ideas and to formulate great programs in language that will capture the hearts and minds of the people, as Wilson could. Carter can say the most important things in the dullest way, particularly in public addresses. . . . I want to emphasize that I have enormous respect for Carter as a man, but I do feel that his leadership so far has been inept; he has not been able to rally the country.
> Wilson, by contrast . . . could change history through rhetoric.[11]

This is not to say that Ford and Carter shirked their public duties. They spoke a great deal—at party rallies, press conferences, town meetings, briefings for special-interest groups, White House toasts, national addresses, speeches to the Girl Scouts. Their faces became familiar to the American people even though the people rarely remembered their messages. Thus, if they failed to catch fire it was not because of lagging effort or perhaps even because of what they said. Their difficulties are revealed as much in the details of their language—in how they said what they said—as in congressional voting tallies or in George Gallup's incessant polls. For Ford and Carter, public opinion was typically rhetorical opinion.

On Being Strong

Assurance

No matter how they phrased it, most pundits agreed that Gerald Ford failed to embody presidential power. When handicapping Ford's forthcoming debate with Jimmy Carter in 1976, for example, *Newsweek* asked five political specialists to provide advice for the president. They were unanimous:

John Sears: "In the debates he should not appear to have a foot in both camps. He should not be afraid of appearing provocative."

Larry O'Brien: "The president should work at making himself more commanding on television."

David Garth: "He should demand specifics of Carter."

Harry Treleaven: "The president's biggest problem is that people don't think of him as a leader. That is the image he should try to create."

Robert Goodman: "Ford needs to demonstrate more strength in his grasp of the issues."[12]

Mr. Ford's response was to produce one of the most uncompromising speeches of his career, tacking directly to the course suggested by his political navigators. Unfortunately, one of his most assured sentences was the following: "There is no Soviet domination of Eastern Europe, and there never will be under a Ford administration."[13]

In addition to its obvious political newsworthiness, Ford's gaffe has rhetorical interest as well: His speech was uncharacteristically strong. In his desire to appear presidential, Ford used language forms that were largely foreign to him. His typical speaking style produced the lowest Certainty scores of the presidents sampled (an average of 20 points lower than Harry Truman, for example). Jimmy Carter was also quite tentative (see Figure 6.1). Needless to say, Carter's and Ford's heralded debate was not a battle of the titans but rather a gentle conversation between two men whose by-word was caution, one of whom (Ford) had been termed "a well-meaning, genial Boy Scout"[14] and the other (Carter) was described as having "no fire in his belly."[15]

Admittedly, the nature of Gerald Ford's presidency-on-loan prohibited him from having the usual mandate that so often encourages a chief executive to pound his fist on the nation's podium. Ford's fragile political base is revealed in three speeches that were exceptionally low on Certainty: his "WIN (Whip Inflation Now)" speech on economics, his first State of the Union Address, and his pardoning of draft dodgers. But even on innocuous occasions (like a football awards dinner), Jerry Ford kept it simple and cautious. When he did inject assertiveness into his speeches, the settings were not noteworthy: a commencement speech at Ohio State, a dedication

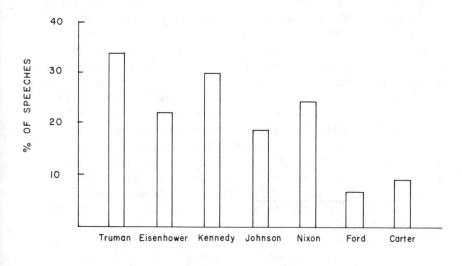

PRESIDENTS

Figure 6.1   Comparative usage of high certainty (≥ 203) by modern presidents (N = 380).

ceremony for Lyndon Johnson's memorial, and an address before the Motherhood Award Committee (the most assured speech he made).

Why Mr. Ford adopted such a low-key style is not clear, although numerous hypotheses are available. John Casserly, as might be expected, lays such timidity at the door of Bob Hartmann: "Direct, tough, straight speeches are deliberately compromised into 'safe' speeches that won't cause too many waves. Hartman and [Paul] Theis appear far less interested in leadership for the nation than in their own personal survival."[16] Other commentators have suggested that Jerry Ford's personal acknowledgement of his intellectual limitations caused him to understate his case; in this scenario, a lifetime of cutting deals in the congressional corridors made him temperamentally unsuited for taking doctrinaire positions in public. John Osborne, author of the *White House Watch: The Ford Years,* suggests another possibility: Ford appeared gauche when overstating his positions and was deliberately restrained by his aides from so doing. "When he makes a conscious effort to be sharp and aggressive in the guise of give-'em-hell Jerry," says Osborne, "he tends to overdo it and make himself appear ridiculous."[17]

Jimmy Carter's diffidence was another matter entirely, but the effect upon his presidency was much the same. Like Ford, Carter avoided the political overstatement, but unlike Ford his caution probably did not result from feelings of personal incompetence because Carter was surely one of our most intellectually dexterous presidents. Numerous authors have attempted to explain Carter's lack of verbal aggressiveness. James Wooten of the *New York Times* reasoned that he was restrained because he was attempting to remove himself (in the public's eyes) from the oratorical bombast of his Southern roots.[18] Political scientists Dan Nimmo and James Combs suggest that he understated his positions in order to retain maneuverability.[19] William Grieder of the *Washington Post* offers an explanation based on a theory of political schizophrenia: "Carter, at ease with his closest friends and advisors, talks tougher than Carter in the public pulpit. . . . some of his closest admirers think he would be more popular, more believeable as a human being and a political leader, if his private manner were more visible."[20] Finally, Eugene Kennedy offers the intriguing suggestion that Carter's was a philosophical decision: "Carter seems a man holding back, as though he had once looked directly into the dark but glowing face of old fashioned power and had vowed never to let it become his master—or he its."[21]

When examining Carter's use of Certainty on a case-by-case basis, his political world view is not easy to understand. Among his least absolute speeches were such important ones as his first State of the Union Address, his speeches on energy, his announcement for reelection, and even his summation during the all-important debate with Ronald Reagan. During this last speech, arguably the most important speech of his entire presidency, a speech that could not have been answered successfully by his opponent under the circumstances, a situation virtually demanding the best weaponry he had in his arsenal, Carter adopted a style suitable, perhaps, for a chat over drinks in the faculty club. Random excerpts from his remarks reveal an almost dreamlike quality to Carter's thoughts on what was virtually election eve:

> First of all, I'd like to thank the League of Women Voters for making this debate possible. I think it's been a very constructive debate. . . .
> I've seen the strength of my nation, and I've seen the crises that it approached in a tentative way, and I've had to deal with those crises as best I could. . . .
> I consider myself in the mainstream of my party. . . . I've [made decisions] with moderation, with care, with thoughtfullness. . . . It's a lonely job. . . . Those listening to my voice will have to make a judgment about the future of this country, and I think they ought to remember the difference.[22]

If this was the modern incarnation of Teddy Roosevelt's bully pulpit, it was a placid incarnation indeed.

Unlike Jerry Ford, whose use of Certainty seemed either random or just plain misguided, Jimmy Carter occasionally—and strategically—increased his assertiveness. For example, his speeches on the topic of strife were typically presented in a firm and resolute manner: high on Certainty, low on Self-Reference and Embellishment (see Table B.9). Intriguingly, these speeches almost universally drew praise from the nation's press and his standing in the opinion polls often rose upon their delivery. His Naval Academy speech in June of 1978, his press conference on Iran in November of 1979, and his remarks on the Soviets' invasion of Afghanistan in January of 1980 were all high on Certainty. In this latter speech, Carter was reminiscent of Truman on Korea, Kennedy on Cuba, Johnson on Vietnam. His words carried both punch and verve and served to galvanize the American people:

> If the Soviets are encouraged in this invasion by eventual success . . . peaceful balance of the entire world *will be changed.* . . .
> *I have already recalled* the United States Ambassador from Moscow back to Washington. . . .
> *We will delay* opening of any new American or Soviet consular facilities. . . . Trade with the Soviet Union *will be severely restricted* . . . *I have decided* to halt or reduce exports to the Soviet Union. . . . Fishing privileges for the Soviet Union in United States waters *will be severely curtailed.*[23]

Here is an active, aggressive son of Annapolis, hands on the helm, vision clear, priorities in order. Unfortunately for Jimmy Carter (fortunate, no doubt, for the American people), such militaristic showdowns did not present themselves often enough to constitute a theme for his presidency. Everyday matters like energy supplies, welfare reform, inflation, and rural development beckoned instead. His engineering mentality, perhaps, precluded him from going beyond his data when making claims about such matters. Such an intellectual habit may have had a curious advantage for the American people: Because of Carter's refusal to overstate, his fellow citizens probably learned more about their nation under his tutelage than they had under any previous president. Unfortunately for Carter, his pedagogy did not typically hearten his constituency because so much of the news he reported was bad.

Carter's inexpediency seemed almost suicidal at times. Three of his least certain speeches (delivered on March 10, 1977, May 3, 1979, and May 15, 1980) were presented to women's groups on the topic of equal rights. For a Democratic president to hold back on such occasions (especially a Democratic president who some feminists viewed suspiciously) seems absurd. Speaking situations of this sort virtually demand the easy lie and the ponderous beating of one's breast. That Jimmy Carter would spurn such political opportunities and avoid the forceful pronouncement except in times of crisis surely places him in an odd chapter in the history of political strategy.

Inspiration

Despite Ford's and Carter's timidity, neither is regarded with total negativity today. No matter how low the public's estimations of their competence sank, both men retained an image of being well intentioned, of loving their country, of being principled in their actions. Neither Ford nor Carter was tainted by Johnsonian hegemony or Nixonian double-dealing. In the presidential pantheon, both Ford and Carter might vie for the title of the nation's first moralist.

These public images were not accidental. Carter used more Optimism than any of his predecessors and Ford used somewhat more than Nixon, Kennedy, and Eisenhower. (Statistically speaking, these differences are more suggestive than probative.) James David Barber predicted Carter's deployment of Optimism when he wrote in 1977, that "a frequent charge against him will be overhope."[24] Even after Carter had been in office 2 years, a columnist said that "the president's optimism is so fulsome that we tend to dismiss it or snicker at the steady stream of superlatives, the monotonous 'superb' in his talk,"[25] so cynical were we as listeners. Numerous commentators have linked the Carter buoyancy to his religious fundamentalism,[26] while Ford's Optimism, in contrast, was explained by personality factors. "Unlike many if not most of his Republican predecessors," wrote one columnist, "Mr. Ford has worked hard at being a 'man of the people.' He likes them. He rarely misses an opportunity to shake hands at an airport fence. He sits through every dreary dinner down to the last chicken leg and final speech. He is able to poke fun at himself with a natural humor and self-deprecation."[27]

Ford and Carter were also among the most abstract of our recent chief executives. Carter was second lowest (to Eisenhower) on Realism and Ford third. When combined with Optimism, such a trait could have served to inspire an audience by encouraging them to go beyond their petulant selves. (See Figure 6.2.) For Ford, however, lack of Realism was often equated in the press with an absence of clearheaded pragmatism and therefore rarely seen as a trait of leadership. (He was accused of "blowing smoke," of producing "Lion's Club rhetoric.")[28] Carter also seemed ill-served by his idealistic talk. His style was termed fit for a "moral presidency" but not one conducive to political action.[29]

Ford's speech to the American Legion in August of 1975 contained the least Realism (158) recorded in this study, almost 40 points below the presidential average for that variable. In that speech, Ford lectured his audience on the assorted meanings of détente; with each paragraph, the level of abstraction increased in an attempt to render inoffensive a phrase that nor-

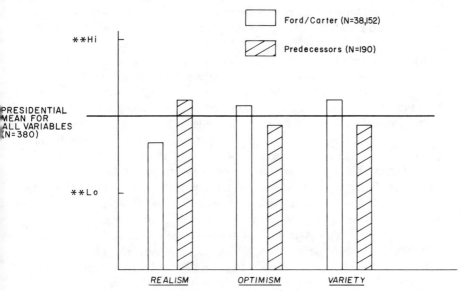

Figure 6.2   Ford's and Carter's soft-spoken style. All differences significant. See Table B.8.
** ± ½ sd from mean. See Table B.1 for exact values.

mally poised Legionnaires on the edges of their seats. Ford explained things as follows:

> To me, detente means a fervent *desire* for *peace*—but not peace at any price. It means the preservation of fundamental American *principles*—not their *sacrifice*. It means maintaining the strength to command *respect* from our adversaries and provide *leadership* to our friends—not letting down our guard or dismantling our defenses or neglecting our allies. It means peaceful rivalry between political and economic *systems*—not the curbing of our competitive *efforts*.[30]

According to his former speechwriter, John Casserly, Ford was frequently seduced by his advisers into producing such oscillating, "gushy, rich rhetoric"[31] that meant nothing to everyone and that so thoroughly confused his stands that his listeners were insulted and he was cheapened by the communicative effort.

Again, James David Barber predicted well when he claimed in 1977 that Jimmy Carter would be likely to "carry over from [1976] campaigning a penchant for idealistic expression, for grand appeals to the best in people."[32] But Carter's preference for abstraction cost him a great deal as president. His preachments soon grew tiresome as Americans began to demand where their oil was. Carter's talk of the nation's troubled conscience and of crises of the spirit—especially when presented in such a steady and unrelenting way—seemed wholly alien to an essentially pragmatic people. The people began to see Carter as a whining, Hamlet-like figure, "more concerned with taking the correct position than with learning how to turn that position into results."[33] When he did chance to increase the Realism in his speeches at Notre Dame, at the Naval Academy, before the nation's governors, at Hubert Humphrey's funeral—we often applauded his effort. But he rarely maintained that level, as if Realism offended his gentle spirit, as if he were "frightened by rhetoric."[34]

Jimmy Carter and Richard Nixon were equally heavy users of the nation's Symbolism. In other times and under other circumstances, a combination of Optimism, Symbolism, and precious little Realism might have produced an attractive confection for a president like Jimmy Carter who wished to establish a new level of dialogue by eschewing the usual political banalities. But the moral fear of Watergate passed, and new, starkly empirical, problems beset the American people. They began to accuse their president of emphasizing style over substance, of not being a leader or a teacher "even for a quiet time,"[35] of making them wonder incessantly "what he means and where he is going."[36] Rather than learn from his press clippings, Carter dipped ever deeper into the well of American symbolism: His third year in office produced twice as much symbolism as his first 12 months on the job.

Carter's speech to the Democratic National Committee in May of 1979 is instructive. In his address, nay, lecture, Carter talked *about* the American people rather than *to* them. In that speech, he used more Symbolism than was found in any of the 380 presidential speeches examined here. The speech is almost a parody of itself. Carter claims that "the times we live in call for plain talk and for political courage" and argues that "slogans will not do the job." He claims that "searching for scapegoats" and "wringing our hands" will not set matters aright in the nation's hamlets, and then reasons that a "failure of will" and a failure "of the political process" itself is to blame for our troubles. He stated that "the bottom line is clear," but he provided no bottom line. Instead, he told the American people about themselves:

> The American people are disturbed, the American people are doubtful, the American people are uncertain about the future, the American people do not have automatic trust in you or me or other Democratic officials. [The American people] see the demagoguery and they see political timidity and they wonder if we who are in office are equal to the challenge.[37]

This was a speech produced by one of the least forceful of our modern presidents, the president best able to analyze the nation's problems but seemingly the president least able to solve them. The doubt, uncertainty, and distrust referred to by Carter here were actually increased by his own academic dissections. Inspiration, true inspiration, comes not from just raising the level of discourse but from linking revered abstractions to practical policy. In other words, Ford and Carter failed to use the language of political leadership.

Optimism and Activity were negatively correlated for both Ford and Carter (see Table B.10), which is to say that their upbeat pronouncements rang hollow because they were unaccompanied by specific, programmatic steps useful for reaching the nirvana the pronouncements foretold. Ford began and ended his presidency on exactly the same note. His first speech in office, for example, contained such hopeful/passive refrains as "America will remain strong and united," "truth is the glue that holds government together," "our long national nightmare is over," "our Constitution works," "let brotherly love purge our hearts of suspicion and hate," and "May God bless and comfort."[38]

These are fitting words; some even have a touch of grandeur for a very special moment in American history. But during the Ford presidency the pattern of "passive postivity" remained constant even when his circumstances were not ceremonial: his national foreign policy address of April 1975 and his speech on privacy and freedom at Stanford University in September of that same year, for example. Even Ford's remarks on election morning of November 2, 1976, contained the rhetorical seeds that caused his campaign to fall on fallow ground: "I believe I offer experienced leadership," "I think my approach could properly be called steady and dependable," "I have been careful never to promise what I could not deliver," and "This is my fondest hope: to continue to serve the people of this country that has blessed me in so many ways."[39] John Osborne commented that Ford "inspired hope, instilled confidence. But he did not and evidently could not inspire ideas, action, purpose."[40] Richard Reeves agrees, but his judgment of Ford's rhetorical shortcomings is harsher:

> Gerald Ford, conditioned not to offend, did not know how to inspire, persuade or force people to go anyplace. He did not have the skills and when he tried to imitate them, as he did in pushing the WIN program, all he could do was offer a parody of leadership. More than that, Ford did not know the someplace he wanted to take or make the American people go, because he did not know where they had been in the last few years.[41]

Although the Optimism–Activity effect was not as great for Carter as for Ford, it was there and it probably did much to build the pleasant-but-incompetent image that haunted his presidency and that forced him to relinquish it to an equally pleasant but seemingly more vigorous septuagenarian.

On Being Oneself

For very specific reasons, a speech by either Jerry Ford or Jimmy Carter is recognizable as such. Both had "style" in the classical sense of that term—the ability to distinguish oneself and one's message. This is not to say, of course, that either had a *graceful* style. We shall see that neither did. But it does mean that they did not resort to formalisms, thereby placing a distinctive stamp on their administrations. These imprintings help us to understand Ford's and Carter's strengths as human beings and their problems as presidents.

Words

Both Gerald Ford and Jimmy Carter had trouble with words, although their problems differed. Ford has been quoted by columnists Rowland Evans and Robert Novak as avowing that Dwight Eisenhower was his favorite predecessor in office because he was a "people's President."[42] Ford's regard for Ike is seen in his middle-of-the-road Republicanism, but it is revealed even more graphically in language—both had significantly higher Variety scores than any of the other presidents sampled. A high Variety score indicates an habitual avoidance of what John Osborne called the simple and unadorned declarative sentence.[43] Commenting upon Ford's speech to the American Legion in Minneapolis during August of 1975 (a speech whose *Variety* score was .542 versus a presidential average of only .488), Osborne aptly characterized Ford's tendency to wander in a thicket of verbalization:

> Once the drafts have been prepared, however, he departs from them only to add a cosmetic emphasis that is unconvincing . . . . the statement in the advance text that "I commend the American Legion" became "I strongly commend." "I am glad" became "I am very, very, happy." "All Americans are proud" became "All Americans are terribly proud." Typically, "I hope" came out "I honestly and sincerely hope."[44]

The real bugaboo in Ford's lexical choices was the connective "and," which he used indiscriminately, as if rhetoric were propelling him rather than the reverse. In an address to the South Florida Bar Association, Ford produced the impressive *Variety* score of .562 with his if-you-didn't-catch-it-the-first-time-listen-again style: "I urge and strongly advocate," "criminals ready to maim and to kill," "notoriously bad or overcrowded [prison] facilities," "protection and consideration [for victims]," and "serious and violent crimes."[45]

Ford's curious rhetorical choices often got him into hot water. *Time* headlined "The Blooper Heard Round the World"[46] when describing his Eastern European gaffe of 1976, while the *New Republic* gleefully described the same linguistic difficulty with "Ford's Boo-Boos."[47] *Vogue* sallied forth with "High-level Bafflegab" when describing Ford, labeling him a typical "Midwestern politician" who disliked verbal elegance and who, like his farm-belt colleagues, had a "pitiful" vocabulary.[48] The University of Michigan apparently had done its best to forewarn Mr. Ford, having awarded him an A in Government but C's in English Composition I and II.[49] In his defense, Ford's staff argued that average Americans could see themselves in Ford's little blunders and mispronunciations and that his linguistic liabilities were, consequently, strengths.[50] One wonders.

Jimmy Carter's linguistic problems were quite different. Unlike Ford who searched for his phrases while saying them, Carter used a technical vocabulary suitable for his former engineering professors at Georgia Tech. Compared with all of his predecessors, Mr. Carter was an absolute egghead whose words typically ran 5.89 characters in length (compared to the Complexity average of 4.65 for the other presidents), with some of his speeches reaching the positively William Buckleyan level of 7.5 characters per word (see Figure 6.3). This one set of verbal statistics may capsulize the difficulties Carter experienced as president and the totally contradictory image he projected: an earnest young fellow from the backwoods of Georgia whose popular speeches bespoke an intelligence rarely seen in the White House.

Jimmy Carter was a pedagogue's dream and a citizen's nightmare. Bruce

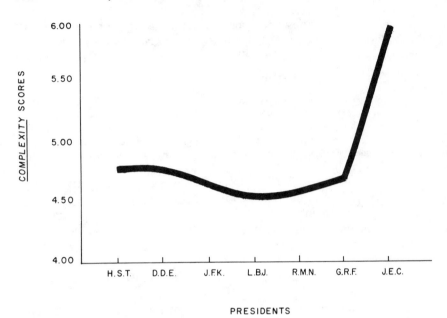

PRESIDENTS

Figure 6.3 Jimmy Carter versus other presidents on complexity. For Carter, N = 152; for each of the others, N = 38.

Mazlish and Edwin Diamond called him a "complexifier," a rare entity in political circles because such persons "tend to turn people off with their refusal to advance yes/no propositions."[51] According to Mazlish and Diamond, Carter recognized this trait in himself and had remarked that "the more simplistic an approach can be, the more the public can be aroused. . . . Although this [complexity] produces an appearance of confusion, in the long term I think it is good."[52] Mazlish and Diamond conclude that Carter's preference for detail caused him to be seen as "fuzzy," "waffling," or "bland."[53]

Apparently, Jimmy Carter was a verbal compulsive, one who demanded precision in language even if his audience was willing to accept (sometimes even demand) simplification. Phrases like "broad-scale exhibition of interest," "publicity accruing," "mutuality of interest," and "transcend obstacles" tripped off his tongue easily when facing an audience of Medal of Science winners.[54] Almost any expert who heard Carter speak on technical matters during his 4 years in office was enormously impressed by his grasp of the issues. Businesspersons who heard Carter refer knowingly to "pension fund regulations," "small business initiatives," "energy pricing policy," an "upward spiral," "synthetic alternatives," and "windfall profits tax" knew that they were in the presence of a mind to be reckoned with.[55]

But Carter's vocabulary was not, unfortunately for him, reserved for small groups of professionals. When speaking before an assemblage of educators, for example, President Carter described a "greatly magnified opportunity for the enhancement of better relationships" and later mentioned that the delegates would be receiving "an encapsulation of what they can do in political motivation" when they returned home.[56] One can only imagine the sea of glazed eyes in the audience that day.

Predictably, Carter did not alter his Complexity when speaking to the American people en masse. No general differences on this variable were observed when his live speeches were compared with those delivered on television (see Table B.9). In either context, he seemed incapable of rendering complex ideas in a simple manner. His natural wont was to report the reality he saw, dotting every "i" and crossing every "t" in his Brobdingagian words. The American people universally fell asleep during his lectures, evidently substantiating Thomas Hughes's analysis: "Carter is unusually intelligent. He is extraordinarily hard-working. He tries to master subjects. The problem is that that is not exactly what we pay our President to do."[57]

Feelings

No matter what audience he faced or what topic he addressed, Gerald Ford's most reliable rhetorical comrade was himself. He averaged almost 13 Self-References per passage, far more than any of the other presidents studied. Since the passages I selected for analysis never included introductory or concluding remarks (where one might normally expect to find such personal flavorings), Ford's tendencies in this regard are all the more noteworthy. Of his 38 speeches 27 exceeded the presidential average on Self-References (see Figure 6.4). Even when he was president, said Charlie Goodell, a friend from back home, Mr. Ford "continued to act as if he were still just a congressman from Grand Rapids."[58] Ford disliked the "Nixon royal WE"[59] and used his speeches to report on the state of Jerry Ford.

Even the most cynical observer has to admit that Ford's personalism was infectious and that it cut against the pretentiousness so often surrounding White House activities. Ford's success in Congress had been purchased by his staunch loyalty to party and by his openness and directness as a human being. He brought these qualities to the White House and depended upon his old congressional relationships to see him through as president. Congressional relationships are, after all, relationships, built with the mortar of interpersonal investment.

In a speech before the American Society of Newspaper Editors, Ford revealed how highly personalized his political world view was:

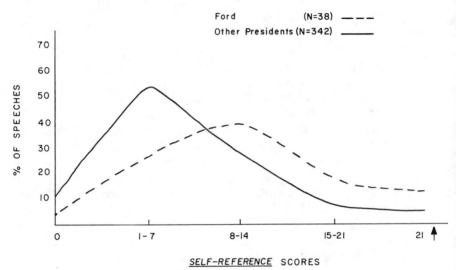

SELF-REFERENCE SCORES

Figure 6.4 Distribution of Self-Reference scores for Gerald Ford versus other presidents. Mean for Self-Reference for the presidential sample was 8.01 (N = 380).

> It is my strong belief that we can achieve unity at home. I see no reason why the Congress and the President cannot work together. That doesn't mean that all 535 Members of the House and Senate will agree with me. But I can assure you that what I have said on more than one occasion, I believe and I will try to implement, that I will work with the Congress, and I know many, if not all, in the Congress will work with me.[60]

Naturally, a good copyeditor could have transformed these 87 meandering words into a single, efficient sentence. But that would have meant removing the 10 Self-References and, in so doing, Gerald Ford's essential political platform—himself—would have been blue-penciled as well.

Jimmy Carter's use of Self References was not quite as high as Ford's, but he did use more of them than any other president except Richard Nixon. Of particular interest are Carter's speeches on pragmatic topics, which contained significantly more Self-References than his other remarks. Like Ford before him, Carter relied on the personal mandate that had brought him to office. A presidential candidate who had no federal experience, no training in foreign policy, and who knew virtually nobody in the Congress, presented himself to the American people in 1976 on a platform consisting of his good heart and a refusal to misspeak. When one heard Jimmy Carter address matters of practical policy, one heard the 1960s in his speech patterns. He was in touch with his feelings, willing to risk self, anxious to develop an I–Thou relationship with his listeners. This Californication of language was too much for New Englander Robert Shrum who quit the Carter campaign (after only 9 days on the job) with the remark, "I am not sure what you truly believe in other than yourself."[61]

Carter's rhetoric was a rhetoric of confession. As Christopher Lydon noted in *Atlantic Monthly*, Carter proudly claimed "that no black group had ever hassled him about his opposition to busing after he told how his own daughter, Amy, went to a mostly black school at home. Jimmy was okay on race! Next question!"[62] But the cynics were more often kept at bay by Carter's personal style, partly because of its novelty as a political strategy and partly because it forced a critic to take on the whole package— self plus policy. Not only would that be uncourtly in the half-civilized world of politics, but it is especially dangerous when one is up against a presidential self. Thus, Jimmy Carter fully expected his listeners on October 24, 1979, to understand that Mid-East policy was Carter policy:

> There's something else we've been working on. It's been mentioned twice tonight already, but *I* want to make it clear, because *I* happen to be the President and *I* want the words to come from *me*. For the first time in 40 years, *I'm* a President that has seen our Nation completely at peace, not a single loss of life, and *I* thank God for that. And *I* hope *I* can leave this office, which you've given to *me*, with that record still intact.
>
> It is not an accident. *I* don't take credit for it *myself*. The American people are deeply committed to peace, but. . . .[63]

A superpersonalized rhetoric makes for a moving target. Just as a critic gets a piece of governmental policy in his or her sights, the political self is attached to another matter of public concern. In the space of only a few minutes during his speech at the 1977 Governor's conference, for example, Carter was able to stand behind every political essence known to contemporary humankind: "I believe in our country. . . . I believe in the system of federalism. . . . I think about the lonely days that I spent campaigning through your states. . . . I know that I'm going to make a lot of mistakes. . . . I've learned a lot about government as a Governor. . . . This is a time, I think, of restoration in our country. . . . I've had a chance to learn about matters concerning defense. . . . Rosalynn and I went down to visit Brazil."[64] A proud, humble, experienced, naive, domestic globe-trotter is a political animal to be reckoned with. However, there is a disadvantage to this type of personalization: When things went wrong, Carter was to blame for them all. (One is reminded of Ronald Reagan's deft, albeit borrowed, campaign query, "Is your life better off now than it was four years ago?"). Carter's confessional style, coupled with his Symbolism and lack of Realism, set him up for a bitter personal loss in 1980. Since "the central idea of the Carter administration is Jimmy Carter himself, his own mixture of traits," and since "the only thing that finally gives coherence to the items of his creed is that he happens to believe in them all,"[65] it is little wonder that Mr. Carter's retirement has been the most secluded of modern presidential retirements. After all, personal bruises take longer to heal than do purely political bruises.

On Fixing Blame

In another era, perhaps, Gerald Ford and Jimmy Carter would not have been lambasted for their miscues as thoroughly as they were. But in a contentious era like the late 1970s, in a nation raised on imperial tough talk, in a media-saturated environment hyped by the rhetoric of presidents and nonpresidents alike, Gerald Ford and Jimmy Carter were unable to go underground. Their public images became the focus of dinnertime conversation from Plains, Georgia, to Grand Rapids, Michigan, and in every hamlet in between. Their rhetorical successes were dutifully heralded *as* rhetorical successes by the media. Their ineptness, loquaciousness, and muddle-headedness were, likewise, replayed on both the 6:00 o'clock and 11:00 o'clock news. Other presidents' speech habits were treated in a similar fashion, or worse, by the people and the media, but Ford and Carter had little with which to distract their style-based critics, the former having had no real policy-creating experience before he became president and the latter having no natural constituency other than the effervescent one he created during the spring and summer of 1976.

It is impossible to calculate, of course, how much of Ford's and Carter's problems of leadership were image-based. Clearly, neither projected well and such projections obviously affected Congress's reaction to policy formulation and the public's reaction to policy once formulated. What reasons for their failure might be offered?

One explanation is that both Ford and Carter lacked rhetorical inventiveness. Jerry Ford, for example, was a paint-by-numbers spokesman, typically adopting the traditional approach to speechmaking: highly Embellished on ceremonial occasions, legalistic when discussing the draft (Variety = .564), ideological with the American Legion (very low Realism). (See Appendix A for further examples.) He appeared to have no natural sense of appropriateness despite his long career as public speaker. Eventually, he even hired a professional comedy writer to fashion natural-sounding humor for him.

Mr. Ford was what he appeared to be. No significant differences were detected when his televised speeches were compared with his live performances. No major changes in language behavior occurred when the topics changed. His speech at the dedication of the LBJ Memorial on September 27, 1974, was low on Realism, Familiarity, and Human Interest and high on Complexity as was his nationally televised speech on inflation the next evening. Mr. Ford seemed to sense that no great purpose could be served by rhetorical cosmetics and that a person once made could not be remade.

There is also evidence that the Ford speechwriting team was uncommonly inept. Its captain was Robert Hartmann, an old Ford protégé whose less-than-winning personality caused him to be disliked by all. Speechwriting in the Ford White House was often a crisis affair, with jealousy among collaborators a constant presence. Hartmann insisted on maintaining the plain, unexciting style in Ford's speeches and eventually drove the most creative talent out of the White House. Typically, a Ford speech was a team effort overseen by an ineffective team leader.

Although he is hardly an unbiased source in this regard, one of Ford's disillusioned ex-speechwriters sharply attacked the uncoordinated effort he usually saw in the White House: "You can't produce a speech with sixteen people editing it as happened in the hardware industry speech I wrote for Chicago. All you have left is bits and pieces. What you have is a string of statements, any of which contradict one another, dangling without logic, feeling or direction. That isn't speechwriting."[66]

The lack of coordination showed. My data revealed a strong negative correlation between Human Interest and Activity for Ford, meaning that his folksiness was undercut by his plodding imagery (see Table B.10). With the exception of Carter, no other president was even remotely similar to Ford on this score. His very first speech in office started him on this rhetorical course and he only occasionally veered from it.

On other occasions, the lack of coordination caused Ford to be high on Certainty but low on Activity (e.g., his speech on the Pacific Doctrine at the University of Hawaii) or exactly the reverse (e.g., his first State of the Union speech). The remarkable thing is that when Ford and his staff took time to work on his speeches, the result was often rewarding. According to Ron Nessen, Mr. Ford's erstwhile press secretary, the chief executive spent some 50 hours crafting his 1976 State of the Union address[67] and the result was an active, realistic, and optimistic speech that was heralded in some quarters as one of Mr. Ford's best.

Perhaps his most illustrious effort was his acceptance of the Republican nomination in August 1976. *Time* called the speech "the best of his presidency and perhaps of his career"[68] and the computer found it to be high on those things that an acceptance speech should be high on: Realism, Certainty, Symbolism, and Familiarity. Gone from his speaking style were the simpering phrases, the cloying personalism, and the mishmash of words. On this one occasion Mr. Ford spoke as the majority of the American people would have their president speak to them—clearly, crisply, definitively:

I come before you with a 2-year record of performance, without your mandate. I offer you a 4-year pledge of greater performance with your mandate.

As Governor Al Smith used to say, "Let's look at the record." Two years ago, inflation was 12 percent. Sales were off. Plants were shut down. Thousands were being laid off every week. Fear of the future was throttling down our economy and threatening millions of families.

Let's look at the record since August 1974. Inflation has been cut in half. Payrolls are up. Profits are up. Production is up. Purchases are up. . . . This year, more men and women have jobs than ever before in the history of the United States. Confidence has returned and we are in the full surge of sound recovery to steady prosperity.[69]

It is tempting to wonder, but impossible to determine, how different the political chronicle might read had Jerry Ford and his writers put forth this sort of rhetorical effort consistently. As a one-time Ford aide remarked, Robert Hartmann may have much to answer for in history.[70]

If Jimmy Carter lost favor with the American people it was not because of insufficient personal effort or because of a lazy speechwriting staff. Carter threw himself into his speechmaking fully, hating it all the while but gutting it out like the modern Puritan he was. With relatively few exceptions, his speechmaking never helped him politically but, perhaps because he was such a willing, cheerful orator, his public presentations never fatally wounded him either. Nevertheless, to be able to say that a president's discourse failed to help him, given the tremendous perquisites of office in a media-saturated era, is to isolate a significant problem.

In the vernacular of his times, Jimmy Carter was unable to get it together. He worked slavishly over his speeches but (1) could not find a consistently attractive public persona and (2) was not able to combine the various elements of language that many Americans expect a president to combine. When looking at the intervariable correlations for the Carter speeches, two distinctive clusters emerged. These alternating faces of Jimmy Carter may reveal why pollster Pat Caddell's research always dredged up such inconsistent images of the president. Remarking on those disparate patterns, Caddell once said, "You would think they were talking about two totally separate people."[71]

Figure 6.5 throws light on the two people calling themselves Jimmy Carter. The presidential cluster reveals an assertive, pragmatic leader who knew how (via Embellishment and Symbolism) to lay it on thick when motivating. His remarks of December 21, 1979, announcing economic sanctions against Iran reveal the presidential Jimmy Carter. His language was harsh: He accused Iran of standing "in arrogant defiance of the world community." His language was unqualified: "In an irresponsible attempt at blackmail, to which the United States will never yield, kidnappers and terrorists, supported by Iranian officials, continue to hold our people under inhumane conditions." His language was even a touch excessive: "The foundation of civilized diplomacy is at stake; the credibility of the United Nations is at stake. And at stake, ultimately, is the maintenance of peace in the region."[72]

Several points need to be made about this presidential Jimmy Carter: (1) The intercorrelations are not particularly high, suggesting that Carter did

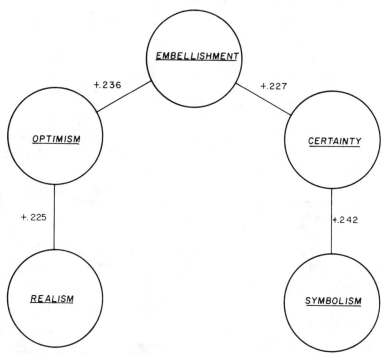

Figure 6.5 Jimmy Carter's weak presidential style (Pearson correlations for selected variables, N = 152). For additional information, see Table B.10.

not combine these rhetorical forces on a daily basis; (2) when he did so, he typically spoke to a live audience without media coverage, thus denying himself the national applause which often accompanies such forcefulness; and (3) of the 152 Carter speeches sampled, perhaps as few as a dozen could be called fulsomely presidential. The media made a good deal out of this inconsistent strength, quoting one citizen as saying: "I want my President to have some class. I'm not ready for a blue-jean image in the White House. I wonder how it looks to the world."[73]

During Carter's stay in the White House his blue-jean image was often seen. His second face (see Figure 6.6) has been described as "a blend of transparent sincerity, friendliness, and unpretentiousness"[74] by one reporter, while another declared that "Although his speeches have not generally been charismatic or inspirational, he has been enormously effective by being natural."[75] Carter's combination of Self-References and Familiarity and his frequent use of Human Interest without Embellishment helped him weather several political storms. The folksy Jimmy Carter was a comparatively new phenomenon on the American political scene. It is hard to

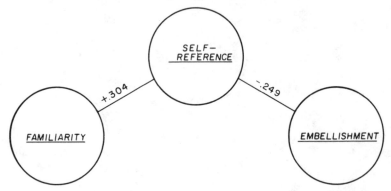

Figure 6.6 Jimmy Carter's folksy style (Pearson correlations for selected variables, N = 152). For additional information, see Table B.10.

imagine a Richard Nixon or a John Kennedy explaining an aide's fiscal indiscretions in the open and unassuming manner used by Carter when describing Bert Lance's:

> Bert Lance is my friend. I know him personally as well as if he was my own brother. I know him without any doubt in my mind or heart to be a good and honorable man. . . . He told the truth. . . . I accept Bert's resignation with the greatest sense of regret and sorrow. He's a good man. . . . And although I regret his resignation, I do accept it. I would be glad to answer any questions you might have about this or other matters.[76]

It was probably Carter's consistent use of Human Interest (the most consistent of all presidents) that made the American people basically like him. But because he could not combine Human Interest with Activity, he was described by senator-turned-psychologist Scoop Jackson as afflicted with "abulia,"[77] the abnormal inability to act. The absence of a strong, positive correlation between these two variables in Carter's speeches made him seem both incompetent and disingenuous.

For example, Carter's support within the black community deteriorated badly during his administration, probably because he failed to launch an aggressive legislative program on behalf of blacks. Ever the scientist, Carter seemed unable to speak categorically. When talking to blacks about human rights, for example, Mr. Carter reminded them that "the endorsement by the President, of course, is not the final step. The Congress must act and the people have to ratify a change in the United States Constitution. As I say, we still have a long way to go." Carter's speech on this occasion was filled with timid declarations of success ("we are making some progress"), frank admissions of work undone ("We are evolving an urban policy"), opaque pledges ("The extrapolation of what you have already accomplished to the future is a goal of yours and also a commitment of mine"), and inspecific, immobilizing abstractions ("we're involved together on a concept of enhancing human rights, here and around the world. And the example you've set is now an inspiration to many throughout the globe.").[78] "Jive," responded some black Americans. "What will you *do* as president," queried others. In many ways, Carter's inactive language reflected his understanding of the presidency as a behemoth hamstrung by special-interest groups and bureaucratic recalcitrance. Even when talking to what should have been for him a "natural" constituency, American women, Carter forsook the language of intense motivation for a pitiable approach that hardly quickened the pulse: "I and my wife and daughter-in-law and others have tried as best we could to join with you in the furtherance of this noble and very necessary change in the United States Constitution. . . . our failure to pass the Equal Rights Amendment hurts us as we try to set a standard of commitment to human rights throughout the world. I hope we can correct that defect by next year at the latest."[79] This is hardly commanding language, especially in a situation begging for an overstatement or two. These women were as aware as Carter of the political difficulties faced by the ERA, but they, unlike him, would have willingly luxuriated for the moment in visions of a dynamic president marching to the barricades on their behalf. As I. F. Stone once said of Carter, "There's no music in him. He just can't lift off. He can fool people for awhile, but he really doesn't know how to inspire."[80]

Jimmy Carter's conception of the presidency simply did not seem grand enough for an era beset by a series of problems—energy, international imbroglios, inflation—that defied simple solution. Mr. Carter did not tell his black audiences that he would jump up and solve their problems because he knew that he could not do so (a fact that many of his predecessors would probably have ignored in the same circumstances). Mr. Carter did not tell the nation's women that he would personally take charge of passing the ERA because he knew that this was impossible, too. Therein lay his problems as president. For Carter, politics was the art of the *probable,* not the possible. He simply did not believe that the presidency was invested with imperial powers, and this belief guided his rhetorical decisions. Jimmy Carter understood the presidency of the latter 1970s. In bespeaking that understanding, he made us wince. Perhaps Lewis Lapham was right when describing Carter as having suffered from "delusions of adequacy."[81]

Conclusion

Gerald Ford, "an Eisenhower without medals,"[82] and Jimmy Carter, who could command nothing more than "the perfunctory civility due the minister at a wedding reception,"[83] gave us a radically new presidency. They spoke softly: with tentativeness, with obscurity, with friendliness, with a jumble of words. Neither Ford's affability nor Carter's supreme intelligence could rescue them from the rhetorical trap they (or we) set for their presidencies. Yet neither Ford nor Carter was a slacker. Both spoke to the American people with unrivaled frequency even though their political losses continued to mount. Both were replaced by new persons with new voices, despite the fact that the messages did not change substantially in either case. Between 1974 and 1980, the American presidency adjusted its political and rhetorical expectations of itself.

This is not to say that the Ford or Carter presidencies were constant. Like most of his forerunners, Jerry Ford learned that the institutional pressures placed on the presidency were considerable. Like most of them, he produced a sterner rhetoric over time: Certainty increased and Self-References decreased as Mr. Ford sought out the presidential posture that was not his by nature (see Table B.9). His adjustments may even have done him some good (as Jimmy Carter painfully learned in the waning days of the 1976 campaign). Despite these changes, however, the American people sent Jerry Ford back to the golf links, hoping to have found in Jimmy Carter a person of sterner stuff.

Jimmy Carter changed during his 4 years in office, too. Those changes will be detailed in the forthcoming chapter. For the moment, however, we might reflect on his presidency as a whole, a presidency that was soft-spoken because it seemed politically expedient, because circumstances made that course inevitable, because his Georgia mafia had insensitive rhetorical feelers, or perhaps simply because that was the way Jimmy Carter wanted to speak. In striving, and failing, to change the level of dialogue with the nation's citizens, Jimmy Carter may have taught us more about ourselves than any of his precursors in the White House. The lesson appears to be this: the American people cannot tolerate for long a passive, thoughtful chief executive. Writing in the pages of *Christian Century,* Richard Hutcheson, Jr., wonders if our rejection of Jimmy Carter and his rhetoric shouldn't concern us all:

> Yet here we encounter a strange anomaly. Carter is being rejected by precisely those people who claim to be, or should be, most in favor of a moral presidency. Intellectual elites that profess enormous concern with moral issues; establishment religious leaders, Catholic, Protestant and Jewish; hundreds of thousands of enlightened citizens who have some awareness of moral questions—these should be the natural constituency of a moral presidency. What has gone wrong?[84]

Notes

1. Arthur Schlesinger, Jr., *The Imperial Presidency* (New York: Popular Library, 1973), p. 395.
2. Haynes Johnson, *In the Absence of Power* (New York: Viking, 1980), p. 301.

3. William Raspberry, "Carter's Presidency Lacking in Passion," column syndicated in the *Austin American Statesman,* July 10, 1979, p. A6.

4. Richard Reeves, *A Ford, Not a Lincoln* (New York: Harcourt, 1975), p. 163.

5. Reeves (1975), p. 163.

6. Reeves (1975), pp. 187–188.

7. John Casserly, *The Ford White House: The Diary of a Speechwriter* (Boulder: Colorado Associated University Press, 1977), p. 329.

8. William Siffin, quoted in "Verdict from Experts," *U.S. News and World Report,* January 9, 1978, p. 18.

9. Tad Szulc, "Our Most Ineffectual Postwar President," *Saturday Review,* April 29, 1978, p. 10.

10. "Carter's Year One," *National Review,* February 3, 1978, p. 134.

11. Quoted in Johnson (1980), p. 301.

12. "The Debates," *Newsweek,* September 27, 1976, p. 26.

13. "Presidential Debate," October 6, 1976, *Weekly Compilations of Presidential Documents* (hereafter, *Weekly Compilations*) 12:41 (1976), p. 1449.

14. "Pure Prairie," *Nation,* December 14, 1974, p. 611.

15. Fred Friendly, quoted in "Americans Grade a President," *People,* January 9, 1978, p. 12.

16. Casserly (1977), p. 237.

17. John Osborne, *White House Watch: The Ford Years* (Washington: New Republic Books, 1977), p. 420.

18. James Wooten, "The President as Orator," *New York Times,* January 26, 1978, p. 15.

19. Dan Nimmo and James Combs, *Subliminal Politics* (Englewood Cliffs: NJ: Prentice-Hall, 1980), p. 73.

20. William Grieder, "Can a Real Christian Make It as President?" *Washington Post Magazine,* November 5, 1978, p. 15.

21. Eugene Kennedy, "Political Power and American Ambivalence," *New York Times Magazine,* March 19, 1978, p. 84.

22. "Presidential Debate," October 28, 1980, *Weekly Compilations,* 16:44 (1980), p. 2501.

23. "Soviet Invasion of Afghanistan," January 4, 1980, *Weekly Compilations,* 16:2 (1980), p. 26. Italics mine.

24. James David Barber, *The Presidential Character: Predicting Performance in the White House,* 2nd edition, (Englewood Cliffs, NJ: Prentice-Hall, 1977), p. 358.

25. Grieder (1978), p. 11.

26. See, for example, William Lee Miller, *Yankee from Georgia: The Emergence of Jimmy Carter* (New York: Times Books, 1978).

27. John Mashek, "A 'Nice Guy' as President: His Strengths, Weaknesses," *U.S. News and World Report,* August 11, 1975, p. 19.

28. Assorted remarks quoted in Casserly (1977), p. 89.

29. See Richard G. Hutcheson, Jr., "Jimmy Carter's Moral Presidency," *Christian Century,* November 21, 1979, p. 1155.

30. "American Legion," August 19, 1975, *Weekly Compilations,* 11:34 (1975), p. 871. Italics mine.

31. Casserly (1977), p. 188.

32. Barber (1977), p. 537.

33. James Fallows, "The Passionless Presidency," *Atlantic Monthly,* May 1979, p. 35.

34. "Drawing the Battle Lines," *Time,* August 25, 1980, p.21.

35. "The State of Mr. Carter's Country," *New York Times,* January 22, 1978, pp. 4–18.

36. James Reston, "Carter and the Press," *New York Times,* April 12, 1978, p. 25.

37. "Democratic National Committee," May 25, 1979, *Weekly Compilations,* 15:21 (1979), p. 948.

38. "Swearing in of the President," August 9, 1974, *Weekly Compilations,* 10:32 (1974), p. 1024.

39. "Radio Address on the Presidency," November 2, 1976, *Weekly Compilations,* 12:45 (1976), p. 1674.

40. Osborne (1977), p. xv.

41. Reeves (1975), pp. 187–188.

42. Rowland Evans and Robert Novak, "Jerry Ford: The Eisenhower of the Seventies?" *Atlantic Monthly,* August 1974, p. 28.

43. Osborne (1977), p. 176.

44. Osborne (1977), pp. 176–177.

45. "Dinner of the South Florida Chapter of the Federal Bar Association," February 14, 1976, *Weekly Compilations,* 12:8 (1976), p. 219.

46. "The Blooper Heard Round the World," *Time,* October 18, 1976, pp. 13–14, 17–18.

47. John Osborne, *New Republic,* October 23, 1976, pp. 8–10.

48. "High-level Bafflegab," *Vogue,* December 1974, p. 128.

49. John Hersey, *The President* (New York: Knopf, 1975), p. 131n.

50. Paraphrased in Reeves (1975), p. 45.

51. Bruce Mazlish and Edwin Diamond, *Jimmy Carter: An Interpretive Biography* (New York: Simon and Schuster, 1979), p. 264.

52. Quoted in Mazlish and Diamond, p. 264.

53. Mazlish and Diamond (1979), p. 264.

54. "Remarks at Presentation Ceremony," November 22, 1977, *Weekly Compilations,* 13:48 (1977), p. 1799.

55. "Remarks to White House Conference on Small Business," January 13, 1980, *Weekly Compilations,* 16:13 (1980), pp. 70–71.

56. "Remarks at White House Meeting of Humphrey Scholarship Program," December 5, 1978, *Weekly Compilations,* 14:49 (1978), p. 2158.

57. Thomas Hughes, "Carter and the Management of Contradictions," in Steven Shull and Lance LeLoup, eds., *The Presidency: Studies in Policy Making* (Brunswick, OH: Kings Court, 1979), p. 267.

58. Quoted in Reeves (1975), p. 26.

59. Casserly (1977), p. 31.

60. "Remarks to American Society of Newspaper Editors," April 16, 1975, *Weekly Compilations,* 11:16 (1975), p. 389.

61. Quoted in Christopher Lydon, "Jimmy Carter Revealed," *Atlantic Monthly,* July, 1977, p. 56.

62. Lydon (1977), p. 54.

63. "Remarks at Fund-Raising Dinner for Carter/Mondale," October 24, 1979, *Weekly Compilations,* 15:43 (1979), p. 2017. Italics mine.

64. "Remarks at National Governor's Conference," March 1, 1977, *Weekly Compilations,* 13:10 (1977), p. 279.

65. Fallows (1979), p. 42.

66. Casserly (1977), p. 194.

67. Quoted in Osborne (1977), p. 260.

68. "The Making of a Fighting Speech," *Time,* August 30, 1976, p. 18.

69. "President's Remarks Accepting the Nomination," August 19, 1976, *Weekly Compilations,* 12:34 (1976), p. 1269.

70. Casserly (1977), p. 329.

71. Quoted in "In Elections," *Time,* September 15, 1980, p. 19.

72. "Economic Sanctions against Iran," December 21, 1979, *Weekly Compilations,* 15:51 (1979), pp. 2277–2278.

73. Max Naylor, quoted in Douglas Kneeland, "Mixed Reviews," *New York Times,* February 13, 1977, p. 26.

74. "Jimmy the Persuader," *Newsweek,* March 19, 1979, p. 25.

75. Hedrick Smith, "Carter to Date," *New York Times,* April 24, 1977, p. 4:1.

76. "President's News Conference," September 21, 1977, *Weekly Compilations,* 13:39 (1977), p. 1390.

77. Quoted in Szulc (1978), p. 10.

78. "Remarks to Congressional Black Caucus," September 24, 1977, *Weekly Compilations,* 12:14 (1977), p. 1417.

79. "Remarks to National Women's Political Caucus," March 30, 1977, *Weekly Compilations,* 12:14 (1977), p. 474.

80. Quoted in Wooten (1978), p. 15.

81. Lewis Lapham, "King Frederick's Mules," *Harper's,* March 1980, p. 22.

82. "The President up Close," *Newsweek,* October 18, 1976, p. 36.

83. Lapham (1980), p. 18.

84. Hutcheson (1979), p. 1162.

JIMMY CARTER'S
RHETORICAL ODYSSEY

The most perceptive commentary yet written about Jimmy Carter is Betty
Glad's *Jimmy Carter: In Search of the Great White House.*[1] In her book,
Glad analyzes why Carter so impressed small town Americans in early 1976
that the media were forced to treat him as a serious candidate for the presidency. In trying to explain Carter's appeal, Glad lauds his "anonymity"
because it "gave Carter an extraordinary freedom to present himself and
his themes, sometimes in an emotionally rich, fablelike form. Moreover,
his technique of sending out so many different signals about where he stood
politically as well as what he was like perpetuated the ambiguity."[2] Glad
reveals that Carter managed to buffalo even seasoned political reporters
during the 1976 campaign, with some viewing him as a new conservative and
others viewing him as a new dealer. Glad reports that "the voters, too, seem
generally to have interpreted Carter to fit their predispositions. Surveys
taken by *The New York Times* and CBS throughout the primaries indicated
that conservative voters saw a conservative Carter, moderates a moderate
Carter, and liberals a liberal Carter."[3] Glad contends that Carter had the
"ability to connect, seemingly on a personal and intimate basis, with many
different types of people, whether individually or in groups."[4] Women appreciated Carter's tendency to stop "for a tender second over a hand clasp,"
college students regarded him as "innocent of demagoguery," and Carter
was even able to get a group of potentially hostile south Georgia sheriffs
"to eat out of his hands through his soft, schoolmarmish ways."[5] It is little
wonder, then, that so many different people asked so often where Jimmy
Carter was even as he stood in their midst. Betty Glad explains in delightful
detail:

He took his search for a common ground with audiences sometimes to absurd extremes: While campaigning in Idaho in 1976, he told one audience that he identified with them because the major products of Idaho and Georgia were raised underground—Idaho potatoes and Georgia peanuts. Later he noted that both Oregon and Georgia have important lumber industries. To a West Virginia crowd Carter said: "You have tremendous coal deposits under your surface lands. As you know peanuts grow under the ground also, so I have a lot in common with you there." (Norman Mailer, who was in the audience, thought he was telling a bad joke.) During a visit to the West Coast in August, 1976, Carter observed that even Hollywood reminded him of Plains. When a startled listener asked him "Why?" Carter explained that both towns had trees. And in September at Brooklyn College, Carter found himself "much at home," observing that "both a neighborhood and a small town have their own special character, their own distinctive life. I don't come from Americus, or Vienna, or Cordele. I come from Plains. You come from Flatbush—and not Sunnyside or Bay Ridge or Brooklyn Heights. We feel most at home where our roots run deep."[6]

To listen to one speech by Harry Truman was, in a sense, to listen to them all. To understand Jimmy Carter, on the other hand, one must examine his speechmaking in great detail, for the "real Jimmy Carter" was a labyrinthine fellow hidden within his publicness. The Carter presidency is best revealed in the broad expanse of his rhetoric because the several alterations in his rhetoric throw bold light upon the painful policy decisions he could not make or, having made, could not enforce. In trying to be all things to all people, Jimmy Carter succeeded in becoming painfully little to most of them, even though they remained oddly fond of the Jimmy Carters found in his political menagerie. The sample of Carter's speeches studied here (152 in all) seems sufficient to track this elusive creature. In this chapter, then, I examine how Carter altered his public image during his 4 years in office, and how, ultimately, speech failed him as a president. In examining a single presidency in special detail, we shall also be learning something about institutional pressures generally.

In Search of a Rhetoric

Jimmy Carter never found his presidential voice, but this is not to say that he did not try. Mr. Carter sought to please. He did not fix upon a single mode of speech just as he did not fix upon a single approach to energy supplies or Iran. Carter's was a supple intelligence, one that acknowledged and accepted (perhaps too soon) the endless adaptations that make politics political. He entered the presidency as an outsider to Washington and, after some tortuous twists and turns, sought peace with the Congress. He was elected to the presidency because of his special feeling for the American people, but probably achieved his greatest success via his international initiatives (especially in the Middle East). Carter's presidency, like the man himself, was an undulating phenomenon.

Over time, Carter significantly increased his use of Symbolism and significantly decreased his use of Realism (see Figure 7.1). In other words, the presidency increasingly returned Carter to his roots as a Bible-toting moralist, making him more deft at explaining the nation's cultural crises than in deregulating its supply of natural gas. Although he always had a leaning toward preachment, his early presidency seemed to belie this tendency. His inaugural address, for example, was not especially histrionic; it was among the five most realistic televised speeches he gave while serving as president. In it, he warned that *"more* is not necessarily *better,* that even our great Nation has its recognized limits, and that we can neither answer all questions nor solve all problems." Rather than revel in hallowed Symbolism, Carter warned that "we cannot dwell upon remembered glory. We cannot afford to drift. We reject the prospect of failure or mediocrity or an inferior quality of life for any person. Our government must at the same time be both competent and compassionate."[7]

As the pressures of governing mounted for Mr. Carter, as viable political platforms gave way, as frustration melded with frustration, Carter ascended the ladder of abstraction. Whereas during his first 2 years in office he addressed political groups quite pragmatically (e.g., his rally speeches

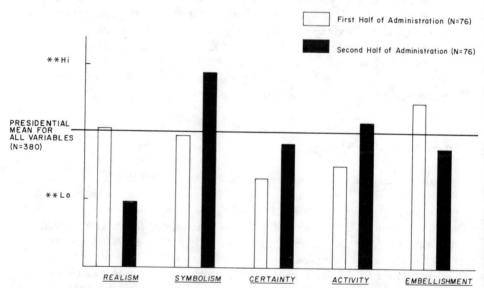

Figure 7.1   Changes in Jimmy Carter's rhetoric over time. All differences significant. See Table B.9. ** ± ½ sd from mean. See Table B.1 for exact values.

of March 1, 1977; April 28, 1978; and September 23, 1978), his later addresses to Democratic gatherings showed an increase in Symbolism. When
addressing the Democratic National Committee on September 26, 1979, for
example, Carter punctuated his remarks with phrases like "an America that
is strong," "an America at peace," and "responsibility to America," all
of which were standard chants in the nation's litany. But he also went on
to ensure that all listeners, potential as well as actual, felt included in his
rhetorical embrace: "Americans who are concerned," "Americans . . . who
work inside government," "hard-working Americans," "American Jews,"
"American blacks."[8] As his presidency matured, such phrases tripped off
Jimmy Carter's tongue easily, without embarrassment on his part, and his
earnest facial expression resembled that of a newly decorated Eagle Scout.

A particularly striking finding is depicted in Figure 7.2, which compares
Carter's use of Realism with his personal popularity (as measured in public
opinion polls). The parallel, decelerating curves graphically reveal the political problems Jimmy Carter experienced. As he increasingly skirted dis-

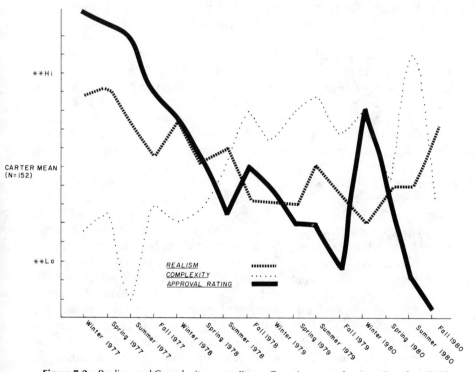

Figure 7.2   Realism and Complexity versus Jimmy Carter's approval ratings. Based on CBS/
New York Times polls.

cussions of current issues, his approval rating dropped. Even a sharp rise in Realism during his last 6 months in office proved insufficient to save him from political defeat. As his ratings in the polls plummeted, Carter seemed to feel that just a bit more explanation by him, or a slightly more complete theoretical case, would make the people understand him and, by understanding him, accept him.

Yet when announcing his anti-inflation program in March of 1980, Carter seemed determined to make listening difficult. Only a person intent on political suicide would, on national television and radio, use a sentence like the following: "To help curtail the excessive uses of credit and by dampening inflation they [his new policies] should, along with the budget measures that I have described, speed prospects for reducing the strains which presently exist in our financial markets." Later in his speech, Carter numbingly referred to "unfair economic distortions," a "tripartite advisory committee," and a "commendable spirit of restraint and cooperation."[9] Compared with Ronald Reagan's speeches on economics, which employed colorful visual aids understandable by prepubescents, Mr. Carter's speeches were hopelessly foggy. When reading his speeches, it is easy to understand why the Realism curve and the Approval rating curve in Figure 7.2 are so closely related.

Figure 7.2 also depicts a less compatible set of variables. Complexity and presidential popularity raced in opposite directions during the Carter years, with each six-syllable word presumably costing him two points in the polls. The remarkable rise in Complexity depicted in Figure 7.2 sheds direct light on Carter's understanding of leadership: His job was to teach and thereby to lead—if the people did not believe something, it was because they did not understand it. As his presidency unfolded, Mr. Carter rang the school bell earlier and more insistently. During his last 2 years in office, for example, *only* 3 of his speeches—out of the 76 studied—dropped below the presidential average for Complexity. His State of the Union address of January 23, 1979, was typical of his classroom cadence: "In less than a lifetime, world population has more than doubled, colonial empires have disappeared, and a hundred new nations have been born. Mass communications, literacy, and migration to the world's cities have all awakened new yearnings for economic justice and human rights among people everywhere."[10]

According to some members of the Carter White House, the President's "encyclopedic knowledge of issues, and his gift for almost total recall from his voluminous briefing books"[11] gave his speechmaking a lecturish quality. His aides felt that "he is simply too rigid too often, secure in the belief that he knows more about his subject than anyone else."[12] His aides could not deny, however, that Carter was right when he said (in that same State of the Union speech) that "the problems we face today are different in nature from those that confronted earlier generations of Americans. They are more subtle, more complex, more interrelated."[13] Deep inside of themselves, the American people also recognized the truth of Carter's remarks, and they probably knew that these remarks deserved to be addressed with a verbal complexity suited to the difficulties of their age. But Carter's professorial presidency just did not feel good to them and so, like all students, they skipped class whenever they could and pilloried their teacher for being the teacher he was.

When he increased his Complexity and Symbolism and decreased his Realism, Mr. Carter was reverting to his natural style. But other temporal changes were more novel for him. Over time, Carter significantly expanded his use of Certainty and Activity, but depended less and less on Embellishment. In so doing, Jimmy Carter retold a story of rhetorical inevitability apparently situated in the Oval Office itself.

In August of 1978, *Time* magazine asked, "Is a new Jimmy Carter emerging—tougher, demanding more of his staff, focusing more sharply on issues?" *Time* concluded that this was indeed the case and credited the change to Carter's newly appointed "Secretary of Symbolism," Gerald Rafshoon. According to *Time*, Rafshoon's job was to get Carter to "assert more control over his Administration in public."[14] The *New York Times Magazine's* Martin Tolchin wrote a feature story about Rafshoon (entitled "New Pro in the White House") and credited him with the "President's new-found image of toughness."[15] According to Rafshoon, his job was simply to let loose the essential Jimmy Carter: "The two things I've always known about him [Carter] are his competence and his toughness. I'd like people to see more of that side."[16] On another occasion, Rafshoon said, "I simply stand between Jimmy Carter and mushy statements."[17]

And stand staunchly he did. Carter's last 2 years in office brought forth some of his most decisive addresses: his disarmament speech of June 18, 1979; his "crisis of confidence" speech the next month; and his town meeting in Burlington, Iowa, of that August during which Mr. Carter declared, "Our Nation has never been afraid to face a challenge. We have never been unable to overcome an obstacle or to meet a problem and solve it. And our country has always been able, when we were united, to answer any difficult question."[18] A month later Mr. Carter told the Russians to remove their troops from Cuba; 2 months later he demanded that the Iranians return our countrymen and countrywomen ("this Nation will never yield to blackmail. . . . The actions of Iran have shocked the civilized world. . . . There is certainly no religious faith on earth which condones the sustained abuse of innocent people.");[19] and 3 months later he delivered his most unyielding State of the Union message. *Time* characterized this latter address as "one of the best received speeches of Carter's presidency. It was firm, measured, strongly felt. He was stopped by applause 20 times."[20] Gerry Rafshoon did what he had set out to do, which was, in his own words, to "save the President's ass."[21]

Rafshoon's vernacular was contagious. During the presidential primary season of 1980, Jimmy Carter declared that he would whip the same portion of Teddy Kennedy's anatomy that Rafshoon had saved for him. Unfortunately for Carter, Rafshoonian certitude could not salvage a presidency afflicted with vagueness and loquaciousness. Being sure about principles just does not impress in politics as does being sure about policy: Certainty without Realism made Carter appear sonorous rather than serious. As if sensing these disparities, columnist Anthony Lewis asked in August of 1979 why Mr. Carter had become "a strident, fist-thumping character? Why should a man at ease with himself have taken so defensive, even petulant, a tone in public over recent weeks? Why had he adopted such Nixonian techniques as making his Cabinet members resign en masse and giving them a childish personnel questionnaire?"[22]

Lewis has his finger here on an unnatural graft in Carter's rhetoric—institutional rigidity laid atop Mr. Carter's own language of sentiment. As we saw in Chapter Two, most of our recent presidents became more rigid as their presidencies progressed. In using this style, Carter adopted an approach that had often sent the American people marching on some glorious, militaristic errand. During his latter days in office, Mr. Carter's remarks sounded suspiciously like the might-makes-right strains (described by Robert Jewett in *The Captain America Complex*), which have propelled us into conflict so often in our nation's history.[23] Fortunately for us all, Mr. Carter had the wisdom to let his policy decisions lag behind his rhetorical inclinations. Yet one cannot help but wonder what it is about the presidency that ultimately makes its sounds of fury so attractive to the occupants of that office.

The Seasons of a Presidency

Naturally, every presidency is unique and must be judged by individual standards. But a careful look at Carter's public persona across time may tell us something about the possibilities (and impossibilities) of the institution itself. The speeches a president delivers become a diary, a record of what he knew and wished for, as well as what he did. Heretofore, no attempt has been made to lay out a given presidency end to end to see how it opened and closed, to see how its themes developed, to see how it was affected by the political winds.

Appendix C presents a tolerably complete synopsis of the Carter administration.[24] Appendix C also shows that any presidency ultimately confronts international and domestic events over which the chief executive seems to have little control. Surely Iran, Afghanistan, coal strikes, Proposition Thirteen, OPEC recalcitrance, Bert Lance, and Billy Carter were not uppermost in Jimmy Carter's mind when he recited the oath of office on January 20, 1977. Nor could he have imagined then that his popularity would drop 10 percentage points a year during his one-term presidency. No Democratic president, surely, would have predicted that labor leaders like George Meaney, feminist leaders like Bella Abzug, and congressional leaders like Tip O'Neill would eventually take turns criticizing him. No first-term president would imagine that he would later be forced to make his reelection bid from the safety of the Rose Garden or, cruelest of all, that he would be forced into presidential debate with a former movie actor. These and other untoward things happened to James Earl Carter and, furthermore, he had to talk about them all.

A presidency, in short, has rhetorical seasons. Figures 7.3–7.5 reveal Jimmy Carter's winters (and summers) of discontent. By examining these risings and fallings across time, we are afforded a unique understanding of

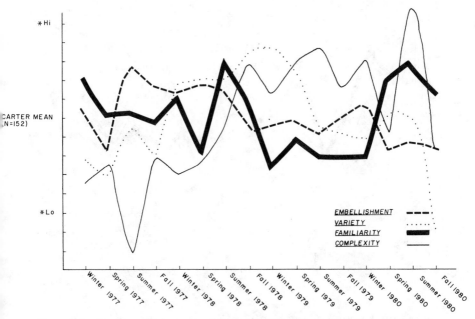

Figure 7.3 Developmental aspects of Jimmy Carter's style: I. *±1 sd from mean. See Table B.13 for exact values.

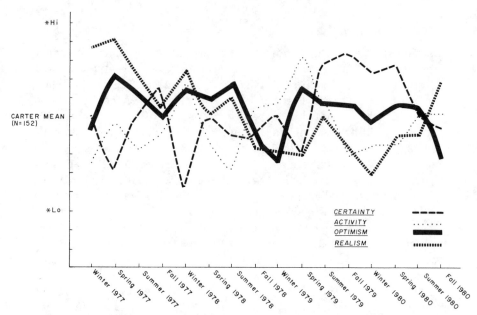

Figure 7.4 Developmental aspects of Jimmy Carter's style: II. *±1 sd from mean. See Table B.13 for exact values.

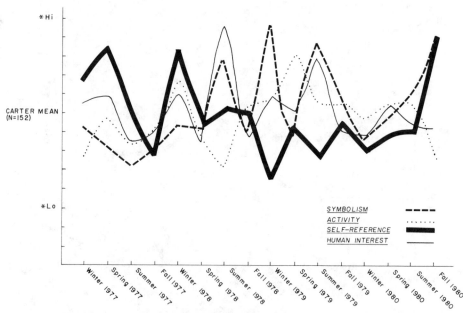

Figure 7.5 Developmental aspects of Jimmy Carter's style: III. *±1 sd from mean. See Table B.13 for exact values.

the Carter presidency. One pedestrian fact should be noted immediately: Jimmy Carter's speechmaking varied considerably during his 4 years in office as he sought to adjust to the political and psychological circumstances of the job. Naturally, some variables (like Optimism) were less affected by time than others. Also, some language factors (like Self-Reference) behaved erratically while others assumed a steady pitch downward (like Realism) or upward (like Complexity). Taken together, the 10 language variables describe the following sort of evolution:

1977 Probably his best year in the presidency. His speeches were as realistic as they ever became, his language was fairly simple, and his highly personalized campaign style gave way gradually to a more dignified, presidential approach. His national phone-ins, town meetings, and fireside chats allowed him to strike a new rhetorical pose in the White House. Although his comparatively low levels of Activity and Certainty caused his image to suffer a bit when contrasted to his imperial forebears, his was a new sort of voice in Washington and most Americans listened to it patiently.

1978 This was a transition year, rhetorically speaking. The sharp peaks and valleys in many of the curves suggest a president desperately looking for something that would work. Human Interest sharply fluctuated as Carter first tried a homespun and then an ex cathedra style. The great amount of Variety also suggests a president unsure of himself. Coupled with his jumble of words was Carter's ominous rise in Complexity, a trend which never really abated thereafter and that probably did more than most variables to confuse the voters.

1979 1979 brought SALT II, the Ayatollah Khomeini, MX missiles, Teddy Kennedy, a Soviet invasion, the pope, and a Chrysler bailout. It also brought a sharp rise in Jimmy Carter's Symbolism and Certainty (at about the time of Camp David), a slight increase in Realism at this same time, and a roller coaster–like drop in Variety as the president effected a simpler, surer message. The winter of 1979 was particularly difficult for Carter as his use of Optimism and Self-Reference reached their lowest levels, and Variety and Symbolism reached their highest. Toward the end of that year, however, Iran and Camp David—and Carter's uncharacteristic deployment of Certainty—permitted the president to jump 21 percentage points in the opinion polls. 1980 looked like it would be a good year for Mr. Carter.

1980 But 1980 was not to be appeased. High interest rates, a failed rescue mission in Iran, and more of Billy Carter's shenanigans cost the president a good deal. As election day approached, Carter cranked up the Symbolism machine, eschewed his characteristic Complexity for Familiarity, and even made a last-gasp effort in the area of Realism. The two aspects that create the most splendid campaign fireworks, however, are Certainty and Activity. When he needed these rhetorical resources most they slipped through his fingers. In the fall of 1980, Mr. Carter tried to sell us himself (via Self-References) but the voters were not buying.

The wide swings in behavior depicted in Figures 7.3 through 7.5 surely reveal a president who tried—desperately. Perhaps that was his problem. His administration was never able to generate in the minds of the American people a single, consistent image. Carter's was an experimental presidency; timidity alternated with ferocity, pragmatism with preachment. The result was confusion for the voters and censure from the critics: "Carter seems like one of the boys on the corner. He doesn't appear to understand what leadership is. Making a change in his style is like a zebra opting to have spots instead of stripes—it doesn't make a significant difference."[25]

Mr. Carter's public diary of rhetoric is a difficult one to read. Table 7.1 contains representative selections from the pages of his presidency. When scanning them collectively in this way, it is hard to imagine that his remarks emanated from the same presidential pen. Perhaps it was this ambiguity of authorship (and corresponding ambiguity of purpose) that ultimately cost Mr. Carter his job.

Table 7.1 also presents stark evidence of how hard a president must work. Jimmy Carter was expected to be friend of the farmer, defender of the free world, companion to his brother, student of technology, admirer of the Poles, humble son of the South, and lionizer of Clarence Mitchell. The difficulty, of course, is that all of these roles had to be played in public,

TABLE 7.1

THE CARTER RHETORICAL DIARY

Period	Dominant rhetorical features	Sample[26]
Winter 1977	High Realism, low Activity and Complexity	I don't believe I could have chosen a woman to be Vice President who cares any more about day care centers, care for those who are deprived, women's rights, than Fritz Mondale. And this is something that ought to be recognized. In some of our major departments we have 50% women at the top levels; in some we have much less than that. I understand that we have got a long way to go. And when we double or triple what has been done with the previous Presidents, even Lyndon Johnson, even John Kennedy, we are not bragging about it. But I think it would be good for you to recognize it. (3/10/77, Women's Group)

Table 7.1 (*continued*)

Period	Dominant rhetorical features	Sample[26]
Spring 1977	High Optimism and Self-Reference, low Certainty	I'm very grateful that you would come and meet with me this afternoon, now. And we have a chance, I think, to make our country even greater than it has been in the past. It depends not on the identity of the president but on the common thrust and strength of our people. And I'm one of you, and you're part of me, and that realization gives me a quiet confidence that I can serve in such a way as not to embarrass you. (5/13/77, Reception for Southern Baptists)
Summer 1977	High Embellishment, low Symbolism and Complexity	I urge all nations, and especially the major industrial countries, to reduce energy waste along with us and to pursue economic growth and stabilization policies along with us, leading to an expanding, noninflationary world economy, growing international trade, and an improved pattern of world trade balances. The International Monetary Fund has played already a vital role in keeping the international monetary system both flexible and effective. I'm particularly grateful for the enlightened fiscal discipline which the Fund and the Bank encourage throughout the world with their loans. (9/26/77, Economics Conference)
Fall 1977	Low Self-Reference, Variety, Complexity	We must face an unpleasant fact about energy prices. They are going up whether we pass an energy program or not, as fuel becomes more scarce and more expensive to produce. The question is, who should benefit from those rising prices for oil already discovered? Our energy plan captures and returns them to the public, where they can stimulate the economy, save more energy, and create new jobs. We will use research and development projects, tax incentives and penalties, and regulatory authority to hasten the shift from oil and gas to coal, to wind and solar power, to geothermal, methane, and other energy sources. (11/8/77, Address to Nation)

(continued)

Table 7.1 (*continued*)

Period	Dominant rhetorical features	Sample[26]
Winter 1978	High Realism and Self-Reference, low Certainty	I was overwhelmed with the response of the Polish people when we discussed the historic ties that have long bound our countries together. As a southerner from Georgia, my own earliest studies of both Georgia and United States history have included in a major way the reports of the great heroism and dedication of Kosciuszko and Pulaski. My own son Chip's wife is from Pulaski County in Georgia, named in honor of the Polish patriot who helped us win our independence. And we discussed quite freely both with servants in the beautiful mansion we stayed and those in the government, the common effort that we had made in the world wars, when Poland was so nearly destroyed. (2/6/78, Reception for Polish Americans)
Spring 1978	Low Familiarity and Activity, high Variety	Well, as President, I face difficult and sometimes almost insoluble problems. And I need Jennings Randolph in Washington to help me to serve our people, those who live here and those who live around the country. This is not going to be an easy election year. It will not be an easy campaign for Jennings Randolph. And I know that you've sacrificed coming here, contributing to his campaign financially. And I would hate for any one of you to go away thinking that you've done all that he or I expect from you. (5/26/78, West Virginia Rally)
Summer 1978	High Familiarity, Human Interest and Symbolism, low Activity	I was concerned when I became President, as a farmer, about farmers. We've got a good sound administration. Bob Bergland, Secretary of Agriculture—he's not a college professor or economist exercising his theories in the Agriculture Department in Washington; he's a dirt farmer. When he came back from the war, he couldn't make a living at home. He had to go down to Florida as an itinerant farmworker. He went back up to northern Minnesota and borrowed money and rented some land and, eventually, built up a farm in his own family of about 600 acres. (8/5/78, Remarks at Growers Warehouse)

Table 7.1 (*continued*)

Period	Dominant rhetorical features	Sample[26]
Fall 1978	High Variety and Complexity	In distributing the scarce resources of our foreign assistance programs, we will demonstrate that our deepest affinities are with nations which commit themselves to a democratic path of development. Toward regimes which persist in wholesale violations of human rights, we will not hesitate to convey our outrage, nor will we pretend that our relations are unaffected. In the coming year, I hope that Congress will take a step that has been long overdue for a generation, the ratification of the Convention of the Prevention and Punishment of the Crime of Genocide. As you know, the genocide convention was also adopted by the United Nations General Assembly 30 years ago this week, 1 day before the adoption of the Universal Declaration. It was the world's affirmation that the lesson of the Holocaust would never be forgotten, but unhappily, genocide is not peculiar to any one historical era. (12/6/78, Human Rights Ceremony)
Winter 1979	High Symbolism and Variety; low Optimism, Self-Reference, and Familiarity	We have won at last the first step of peace, a first step on a long and difficult road. We must not minimize the obstacles which still lie ahead. Differences still separate the signatories to this treaty from one another, and also from some of their neighbors who fear what they have just done. To overcome the differences, to dispel broader peace with justice for all who have lived in a state of conflict in the Middle East. We have no illusions—we have hopes, dreams, and prayers, yes, but not illusion. (3/26/79, Peace Treaty Ceremony)
Spring 1979	High Activity and Complexity	The times we live in call for plain talk and call for political courage. Slogans will not do the job. Press conferences will not solve serious problems that we face in inflation, in energy, in maintaining peace in a troubled world. We have already wasted years, as you know, under Republican leadership, looking

(continued)

Table 7.1 (*continued*)

Period	Dominant rhetorical features	Sample [26]
		for quick fixes, often just before a national election. This is a time to tell the American people the truth. The days of the quick fix and the painless solution, if they ever existed, are gone. . . . The bottom line is clear. We need positive political solutions in America today, not just a sustained record of negative notes to appease some special, powerful political group back home. (5/25/79, Democratic National Committee)
Summer 1979	High Certainty, Symbolism, Human Interest, and Complexity	Our nation has never been afraid to face a challenge. We have never been unable to overcome an obstacle or to meet a problem and solve it. And our country has always been able, when we were united, to answer any difficult question. God's blessed us in many wonderful ways, with rich land, a democratic, free government, a pride in the individualism of each person, the right to be different, the right to speak our minds, the right to control our own Government, the right to unify ourselves in times of challenge, and I have to say that this is one of those times when our people must be unified. (8/22/79, Iowa Town Meeting)
Fall 1979	High Certainty	I want the American People to know and I want the world to know that we will persist in our efforts, through every means available, until every single American in Iran has been freed. We must also recognize now, as we have never done before, that it is our entire Nation which is vulnerable, because of our overwhelming and excessive dependence on oil from foreign countries. We have got to accept the fact that this dependence is a direct physical threat to our national security, and we must join together to fight for our Nation's energy freedom. (11/28/79, Press Conference)
Winter 1980	Low Realism, high Complexity	Clarence Mitchell is the symbol of the strength of this organization. A modest man, he's always eager to give other people credit, as he did a few minutes ago. This is a night to honor him. He, in an excessive degree of

Table 7.1 (*continued*)

Period	Dominant rhetorical features	Sample[26]
		generosity, tried to give me credit for things; that's typical of him. But he's always known how to be successful. And the reason he has been successful is that he's been eager to give other people credit for what he himself has accomplished. (1/27/80, Civil Rights Conference)
Spring 1980	High Certainty and Familiarity	It's time for us to look forward, not backward. It's a time for us to heal existing wounds that are created in any tough Democratic Party election campaign and not create new wounds. It's incumbent on you and me to heal existing wounds, not to create new wounds in our party. It's time for us to pull the different elements of our party back together; to be generous in victory, to be united, to be determined, and not to fail. I do not intend to lose this election in 1980. (5/19/80, Party Rally)
Summer 1980	High Certainty and Familiarity	And now I'd like to say a word about my brother's relations with Libya. As all of you know by now, Billy is a colorful personality. We are extremely close. I love him, and he loves me. Billy is extremely independent. On occasion he has said, "I don't tell Jimmy how to run the country, and he doesn't tell me how to run my life." When I was elected President, Billy was thrust into the public limelight. Media attention made him an instant celebrity. He was asked to make a number of television and other speaking engagements, and he even put his name on a new brand of beer. (8/4/80, Press Conference)
Fall 1980	High Realism, Symbolism, and Self-Reference; low Activity and Variety	It's a lonely job, but with the involvement of the American people in the process with an open government, the job is a very gratifying one. The American People now are facing next Tuesday a lonely decision. Those listening to my voice will have to make a judgment about the future of this country, and I think they ought to remember the difference. If one vote per precinct had changed in 1960, John Kennedy would never have been president of

(continued)

Table 7.1 (*continued*)

Period	Dominant rhetorical features	Sample [26]
		this nation. And if a few more people had gone to polls and voted in 1968, Hubert Humphrey would have been president, Richard Nixon would not. There is a partnership involved in our nation to stay strong, to stay at peace, to raise high the banner of human rights, to set an example for the rest of the world, to let our deep beliefs and commitments be felt by others in all other nations. Here's my plan for the future. I ask the American people to join me in this partnership. (10/28/80, Presidential Debate)

had to be played in near simultaneity, and had to be played well, each and every one of them. All of the Jimmy Carters we met were applauded politely but no one of them remained with us long enough, or seemed sure enough of himself, to capture our ardor or respect. In toto, and that is how a president is judged, Mr. Carter's failure to blend his selves into a consistent, pleasing whole may have resulted from his personal inadequacies as a leader, from the standards of judgment employed by a fickle citizenry, or, perhaps, from a presidential institution so besieged by political pressures that, like some crazed, fictional scientist, it creates and then destroys mutation after mutation.

Problems Aplenty

Studying the persuasive difficulties Jimmy Carter experienced as chief executive may explain why his presidency ultimately foundered. Such an examination may also reveal hazards native to the insitution itself. The following section, then, is a kind of rhetorical postmortem of a presidency.

Coordination

Basic to Mr. Carter's problems were ones of coordination. That is, he was often out of sync with himself. While portions of his remarks suited his listeners from time to time, other portions left them vaguely discomfited. Political scientist Aaron Wildavsky explains: "The president calls upon the citizenry to sacrifice, without explaining why or telling them how. The gap between the rhetoric of crisis and the paucity of action leaves President Carter's listeners dissatisfied—as if drinking their medicine from empty cups, invited to a party but always knocking at the wrong door."[27] Figure 7.4 shows that Mr. Carter could not successfully combine strength with enthusiasm. Figure 7.4 also reveals an even more problematic situation: When Carter was tough, he was tough about ideas, not about action. With few exceptions, the Certainty and Activity curves pass each other by until they die a twin death in the 1980 campaign. Figure 7.4 indicates that Certainty and Realism had similar aversions, with Mr. Carter fulminating about concepts (like "human rights") rather than grounding his strongest remarks in the world of everyday policy (like the Equal Rights Amendment).

What could cause such rhetorical miscues? One suggestion is made by James Fallows, who claims that too many hands were involved in the president's speech preparation. He cites as an example Carter's stern address at the U.S. Naval Academy in June of 1978. Fallows reports that Mr. Carter's speech preparation consisted of stapling a memo by Cyrus Vance to one written by Zbigniew Brzezinski. According to Fallows, the speech "had an obvious break in the middle, like the splice in a film; as one newsman who had read the advance text said, after hearing Carter come to the end of conciliatory material and move into the Brzezinski section, 'And now— War!' "[28] Although the Annapolis speech received much favorable press (no doubt because of its high Certainty quotient), it got the president "into hot water with the experts; he was widely criticized for inadvertently using undiplomatic words and inflammatory phrases which exacerbated U.S.-Soviet relations"[29] (no doubt because Mr. Carter's low Activity score beclouded his policy preferences). While it is impossible to determine how many of Carter's speeches suffered because of mixed parentage, one member of the House of Representatives claimed that "every night is Amateur Night at the White House,"[30] while a student of the presidency has avowed that "no recent American president—not even Jerry Ford—had had so poor a working relationship with speechwriters."[31]

Another kind of coordination problem was more cerebral. Hedrick Smith reports one insider's opinion that Carter's "greatest strength is his intelligence in attacking and analyzing problems. His greatest weakness is his lack of conceptual structure."[32] That may have been too strong a statement, but it would have been accurate to say that Carter demonstrated a consistent inability to blend the right rhetorical humors. His "crisis of confidence" speech of July 15, 1979, illustrates. In his remarks, Carter asserted that a "national malaise" had befallen the American people and that only a change of heart—not just a change in energy policy—could set matters aright. This speech, low on Activity but high on Certainty, was reported to be an attempt by Carter to return "to the homilies and populist rhetoric of his 1976 campaign in an effort to save his Presidency and to try to restore what he feels is his lost contact with the American people."[33] In the speech, Mr. Carter presented a tour de force of the nation's urgent problems, including the following: "We are losing our confidence in the future. . . . too many of us now tend to worship self-indulgence and consumption. . . . there is a growing disrespect for government and for churches and for schools. . . . the gap between our citizens and our Government has never been so wide." Another of Mr. Carter's statements was ironically self-reflective: "What you see too often in Washington and elsewhere around the country is a system of government that seems incapable of action."[34]

Despite its rich philosophical texture, Carter's speech forsook the bombast (that is, Certainty *plus Activity*) demanded in July of 1979. The three most important ingredients of political discourse—Certainty, Activity, and Optimism—seemed alien to Carter. As a result, the American people never quite caught his drift. They had, according to Eugene Kennedy, "two sided reactions to the President—to their agreement with him and confusion about him, to their relief and impatience—they merely reflect the way people always feel when someone delivers more than one message at the same time. . . . The President cannot make a claim to new leadership, and then insist that the populace instruct him in the exercise of that leadership, without generating bewilderment and dismay."[35]

With very few exceptions after the winter of 1978, Realism and Activity also were never truly coordinated by Carter. Figure 7.4 reveals the disparity between these elements, with Carter promising to do more and more as time went on but backing up his remarks with less and less concrete evidence. Figures 7.3 and 7.5 indicate that Carter was also more preacher than politician after the first few months of 1978. Wordiness, and a fondness for basic American values, weakened his rhetorical impact. Although it was only the Republicans who claimed in April of 1977 that "Carter is all symbolism and little substance,"[36] such feelings became more widespread as the Carter administration wore on the American people. The Realism–Variety disparity caused Carter to sound increasingly airy, while the Symbolism–Realism switch after the spring of 1978 made him seem more American Legionnaire than American leader.

Problems in role coordination are also evident in Figure 7.5. Beginning with the fall of 1978, Mr. Carter never closed the gap between self and policy, causing him to seem an insignificant figure in the political cosmos his speeches described. Naturally, some of the decrease in Self-Reference was due to the processes of institutionalization described in Chapter Two (a notion also revealed in Figure 7.5, as Mr. Carter finally broke free in the campaign of 1980 and placed himself once again on center stage). But the fact that so few Americans associated Carter with specific policy stands, thereby presuming that he was "fuzzy on the issues," may have been perceptions manufactured by Mr. Carter's own rhetoric.

It is also interesting to note (in Figure 7.5) that Human Interest dominated Carter's discourse in his middle 18 months in office. Although only an incidental finding, the curves depict Mr. Carter slipping farther and farther into the background, allowing "the people" to appear to dominate his interests. No doubt such language choices made him seem a humble and benevolent fellow, but they also made it seem unlikely that he was generating the action of the moment. This is not to say that a president should become an egomaniac, but a chief executive does need "to speak in an idiom and relay a message that at once certifies his own common humanity *and* his uncommon mastery of turmoil and complication."[37] Jimmy Carter was accused of being many things, but a "master of turmoil and complication" was not among them.

Timing

Another major set of problems for Mr. Carter were those related to timing. As revealed in Figures 7.3 through 7.5, the president adapted his remarks carefully during the summer of 1978, as the all-important off-year elections heated up. Human Interest, Optimism, and Familiarity all went up, as Carter again cozied up to the voters as he had in 1976. Unfortunately, the summer of 1978 was also precisely the time when he employed the least amount of Activity during his 4 years in office. Even on the stump, Mr. Carter chose to be philosophical and friendly rather than specify what he was doing as president.

A campaign speech in North Carolina demonstrates. Instead of declaring (in typical political argot) that he had created jobs as president, he said "I formed a partnership to try to do something about it." Instead of predicting that his Civil Service Reform Bill was going to sail through Congress, Mr. Carter said meekly that it was "on the verge of being passed." Instead of declaring that there would be peace in our times because of his efforts, he became metaphorical: "We put our arms around the shoulders of our close friends, who might be living next to one another in a state of war." His ruminating style also seemed ill-advised when he admitted that the governmental bureaucracy in Washington "was a lot worse than I thought it was" and that unemployment was, contrary to his hopes, not going down as quickly as he had originally predicted.[38] Commenting upon Carter's passivity, Eugene Kennedy noted: "Genuine leaders act, and they do so because they understand their people, they understand that the people will allow them to make mistakes but they will not tolerate indecision, endless meditation, or an attempt to lay on them a style of moralizing as self-serving and inappropriate as that in a Somerset Maugham minister."[39]

To his credit, if expediency be such, Mr. Carter succeeded in rallying his persuasive resources during the 1980 reelection campaign. Figures 7.3–7.5 document the prodigious changes he made: Complexity and Variety down; Realism, Self-Reference, and Symbolism up. In making these alterations, he again appropriated the direct and personal style that had brought him to office 4 years earlier. The simple refrains perfected on the hustings in Georgia returned on October 6, 1980, when he told Chicago voters that

> this is a crucial election. It's not just an election between two candidates. It's not just an election between two parties—and you know the differences between the Republican and Democratic Party. This is an election between two futures that will have an impact on whether this country continues to strive for justice and compassion, whether we build or not for peace in the future, and whether or not we have a solid economy that provides a job for every person who wants to work in this country. That's what the Democrats stand for.
>
> I have confidence that you and the people of this Nation will make the right judgment and the right choice on November the 4th, because I know the people of this country, like the people of Chicago, are builders. The same spirit that built the magnificent skyline of this city is building a new future for our Nation.[40]

There was a difference in political climate between 1976 and 1980, however. While "striving for human justice" and "building a new national spirit" sounded like useful ways to spend their time 4 years earlier, the voters in 1980 were looking for more concrete Activity, the specifications for which Mr. Carter chose not to offer. As a result, Ronald Reagan jumped into the breach, accusing Mr. Carter of political (he could have added rhetorical) inaction. Jimmy Carter was unable, or unwilling, to respond to Reagan's challenge by posing a new raft of policy. Despite the considerable alterations Carter effected in his rhetoric for the campaign, his low Activity scores uncovered an administration that did not know where it had been or where it intended to go.

Attitude

A final set of problems faced by Mr. Carter during his tenure in office might be termed attitudinal. Had Earl Stanley Gardner chronicled the Carter presidency, he might well have called it *The Case of the Reluctant Rhetor.* From the available anecdotal evidence, it appears that Carter both disliked and distrusted speechmaking. While at Annapolis, his experiences with after-dinner speaking were, he declared, the "most fearsome" he underwent as a midshipman.[41] Later, the president's rather sorry speaking abilities were apparently so obvious (and painful) to him that they were not to be discussed. "I've been told never to bring it up,"[42] reported one aide. According to his former speechwriter, James Fallows, Mr. Carter refused to learn how to speak more effectively. "It seemed to me the height of arrogance," said Fallows, "that Carter refused oral practice before his campaign debates with Gerald Ford. To the day I left the White House, he never really practiced a speech."[43]

In feeling as he did, Mr. Carter continued a relatively long American tradition of distrust of words and wordsmiths. The antirhetorical frontiersman is a cherished American archetype. Jimmy Carter's engineering training made him naturally suspicious of verbal camouflage and the several arts of public oratory. Mr. Carter was not one to sit for hours polishing a speech text, all of which resulted in his dense, at times opaque, remarks.

Figures 7.3–7.5 show that by the fall of 1978 Mr. Carter's Complexity had finally sapped the life out of his Optimism, Human Interest, Familiarity, and Self-Reference. His comparatively plainspoken early presidency gave way to a style of speech that could only be described as cordial obfuscation. This is not to say that Jimmy Carter was trying to conceal the truth from his listeners; the case was quite the opposite. He told them exactly what conditions were like, which meant discussing things like oil depletion allowances, photovoltaic cells, price escalation clauses, and strategic nuclear balance. Were his use of such phrases challenged (which, as has been mentioned, was unlikely), Mr. Carter would have indignantly explained that oil depletion allowances and price escalation clauses were modern realities and the American people had better learn about them. End of lecture.

Inspiring words are often small words. And Mr. Carter surely remembered such words from his days spent listening to Baptist homilies. But as his presidency continued, he depended upon such language less and less and the American people became more and more bewildered by him.

The 15 months between April 1, 1978, and July 1, 1979, may have been Mr. Carter's most difficult in office. Figure 7.3 indicates that Variety (or wordiness) peaked during this period and Self-Reference, Optimism, and Familiarity reached their lowest points. According to one set of researchers, Variety is positively correlated with anxiety, indicating that psychological pressures cause one to ramble when speaking.[44] Mr. Carter's high Variety scores coincided with his precipitous drops in the opinion polls, with the travels (and travails) of the Shah of Iran, with Billy Carter's anti-Semitic remarks, and with the highest inflation rate in 4 1/2 years. Thus, his speechmaking may have reflected some amount of enervation. As Eugene McCarthy puts it, Mr. Carter was an "oratorical mortician" who interred his "words and ideas beneath piles of syntactical mush."[45]

High Variety scores are generated for a number of other reasons as well:

because the speaker uses informal rather than formal oratory, because he or she has an unusually rich vocabulary, because of a refusal to parrot the glib phrases of formula politics, or because the complexity of one's task requires one to dot every "i" and cross every "t" so as not to be misunderstood. All of these reasons could have been Jimmy Carter's reasons. Whatever the reason, William Safire precisely captured his style when he Carterized the Gettysburg Address in the following manner: "Exactly two hundred and one years, five months and one day ago, our forefathers—and our foremothers, too, as my wife, the First Lady, reminds me—our highly competent Founding Persons brought forth on this land mass a new nation, or entity, dreamed up in liberty and dedicated to the comprehensive program of insuring that all of us are created with the same basic human rights."[46]

Figure 7.3 also reveals that Mr. Carter snapped out of this rhetorical tailspin after July of 1979 and developed a less encumbered style. It would be the worst sort of Monday-morning quarterbacking (and rhetorical determinism), however, to suggest that Carter's middle 15 months caused his eventual downfall. But during this period he gave 10 major national addresses and thereby risked displaying himself as increasingly besieged. The quick downturn in Variety commencing in the summer of 1979 may have been, for Jimmy Carter, too little too late.

Unpacking the Presidency

One final way of understanding Jimmy Carter is to examine how he addressed certain topics during his 4 years in office. The period between January 1976 and November 1980 was a fairly turbulent one for the American people. Their domestic and international visions were humbled during that time; they began to realize that they owned precious little oil as a nation; they learned that a small, turbulent country could hold their psyches hostage for more than a year; they came to regard inflation as a long-lost relative who came to dinner and stayed a decade. Jimmy Carter had to deal with these problems and more as president. How he did so tells us both about him and about anyone who presumes to govern the American people in the current age. We shall see that three major forces took their tolls on Jimmy Carter and his presidency.

The Press

Almost every recent American president has left office cursing the Ben Bradlees and Scotty Restons of the world. Too polite a man to curse in public, Jimmy Carter nevertheless learned how difficult it was to placate the press. Whenever he spoke, Jimmy Carter kept a wary eye on those who tell the people what the president has just told them. Jimmy Carter's handling of the human rights issue illustrates how the media may have affected his speaking.

Consider the following speeches, one delivered in March of 1977 and the other in May of 1979:

1977

> Your forceful voices in constantly espousing the cause of human rights would help me a great deal and help the Members of Congress and help the other leaders of our nation to establish a corps of moral commitment that can restore the legitimate pride in our country, to the extent that it has diminished, the United States of America as the rallying point for human rights around the world. We've not enjoyed that position in recent years. But I'm determined that once again, we'll be a light for those who believe in human rights all over the globe.[47]

1979

> Our economy has added 250,000 jobs for black and other minority teenagers since I became President. This year, we've committed $3.4 billion for youth employment and training—twice what we were spending 3 years ago. . . . We're going to make sure these programs work. And we're going to look for ways to get private business to do its part as well. . . . The struggle for civil rights is not over. Talk to the Members of the Congressional Black Caucus. They are deeply concerned about the attitude in the United States Congress toward civil rights. We've made progress, but we've not achieved what we need to accomplish.[48]

Figure 7.6 shows how differently Jimmy Carter spoke about Human Rights during his latter years in office. Gone by 1979 was the buoyant, moralistic prose of his early days on the job. By 1979 the press corps's eyes glazed automatically should Mr. Carter be even tempted to speak of equal rights in the wordy, upbeat manner of his early days, his honeymoon days. By 1979 they were looking for bottom lines in an administration that seemed to have few. The press accused Carter of demagoging the human rights issue at the expense of enacting workable political programs. The hardheadedness Mr. Carter shows in the second of the two illustrations above may thus have been the result of the increasingly bad news the newspapers reported in 1979, news in which Jimmy Carter figured prominently.

As time went on, Carter also made alterations in his rhetoric of national defense. His first six speeches on that topic were moderately assured, practical, and programmatic. In Figure 7.7 we see that things changed. Realism dropped dramatically and Certainty soared off the chart. Activity made a modest gain. The result was a hortatory style, a style to which national defense has long been suited in the United States. Often, the American people rally around when the talk about defense becomes tougher. The press, sometimes unwittingly, leads the cheers.

It could be argued that events themselves (e.g., Iran and Afghanistan),

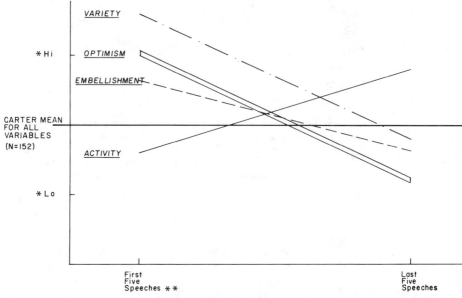

Figure 7.6   Changes in Carter's language on the topic of human rights (N = 10). * ± ½ sd from mean. See Table B.13 for exact values. **Information on speeches in Appendix A.

not media demands, prompted Mr. Carter's transformation. Other evidence (admittedly anecdotal) suggests the contrary. Consider, for example, Carter's speech delivered during June of 1978 at the U.S. Naval Academy. Prior to that speech, the Carter presidency was groping for a firm stand on something. Annapolis provided both the stand and the topic. The speech delivered there was high on Certainty (higher than all but one national address he had delivered to that point), but it was also fairly high on Realism and low on Activity (presumably because Mr. Carter wished to put the Russians on warning without resorting to ideological saber rattling.) The reviews were favorable and all concentrated on Carter's assuredness. TRB of the *New Republic* thought that the speech was "the best I ever heard him make."[49] *Time* openly admired Carter for talking "straight to Moscow in some of the harshest words of any U.S. President since John Kennedy in 1961."[50] *America* appreciated Carter for reminding "us that the pursuit of detente does not mean a retreat from the contest."[51]

In his review of the speech, however, TRB went on to suggest that Carter's high Realism and moderate Activity were also worthy of praise: "At an awesome moment in history he was calm, restrained, reassuring. There was no bombast. It would have been so easy to slop over and throw in the 'lift of a driving dream' or some other meretricious purple phrase. He

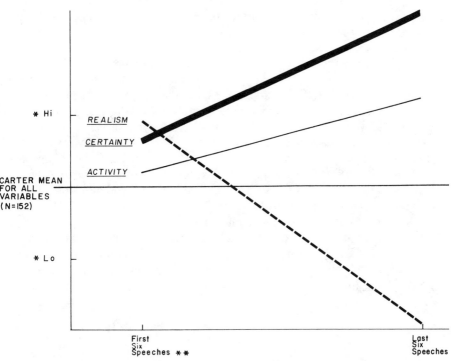

Figure 7.7 Changes in Carter's language on the topic of national defense (N = 12). * ± ½ sd from mean. See Table B.13 for exact values. **Information on speeches in Appendix A.

didn't.''[52] He did later. As Ronald Reagan appeared on the scene to capture some of the press's attention and as the press reminded the nation's citizens that their allies thought they had a weakling for a chief executive, Mr. Carter responded by stoking up the furnace of moral authority—before the servicemen on the *USS Nimitz,* before the American Society of Newspaper Editors, and before the members of the Business Council.[53] Although it would be foolish to suggest that the nation's media led Jimmy Carter by the nose on matters of national defense, it is surely true that his speeches on that topic were those they covered most appreciatively.

Modern Complexity

Most modern presidents are confronted with domestic and international problems whose causes are so complicated and whose solutions so hard to discern that sometimes making do is all that can be done. Take, for example, the problem of energy resources, where technological intricacies are equalled only by geopolitical entanglements. There is an economics of energy, a politics of energy, a military perspective on energy and, lately, a rhetoric of energy.

Early in his presidency, Jimmy Carter happened upon what appeared to be the perfect solution to the nation's energy woes: put on a cardigan sweater, sit by a roaring fire, and chat with the voters. In early 1977 it may have seemed to Mr. Carter that phrases like "the moral equivalent of war" would arouse the people sufficiently to keep them from turning up the thermostat. As we see in Figure 7.8, Jimmy Carter's early speeches on energy were simple, pragmatic, and sure-footed. The showmanship of Mr. Carter's speech-at-the-hearth was justified in those days by the topic he addressed. Said Jody Powell: "Television may not be too deep, but it's broad as hell. When you have a subject like energy that is not chatty, you need something to indicate that this is serious business."[54]

It did not take the American people long to learn exactly how serious the topic was, and it did not take Mr. Carter long to learn how very little could be said about energy with both Certainty and Realism. As time went on, his speeches on this topic became increasingly convoluted, cautious predictions substituting for the brave phrases of his early days in office. As we

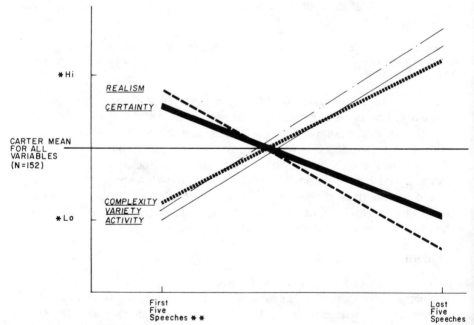

Figure 7.8 Changes in Carter's language on the topic of energy ($N = 10$). * $\pm \frac{1}{2}$ sd from mean. See Table B.13 for exact values. ** Information on speeches in Appendix A.

see in Figure 7.8, it was not long before the Realism and Activity curves passed each other by, signalling that even though the American people were demanding action, world events permitted only theoretical discussions of energy. The Certainty curve also plummeted past the Complexity and Variety curves, as Mr. Carter found it wise to retreat to a world of words rather than commit himself to a policy that rapidly changing events could vitiate within moments. In his energy speech of January 13, 1980, we thus hear the tentativeness and frustration of one who knew, by that time, that he was wrestling with a hydra-headed set of issues: "That's one of the main reasons why I have been almost obsessed with energy since the first day I came into this office, and have worked for almost 3 years, constantly with the Congress to hammer out, over the most difficult possible obstacles, a comprehensive energy policy. And we are just on the verge of success, and that's why our Nation as a whole, and you individually, must face up to this very difficult task."[55]

Economics proved no simpler a topic to deal with. In the latter 1970s and early 1980s, almost nobody in public life seemed able to say anything sensible about the world's economy. The single variable graphed in Figure 7.9 tells Mr. Carter's (and the nation's) economic story as vividly as anything could, its single downward slope perhaps being the mental picture the voters carried with them to the polling booths in November of 1980. Excerpts of Mr. Carter's speech of October 1979 to members of the AFL/CIO indicate that even a naturally cheerful person like Jimmy Carter could not com-

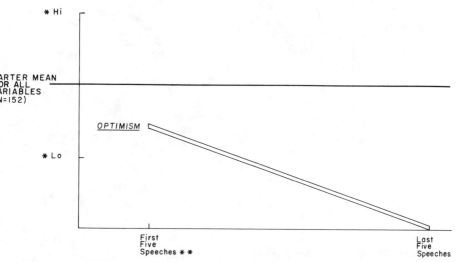

Figure 7.9 Changes in Carter's language on the topic of economics ($N = 10$). * ± 1/2 sd from mean. See Table B.13 for exact values. **Information on speeches in Appendix A.

pletely hide the realities of his day as he referred to "rapidly rising energy costs," "the unemployment rate is still too high," "interest rates have been rising," "building dropped to practically zero," "millions of people out of work."[56] Naturally, these phrases were interspersed in the speech with promises of a better day, but in late 1979 Mr. Carter's listeners were not as willing to read between his lines.

An equally revealing look at Carter's economics speeches is presented in Figure 7.10, which shows how diligently he sought a formula that would work. He pulled out every stop he knew. He tried active but cautious, cautious but realistic, realistic but passive, and most of the remaining permutations as well. Fluctuating in speaking styles as he did, Jimmy Carter may well have demonstrated the state of the rhetorical art on economic matters.

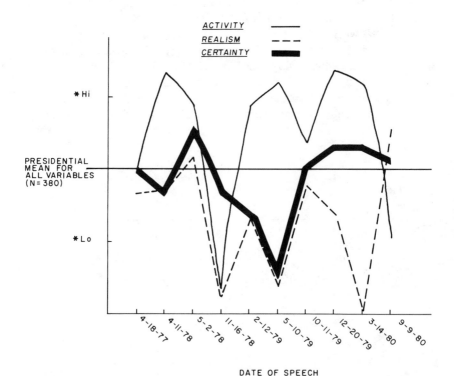

DATE OF SPEECH

Figure 7.10   Speech-by-speech changes by Carter on the topic of economics ($N = 10$).
* ± ½ sd from mean. See Table B.1 for exact values.

Institutional Realities

As we saw in Chapter Two, political candidates and presidents are often rivals in the same family. Presidents are the older children, the responsible ones—appropriately chary, rarely intemperate, in a word, mature. Candidates, colorful and irresponsible as they are, say things like "I'll never lie to you." Even if they then proceed to tell a lie, they are rarely brought on the carpet because they are, after all, merely youngsters.

Jimmy Carter's addresses on the topic of social welfare indicate how quickly the political reality of leading all the American people settles into a president's consciousness. For some, Figure 7.11 presents distressing facts. As his administration progressed, Mr. Carter substituted glad-handing and wordiness for practical programs in the area of human services. But early in 1977, Mr. Carter spoke as he did while campaigning. Yes, the nation was experiencing hard economic times but, no, he would not sacrifice the welfare of its needy citizens. In 1977 he was specific, simple, clearheaded:

> We've already proposed to the Congress a program for the screening, the health screening of poor children, and within just a few years we will multiply five times the number

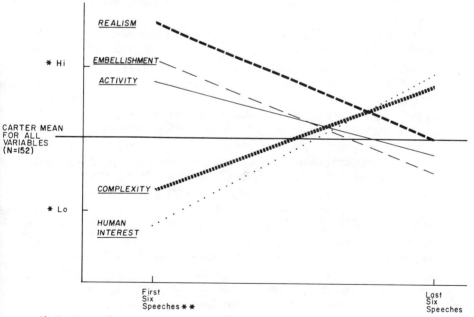

Figure 7.11 Changes in Carter's language on the topic of social welfare (N = 12). * ± ½ sd from mean. See Table B.13 for exact values.

of poor, young children who have a chance to see a doctor early in their life so their potential handicap or affliction might be prevented or corrected.

We now have 35 percent of the young children in this country who are not even immunized or inoculated against preventable diseases. When I was a child many years ago, almost 100 percent of all American children were immunized. We have started a new program now under Joe Califano's leadership and have asked the Congress for authority to increase greatly this immunization program so that within just a short time we intend to approach the 100 percent level again.[57]

Just a little over 3 years later, the change in Carter's remarks was stark. He sounded less like a student of social welfare than of sociology as he told the White House Council on Familes that "our people are more mobile. . . . People are uprooted. . . . Television . . . affects families in ways that we are only now beginning to understand. . . . Some laws, some government policies, tend to disrupt family structures." Instead of concentrating on administration policy as he had 3 years earlier, Mr. Carter reached into the more distant past, telling his audience, "My father didn't finish high school. Neither did his father, nor any other in our family for five or six generations back." A bit later in that same speech, he moralized that the family is "the first place that we learn to care and nurture the child, and to recognize its centrality in any society. That has always been the special responsibility of the family. It's here that the motivation and the morals and goals of life are first shaped."[58]

Carter's retreat on the topic of social welfare made political sense. Growing dissatisfaction with big government and its wasteful programs (as the rhetoric of the day had it) helped Mr. Carter pick his new course. Three years of experience in the White House caused him to realize that political action takes longer to effect than to conceive or articulate. The drop-off in Realism and Activity and their replacement by more timid phrases results from the constraints imposed upon a sitting president who faces a maze of special-interest groups—public as well as private—demanding that he spend the nation's money elsewhere. On the topic of social welfare, Jimmy Carter ended his presidency by using what Betty Glad called "the hedge,"[59] thereby hoping to win the people's hearts without becoming mired down in the details of potentially unpopular social programs.

When speaking about political matters, Mr. Carter also became role-constrained. Figure 7.12 shows that as time went on Carter took himself off center stage and wrapped himself in the nation's bunting. As we saw earlier, institutionalization encourages a chief executive to view himself as presiding over the American people rather than having a first-person relationship with them. That a disarmingly direct person like Jimmy Carter could also fall into this pattern is especially noteworthy. Speaking to a political gathering in Wisconsin in 1979, Mr. Carter cast himself in the role of spokesperson for all the American people, and, in a sense, thereby became personally

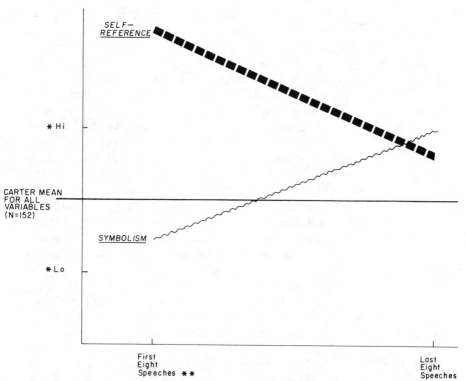

Figure 7.12   Changes in Carter's language on the topic of politics (N = 16). * ± ½ sd from mean. See Table B.13 for exact values. **Information on speeches in Appendix A.

responsible to none of them: "We are a Nation that believes in justice. . . . We're a Nation which believes in strength. . . . We're a Nation which recently has been involved more and more deeply in trying to bring peace to Southern Africa. . . . We've now opened our arms to embrace as friends, as new friends, a billion people who live in China. . . . I thank god that . . . those struggling Nations look on us as a friend and not as an enemy, as an equal and not a superior, as a Nation to be trusted, as a Nation to be sought out as a source of help."[60] By thus making president and nation iso-morphic, Carter reveals both the greatest strength and greatest weakness of a presidential form of government.

Conclusion

Jimmy Carter's rhetorical odyssey was not a particularly remarkable one. His public statements began no wars and ended none. His persuasion did not cause the American people to lurch off in some brave new direction nor could it even forestall a nearly uninterrupted 4-year slide in the public opinion polls. Although he spoke with great frequency as president, he rarely spoke impressively. His best moments included his refreshingly candid town meetings, his touching defenses of Bert Lance and Billy Carter, his graceful hosting at the Egyptian–Israeli peace conference, and his fascinating description of the nation's crisis of confidence. His failures loomed larger: his quixotic speech about Russian troops in Cuba, his dispirited eulogy for Hubert Humphrey, his hopelessly complex explanations of energy (we did not have enough) and inflation (we had too much), and his lackluster acceptance speech at the 1980 Democratic National Convention. Francis X. Clines, writing in the *New York Times,* probably provided the most devastating obituary of the Carter administration when he quotes a Carter staffer as saying, "This Administration doesn't have the commercial potential of the Nixon people. Our crowd is more likely to produce scholarly, relatively unreadable tomes, and memoirs published overwhelmingly by university presses."[61]

Looking at a presidency, even a modest presidency, across time tells an institutional story. Indeed, it is the very ordinariness of Mr. Carter's rhetorical problems that instruct us best. As we have seen here, Carter altered his strategies in major ways throughout his time in office, searching for something that would work. As Betty Glad noted, in his campaigning Carter had "shown an almost Protean flexibility in the selection of strategies and rhetorical appeals."[62] When serving as the nation's thirty-ninth president, Jimmy Carter bobbed and weaved as best he could but, unfortunately, all eyes were on his footwork. Scrutinizing the president and dissecting what he says have become popular sports. Encouraged by the press, citizens now listen to a president while simultaneously critiquing his speech, turning the presidency into both event and metaevent. As a result, Jimmy's "Protean flexibility" became obvious.

Mr. Carter's experience in office suggests that the presidency may finally have become a thoroughly rhetorical institution. When viewed in light of what was possible between 1977 and 1980—given the nation's economic doldrums, the tinder box of international relations, and the technological complexity of modern political issues—the Carter presidency may appear in the 1990s to be more adequate than it seems now. By using rhetorical criteria exclusively, however (the same criteria people used when labeling the Kennedy presidency a success even though its programmatic accomplishments were modest), Jimmy Carter failed. We know this because his sermons put us to sleep, because the nation's comics mimicked his speaking style, and because the press gleefully reported Carter's persuasive liabilities to us, thereby increasing their impact upon us. It may have finally become true that, unless the voters can estimate how well a presidency is doing *rhetorically,* they cannot gauge it at all.

There may be an equally ominous message in Mr. Carter's increase in Certainty and decline in Self-Reference. What is it about presidents, world events, political pressures, the media, or voters' expectations that causes so many chief executives to begin their terms sounding like Unitarian ministers, only to leave office sounding like Roman Catholic pontiffs? What is it that requires (or permits) a president to sound so sure of himself at precisely the point during his administration when he knows that little is certain in the nation he governs? Was it presidential ego, or frustration, that precipitated such changes in Mr. Carter? And, if even Jimmy Carter can fall victim to such institutionalization, could anyone resist it? This latter question is a rhetorical question both in form and in substance and, as such, may well be the only question worth asking of the presidency today.

Notes

1. Betty Glad, *Jimmy Carter: In Search of the Great White House* (New York: Norton, 1980).
2. Glad (1980), p. 362.
3. Glad (1980), p. 363.
4. Glad (1980), p. 364.
5. Glad (1980), p. 364.
6. Glad (1980), pp. 484–485.
7. "Inaugural Address," January 20, 1977, *Weekly Compilations of Presidential Documents* (hereafter, *Weekly Compilations*), 13:4 (1977), p. 88.
8. "Remarks at Fundraising Dinner," September 26, 1979, *Weekly Compilations,* 15:39 (1979), pp. 1768, 1769.
9. "Anti-Inflation Program," March 14, 1980, *Weekly Compilations,* 16:11 (1980), pp. 478, 479.
10. "State of the Union Address," January 23, 1979, *Weekly Compilations,* 15:4 (1979), p. 106.
11. "Jimmy the Persuader," *Newsweek,* March 19, 1979, p. 25.
12. *Newsweek,* March 19, 1979, p. 25.
13. *Weekly Compilations,* January 23, 1979, p. 103.
14. "Packaging a New Carter," *Time,* August 21, 1978, p. 16.
15. Martin Tolchin, "New Pro in the White House," *New York Times Magazine,* December 17, 1978, p. 30.
16. "Events will Dominate," *U.S. News and World Reports,* July 24, 1978, p. 22.
17. Quoted in Tolchin (1978), p. 30.
18. "Remarks at a Town Meeting," August 22, 1979, *Weekly Compilations,* 15:34 (1979), p. 1495.
19. "The President's News Conference," November 28, 1979, *Weekly Compilations,* 15:48 (1979), pp. 2167, 2168.
20. "New Moon on Capitol Hill," *Time,* February 4, 1980, p. 14.

21. Quoted in James Wooten, "Can Rafshooning Save Jimmy Carter?" *Esquire*, March 3, 1979, p. 26.

22. Anthony Lewis, "The Carter Mystery: I," *New York Times*, August 13, 1979, p. 17.

23. Robert Jewett, *The Captain America Complex* (Philadelphia: Westminister, 1973).

24. Materials presented here were gathered, in part, from the various *Yearbooks* for *Collier's Encyclopedia* (New York: Macmillan) and from the CBS/*Times* polls reported regularly in the *New York Times*. A fairly complete synopsis of these polls is reported in the *New York Times* of August 12, 1980, p. 2.

25. Henry Graff, quoted in "Now, for the Hard Sell," *Time*, August 6, 1979, p. 13.

26. The complete texts of the speeches can be found in *Weekly Compilations of Presidential Documents* as follows, respectively, "Remarks to Ad Hoc Coalition for Women," 13:11 (1977), p. 340; "Remarks to Baptist Brotherhod Commission," May 13, 1977, 13:20 (1977), p. 718; "Remarks to World Bank Group," September 26, 1977, 13:40, (1977), p. 1423; "National Energy Plan," November 8, 1977, 13:46 (1977), p. 1738; "Reception Honoring Polish Americans," February 6, 1978, 14:6 (1978), p. 282; "Remarks at Fundraising Reception," May 26, 1978, 14:21 (1978), p. 1001; "Remarks at Growers Cooperative Warehouse," August 5, 1978, 14:32 (1978), p. 1391; "Remarks at White House Meeting on Human Rights," December 6, 1978, 14:49 (1978), p. 2161; "Remarks at Peace Treaty Ceremony," March 26, 1979, 15:13 (1979), p. 518; "Remarks to Democratic National Committee," May 25, 1979, 15:21 (1979), p. 949; "Remarks at Iowa Town Meeting," August 22, 1979, 15:34 (1979), pp. 1495–1496; "Remarks at News Conference," November 28, 1979, 15:48 (1979), p. 2168; "Remarks at Leadership Conference," January 27, 1980, 16:5 (1980), p. 222; "Remarks at National Campaign Headquarters," May 19, 1980, 16:21 (1980), p. 939; "Remarks at News Conference," August 4, 1980, 16:32 (1980), p. 1478; "Presidential Debate," October 28, 1980, 16:44 (1980), pp. 2501–2502.

27. "The State of the Presidency," *New York Times Book Review*, April 27, 1980, p. 24.

28. James Fallows, "The Passionless Presidency," *Atlantic Monthly*, May 1979, p. 43.

29. "Can a Real Christian Make It as President?" *Washington Post Magazine*, November 5, 1978, p. 13.

30. Unnamed source quoted in Charles Mohr, "Carter's First 9 Months," *New York Times*, October 23, 1977, p. 36.

31. Remarks based on a series of interviews with presidential speechwriters as reported by J. Jeffery Auer, "The President as Public Persuader." Paper read at the Annual Convention of the Central States Speech Association, April 11, 1980, p. 5.

32. Former campaign official quoted in Hedrick Smith, "Carter and the 100 Days," *New York Times*, April 29, 1977, p. 16.

33. Hedrick Smith, "Part Homily, Part Program," *New York Times*, July 16, 1979, p. 1.

34. "Address to the Nation on Energy and National Goals," July 15, 1979, *Weekly Compilations*, 15:29 (1979), pp. 1237, 1238.

35. Eugene Kennedy, "Carter Agonistes," *New York Times Magazine*, August 5, 1979, p. 27.

36. "How Carter Spruces up His Image," *U.S. News and World Report*, April 11, 1977, p. 43.

37. Meg Greenfield, "Carter and the PR Trap," *Newsweek*, January 26, 1981, p. 84.

38. "Remarks on Arrival at the Asheville Airport," September 22, 1978, *Weekly Compilations*, 14:39 (1978), pp. 1576, 1577.

39. Kennedy (1979), p. 38.

40. "Remarks at a Voter Registration Rally," October 6, 1980, *Weekly Compilations*, 16:41 (1980), p. 2090.

41. James Wooten, *Dasher: The Roots and the Rising of Jimmy Carter* (New York: Summit, 1978), p. 166.

42. Unnamed aide quoted in James Wooten, "The President as Orator," *New York Times,* January 26, 1978, p. 15.

43. Fallows (1979), p. 44.

44. See Joan M. Preston and R. C. Gardner, "Dimensions of Oral and Written Language Fluency," *Journal of Verbal Learning and Verbal Behavior,* 6 (1967), pp. 936–945.

45. Quoted in Wooten (January 26, 1978), p. 15.

46. "Carter's Gettysburg Address," *New York Times,* December 5, 1977, p. 37.

47. "Remarks to National Women's Political Caucus," March 30, 1977, *Weekly Compilations,* 13:14 (1977), p. 474.

48. "Address at Cheyney State College," May 20, 1979, *Weekly Compilations,* 15:21 (1979), pp. 910–911.

49. TRB, "Carter's Best Speech," *New Republic,* June 17, 1978, p. 3.

50. "Talking Tough to Moscow," *Time,* June 19, 1978, p. 32.

51. "A More Certain Trumpet," *America,* June 24, 1978, p. 496.

52. TRB (1978), p. 3.

53. These speeches can all be found in *Weekly Compilations* as follows, respectively: "Remarks on Board the *USS Nimitz,*" May 26, 1980, 16:22 (1980), pp. 969–972; "Remarks to American Society of Newspaper Editors," April 10, 1980, 16:15 (1980), pp. 631–637; "Remarks to Members of the Business Council," December 12, 1979, 15:50 (1979), pp. 2232–2237.

54. Quoted in "President McLuhan," *The Nation,* February 11, 1978, p. 132.

55. "Remarks to White House Conference on Small Business," January 13, 1980, *Weekly Compilations,* 16:3 (1980), p. 71.

56. "Remarks to Building and Construction Trades Department," October 11, 1979, *Weekly Compilations,* 15:41 (1979), pp. 1868, 1869.

57. "Remarks to White House Conference on Handicapped Individuals," May, 23, 1977, *Weekly Compilations,* 13:22 (1977), p. 797.

58. "Remarks to White House Conference on Families," June 5, 1980, *Weekly Compilations,* 16:23 (1980), pp. 1034, 1035.

59. Glad (1980), p. 306.

60. "Remarks at a Jefferson-Jackson Day Dinner," March 31, 1979, *Weekly Compilations,* 15:14 (1979), pp. 575, 576.

61. Quoted in Francis X. Clines, "About Washington," *New York Times,* December 15, 1980, p. 18.

62. Glad (1980), p. 489.

THE GREAT COMMUNICATOR
AND BEYOND

Ronald Reagan did not burst upon the American political scene. He did a slow dissolve, fading from the fanciful atmosphere of studio back lots into that tempestuous, often churlish, location known as California politics. Then on to the White House, where the scripts were more unsettling and the resident players less predictable, but where the klieg lights were just as warming, the camera operators just as convivial, and the audiences likely to respond just as appreciatively to the planned spontaneity that had become, by that time, the Reagan style.

In many ways, only a message analyst could hope to understand the essence of the Reagan presidency. The emphasis Ronald Reagan has placed on rhetoric during his first 2 years in the White House seems to invite study of what he does best—communicate. And it is massively significant that he has been called The Great Communicator—not The Nation's Orator, or a Master Stylist. For Ronald Reagan lives not by words alone. He lives or rather thrives, because of that complex of factors constituting modern communications—skilled advance agents; sophisticated polling techniques; a panoply of media events; blue suits and undyed hair; a throaty laugh; first-name exchanges with members of the press corps; a handsome, faintly regal, wife; and the God-given ability to dominate by force of personality almost any social gathering in which he finds himself. Ronald Reagan is no Bryan or Lincoln or Stevenson. He impresses by means of dramatic action, not by means of deftly chosen words. His pleadings find favor because Ronald Reagan himself is attractive. He is welcomed into our homes—more frequently and more openly than most of his predecessors—because he seems so removed from what he is fundamentally: a rhetorical wizard.

All of this may hardly seem new. As the Reagan presidency reached the end of its second year, it impressed most people, certainly most journalists, as a communication-intensive presidency. Newspaper and magazine headlines alone were revealing:

Wall Street Journal: "Reagan Misstatements Accumulate But so far Do Little Harm"

New York Times: "Marketing the President"

Newsweek: "Reagan's Articulation Gap"

U.S. News and World Report: "Silver Tongue Pays off for Reagan"[1]

It is hardly surprising that the press latched onto the rhetorical dimensions of the Reagan presidency, since the media perceive modern Americans as more interested in showmanship than in the show. Ronald Reagan and media commentators alike understood things like audience share, symbolic appeal, and image packaging. Hence, they often exhibited a kind of fraternal sympathy, or at least empathy, for this actor turned president. Mark Crispin Miller provides a case in point: "In a paradigmatic encounter with Reagan last January, Dan Rather sounded more like a publicist than an interviewer, talking about 'perceptions' and 'signals,' at one point making this assessment: 'This is going to be a continuing problem for you, *getting people to believe* that you really do know what's going on in the interior of your Administration.'"[2]

Mr. Reagan's adeptness was the product of an adulthood spent in front of the evolving motion picture camera. Having begun his career as an actor, Reagan naturally regarded a public speech as "a theatrical event," according to his biographer, Lou Cannon.[3] Cannon also recounts how Reagan's work for the General Electric Corporation between 1954 and 1962 (he served as a touring spokesperson after his film career had ended) marked his transition from the poetic to the rhetorical. During this time, says Cannon, "Reagan made the most of a unique opportunity to develop and polish a basic speech before captive audiences,"[4] thereby learning the difference between encouraging an audience to suspend disbelief and prompting them to believe him implicitly. Cannon goes on to suggest that Ronald Reagan's altered political philosphy (from Left to Right) was a natural result of these public encounters. Because his GE speeches were presented almost exclusively to service clubs and to corporate audiences, and because Ronald Reagan's natural predisposition was to please his auditors, he found himself traveling a political path blazed by his own applause lines. Cannon describes this rhetorical–philosophical process as being virtually self-reflective: "Reagan believes what he says, and [because of the GE experience] he wound up believing what he was saying."[5] If Cannon is correct, and if Mr. Reagan had instead passed his time in the 1950s by talking to the Americans for Democratic Action, he would have spent the 1960s on the barricades with Tom Hayden and the 1970s as Jerry Brown's soulmate.

It is also significant that Reagan's introduction to the national political scene came as the result of his suasory abilities. His pretaped campaign speech for Barry Goldwater presented on October 27, 1964, was the only bright light in that year's Republican bleakness. But from that bleakness rose a rhetorical giant, one who has been described as "the most effective American political orator since Franklin Delano Roosevelt,"[6] who has been likened to Winston Churchill as a "combination orator-rhetorician-leader and *performer*,"[7] whose listeners are said to "sense a whiff of the Kennedy magic and glamour."[8]

But what, specifically, is the source of Reagan's attractiveness? How is it that his party was able to suffer significant losses in the off-year elections of 1982 without Ronald Reagan himself being drubbed in the public opinion polls? On what authority can one say that Reagan was Kennedy-like? What do people mean when they claim that Ronald Reagan thinks like Barry Goldwater but sounds like FDR? Complete answers to questions of this order will have to be delayed. The data base available to me—24 speeches from Mr. Reagan's first year in office—is hardly sufficient to permit a complete understanding of his persuasiveness. But the findings to be presented here are interesting indeed. They tell us that Mr. Reagan's speaking style is highly distinctive, that he has some communicative strengths that far outstrip the considerable talents of his predecessors in office, and that his stylistic (i.e., word-based) liabilities are more than compensated for by his communicative instincts—that is, by his penchant for using staging, timing, and personal flair to offset the intellectual and political problems created by his words alone.

Ronald Reagan is a twenty-first-century chief executive. He knows, and what is more important, he *feels* what it takes to lead a people housed in bungalows connected to the White House by endless loops of thin black cable. It was thus a twenty-first-century compliment paid to Mr. Reagan by his aides when one of them said: "The staff doesn't presume to tell him, if it's a question of how you persuade people. No one challenges him, because he's far better than anyone on the staff."[9]

The Great Communicator

Ronald Reagan's inaugural address was less a ceremonial event than it was his first campaign speech of 1983. It was hardly eloquent, although it did make people feel good about themselves; it was not stirring in the traditional sense, but it did give many Americans a feeling of calm; it was not particularly emotional, although it misted some eyes. The more effete of Mr. Reagan's inaugural critics sharply rebuked him for being, well, too Reaganesque. But Reagan's address typified the rhetorical character of his presidency. One of his passages was especially suggestive:

> We hear much of special interest groups. Well, our concern must be for a special interest group that has been too long neglected. It knows no sectional boundaries or ethnic or racial divisions, and it crosses party lines. It is made up of men and women who raise our food, patrol our streets, man our mines and factories, teach our children, keep our homes, and heal us when we're sick—professionals, industrialists, shopkeepers, clerks, cabbies, and truckdrivers. They are in short, "We the people," this breed called Americans.[10]

Clearly, this is the stuff of grade-B movies, electoral pap at its worst, obvious in its politicalness, devoid of captivating imagery. But this is also pure Ronald Reagan, prairie orator that he is. From a technical standpoint, Ronald Reagan does very little with language per se. His masterstroke lies beyond his words—there in his smile, in his soft voice, in his physical presence. Ronald Reagan communicates sentiments, not ideas. He gives us the sense that he has something special up his sleeve and yet that he is but one American among many. There are three special "senses" in Reagan's rhetoric, three dimensions to his political art.

Sense of Momentum

Reacting to Ronald Reagan's inaugural address, *New York Times* columnist Hedrick Smith observed that "the time imperative presses him (Reagan) to produce an immediate sense of forward motion, to produce the feeling that he has taken charge and begun to halt the drift and uncertainty that caused such an explosive burst of voter frustration against the Democrats. And he has signaled that he intends his first days in office to convey a sense of urgency."[11] Note that Smith talks here about a sense of forward motion, the feeling that Reagan has taken charge, and a sense of urgency. In the 12 ensuing months, Reagan obliged Smith by producing the highest Activity level of any modern president while using less Realism than any of the last eight chief executives (see Figure 8.1). In other words, Mr. Reagan's revolution was in some measure a revolution of the emotions. His language suggested a president vigorously pursuing ends, but a programmatically reticent president as well. Thus, it is interesting that presidential scholar Thomas Cronin points up Reagan's "can-do spirit" as being among his greatest assets.[12] But it is even more revealing that a "can-do spirit" is fully oxymoronic since "doing," presumably, involves some amount of *doing*.

This image of Ronald Reagan as the nation's First Cheerleader is not far

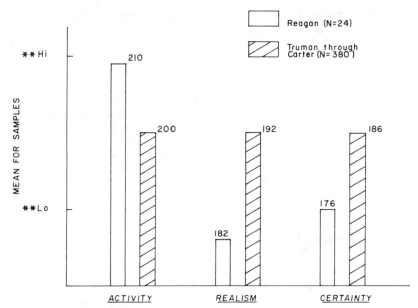

Figure 8.1   Distinctive features of Ronald Reagan's style. All differences significant. See Table B.8. ** ± ½ sd from mean. Table B.1 for exact mean.

off the mark. Cheerleaders, after all, rarely suggest exactly which *procedures* the defense might employ in taking the ball the other way. Like most other presidents, Ronald Reagan is a practical politician. Like them, he realizes that a president–cheerleader can only point the team in the appropriate direction and then hope for the best. Unlike many presidents, however, Reagan's ambiguities and abstractions give listeners the sense that pointing is doing.

In his speech on the economy of February 18, 1981, for example, Mr. Reagan used very little Realism but still managed to give his listeners the impression that change was in the wind. He mentioned that his "aim will be to provide the most effective defense for the lowest possible cost"[13] but failed to say how such capabilities would be achieved. He promised that "as we negotiate, our security must be fully protected by a balanced and realistic defense program,"[14] but he avoided a discussion of how much money and how many armaments would be involved. In another portion of the speech, Mr. Reagan manfully attacked fraud and waste in government, describing it as "an unrelenting national scandal, a scandal we're bound and determined to do something about,"[15] without saying when, where, or how it would be done.

Here, and elsewhere, Reagan talked about doing and thereby "did." Mr.

Reagan knew full well that the practical language of doing (Activity plus Realism) was not meant for his public platform but meant, instead, for the corridors of Capitol Hill. He appears to have reasoned that the people, alternatively, could be heartened considerably by a president who did something about a problem and, by defining it, seemed to solve it. It is not surprising, therefore, that Mr. Reagan preferred to deal with what one of his aides called "thematics,"[16] statements of philosophy rather than statements of policy. It is also not surprising that Lou Cannon isolated Reagan's "patriotism" and "enormous idealism" as numbering among his greatest rhetorical strengths.[17] And it is certainly not surprising to hear Mr. Reagan's speechwriters claim that the public forgives his mistakes "because they sense his 'thrust' toward a larger truth."[18] (This latter quotation is interesting in that the word "thrust" counts toward the Activity score in my computer program while the word "truth" does not contribute to a speaker's Realism score.) Presumably, Aram Bakshian, Jr., would not be surprised by the findings just reported, for, as Mr. Reagan's head speechwriter, he knew that "speechwriting is to writing as Muzak is to music."[19]

Reagan's active–unrealistic approach stood him in good stead throughout his first year in office with most audiences. He first speech on the economy followed this pattern and was accurately described by *Newsweek* an "an effective piece of exhortation" whose "lack of specifics was by design."[20] His remarks at the Department of Defense's dedication ceremony on September 10, 1981, also employed this style, as Reagan provided a blow-by-blow description of General Douglas MacArthur's wartime duties and thereby identified himself with MacArthur, a figure of energy and inspiration. Mr. Reagan also attempted to use this same strategy of dynamic circumspection when he spoke to the NAACP convention in July of 1981. Although they received him politely, the delegates to that convention complained that "he didn't give us anything."[21] As *Time* reported, Mr. Reagan's avoidance of such topics as Aid to Dependent Children, school lunches, Medicaid, and job training caused many blacks to wish openly for something more than symbolic energy from their president.[22] With this notable exception, however, the Reagan formula worked.

Figure 8.1 also reveals another important aspect of that formula. Ronald Reagan used less Certainty than any of the other presidents studied here. This finding may seem surprising since Mr. Reagan is often thought of as something of an ideologue. The key to the riddle, of course, is that Mr. Reagan is a political ideologue and, more important, a presidential ideologue, which largely prevented him from being, especially in 1981, a verbal ideologue. These distinctions are ones that Mr. Reagan learned prior to 1981, however.

Hedrick Smith recounts that when Ronald Reagan served as governor of

California he learned how necessary it was to temper his talk: "He struck compromises and made deals with political opponents, reversed campaign slogans, and swallowed what he had labeled unthinkable before he took office."[23] Reflecting upon Reagan's early days in the presidency, Rowland Evans and Robert Novak noted that Mr. Reagan was "pursuing radical goals but using nonradical language."[24] Both accounts seem essentially correct. By using little Realism in his speeches, Reagan could invoke the various political deities and surround himself with the philosophical trappings of the New Right. By choosing his words carefully (low Certainty), however, Mr. Reagan could avoid being caught in a blind alley by the partisans on the Left or by the practical politicians in the middle. Even during his campaign for the presidency, Ronald Reagan is said to have "fashioned a rhetoric of implied force that is not only fervent in its insistence on greater military power but also vague as to how he would employ such power as president."[25]

As his presidency began to unfold, Mr. Reagan found it wise to stick to this same, safe course of cautious preachment. When the hostages arrived home from Iran, for example, President Reagan mentioned enough about their conditions to suggest his (attitudinal) repudiation of the Iranian captors but did not preclude further (behavioral) dealings with that country: "We're now aware of the conditions under which you were imprisoned. Though now is not the time to review every abhorrent detail of your cruel confinement, believe me we know what happened. Truth may be a rare commodity today in Iran; it's alive and well in America."[26] Even when speaking to an adoring group of fellow conservatives in March of 1981, Mr. Reagan saw fit to remark: "I hope our political victory will be remembered as a generous one and our time in power will be recalled for the tolerance we showed for those with whom we disagree."[27]

This is not the language of the Moral Majority, a group that, presumably, combines generous amounts of Realism, Certainty, and Activity in its public remarks. Unlike a sitting president, a special-interest group like the Moral Majority can fire its rhetoric to a white hot glow. It is small wonder, then, that many members of the Moral Majority soon became disillusioned with the Reagan presidency as it became caught up in the political realities of government-as-usual. Nellie Gray, leader of a Right to Life march in Washington, was one who became disaffected when the newly elected Ronald Reagan refused to participate in the march. Instead, he politely agreed to chat with her behind closed doors in the White House, an invitation Ms. Gray refused—ostensibly because she was able to predict the careful words she would hear, words containing only the sense of momentum.[28] As one commentator observed, once he became president Ronald Reagan could not afford "to do freely, without discipline, what he has done best all these years—play to sympathetic conservative audiences, occasionally giving them what some of his campaign aides have graphically termed 'a piece of red meat' in the form of hot political rhetoric. Careless words can upset diplomacy abroad or undercut credibility at home, especially for a leader who banks heavily on his speeches to generate the momentum behind his program."[29]

A comparison on this aspect of verbal tentativeness between Ronald Reagan and Barry Goldwater seems irresistible. Table 8.1 presents the four main differences between their speaking styles. While a content analysis would probably reveal important similarities in the philosophical positions adopted in their speeches, a *language* analysis points up marked differences. Reagan: cautious, resilient, personal. Goldwater: resolute, pessimistic, detached. These differences are highly significant statistically but, what is more important, they signal an important socioemotional difference between the two men. For example, when commenting on the need for increased defense allocations, Barry Goldwater warned:

> And what of this, the most perilous statistic of all? Under our present defense leadership, with its utter disregard for new weapons, our deliverable nuclear capacity may be cut down by 90 per cent in the next decade. Let me repeat that. The figure is startling, and yet undeniable.[30]

Commenting on similar matters, Ronald Reagan told a story:

> I received a letter from a young lad who's a sailor on one of our submarines. He said he was writing, and he was writing on behalf of his 180 shipmates. And he said he just wanted us to know how good it felt to be an American. And he said, "We may not have the biggest Navy in the world, but we've got the best."[31]

Lou Cannon amplifies on these communicative differences when he characterized Goldwater as "blunt, impatient, honest and profane, with a pro-

TABLE 8.1

RONALD REAGAN VERSUS BARRY GOLDWATER
ON FOUR ASPECTS OF LANGUAGE

	Reagan $(N = 24)^a$	Goldwater $(N = 20)^b$
Certainty	175.9	194.5
Optimism	220.4	204.7
Self-Reference	8.38	4.20
Human Interest	28.3	22.8

^{a} First year in office only.
^{b} Campaign speaking of 1964 only.

clivity for the self-destructive phrase ('let's lob one into the men's room of the Kremlin') that alarmed even some of his own supporters."[32] "Reagan inspired," says Cannon, "where Goldwater tended to terrify. Reagan's . . . manner was reassuring, replete with self-deprecating little jokes and that winning smile."[33] Conservatives, who recognized right-wing imprecations when they heard them, were understandably confused by a Reagan presidency. It was probably thus a rhetorical marker of the times that John Lofton, editor of the *Conservative Digest*, surmised: "Sometimes I wonder how much of a Reaganite Reagan is, and unfortunately those times are becoming more frequent."[34]

Sense of Place

Everyone, it seems, has sensed that Ronald Reagan is a master of the suasory arts. But few have been able to put their fingers on exactly those features of language that make him special. My data suggest that Reagan's real strength is his ability to show that he belongs to the people of this nation, that he speaks a language of them and for them.

Figure 8.2 reveals one of the most dramatic findings of this study. Ronald Reagan's use of Embellishment is the lowest of all the chief executives surveyed; he is a man without adjectives. His remarks carry punch because his

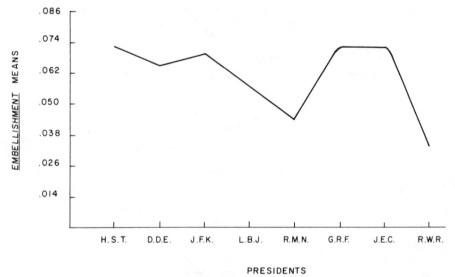

Figure 8.2   Ronald Reagan compared to other presidents on embellishment. Based on sample sizes of $N = 38$, except for Carter ($N = 152$) and Reagan ($N = 24$).

nouns and verbs stand alone, making his style almost aphoristic. Reagan's language virtually never calls attention to itself. This makes Ronald Reagan the sort of American whom Tocqueville wrote about, a person whose faith in certain simple values was so strong that his words needed no adornment. Mr. Reagan's speech welcoming Prime Minister Margaret Thatcher to the United States exemplifies this:

> Great Britain and the United States are kindred nations of like-minded people and must face their tests together. We are bound by common language and linked by history. We share laws and literature, blood, and moral fiber. The responsibility for freedom is ours to share. When we talked in London just over 2 years ago—when neither of us was in office—I was impressed by the similar challenges faced and by our determination to meet those challenges. You have said that we enter into a decade fraught with danger, and so we have. But the decade will be less dangerous if the West maintains the strength required for peace, and in achieving that goal, there is one element that goes without question: Britain and America will stand side by side.[35]

We see here a president whose short, crisp sentences are unburdened by modifying structures, a president who, when he did use adjectives, used words like "common," "similar," "dangerous," and "kindred." Trite expressions ("side by side," "determination to meet those challenges," "decade fraught with danger," etc.) reign supreme here because Ronald Reagan is a communicator whose body, voice, and smile do the necessary emotional embellishing. Unless she were unconscionably plutocratic, even Margaret Thatcher might have been disarmed by this common American speech. When listening to Mr. Reagan welcome her, she might have been moved to agree with Mark Crispin Miller, who observed that "even at the dressiest affairs, and on the grandest state occasions, he [Reagan] has us thinking that he wears white socks and carries a pen-knife."[36] Margaret Thatcher night also have been reminded on this occasion of the American cabdriver who in 1980 explained his preference for candidate Reagan with the observation, "He's the only politician I can understand."[37]

Figure 8.3 indicates that Reagan's low Embellishment scores were often accompanied by multiple Self-References and by generous amounts of Familiarity. This figure also indicates that when he did use Embellishment, he counteracted such decorativeness with Human Interest words. In either instance, then, Reagan demonstrated that he belonged to the people of the United States and that he understood their ambivalence about verbally adept politicians. Mark Crispin Miller's characterization of this style evokes memories of the Western sheriffs Reagan had portrayed during his acting career on *Death Valley Days*: "He speaks quietly, a little hesitantly, with his eyes to the ground, as if not used to public speaking; and he often punctuates his statements with a folksy little waggle of his head and shoulders so that we won't take his speechifying too seriously."[38]

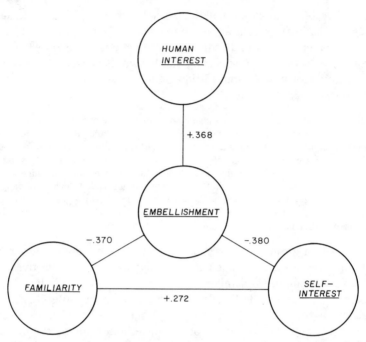

Figure 8.3   Ronald Reagan's homespun style (Pearson correlations for selected variables, N = 24). For additional information, see Table B.10.

The advantages of Mr. Reagan's personal, indigenous style are several: (1) It allowed him to gloss over unpleasant facts and contradictory instances. As the *Wall Street Journal* observed, "He's got his anecdote, and nothing can spoil it"[39] (2) It confounded those bent on accusing him of being a far-right fanatic: "On camera or on the stump, Reagan can be magical in his appeal. He projects as a highly moral, honest, sincere, and purposeful citizen-politician. He exudes an air of simple virtue."[40] (3) It allowed him to be reductionistic about massively complicated topics, like the economy, without risking censure. One of his least embellished speeches, his gloomy economic forecast of February 5, 1981, was praised by the *New York Times* as a "plain-spoken audit," "uncomplicated," and a "stark description,"[41] even though the daily reportage of that same publication proved that any uncomplicated discussion of the 1980s economic scene was sophistic at best. (4) Most important, Reagan's language allowed him to appropriate a rhetorical tradition that had normally been the property of his political rivals. A homespun style, after all, is a Democratic style. Typically, Republicans only tolerate the rabble; when they make political solicitations, Republicans do so in the language of tax forms. One senses none of that in Ronald Reagan: "Though he had left the party of Franklin Roosevelt, he refused to abandon the words and phrases which provided a shared language and a common bond with his fellow citizens. When Reagan spoke, ordinary Americans did not have to make the mental translation required for conservative Republican speakers. He undermined the New Deal in its own vernacular."[42]

Another clue to Reagan's magic is provided by the data reported in Figure 8.4, where we find him at the top of the Variety curve (suggesting that he typically sought alternative phrasings for his ideas). This finding may seem curious, especially when we remember that it was Dwight Eisenhower who had previously scored highest on Variety. Clearly, Eisenhower and Reagan spoke differently. Two explanations for this apparent anomaly are available: (1) Whereas Eisenhower wandered among a forest of *ideas* when speaking, Reagan varied only his manner of presentation and (2) whereas Eisenhower was comparatively high on both Variety and Embellishment, Reagan was high only on Variety.

With regard to the first point, Mr. Reagan, strange as it may seem, has

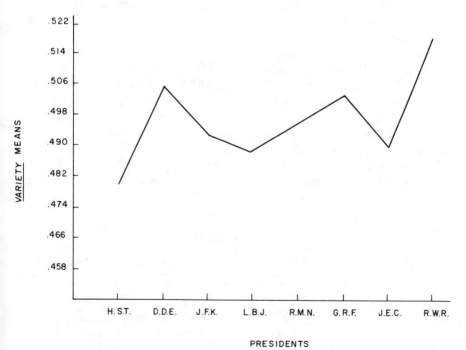

Figure 8.4 Ronald Reagan compared to other presidents on Variety. Based on sample sizes of N = 38, except for Carter (N = 152) and Reagan (N = 24).

a gift for metaphor. Perhaps "gift" is an overly strong characterization, for his imagery is decidedly pedestrian. That, of course, is the point. Reagan's style is often called easy-going because he never reaches beyond himself or his culture when speaking. Predictably, his cultural reach permits use of such hackneyed phrases as "economic might," "spending targets," and "monuments to the policies of the past."[43] None of Reagan's imagery startles; none impresses. His words never force his listeners to imagine things they are incapable of imagining or require that they make a taxing intellectual association. His images are drawn from common labor ("We must chart a different course"), from transportation ("we've come to a turning point"), from strife ("we've tried to fight inflation"), and from human association ("inflation and unemployment—they go hand in hand.")[44]

Nothing poetic here. In fact, Reagan's tropes are so ordinary that they may not even be initially recognized as classical metaphorical structures. His language is drawn from life as it is lived most simply. Because Mr. Reagan's listeners hail from a technocratic society, they understand economic "pump primers." Because his listeners' children are assaulted in the schoolyards by drug dealers, they will regard an economic "quick fix" as undesirable. And because his hearers identify with the Judeo-Christian tradition, they will realize how a growing economy can make their "burden lighter."[45]

Admittedly, the Reagan examples above were taken from a speech on the economy, hardly a topic inspiring flights of fancy. But this speech of February 5, 1981, was not atypical. In almost all of his speeches, Reagan could be starkly contrasted to two orators—John Kennedy and Martin Luther King, Jr.—who created quite different effects through language. Table 8.2 compares three speeches—Reagan on the economy, Kennedy at a civic reception, and King at the 1963 march on Washington. In the excerpt below, Kennedy differs from Reagan in both Variety and Embellishment, substituting an exhilarating style for a varied one and achieving his effect through

TABLE 8.2

STYLISTIC COMPARISON OF KENNEDY, KING,
AND REAGAN ON SELECTED VARIABLES

	Kennedy speech of 5/4/62	King speech of 8/28/63	Reagan speech of 2/5/81
Variety	.418	.508	.550
Embellishment	.092	.111	.010

the simple repetition of key phrases and the heavy use of adjectival constructions:

Florida, Alabama, Louisiana, and Texas are going to be the center of a *great national effort* which will, we believe, someday give us leadership in space which will make the *most profound* differences to this city and State and section.

And I want to emphasize how *important* it is that this city and State prepare itself for the *great technological* changes which are going to take place in *all* our lives. We are going to need in the coming months and years, in order to maintain our position in the world, the *best* schools and the *best* colleges, and the *best* research centers and the *best* engineers, and the *best* scientists—and the *best* citizens that a *free* democracy can possibly produce.[46]

King operated differently. Like Kennedy (and unlike Reagan), he used Embellishment. Unlike Kennedy (and like Reagan), he used a good deal of imagery. Unlike Reagan, he used images which portrayed him as a man of a special time from a special place. Unlike Reagan, King sought to move his listeners beyond the confines of ordinary existence. His words remind us therefore of the difference between conversation and eloquence:

Let us not seek to satisfy our *thirst* for freedom by drinking from the *cup of bitterness* and hatred. We must forever conduct our struggle on the high *plane of dignity* and discipline. We must not allow our creative protest to degenerate into physical violence. Again and again we must rise to the *majestic heights* of meeting physical force with soul force. . . .

I am not unmindful that some of you have come here out of excessive trials and tribulations. Some of you have come fresh from narrow jail cells. Some of you have come from areas where your *quest for freedom* left you battered by the *storms of persecution* and staggered by the *winds of police brutality*. You have been the victims of creative suffering. Continue to work with the faith that unearned suffering is redemptive.[47]

Sense of Tradition

Radical though his legislative priorities are, Ronald Reagan is no rhetorical insurgent. His instincts in speechmaking force him down well-worn paths, as we have seen earlier. Figure 8.5 reinforces this picture, revealing an unprecedented set of correlations for the variables depicted. Reagan lards his speeches with positivity and cuts back on the tools of the superpatriot (Certainty and Symbolism). No other president emphasized these priorities to the extent that Ronald Reagan did. In part, this may be due to his unusual public history, a history that showed him that a winning smile can do much in politics. As his old nemesis in California, Pat Brown, once remarked, "Philosophically and politically, Reagan pours his energies into attempts to denounce, restrain, or cut back. But personally, Reagan con-

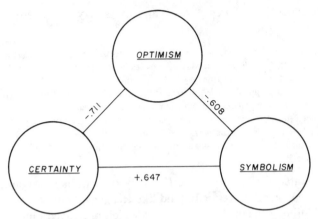

Figure 8.5   Ronald Reagan's celebratory style (Pearson correlations for selected variables, N = 24). For additional information, see Table B.10.

veys an impression of positiveness. . . . Unlike Goldwater, Reagan never suffered from a reputation of shoot-from-the-hip negativism.''[48]

Like Dwight Eisenhower, Ronald Reagan likes to use private speech for deliberation and public speech for celebration. A speech he delivered in June of 1981 at a Champions of American Sport reception in the White House showed him at his most comfortable. His speech contains no partisanship (no essential philosophical proposition, for that mater), but merely the sentiments of a man who learned a simple creed on the gridiron. Portions of the speech could be extracted at random and arbitrarily interchanged without violence being done to this upbeat, noncontroversial message:

> Sports have played an indispensable role in the development of American character . . . if it hadn't been for football, track, and swimming, I might not have been able to go to college . . . . the men and women of sports have done much to bring this country together. . . . what American can forget the pride that swept this country last year when our U.S. ice hockey team beat the Russians? . . . If there was ever a golden age of sports, this is it. . . . I want to thank all of you—the sports men and women this afternoon—for adding a bit of joy and inspiration to our lives.[49]

Speeches of this sort were Ronald Reagan's favorites. But they were not necessarily the Reagan speeches seized upon for commentary by the press. More often than not, the press focused upon the rhetorical news—the comparatively few outbursts he made during his first year. Mr. Reagan had promised a political revolution, after all, and the press was determined to find a stylistic revolution to complement it. One of his more assured, accusatory speeches was that given at West Point in May of his first year in office, and the *New York Times* made a point to comment on its "tough, martial language."[50] That same journal also gave prominent attention to Mr. Reagan's inaugural address, citing its "ringing denunciation of overgrown government" as its most distinctive feature.[51] Generally, however, speeches of this sort were rare during Reagan's first year on the job. Virtually every negative, assured speech was given in innocuous, ceremonial surroundings. More typically, Mr. Reagan sighted fair weather when he spoke. Reflecting on Reagan's first hundred days in office, Steven Weisman noted that not once "has Mr. Reagan called for sacrifice."[52] "Jimmy Carter talked about accepting shortages, and look where it got him," Weisman notes a Reagan aide as having observed.[53]

Most people who study Reagan's speaking quickly learn how limited he is without a script. His aides blanch visibly when he is unexpectedly accosted by a reporter (for fear of what might slip out). Press conferences are particularly difficult for Mr. Reagan. He has difficulty adjusting to a steady stream of disconnected queries, to reporters' individualized questioning styles, and to the lack of time for telling the anecdotes he tells so well. In such encounters, declare Melinda Beck and Eleanor Clift, the president "operates from a visceral sense of foreign policy while doing less homework than some of his predecessors. . . . The result: gaffes and the kind of bold campaign-style rhetoric that borders on excess."[54]

Figure 8.6 shows rather graphically why Ronald Reagan appreciates ceremonial speaking. Compared with press conferences and formal briefings, such speeches permit the safe overstatement, the invocation of national symbols, and the deployment of folksy terminology. Speeches of this sort allow Reagan to return to the simple themes of his GE days. "Because he believed in these pieties," says Lou Cannon, "he could get away with saying what other politicians were unable to say."[55] Ceremonial settings, of course, also permit the use of a script, a script that an experienced speaker like Ronald Reagan had long since committed to memory. "Even those who did not share [his] vision were apt to be stirred by Reagan" in such settings, observes Cannon.[56] Adds Wayne Valis: "Reagan can make an adequate script good; good material he makes excellent."[57]

Ronald Reagan is hardly a brilliant speaker. But he is, unquestionably, a great communicator. We see this in his ability to give listeners a sense of forward movement without overcommitting himself. We see this in his pellucid language and homely figures of speech. But mostly we see this in his ability to tell the American tale to Americans in ways they find comforting, moving, heartening. In telling such tales he typically uses no linguistic trickery, no histrionic formula. Most important, he says such things without the slightest self-consciousness. It is this latter aspect that keeps Reagan's critics

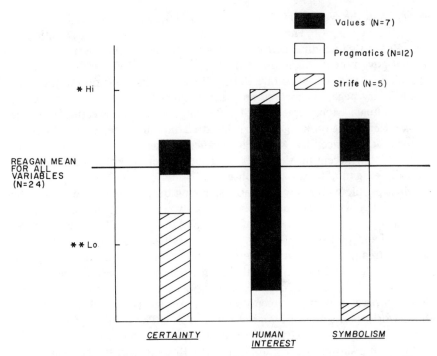

Figure 8.6   Topic-related differences in Ronald Reagan's speaking. *Scores at + ½ sd from mean, which are, respectively, 184.7, 43.1, 6.11. **Scores at − ½ sd from mean, which are, respectively, 167.1, 30.3, 1.73. Means included in Table B.8.

at bay. They seem to reason that any grown man who could offer the following words without batting an eye is too deadly a political opponent to confront unthinkingly, a combatant who will not engage in verbal repartee but who repairs instead to a stronghold fortified by the childhood myths of the American people themselves:

We have every right to dream heroic dreams. Those who say that we're in a time when there are no heroes, they just don't know where to look. You can see heroes every day going in and out of factory gates. Others, a handful in number, produce enough food to feed all of us and then the world beyond. You meet heroes across a counter. And they're on both sides of that counter. They are entrepreneurs with faith in themselves and faith in an idea, who create new jobs, new wealth and opportunity. They're individuals and families whose taxes support the government and whose voluntary gifts support church, charity, culture, art, and education. Their patriotism is deep. Their values sustain our national life.[58]

And Beyond

Beyond Ronald Reagan? It is somewhat hard to imagine, halfway through the Reagan presidency, what the Oval Office would be like without the Great Communicator residing there. This consumate actor–politician has brought so many interpersonal skills to his job that one has to be pinched to be reminded that there is more to the presidency than winsomeness. The real question in the mid-1980s is whether the American people can ever get beyond Ronald Reagan. To get beyond Ronald Reagan, the American people would have to get beyond purposeful facial expressions and nonchalant humor. To get beyond Ronald Reagan, the American people would have to distinguish more sharply between genuine economic advancement and earnest promises, between the dangers of nuclear destruction and a comforting rhetoric of military strength, between institutionalized prayers in the schools and cordial civic piety, between an Equal Rights Amendment and White House receptions for women's leaders, between drastic cuts in Social Security and speeches in praise of the elderly.

To this point, the majority of the American people has demonstrated none of these capacities, perhaps because they implicitly realize that the economic, military, and social uncertainties of the 1980s often permit little more than well-turned phrases by a gifted phrase-maker. The American people themselves are unsure about solutions for employment, Russia, religion, women, and senior citizens. And so they have hired a person to say something about these complexities, hoping that he will assure them, hoping somehow that he will make their emotional lives better, hoping that he will at least prove to be an interesting distraction as events sort themselves out. One senses, as one listens to people talk about Ronald Reagan, that they know what is politically possible in the 1980s—precious little—and that they therefore treat Mr. Reagan's speeches as the state of the art.

In eagerly assuming the public platform, Ronald Reagan operated no differently than his immediate predecessors in office. Throughout this book, we have seen presidents resort to words when events would not yield to them—Truman with Korea, Kennedy with Laos, Johnson with Vietnam, Carter with Iran. Throughout this book, we saw patterns of language linked to the changing fortunes of the presidents studied. My hope is that hereafter it will become increasingly difficult for cultural commentators to give short shrift to presidential speechmaking. The simple fact of the matter is that people listen when presidents speak. Even if it is Richard Nixon talking to the Washington Redskins, people listen. Even if it is Jerry Ford lionizing his WIN buttons, people listen. Even if it is Dwight Eisenhower in a Teamster's hat, people listen. They may listen skeptically, they may even listen cynically, but they never leave an American president standing alone on an airport's tarmac.

It has been fashionable, heretofore, to discount presidential speeches, to treat them as the semblance rather than the substance of political leadership. It has also been fashionable to ignore the details of presidential messages, to gloss over the *ways* presidents say things in order to get at their manifest meanings. This study cautions us against adopting such fashions. We have seen, here, important clues about the changing fortunes of presidential governance, clues imbedded within the specifics of language. By means of language, presidents have also defined for themselves a role different from those assumed by other societal spokespersons. We have witnessed television's tangible effects—on presidents generally, on Lyndon Johnson particularly. We have seen how rigidities of office are transmuted into rhetorical rigidities as a presidency matures, and particularly how Jimmy Carter matured. We have seen how the office changed presidents' natural ways of saying things, particularly Richard Nixon's way of saying things. We have seen certain rhetorical habits characterize entire presidencies and also set the limits of what those presidencies could accomplish. We have seen presidents like Ronald Reagan turn to rhetorical activity when economic and political activity were denied them. We have seen Richard Nixon opt for rhetorical consistency when his world seemed least consistent; and we have seen Jerry Ford, an amiable president without a mandate, stand atop the only available platform—himself. In these ways and more, American presidents sought rhetorical havens when other sources of refuge were unavailable.

Throughout this study, I have attempted to trace why people felt as they did when listening to their chief executives. Some of these inquiries have been heartening—as when Lyndon Johnson, and even Ronald Reagan, insulated themselves from the strident thumpings of a Barry Goldwater, and when the presidents spoke for the people, rather than for themselves, when strife was at hand. Other inquiries prompt questions. Was it good to have a president like Richard Nixon whose iron self-control could not be broken, not even when he spoke extemporaneously? Was it to the nation's credit that Dwight Eisenhower befuddled and confused (himself as well as his listeners) without suffering politically? Should contemporary Americans be pleased that Harry Truman's formality gave way to Jimmy Carter's folksiness?

We have also observed that, increasingly, our presidents are speaking, even though those speeches do not often add appreciably to the pool of understanding. Presidents speak because speechmaking provides political advantage—as when John Kennedy simultaneously assured blacks of his concern for their welfare and promised whites that his civil rights policies would be judicious; as when Lyndon Johnson punctuated his commitment to broad-based educational opportunities by speaking in the doorway of a one-room schoolhouse; as when Jimmy Carter briefly resurrected a faltering presidency by adding firepower to his statements on the Middle East. Via speechmaking, presidents can act, even when more tangible actions are rendered impractical. Via speechmaking, presidents can reestablish their authority (e.g., Nixon during the early days of Watergate), animate dormant ideas (e.g., Ford during the bicentennial), and send aloft political trial balloons without making irrevocable commitments (e.g., Reagan on tax cuts). Via speechmaking, presidents can appear brave when they are fearful, buoyant when they are depressed, challenged when life has become routine for them. Via speechmaking, presidents can stumble on to novel political solutions that benefit both their presidencies and their constituents' lives. As Dean Acheson once said of presidential speechmaking, "This is often where policy is made, regardless of where it is supposed to be made."[59]

That is the up-side of presidential speechmaking. Its down-side is equally apparent. Too often, presidents seem to reason that rhetorical palliatives are the only palliatives that count. Just as surely, they spend too much time speaking in public and far too little time thinking in private. This latter charge is one which virtually every president acknowledges upon leaving office, yet which all of them deny while serving as chief executive. Because they nourish themselves on a daily diet of rhetoric, presidents are easily led to believe that the basic problems in life are stylistic, that their most helpful advisers are their media chiefs, and that all ideas not found in their own speeches are worthless at best, antithetical to the national good at worst. A presidency dominated by symbolic concerns is a presidency likely to become jealous of its rhetorical rivals (often the press) and also likely to confuse political preening with leadership. Speechmaking, in short, can seduce both listeners and speakers.

A book of this sort prompts the inevitable question: Who has been our best presidential persuader? To answer such a question is to confront matters of axiology: What does one want from a president? from human communication generally? Not surprisingly, questions of this sort admit to multiple, often contradictory, answers.

For example, one could easily make the case that Harry Truman maximized the benefits of speechmaking. Possessing few native talents, Truman used communication in its most pristine form—to tell people what he thought. Like the great Anglo-American orators of the nineteenth century, Truman spoke in order to be heard, even though his message frequently flew in the face of popular opinion. Harry Truman's forthrightness, like the forthrightness of the great Irish orator, Daniel O'Connell, stirred many, angered many. Truman used speech to take risks (on the back of his campaign train, before striking miners, and when relieving MacArthur) and to establish himself as a political entity to be feared. For these reasons, Harry Truman was the greatest presidential persuader.

Using other criteria we can see Dwight Eisenhower—despite his intrusive syntax and wandering intellect—as a masterful communicator. As Robert T. Oliver notes in his fascinating book, *Communication and Culture in Ancient India and China,*[60] Americans' penchant for rhetorical boldness is culturally distinctive. Surveying the Oriental mindset relative to speechmaking, however, Oliver observes that interpersonal solidarity, not personal dominance, is also a worthy persuasive goal. For Orientals, says Oliver, public speech is used to bring honor to both speaker and listener, to celebrate social values too often ignored, to bestill the hearts of a community undergoing stress. From such a standpoint, Ike was a fine speaker, inspiring confidence that someone was in charge of 1600 Pennsylvania Avenue, that people need not be troubled by the mindless political squabble, and that by listening to their war hero turned president they could sleep peacefully at night. In these ways and more, Dwight Eisenhower was the greatest presidential persuader.

So, too, was John Kennedy. To judge him as such, one would have to travel to Europe for an appropriate set of communicative standards; one would have to focus more discreetly on the building blocks of ideas—language—and view the creative function of speechmaking as its primary function. John Kennedy emerged from the rhetorical tradition of eighteenth-century writer Hugh Blair, who held that ornamentation alone separated the great idea from the near-great idea.[61] Kennedy assumed the proportions of the palace orators, using speech to display notions that would have remained unnoticed if dressed in plainer garb. If Eisenhower appealed to the heart, and Truman to the solar plexis, Kennedy appealed to that portion of the brain containing the imagination. In listening to him, the American people felt their wits become enlivened. Yes, John Kennedy was the greatest presidential persuader.

Lyndon Johnson spoke American. American (as opposed to English) is a language rich in proletarian imagery. It is also a language useful for scheming schemes that can be put into operation soon—tomorrow if possible. Arm-waving, spittle-spewing, sweat-dripping orator that he was, Lyndon Johnson knew his craft well. It disappointed him that he did not know John Kennedy's craft, but his disappointment did not prevent him from speaking at every hither and yon in the continental United States. Johnson's rhetorical tradition was the tradition of those who hawked the wonders of the American West to the city folks in St. Louis; it was the tradition of the abolitionists and the suffragettes; it was the tradition of the Sunday chautauqua meetings. This tradition prided itself on finding practical solutions to knotty theoretical problems, on energizing people whose lives had become tedious, on skillfully passing through the horns of some intractable political dilemma. When speaking, Lyndon Johnson reflected this history and for these reasons was the greatest presidential persuader.

Problematic though it would be for many to admit it, Richard Nixon was a marvelously skilled communicator. Nixon knew what people felt when listening to politicians speak. He knew they respected pugnacity; he knew they rooted for the underdog during athletic and electoral contests alike; he knew that Americans especially detested metaphysics. Unlike that of his predecessor, Nixon's rhetorical tradition was the white-collar tradition of the Harvard and Yale debating societies, of Clay and Webster, of Clarence Darrow. Mr. Nixon could have easily written rhetorical primers for students disputants. If he had, he would have had them memorize the standard lines of argument: Learn how to spot an opponent's logical fallacies, give no quarter during debate, and spend off hours with fellow strategists. On the basis of technical skill alone, Richard Nixon could be declared the greatest presidential persuader.

Gerald Ford would probably be the first to declare himself out of the running for the rhetorical honor being adjudicated here. He would acknowledge that he possessed few performance skills. He would admit that he was not a wordy man but he would also remind us that he appreciated the personal immediacy of speech and that he tried to reach his listeners when speaking to them. He might think to mention that he was educated at a land-grant university in the midwest, the kind of institution that has traditionally provided speech instruction to its undergraduates. Moreover, he might remind us that his speaking had improved considerably over the years and that he gave more speeches during a single year (1976) than had any president previously in American history. Judged by absolute standards, Jerry Ford was not a masterful orator. But judged by the rhetorical tradition embodied in 4-H speaking contests, in Dale Carnegie self-improvement courses, and in Toastmasters' Clubs, even Jerry Ford could claim that enthusiasm and improvement entitled him to be called the greatest presidential persuader.

Yet another rhetorical tradition makes an argument for Ronald Reagan. That tradition, American pragmatism, holds that no idea, however convoluted, is incapable of being made simpler and thereby of being made the possession of another. This is the tradition of the Basic English movement, of the 5-foot stack of *Harvard Classics*, of *Reader's Digests* condensed novels. Ronald Reagan is a semantic egalitarian who resolutely insists that no philosophical concept is so subtle that it cannot be turned into a political slogan. In this sense Ronald Reagan is the Mortimer Adler of American politics. Clarity, clarity, and once again, clarity, are Reagan's watchwords.

He has made reductionism an art form and has thus become the greatest presidential persuader.

Virtually nobody would place Jimmy Carter atop the rhetorical pantheon being discussed here. None of the traditions mentioned would claim Mr. Carter as its own. Defenders of these traditions would correctly assert that Carter was dense compared with Reagan, timid compared with Truman, awkward compared with Eisenhower, artless compared with Kennedy. Others would observe that Mr. Carter was transparent compared with Nixon, dispirited compared with Johnson, and cold compared with Ford. Such critics would have no difficulty documenting their claims, for Carter's speechmaking was a treasure trove of misdelivered lines, witless pauses, and hopelessly technical verbiage. Should anyone doubt Carter's ineptitude, he or she would only have to listen to Mr. Carter himself: "In the 1980 campaign I tried to warn the American people about President Reagan's policies. He was a much better communicator than I was, a better salesman. . . . I have the inclination to explain both sides of an issue to the public and then draw a conclusion. This often is lost in the heat of a political campaign because people want simple answers to complicated questions. They want magic solutions to long-standing problems."[62]

One of the quickest orthodoxies ever established in American political history is that Jimmy Carter failed as president because he failed rhetorically. Just a few years after his presidency, nobody denies that, not even Mr. Carter himself. And surely the data presented in Chapters Six and Seven of this book substantiate that claim. Whether they isolated his curious sense of timing, his refusal to rehearse, or his paralyzing abstractions, critics of the Left, Right, and Middle agreed that Jimmy Carter was a communicative disaster area. Case closed.

Mr. Carter's case is worth reopening. We might well examine what it means to say that a president has failed in his job because he could not speak well. It is wise to ask how important rhetoric really is to us. Is the presidency, now, a job in which a man of supreme intelligence (surely Jimmy Carter was that) cannot function effectively unless he is also a person of consummate suasory skill? Can we still take the measure of a chief executive without gauging his ability to read fluently from a TelePrompTer? Have opinion polling and instant commentary made our presidents so process-centered that they themselves can no longer find the fiber of their administrations? Have we, in short, produced a rhetorical presidency?

It is likely that we have. The rhetorical traditions of Mr. Carter's predecessors (and successor) provide few accolades for him, but these traditions bind our minds and hearts tightly these days. There is yet another tradition, however. It holds that public communication's noblest goal is to enlighten, that talk should challenge rather than mollify, that presidential speechmaking should edify citizens as well as effect political compacts, that a chief executive should gather and explain options—each and every one of them—whether these options are pleasing to listeners or not.

This was Woodrow Wilson's tradition and Jimmy Carter's "natural" tradition as well. It was not the tradition of nay-saying, but it was the tradition of the social commentator and the academic. It was a tradition that proved intuitively attractive to the empiricist-moralist that was Jimmy Carter. It was hardly a tradition he followed consistently, however, for Jimmy Carter was an extraordinarily expedient politician, too. But it was the tradition he exploited effectively when running for the presidency in 1976 and the tradition he returned to in mid-July of 1979 when describing to the nation its crisis of confidence. Upon listening again to some of the words he spoke then, we can easily imagine ourselves in the lecture hall of a prominent sociologist. We have to be prodded to remember that Mr. Carter's central topic that day was petroleum supplies—who had them, why they had them, and how we could get more of them. Yet, as it had on so many occasions, Jimmy Carter's rhetoric contained its own distraction:

> The symptoms of this crisis of the American spirit are all around us. For the first time in the history of our country a majority of our people believe that the next 5 years will be worse than the past 5 years. Two-thirds of our people do not even vote. The productivity of American workers is actually dropping, and the willingness of Americans to save for the future has fallen below that of all other people in the Western world.
>
> As you know, there is a growing disrespect for government and for churches and for schools, the news media, and other institutions. This is not a message of happiness or reassurance, but it is the truth and it is a warning.
>
> These changes did not happen overnight. They've come upon us gradually over the last generation, years that were filled with shocks and tragedy.
>
> We were sure that ours was a nation of the ballot, not the bullet, until the murders of John Kennedy and Robert Kennedy and Martin Luther King, Jr. We were taught that our armies were always invincible and our causes were always just, only to suffer the agony of Vietnam. We respected the Presidency as a place of honor until the shock of Watergate.[63]

These are ugly words. Upon hearing them we instinctively yearn for simpler times, simpler issues, simpler voices, voices with Harry Truman's Certainty, Richard Nixon's Realism, or Jerry Ford's Optimism. It is probably something short of the great American tragedy that Jimmy Carter was denied a second term in office, but it may have been at least a minor tragedy that Mr. Carter was punished so severely for speaking as he did and even more tragic that he believed his critics, more tragic, still, that he allowed himself to be tossed about on the political tides.

Presidential persuasion is a useful thing. It can be a great thing. But it is only one thing. And the American presidency is many things. Presidents and people alike will have to decide what role persuasion will have at the highest level of government and who will be its master. Jimmy Carter was not the greatest presidential persuader. That fact should give us all pause.

Notes

1. Rich Jaroslovsky, *Wall Street Journal*, June 15, 1982, p. 33; Sidney Blumenthal, *New York Times Magazine*, September 13, 1981, pp. 43 ff.; Melinda Beck and Eleanor Clift, *Newsweek*, June 29, 1981, p. 20; Alvin P. Senoff, *U.S. News and World Report*, March 2, 1982, p. 29.
2. Mark Crispin Miller, "Virtu, Inc.," *The New Republic*, April 7, 1982, p. 32.
3. Lou Cannon, *Reagan* (New York: Putnams, 1982), p. 36.
4. Cannon (1982), p. 72.
5. Cannon (1982), p. 94.
6. Robert Lindsey, "Creating the Role," in Hedrick Smith *et al.*, eds., *Reagan the Man the President* (New York: Macmillan, 1980), p. 24.
7. Wayne Valis, "Ronald Reagan: The Man, The President," in W. Valis, ed., *The Future under President Reagan* (Westport, CT: Arlington House, 1981), p. 34.
8. Hedrick Smith, "Mr. Reagan Goes to Washington," in Smith *et al.* (1980), p. 150.
9. Quoted in Blumenthal (1981), p. 110.
10. "Inaugural Address," January 20, 1981, *Weekly Compilations of Presidential Documents* (hereafter *Weekly Compilations*), 17:4 (1981), p. 2.
11. Hedrick Smith, "Reformer Who Would Reverse New Deal's Legacy," *New York Times*, January 21, 1981, p. B2.
12. Quoted in Smith (1980), p. 150.
13. "Program for Economic Recovery," February 18, 1981, *Weekly Compilations*, 17:8 (1981), p. 134.
14. *Weekly Compilations* 17:8 (1981), p. 134.
15. *Weekly Compilations* 17:8 (1981), p. 134.
16. Quoted in Jaroslovsky (1982), p. 33.
17. Cannon (1982), p. 14.
18. Quoted in Francis X. Clines, "The Voices that Blend into Reagan's Speeches," *New York Times*, October 8, 1982, p. 14.
19. Clines (1982), p. 14.
20. "Reagan Readies the Ax," *Newsweek*, February 16, 1981, p. 20.
21. "He Didn't Give Us Anything," *Time*, July 13, 1981, p. 11.
22. *Time*, July 13, 1981, p. 11.
23. Smith *et al.*, (1980), p. 97.
24. Rowland Evans and Robert Novak, *The Reagan Revolution* (New York: Dutton, 1981), p. 245.
25. Smith *et al.* (1980), p. 98.
26. "Freed American Hostages," January 27, 1982, *Weekly Compilations*, 17:5 (1981), p. 50.
27. "Remarks to Conservative Political Action Conference," March 20, 1981, *Weekly Compilations*, 17:12 (1981), p. 330.
28. This story is related in Evans and Novak (1981), p. 216.
29. Smith *et al.* (1980), p. 181.
30. "The Defense Lag," August 10, 1964, *Vital Speeches of the Day*, 30:22 (1964), p. 677.

31. "Salute to a Stronger America," November 13, 1981, *Weekly Compilations*, 17:47 (1981), p. 1258.

32. Cannon (1982), p. 98.

33. Cannon (1982), p. 98.

34. Quoted in Smith *et al.* (1980), p. 180.

35. "Remarks at Welcoming Ceremony," February 26, 1981, *Weekly Compilations,* 17:9 (1981), p. 194.

36. Miller (1982), p. 28.

37. Quoted in Cannon (1982), p. 372.

38. Miller (1982), p. 29.

39. Anthony Beilenson, as quoted in Jaroslovsky (1982), p. 33.

40. Smith *et al.* (1980), p. 152.

41. Hedrick Smith, "Blunt and Simple," *New York Times*, February 6, 1981, p. A12.

42. Cannon (1982), p. 99.

43. "President's News Conference," October 1, 1981, *Weekly Compilations*, 17:40 (1981), p. 1064.

44. *Weekly Compilations*, 17:40 (1981), p. 1064.

45. "The Nation's Economy," February 5, 1981, *Weekly Compilations*, 17:6 (1981), p. 96.

46. "Remarks in New Orleans at a Civic Reception," May 4, 1962, *Public Papers of the Presidents 1962* (Washington, D.C.: U.S. Government Printing Office, 1963), p. 362. Italics mine.

47. Martin Luther King, Jr., "I Have a Dream," in Roy L. Hill, ed., *The Rhetoric of Racial Revolt* (Denver: Golden Bell, 1964), pp. 372, 373. Italics mine.

48. Edmund G. Brown, *Reagan: The Political Chameleon* (New York: Praeger, 1976), p. 20.

49. "Remarks at a White House Reception," June 22, 1981, *Weekly Compilations*, 17:26 (1981), pp. 667, 668.

50. Howell Raines, "Era of Self Doubt is Over," *New York Times*, May 28, 1981, p. 1.

51. Hedrick Smith, "A Hopeful Prologue," *New York Times*, January 21, 1981, p. 1.

52. Steven Weisman, "A Test of the Man and the Presidency," *New York Times Magazine*, April 26, 1981, p. 56.

53. Weisman, (1981), p. 56.

54. Beck and Clift (1981), p. 20.

55. Cannon (1982), p. 371.

56. Cannon (1982), p. 14.

57. Valis (1981), p. 35.

58. "Inaugural Address" (1981), p. 3.

59. Quoted in Arthur Schlesinger, Jr., *A Thousand Days: John F. Kennedy in the White House* (Greenwich, CT: Fawcett, 1965), pp. 632–633.

60. Robert T. Oliver, *Communication and Culture in Ancient India and China* (Syracuse: Syracuse University Press, 1971).

61. See Hugh Blair's *Lectures on Rhetoric and Belles Lettres*, two volumes, H. Harding, ed., (Carbondale, IL: Southern Illinois University Press, 1965).

62. Quoted in Wesley G. Pippert, "Reagan is One; Carter is Not," *San Antonio Light*, November 16, 1982, p. 15A.

63. "Address to the Nation on Energy and National Goals," July 15, 1979, *Weekly Compilations*, 15:29 (1979), p. 1237.

CHAPTER
NINE

A POSTSCRIPT ON PURPOSE
AND PROCEDURE

This volume constitutes an experiment. It is an experiment in a particular kind of discernment. Using a computer to understand presidential behavior, especially presidents' communicative behavior, may seem an alien thing to do. To arrest in time a dynamic process like the spoken interchange shared by a leader and his people may appear to be the worst sort of scholasticism. To pore over the written text of a speech, after all, is to examine little more than the residue of an emotional, multilateral conversation long since ended. The printed marks on paper examined by the computer constitute only an oblique record of the personal, political, and rhetorical decisions faced and somehow resolved by an enormously busy chief executive. Such computerized analyses provide fertile ground for several forms of intellectual sin: psychologism, intentional fallacies, scientism, post hoc reasoning, and reductionistic logic. To convert words into numbers, as we have done here, is itself a process fraught with uncertainty, a process rendered even more troublesome when one infers political consequences from such rarified, numerical data. Alas, these problems are sufficient to convince one to look for another line of work.

Several things made me persevere, however. I assumed, for example, that to see is to distort. I assumed that all forms of scholarly inquiry require that one wall out in order to understand what one has walled in. Traditionally, students of the American presidency have examined such things as fluctuations in the gross national product, legislative success records, White House intrigues, presidential work habits, mythical–cultural routines, diplomatic imbroglios, relationships between press and president, psychological styles of leadership, intra- and interparty affiliations, and so

238

forth. In deciding to study such things, these scholars have chosen not to study other things. But they have done more than that. In studying these things, they have presumed that the objects of their inquiries were somehow more important than the objects of others' inquiries. In a sense, the various methodologies they employed when studying the presidency were only secondarily biasing. One distorts life by choosing to witness it rather than simply live it. *How* one witnesses life is a matter of lesser moment.

My argument is that choosing to see how presidents speak is useful, even though it is not the only approach. I have tried to be appropriately cautious when stating or implying cause-and-effect relationships between presidential words and national consequences. But I have also insisted that presidential words are important, more important today, perhaps, than at any other time in American history. In the past, scholars of the presidency have been chary about rhetorical matters. They have been reluctant to indulge inquiries into such faintly feminine matters as word choice, staging and timing of presidential announcements, and problems of delivery, repartee, and pancake makeup. Presidential scholars have, instead, attended to such robustly masculine issues as power blocs, body counts, scientific polling techniques, legislative arm twisting, pork barrel deals, explosive cabinet meetings, political payoffs, platform battles, and other matters that reinforce the image of politcs as a civilized brutality suitable only for one bearing the ancestral traces of blood lust. For such observers, overly delicate matters like syntax and imagery detract from politics' essence and they cannot, therefore, countenance inquiries into such matters.

Not all scholars feel this way, and recent years have been especially inviting to rhetorical studies of American presidents. Popular commentators, too, have become interested in such matters. Television newscasters such as Erik Sevareid, Howard K. Smith, and David Brinkley have operated more frequently as rhetorical critics than as political critics when unraveling the presidential message for their viewers, thereby treating politics as a kind of metareality. Print journalists typically follow suit, although their commentaries about presidential speechmaking are less instantaneous and their purposes in providing them less overtly cynical. Journals of opinion like *Nation* and *National Review* have still other purposes when assessing presidential persuasion, often using a chief executive's words as a springboard for their own more particularized political goals. In short, there exists more than enough analyses of presidents' public addresses, although a wary consumer will espy in them a wide range of both precision and insight.

My purpose in this volume has been to provide a history of presidential discourse, a history whose data base and method of construction were intentionally opened to public inspection. I have attempted to detail how presidents talked and why they talked as they did. I have tried not to be precious when looking for these explanations, and therefore have relied upon both scholarly and journalistic observers to help me understand what I found. Unfortunately, not all of these commentaries were helpful, perhaps because presidential speech often acts as a kind of Rorschach inkblot upon which commentators impose their own versions of political reality. For any given presidential speech, one can find in print virtually any desired interpretation or exposé—all earnest, some helpful. It is probably natural that one would find such a range of sense and nonsense surrounding presidential rhetoric, party because presidential rhetoric is itself composed of sense and nonsense, and partly because presidential rhetoric necessarily deals with the full panoply of human wants and fears: security, conquest, love, anxiety, deliverance.

Scholarly investigations of presidents' speeches can probably be depended upon for two things: distance and precision. Popular commentaries, in contrast, provide other things. Consider, for example, the analyses of Hedrick Smith of the *New York Times*, surely one of the most astute observers of American presidents. When he listens to a president speak, Mr. Smith does some of the things done here. For example, he listens for tidbits of rhetorical "news," locutions differing radically from those he has heard previously from this (or another) president. He listens for "generic imprints," features imposed on the discourse by the discourses to which it is heir. He listens for subtle hints suggesting the president's current political motivations or his most pressing psychological needs. When listening for such things, Mr. Smith consults his own experiences with this particular president, thereby making-conscious remembrances ordinary listeners cannot capture or, recalling them, know not what to do with them.

Throughout Jimmy Carter's administration, Hedrick Smith penned regular analyses of the presidential rhetoric he heard, undoubtedly employing roughly the same methodology employed by me in this study. Although his data bank of presidential speeches was not committed to computer tape, and although he did not listen for exactly the same features of language each time he listened (as DICTION does), he did listen astutely and sensitively, as revealed in Table 9.1.

Smith's observations are well informed because he is a tolerably good student of rhetorical history. When listening to Mr. Carter's inaugural address, for example, Smith mentally consulted the other inaugurals he had previously catalogued and noted correctly (correctly, according to DICTION) the diminished "boldness" of Jimmy Carter's first speech. Similarly, he seized upon the "cautious," "low-keyed," "matter-of-fact" tone as being a significant aspect of Carter's second State of the Union address and also detected how different that tone was from the tone in Mr. Carter's "uncompromising" speech on energy in November of 1977. Significantly,

Smith captures the interesting blend of high Certainty and Human Interest that made Carter's "crisis of confidence" speech "part sermon, part warning."

On other matters, however, DICTION and Smith do not agree. Contrary to what Smith reports, I discerned no specific similarity between Carter's second State of the Union speech and his inaugural, nor do my results for the variable Realism support Smith's claim that Carter "presented the nation with a balance sheet of its problems." In addition, my analyses depict the November 1977 speech on energy as being less platitudinous than Smith's commentary suggests. It contained much more Realism than any of the other speeches presented in Table 9.1, and significantly more than Mr. Carter habitually used elsewhere.

My purpose is making these observations is surely not to quibble with Hedrick Smith. Rather, my purpose is to emphasize that data like those assembled in this study permit one to be especially precise about the nuances of rhetorical style; they allow one to isolate features of language contributing to a given communicative effect; and they permit one to make specific comparisons and contrasts. In addition, such research techniques allowed me to highlight the problematic—that is, to determine, for example, which features of Mr. Carter's speeches were least well understood or which provoked the sharpest controversy among observers of those speeches. DICTION is helpful because it is fast, unerring, and because it has a capacious memory. More important, however, it is helpful because it is capable of attacking a message from so many different vantage points simultaneously, thereby permitting one to apprehend some of the tremendous complexity of verbal style. Finally, all of these features permit the scholar to make a more complete textual inspection than could be made by even a wise and sensitive observer like Hedrick Smith.

Some students of language complain that a computer program like DICTION distorts human communication because it lumbers through a message, insensitve to matters of context. They argue, for example, that a statement like "I've decided to send troops to Central America" would be fundamentally misunderstood by DICTION because it would regard its sedentary verb ("decide") as negating its dynamic verb ("send"), thereby overlooking the important fact that troops were indeed being shipped off to war. Similarly, they would assert that those negations that fundamentally change a statement's meaning (e.g., "I won't accept the view that America is on the decline"), would be stupidly overlooked by a computer programmed only to inspect contextless instances of a given word (e.g., the word "decline").

In my opinion, criticisms like these overlook two important matters. First, DICTION uses multiple searching devices, thus permitting the researcher

TABLE 9.1

COMPARISON OF DICTION RESULTS WITH HEDRICK SMITH'S COMMENTARIES

Speech	Certainty	Realism	Human interest	Smith commentaries (*New York Times*)
Carter's inaugural address	185.5	177.5	50.0	With his sense of the moment, this first President from the deep South in more than a century has chosen modest
Predecessors' inaugurals (*N* = 7)	216.8	199.9	35.3	beginnings and has forsaken the traditional boldness of inaugural rhetoric that contributed to the now fallen mystique of the Presidency. . . . His Inaugural Address was less rallying cry than sermon. It was a call to the American spirit, a moral appeal for decency and unity that tacitly acknowledged the grudging and wary refusal of the American public to be further seduced by the promises of politicalness. (1/21/77,p. 1:6)
Carter's second State of the Union speech	163.8	188.3	24.0	His own proposals for the year ahead were modest in substance and couched in cautious language. . . . Mr. Carter did little to sharpen the focus of his own objectives or his
Predecessors' State of the Union speeches (*N* = 15)	178.2	189.5	27.8	public philosophy. . . . Rather than offering a rich political sermon, he presented the nation with a balance sheet of its problems and a catalogue of his prescriptions for them. . . . President Carter spoke in subdued, matter-of-fact tones, echoing the low-keyed rhetorical style of his inaugural address and matching the modesty of his objectives. . . . his speech broke with the solemn historical tradition of earlier Presidents who employed stately eloquence or seized upon a momentous occasion to summon their nation to arms to direct it into a new era. (1/20/78,p.A11:3)

Carter's "crisis of confidence" speech	206.8	196.5	53.0	In what was part sermon, part program, part warning, the President returned to the homilies and populist rhetoric of his 1976 campaign in an effort to save his Presidency and to try to restore what he feels is lost contact with the American people. . . . Speaking easily, naturally and confidently, he portrayed himself as a people's President who had lost touch with the people and had begun to regain it in the past 10 days at Camp David. . . . the real test for Mr. Carter will be whether the populist tone of his homilies and the tougher talk on energy will serve the rallying cry that he intended. (7/16/79,p.1:4)
Carter's overall behavior (N = 152)	181.1	199.4	28.1	
Carter's energy speech of 11/8/77	209.6	208.5	18.0	President Carter has made it almost a trademark of his political career not to compromise on crucial issues until the eleventh hour, and in his speech last night he signaled that as far as he is concerned the eleventh hour has not yet arrived for his energy program. . . . the President sought last night to be persuasive with Congress rather than force a showdown. He chose to set out his objectives in broad principles rather than specific legislative provisions. (11/10/77,p. 15:1)
Predecessors' overall behavior (N = 228)	188.4	195.0	27.5	

to say more complicated things about a given text. In a given situation, for example, it could be massively important that a president had "decided" to export troops (thereby suggesting that some amount of reflection had taken place prior to his making such a momentous decision), as opposed to arbitrarily and impulsively "sending" them. Not only would the implied "deciding" redound to the advantage of the president, we can assume, but it would also engender fewer feelings of calamity among citizens worried that precipitous actions were being taken in their behalf by the chief executive.

Second, DICTION (and other programs like it) helps the scholar get at the substructure of a given message so that a speaker's basic communicative agenda can be discerned. That is, no amount of analysis can deny the fact that "decline" was very much on the mind of the speaker in the second example cited above. Yes, it is important that this speaker has dissociated himself or herself with that decline, but it may be even more significant that talk of "decline" was in the wind in the first place, more important still that our speaker felt it incumbent upon himself or herself to address the matter frontally.

The important thing to keep in mind about any systematic study of verbal style is the matter of scale. Throughout this book, conclusions were drawn only when language *patterns* were discovered. With a sufficiently large data base, with careful selection of messages, and with judicious interpretation of findings, researchers can indeed make informed and sensitive comments about language, based on computerized counts. In political speechmaking, the simple deployment of a given vocabulary, repeated often enough, can constitute political news. Jimmy Carter's "crisis of confidence" speech made waves not because he was wrestling with personal angst, but because he talked about such matters in public. Computers are especially helpful in noting that a particular vocabulary has been used (e.g., a vocabulary of urgent crisis), remembering when and where that vocabulary was deployed, and then calling the researcher's attention to interesting deviations from such language patterns.

In short, a computer does nothing that a sensitive listener could not do if he or she had the time. Most of use do not have the time. Most listeners allow political speech to sweep past them, occasionally making a mental note of a particular verbal felicity or a peculiar political passion, but more often allowing that message to drop into the mind's dustbin reserved for political talk. When listeners next confront a new speaker, however, they unquestionably use that dustbin of feelings and thoughts to help them categorize and evaluate the new phenomena confronting them. Few of us are actively aware that we make such comparisons or that communicative effects are typically additive effects—part this, part that. Nevertheless, these pieces and parts eventually constitute our communicative histories—useful arrays of blurred memories, idiosyncratic listening styles, distinctive political biases, and half-formed expectations.

DICTION, then, has been designed to simulate some of the mental processes used by political listeners. Like listeners, DICTION pays attention to some words, not all of them. Like listeners, DICTION interprets all new political messages in view of the political messages it has "heard" earlier. Like listeners, DICTION's confidence in its conclusions about a political speaker increases with the number of speeches it listens to. And like listeners, DICTION puts a good deal of stock in what might be called political tone although it treats tone as the direct product of identifiable word groupings. Therefore, to say that computerized language analysis can tell us nothing about political discourse is to say that word groupings are used by speakers and responded to by listeners in random ways, a conclusion that seems patently wrong.

DICTION's use, of course, need not be restricted to presidential speeches. But it seemed to me that there was a particular need in the area of presidential studies for an investigation of this sort. All too often in the past, presidential studies have been either (1) personality based or (2) macro-theoretical, with anecdotal evidence shoring up the former and historical–philosophical intuitions sustaining the latter. From both sorts of examinations, we have learned much. However, Bernard Hennessy has argued that we have not yet learned all that we need to know: "Must presidential studies be a combination of 'great man' biographies, tieresome autobiographies, backstairs gossip, and journalism both good and bad? Even the best—e.g., Neustadt's *Presidential Power*—seem to lack the conceptualization, the hypothesizing, the patient collection of data, the discovery of pattern or lack thereof, and the explanations with an explicit or implicit framework of causality. . . . [I ask] the question of all presidential experts: will you ever be able to get past biography."[1]

Hennessy's charges are both fair and unfair and his implied conceptual model both compelling and flawed. He is correct, for example, in arguing that more dross has been written about American presidents than about any other popular subject. He is correct, too, when he asserts that students of the presidency have not been sufficiently interested in systematic questions heretofore. Surely he is right about the shallow evidence sometimes used to support claims made about the presidency. Indeed, it was out of an attempt to correct such deficiencies that this book was written. My conviction has been that conclusions about presidential behavior cannot be fully trusted if they are exclusively impressionistic or if they are drawn in the absence of an institutional data base.

But I also believe that Professor Hennessy has overstated his position.

While there surely are institutional aspects to presidential behavior (a good many of which have been described here), it is also true that the presidency is a human institution and to some extent an idiosyncrasy-based institution as well. In this volume, we have witnessed different presidents respond in different ways to like circumstances. No matter how hard he tried, Richard Nixon could never have been mistaken for Harry Turman, nor could Lyndon Johnson have disguised himself as John Kennedy. In some measure, the presidency recreates itself on each inaugural morning. It does so because people, even political people, will not completely submit themselves to another's lash. And so the story of a presidency must be, in part, a biographical story, even though it cannot be understood apart from other presidential stories. After intensively studying hundreds of presidential messages, I have become disillusioned with any simple conceptual model of presidential behavior. For example, no theory of presidential persuasion with which I am familiar could have predicted how Jimmy Carter would speak on October 28, 1978, when, at 7:43 P.M. in Portland, Maine, he addressed a Jefferson-Jackson Day dinner. His speech that evening contained no brave new declaration or startling political revelation. Much of it is filled with the banalities expected from an institutionally encrusted chief executive. What was newsworthy was how Jimmy Carter spoke that evening: He violated many of his political instincts and, momentarily at least, forsook several rhetorical habits as well. He was tired; he was petulant; and he was remarkably honest. He did not talk like a sitting president.

The introduction to Mr. Carter's speech especially has haunted me for some time, largely because it stands in contradistinction to the political fare analyzed in this book, thereby demonstrating how much we still have to learn about presidential communication. The style of Mr. Carter's words is worth pondering, for it poses questions about the presidency—its hardships, its seductiveness, its compromises, its possibilities—for which answers are not yet available. Perhaps if we could understand this one speech we would also understand how biography and bureaucracy become fused in presidencies, why these forces take the curious permutations they do, and what it means for our way of government when our leaders address us thusly:

> I don't have much time with you. I wanted to talk soberly and frankly tonight. I don't care whether you applaud or not.
>
> I didn't come up here to waste my time. I've had a long week. The duties of my office are sometimes burdensome, sometimes create loneliness, always serious. My decisions affect the future of our Nation, in fact, many other nations around the Earth. This could have been my one day off this week, but I wanted to come here because I, as the President of our country, and as the leader of the Democratic Party, am very interested in what happens in Maine 10 days from now on November 7.
>
> I can't carry an election for you. I can't stay here and hold your hand to make sure

that Bill Hathaway is the next Senator from Maine or that Joe Brennan is the next Governor, Mark Gartley and John Quinn your next members of Congress. I can't do that.

I thought a lot about Maine. My son's been up here to campaign for these candidates. He didn't have to. The Vice President's been up here to campaign. He didn't have to. My wife has been up here to campaign with Bill Hathaway and with the other candidates. She didn't have to. We believe in them.[2]

Notes

1. Bernard Hennessy, "Review of *The Washington Reporters* and *Portraying the President,*" *American Political Science Review*, 75 (1981), p. 1046.

2. "Remarks at the Annual Jefferson-Jackson Day Dinner," October 28, 1978, *Weekly Compilations of Presidential Documents*, 14:44 (1978), p. 1897.

STYLISTIC PROFILES
OF PRESIDENTIAL SPEECHES

The DICTION program analyses only the middle-most 500 words of the verbal samples submitted. Thus, the profiles presented here describe only a portion of the messages described.

For all charts in the appendix, Hi ≥ 80th percentile, Lo ≤ 20th percentile for the president and variable mentioned, and * = highest or lowest case for the group.

Profile of Harry Truman's Presidential Addresses (1945–1953)

#	DATE	TOPIC	SITUATION	Activity	Realism	Certainty	Optimism	Symbolism	Self-Reference	Familiarity	Human Interest	Embellishment	Variety	Complexity
1	4/25/45	Justice	U.N. conference	Lo	Hi		Hi			Lo*		Hi	Hi*	Hi
2	8/9/45	Warning to Japan	National (address)		Hi	Hi*	Lo		Lo	Hi	Lo		Lo*	Hi
3	10/10/45	American ingenuity	Dam dedication				Lo		Lo	Hi	Lo	Lo		
4	10/30/45	Wages and prices	National (address)		Lo*		Lo			Lo	Lo	Hi		Hi
5	12/24/45	American values	Commemorative ceremony				Lo					Lo		Lo
6	1/3/46	Post-war economy	National (address)	Lo					Hi	Hi	Lo			
7	5/24/46	Railroad strike	National (address)						Hi	Hi				
8	1/6/47	State of the Union	National (congress)	Lo		Lo		Hi		Lo	Lo		Hi	
9	6/29/47	Civil rights	N.A.A.C.P. conference			Lo		Hi*		Lo				
10	10/8/47	Moral force of women	National (address)		Hi		Hi	Hi		Lo	Hi		Hi	Lo*
11	2/19/48	Democratic politics	Party dinner	Hi								Hi		
12	3/17/48	Tyranny vs. freedom	Ethnic organization	Hi	Lo			Hi	Hi			Hi	Lo	Hi
13	6/14/48	Congressional bills	Press organization				Hi		Hi	Hi*				
14	9/20/48	Democratic party	Party rally	Hi		Lo	Lo		Hi				Hi	Hi
15	1/20/49	Values of democracy	National (inaugural ceremony)	Hi*	Hi		Hi	Hi	Lo	Hi	Hi	Lo*	Lo	Hi*
16	2/24/49	Taft-Hartley Act	Party dinner		Hi	Hi		Hi	Hi	Lo			Hi	Lo

No.	Date	Educational needs	Rollins College	Lo	Hi1*								
17	3/8/49	Educational needs	Rollins College				Lo		Hi		Hi		Hi
18	6/11/49	Lasting peace	Memorial ceremony	Hi			Lo		Hi		Hi		Hi
19	7/13/49	Economic situation	National (address)	Hi		Hi	Hi		Hi	Lo	Hi	Lo	
20	12/24/49	Love of fellow man	Commemorative ceremony	Lo				Hi			Hi		Lo
21	1/5/50	State of the Union	National (congress)	Lo*	Hi*		Lo		Hi	Hi	Hi	Lo	
22	2/15/50	Organized crime	Police conference	Lo		Hi		Hi		Lo	Hi		
23	4/20/50	Press and truth	Newspaper organization	Lo		Hi	Hi		Hi*		Hi*		
24	5/15/50	Democratic party	Party conference	Lo	Lo		Lo						
25	7/19/50	Communists in Korea	National (address)	Hi	Lo					Lo	Lo		
26	9/1/50	Korean War	National (address)			Lo*	Hi			Lo	Lo		Lo
27	9/9/50	Economic controls	National (address)								Lo		
28	12/15/50	Korean War	National (address)	Hi				Lo		Hi	Lo		
29	4/11/51	Relieving MacArthur	National (address)			Hi							
30	5/17/51	Freedom	Citizenship conference	Hi		Hi	Hi	Lo		Hi	Hi	Lo	
31	10/15/51	Peace and freedom	Wake Forest University		Hi	Hi	Hi		Hi	Hi		Lo	Lo
32	11/7/51	Reduction of armaments	National (address)	Hi	Lo	Hi	Lo	Lo*	Lo*	Hi	Lo*		Lo
33	1/9/52	State of the Union	National (congress)										
34	3/6/52	Foreign aid	National (address)	Lo*	Lo		Lo	Hi		Lo		Hi	Lo
35	4/8/52	Steel industry	National (address)		Lo		Lo	Lo				Lo	Lo
36	6/13/52	Civil rights	Howard University	Lo	Hi	Hi		Lo		Lo		Hi	Hi
37	10/16/52	Democratic party	Party rally		Lo					Lo			
38	1/15/53	Leaving the Presidency	National (address)	Lo	Lo	Hi*			Lo				

251

PROFILE OF DWIGHT D. EISENHOWER'S PRESIDENTIAL ADDRESSES (1953–1960)

#	DATE	TOPIC	SITUATION	Activity	Realism	Certainty	Optimism	Symbolism	Self-Reference	Familiarity	Human Interest	Embellishment	Variety	Complexity
1	1/20/53	Peace and freedom	National (inaugural ceremony)						Hi	Lo	Hi			Lo
2	5/19/53	National defense	National (address)		Lo*									
3	6/10/53	Military security	Business convention				Hi					Hi	Hi	
4	7/26/53	Korean armistice	National (address)			Lo				Lo	Hi	Lo		Lo
5	8/4/53	State government	Governors' conference	Hi	Hi			Hi		Hi				Lo
6	9/21/53	Freedom and dignity	Party conference	Lo										
7	10/6/53	Faith in God	Church organization				Hi		Hi	Lo				Lo
8	10/19/53	International cooperation	Dam dedication	Lo*		Hi					Hi		Lo	Lo
9	1/7/54	State of the Union	National (congress)	Hi*	Lo	Lo	Lo					Lo		Hi
10	4/5/54	America's greatness	National (address)		Hi	Lo	Lo		Hi	Hi	Hi*		Lo	Lo
11	5/31/54	American education	Columbia University	Lo					Lo		Lo	Hi	Hi	
12	7/25/54	Government and morality	Church convention	Hi	Hi*	Hi*		Hi		Hi	Hi*		Lo	
13	7/25/55	Geneva negotiations	National (address)				Hi			Hi				
14	2/29/56	Nomination acceptance	National (address)			Lo*			Hi*					Hi
15	4/16/56	Agriculture legislation	National (address)		Lo	Lo			Hi			Hi		Lo*
16	5/25/56	Freedom and justice	Baylor University		Lo	Hi	Hi		Lo		Lo			Hi

No.	Date	Topic	Setting												
17	8/23/56	Nomination acceptance	National (Party convention)	Lo	Lo	Hi	Lo	Lo	Hi	Lo	Lo				Hi
18	10/1/56	Political accomplishments	Party rally				Hi	Lo	Hi	Lo		Hi			
19	10/31/56	Mid-East crisis	National (address)	Hi	Hi		Hi			Lo	Hi		Lo	Lo	
20	1/21/57	Price of peace	National (inaugural ceremony)			Hi	Hi*	Lo	Hi	Lo	Lo	Lo*	Lo	Lo	Lo*
21	2/20/57	Mid-East crisis	National (address)	Hi						Hi		Lo			
22	4/4/57	Education	Educational organization	Lo	Hi										
23	5/14/57	National budget	National (address)							Hi	Lo	Hi		Lo	
24	6/24/57	Power in government	Governors' conference	Lo	Hi	Lo	Hi			Hi	Lo	Lo	Lo		
25	9/23/57	Inflation	Bankers' convention			Lo		Hi							
26	6/18/57	Sherman Adams affair	News conference	Lo		Hi			Hi	Lo		Lo			
27	7/15/57	Crisis in Lebanon	National (address)	Hi	Lo	Lo	Lo	Hi		Lo	Lo	Lo	Lo*		
28	9/11/58	Formosa Straits	National (address)	Hi									Lo	Lo	
29	1/9/59	State of the Union	National (congress)			Lo	Hi				Hi	Hi		Hi	
30	8/6/59	Labor and crime	National (address)	Hi	Hi	Hi	Lo		Lo		Lo	Lo	Lo*	Lo*	
31	12/3/59	Peace and freedom	National (address)				Hi	Hi		Lo*	Hi	Hi			
32	12/23/59	Peace on earth	Holiday ceremony	Hi			Hi			Lo	Hi	Lo			
33	1/7/60	State of the Union	National (congress)	Lo			Hi	Hi		Hi*	Lo	Lo	Hi*	Hi*	Hi
34	5/2/60	International security	Political organization			Lo	Hi*								
35	5/25/60	Summit collapse	National (address)		Lo	Lo	Lo	Hi				Lo			
36	6/5/60	Public service	Notre Dame University		Lo	Lo*	Lo		Hi		Hi*	Hi	Hi*	Hi	Hi
37	7/26/60	America's goal	Party convention	Hi	Lo	Hi	Lo				Lo				Hi*
38	1/1960	Liberty	National (address)				Hi	Lo		Hi	Lo	Hi		Hi	Hi*

Profile of John Kennedy's Presidential Addresses (1961-1963)

#	DATE	TOPIC	SITUATION	Activity	Realism	Certainty	Optimism	Symbolism	Self-Reference	Familiarity	Human Interest	Embellishment	Variety	Complexity
1	1/20/61	International harmony	National (inaugural ceremony)		Hi	Hi		Hi	Lo			Hi		
2	1/21/61	Democratic party	Democratic national committee						Hi*	Hi*			Lo*	Lo*
3	1/30/61	State of the Union	National (congress)	Lo	Lo							Hi*	Hi*	Hi
4	2/13/61	Economic growth	Business conference		Lo	Lo			Lo	Lo			Hi	Lo
5	3/21/61	Labor-Management relations	Labor conference		Hi				Hi*	Hi	Hi*	Lo	Lo	Lo
6	3/23/61	Situation in Laos	Press conference	Lo		Hi					Lo		Hi	Hi
7	4/20/61	Cuba and communism	Press convention	Hi	Hi		Lo			Lo		Lo*		
8	4/27/61	President and press	Newspaper conference	Hi	Lo	Lo							Hi	Hi
9	5/25/61	Freedom	National (congress)						Hi				Hi	Hi
10	5/27/61	Democratic responsibilities	Party ceremony	Lo	Hi	Lo			Hi		Lo			
11	6/6/61	Communist challenge	National (address)		Lo*									
12	7/25/61	Berlin crisis	National (address)			Lo			Hi	Hi		Lo		
13	12/6/61	Foreign trade	Industrial conference	Hi	Lo	Lo			Hi	Lo*		Lo*	Lo	Lo*
14	1/11/62	State of the Union	National (congress)	Hi	Hi	Hi				Lo	Hi	Hi		Hi*
15	3/23/62	Foreign policy	University of California		Hi	Lo	Hi				Hi			Hi
16	4/30/62	Government and business	Business convention			Lo						Lo		

No.	Date	Topic	Event											
				Hi*	Hi	Hi*	Hi*	Hi	Hi		Lo	Lo		Lo
17	5/5/62	New Orleans' hospitality	Civic reception		Hi*	Hi	Hi*	Hi	Hi	Lo	Lo			Lo
18	5/20/62	Medical care	Senior citizens' conference		Lo	Lo	Lo							
19	6/6/62	Peace and conflict	U.S. Military Academy	Lo	Lo		Hi	Lo		Lo	Lo			Hi
20	7/4/62	Liberty	Commemorative ceremony	Lo	Lo		Hi	Hi	Lo	Lo	Hi	Lo		
21	8/13/62	National economy	National (address)	Hi*		Lo				Hi			Hi	
22	9/13/62	Space challenge	Rice University	Lo	Lo		Lo				Hi			
23	9/20/62	Pennsylvania politics	Party rally					Hi	Hi					
24	9/27/62	West Virginia politics	Party rally					Hi*	Hi*	Hi	Lo	Lo		
25	10/22/62	Arms and Cuba	National (address)	Lo	Lo		Lo			Lo	Lo	Hi	Lo	Lo
26	1/14/63	State of the Union	National (congress)	Lo	Hi		Hi	Lo	Lo	Lo	Hi	Hi	Hi	Hi
27	4/20/63	Human knowledge	Boston College	Lo*		Hi		Hi	Hi	Hi	Hi	Hi		
28	6/6/63	Importance of education	San Diego State College	Hi	Hi	Lo	Lo			Lo	Hi	Lo	Lo	Lo
29	6/10/63	World peace	American University		Hi		Hi		Lo		Hi			
30	6/11/63	Southern integration	National (address)	Lo	Hi*	Lo*	Hi	Lo	Lo	Lo		Hi	Hi	
31	7/16/63	Test ban treaty	National (address)	Lo		Lo		Lo		Lo				
32	9/18/63	Tax reductions	National (address)	Hi	Hi	Lo	Hi	Lo	Lo	Lo	Hi			Lo
33	9/28/63	Relations with Russia	University of Maine		Hi			Lo	Lo	Lo	Hi	Hi		
34	10/19/63	Democratic party	Party rally	Lo	Hi	Hi		Hi	Hi	Hi	Hi	Hi	Lo	Lo
35	10/26/63	Robert Frost's contributions	Commemorative ceremony			Hi			Hi	Hi	Hi	Hi	Lo	
36	10/30/63	Philadelphia politics	Party dinner		Hi						Lo			
37	11/15/63	Accomplishments and challenges	Labor convention	Hi			Hi	Hi		Hi	Hi	Hi	Lo	Lo
38	11/22/63	Strength of U.S.	Local meeting	Hi	Hi	Hi	Hi				Lo*	Hi	Hi	

PROFILE OF LYNDON JOHNSON'S PRESIDENTIAL ADDRESSES (1963–1969)

#	DATE	TOPIC	SITUATION	Activity	Realism	Certainty	Optimism	Symbolism	Self-Reference	Familiarity	Human Interest	Embellishment	Variety	Complexity
1	11/23/63	America's future	National (congress)			Lo			Hi	Hi		Lo		Lo
2	11/28/63	Our government	National (holiday ceremony)	Lo							Hi	Hi		Lo
3	1/8/64	State of the Union	National (congress)							Lo				Hi
4	2/26/64	Tax reduction	Bill signing ceremony						Lo	Lo				Hi*
5	4/20/64	World policy	Press convention	Lo	Hi		Hi		Lo				Lo	
6	9/7/64	Brotherhood	Commemorative ceremony		Hi			Hi*	Lo			Lo	Hi	
7	10/18/64	International affairs	National (address)	Lo*	Lo*		Lo							Hi
8	12/2/64	U.S. economy	Business organization	Hi	Lo	Hi			Hi	Lo	Lo			Hi
9	1/4/65	State of the Union	National (congress)	Hi	Lo		Lo		Hi		Hi		Hi*	
10	1/20/65	National goals	National (inaugural ceremony)			Hi	Lo		Lo		Hi		Hi	
11	3/15/65	Voting rights	National (congress)		Hi				Hi	Lo				Lo
12	4/7/65	Vietnam policy	John Hopkins University	Hi				Hi	Lo	Hi	Hi			
13	5/2/65	Dominican Republic	National (address)	Hi	Lo	Lo					Lo			Hi*
14	8/6/65	Voting rights	National (address)	Lo	Lo		Lo				Lo*			
15	8/10/65	Housing and urban development	Bill signing ceremony	Lo		Hi			Lo	Hi	Lo	Hi	Lo	Hi
16	8/29/65	News conference	Press conference		Lo	Hi	Hi					Hi*		Hi

#	Date	Topic	Southwest Texas State University													
17	11/8/65	Higher education	Southwest Texas State University	Hi			Hi	Hi	Hi	Lo	Hi	Hi				Lo
18	4/8/66	Medicare	Bill signing ceremony		Hi		Hi	Hi	Hi	Lo	Lo	Lo			Lo	Lo
19	5/17/66	Vietnam war	Party rally	Hi			Lo			Lo	Lo	Hi			Hi	Lo
20	6/8/66	Youth and education	Student association		Lo		Hi*		Lo*	Hi*	Lo					
21	6/15/66	Medicare	Medical organization		Lo		Hi*	Lo			Hi					
22	6/30/66	Vietnam war	Municipal celebration		Hi		Lo		Hi	Hi						
23	6/30/66	Democratic party	Party dinner	Hi	Hi*		Hi	Hi*	Hi*							
24	10/12/66	Democratic party	Party rally				Hi		Hi	Hi						
25	1/10/67	State of the Union	National (congress)		Lo	Lo	Lo	Lo	Lo							Lo*
26	5/9/67	Democratic party	Party dinner	Lo			Hi			Hi						
27	7/27/67	Rioting in cities	National (address)	Hi	Hi		Lo		Lo	Hi	Hi	Lo				
28	10/7/67	Job of President	Party fundraiser	Hi	Hi		Hi	Hi	Hi	Hi	Lo	Lo			Lo	Lo*
29	1/17/68	State of the Union	National (congress)				Hi		Lo	Lo	Lo				Hi	
30	3/31/68	Vietnam war	National (address)		Hi											
31	4/1/68	Freedom of press	Broadcasters' organization	Hi	Lo		Lo	Hi	Lo	Lo	Lo			Hi		
32	4/5/68	Martin Luther King	National (address)	Hi*	Hi		Hi	Hi	Hi	Lo	Lo*	Lo*	Lo	Lo	Lo
33	4/11/68	Civil rights	Bill signing ceremony	Hi		Lo	Lo				Lo				
34	4/24/68	Democratic politics	Party fundraiser	Lo	Hi	Hi	Hi			Hi	Hi				Lo*
35	6/4/68	International affairs	Glassboro State College		Hi*	Hi*		Lo		Hi	Lo*				
36	6/5/68	Domestic violence	National (address)		Lo*	Hi			Hi	Hi	Hi				
37	10/31/68	Vietnam bombing	National (congress)	Lo	Lo*		Hi		Hi	Lo	Hi				
38	1/14/69	State of the Union	National (congress)				Hi		Hi	Lo				Lo	

PROFILE OF RICHARD NIXON'S PRESIDENTIAL ADDRESSES (1969-1974)

#	DATE	TOPIC	SITUATION	Activity	Realism	Certainty	Optimism	Symbolism	Self-Reference	Familiarity	Human Interest	Embellishment	Variety	Complexity
1	1/20/69	First inaugural	National (inaugural ceremony)	Hi		Hi			Lo		Hi	Lo		Lo
2	1/29/69	State Department's importance	State Department meeting	Lo		Lo			Hi*			Lo		Lo
3	2/7/69	Senate Youth Program	Youth convention		Hi					Hi			Lo	Lo
4	3/30/69	Eulogy for Eisenhower	Funeral service							Hi*	Hi	Hi		Lo
5	3/31/69	Broadcasters' meeting	Press association			Lo					Hi			
6	4/16/69	Women's roles	Women's conference	Lo*			Lo	Hi	Hi				Lo	
7	5/7/69	Republican victory	Party rally	Lo			Hi						Lo	
8	5/14/69	Vietnam war	National (address)	Hi	Lo	Hi	Hi		Lo					Hi
9	6/3/69	Freedom	College commencement			Hi			Lo*		Lo		Hi	
10	8/8/69	Welfare reform	National (address)			Lo	Lo	Hi				Hi	Hi	
11	10/17/69	Cost of living	National (address)	Hi	Hi	Lo			Lo	Lo	Lo			
12	11/3/69	Vietnamization	National (address)	Hi	Hi		Hi	Hi						
13	11/27/69	Thanksgiving Day	Senior citizens' conference	Hi	Hi	Hi					Hi			
14	4/30/70	Cambodia	National (address)	Hi			Hi					Lo	Lo	Lo*
15	5/28/70	Faith in America	Religious crusade		Hi*	Hi*		Hi*	Hi	Lo				Hi*
16	10/19/70	Republican party	Party rally	Hi	Hi	Hi	Hi				Hi		Lo	Lo

#	Date	Topic	Venue												
17	4/7/71	Vietnam war	National (address)	Hi		Lo					Lo	Hi	Lo	Hi	
18	5/26/71	Government and the arts	Art conference			Lo					Lo	Lo	Hi	Hi	
19	8/15/71	Wages and prices	National (address)	Hi	Lo						Lo	Lo			
20	9/3/71	Work and productivity	Milk producers' convention	Hi											
21	11/19/71	National economy	Labor convention	Hi		Lo*		Hi		Hi		Lo	Lo		
22	1/25/72	Peace in Vietnam	National (address)	Hi*	Lo*	Lo		Lo		Lo		Lo	Lo		
23	5/4/72	Eulogy of J. Edgar Hoover	Funeral service		Lo	Hi*	Hi						Hi		
24	7/4/72	American Bicentennial	National (address)	Hi	Hi		Hi	Hi		Hi					
25	8/23/72	Administration goals	Party convention				Hi	Hi		Hi	Hi				
26	1/20/73	National priorities	National (inaugural ceremony)	Hi		Hi	Lo	Hi		Hi	Hi	Lo	Lo		
27	4/30/73	Watergate affair	National (address)	Hi	Lo	Lo	Hi	Lo		Lo	Lo	Lo*	Hi		
28	8/15/73	Watergate charges	National (address)		Lo			Lo	Hi	Lo*		Lo	Lo*		
29	10/12/73	Ford Vice-presidency	National (congress)	Lo		Hi			Hi	Hi		Lo*		Hi	
30	11/25/73	Energy crisis	National (address)			Lo		Lo	Lo	Hi		Lo	Lo		Hi
31	1/30/74	State of the Union	National (congress)			Hi	Lo	Lo							
32	2/23/74	Right to privacy	National (address)		Lo	Lo	Lo	Lo	Lo	Hi*	Hi*	Hi*	Hi*		Hi
33	4/10/74	Michigan republicanism	Party rally	Lo	Hi	Hi		Hi	Lo	Lo	Lo	Lo			
34	4/29/74	Presidential tapes	National (address)	Lo	Lo	Lo	Hi	Hi	Lo	Lo	Hi				
35	5/11/74	International agriculture	Oklahoma State University	Lo	Hi			Hi	Hi						
36	5/25/74	Nation's economy	National (address)			Lo	Lo	Lo		Hi	Hi		Hi	Hi	
37	8/8/74	Presidential resignation	National (address)	Lo		Lo	Lo	Lo*	Hi	Lo*	Hi	Hi	Hi*	Hi*	
38	8/9/74	Presidential resignation	National (address)		Hi	Hi	Hi	Hi	Lo	Hi	Hi*	Hi	Hi		Lo

Profile of Gerald Ford's Presidential Addresses (1974–1977)

#	DATE	TOPIC	SITUATION	Activity	Realism	Certainty	Optimism	Symbolism	Self-Reference	Familiarity	Human Interest	Embellishment	Variety	Complexity
1	8/9/74	National problems	National (swearing-in ceremony)	Lo			Hi	Hi	Hi	Lo	Hi*	Hi		
2	8/12/74	Domestic problems	National (congress)	Hi	Hi	Lo	Hi		Hi				Hi	
3	8/26/74	Economic policy	Farewell dinner	Lo										
4	8/30/74	Education and society	Ohio State University		Hi	Hi		Hi	Hi	Lo	Hi			
5	9/8/74	Nixon's pardon	National (address)	Lo	Hi									
6	9/16/74	Draft evasion	Press conference		Lo	Lo	Lo	Hi	Hi	Lo	Lo	Hi*	Hi*	Hi
7	9/27/74	Lyndon Johnson	Memorial ceremony	Hi	Lo	Hi				Lo	Lo	Lo		Hi*
8	9/28/74	Inflation	National (conference)		Lo					Hi	Lo			Hi
9	10/8/74	Economic legislation	National (congress)	Hi		Lo	Lo	Hi	Hi	Hi			Lo	Lo*
10	10/9/74	Republican politics	Party dinner	Lo*			Hi					Hi		
11	12/10/74	Football awards	Awards dinner		Lo	Lo*			Hi					Lo
12	1/13/75	Energy and economy	National (address)				Lo				Lo	Lo		
13	1/15/75	State of the Union	National (congress)	Hi*		Lo	Lo*				Lo	Lo*	Hi	Hi
14	4/10/75	Foreign policy	National (congress)				Hi	Hi*	Hi*		Hi*			Hi
15	4/16/75	National goals	Newspaper conference								Hi*	Hi*	Lo*	
16	5/27/75	Energy programs	National (address)	Hi		Lo	Lo			Hi	Lo	Lo	Hi	Hi

#	Date	Topic	Event									
17	8/19/75	U.S. military	American Legion convention	Lo	Lo*	Lo	Hi	Hi	Lo		Hi	
18	9/4/75	Republican politics	Party fundraiser				Hi	Hi		Lo		
19	9/21/75	Privacy and freedom	Stanford University				Hi*			Lo		
20	10/6/75	Federal spending	National (address)	Lo		Lo	Lo		Lo			
21	10/29/75	New York City finances	Press organization	Hi*	Hi*						Hi	
22	12/7/75	Pacific doctrine	University of Hawaii	Lo	Hi	Hi	Lo	Lo		Hi	Hi	
23	1/19/76	State of the Union	National (congress)	Hi	Hi	Hi		Lo				
24	1/29/76	Proposed legislation	Mayors' conference			Lo		Lo	Lo	Lo		
25	2/14/76	Medicare benefits	Senior citizens' meeting	Hi	Hi	Lo			Hi	Lo	Lo	
26	2/14/76	Law and justice	Bar association						Hi	Hi*		
27	2/22/76	Faith and patriotism	Religious association					Hi	Hi	Hi		
28	4/6/76	Lyndon Johnson	Dedication ceremony				Lo	Hi	Hi			
29	5/5/76	Motherhood awards	Mothers committee conference		Hi*	Hi	Lo		Hi			
30	5/24/76	Strong economy	Business conference	Hi	Lo	Lo		Lo*	Lo*	Lo	Hi	
31	5/25/76	Foreign policy	Press organization									
32	7/4/76	American freedom	Patriotic rally	Lo	Hi	Hi	Lo*		Lo*		Hi	
33	8/19/76	Nomination acceptance	Party convention	Lo	Hi	Hi	Lo	Hi	Hi	Hi	Lo	Hi
34	8/20/76	Testimony to Bob Dole	Local rally	Hi		Lo	Hi	Hi*	Hi	Lo	Lo	
35	10/6/76	International diplomacy	National (debate)		Hi					Lo	Lo	
36	10/26/76	Tax cuts	National (address)	Hi	Hi			Hi				
37	10/27/76	American senior citizens	National (address)	Hi								
38	11/2/76	Trust in the President	National (address)	Lo			Hi	Hi	Hi	Lo	Lo*	Hi

PROFILE OF JIMMY CARTER'S PRESIDENTIAL ADDRESSES (1977)

#	DATE	TOPIC	SITUATION	Activity	Realism	Certainty	Optimism	Symbolism	Self-Reference	Familiarity	Human Interest	Embellishment	Variety	Complexity
1	1/20/77	National values	National (inaugural ceremony)	Lo	Hi	Hi			Lo	Lo	Hi*	Hi		
2	1/21/77	Energy crisis	Proclamation							Hi	Lo*		Hi	
3	2/2/77	National goals	National (address)	Hi	Lo			Hi					Hi	
4	2/18/77	Democratic strengths	Party rally					Hi	Hi					
5	3/1/77	Governmental cooperation	Governors' conference	Lo	Hi*	Lo			Hi	Hi			Lo	
6	3/10/77	Women in government	Womens' conference			Lo				Hi	Hi	Lo	Lo	
7	3/30/77	S.A.L.T. talks	National (press conference)	Hi			Lo*		Lo			Lo*	Lo*	
8	3/30/77	Human rights	Womens' groups	Lo			Hi	Hi				Hi		
9	4/18/77	Energy program	National (address)						Lo	Lo	Hi			
10	4/21/77	National goals and youth	Student conference		Hi	Lo	Hi	Hi*	Hi*			Lo	Lo	Lo
11	4/28/77	Democratic party	Party conference					Hi	Hi	Hi	Lo	Lo	Lo	
12	5/2/77	Welfare reform	Press conference		Hi				Lo	Hi	Lo		Lo	
13	5/13/77	Church and state	Church conference		Hi	Lo			Hi		Hi*		Lo*	Lo*
14	5/17/77	National problems	Notre Dame University	Hi						Hi				Hi
15	5/17/77	Environmental problems	Arrival ceremony	Lo	Hi									
16	5/19/77	Arms' sales	Press conference	Hi	Lo	Hi	Lo		Lo	Lo	Lo	Lo	Hi	Hi

#	Date	Topic	Event												
17	5/22/77	National problems	Labor convention	Hi	Hi	Hi		Hi	Hi	Hi	Hi				Hi
18	5/25/77	Democratic party	Party dinner	Lo*	Lo		Hi	Hi				Lo			
19	5/23/77	Handicapped persons	Handicapped organization		Hi	Hi	Hi	Lo	Lo		Hi	Lo		Lo	
20	7/25/77	Minority programs	National Urban League	Lo		Lo		Lo	Lo	Lo	Lo		Hi	Hi	Lo
21	7/21/77	Soviet-American relations	Governmental conference				Hi				Hi		Lo	Hi*	
22	8/2/77	Drug abuse	Press conference					Lo						Hi*	
23	8/6/77	Welfare reform	National (press conference)	Hi*	Hi	Hi			Lo*		Lo				
24	8/26/77	Foreign policy	Press conference		Lo	Lo								Hi	Lo
25	9/10/77	Gubernatorial politics	Party rally			Hi	Hi								Lo
26	9/21/77	Bert Lance affair	National (press conference)	Lo*			Hi*	Hi*		Hi*				Lo	
27	9/24/77	Gubernatorial politics	Party rally	Lo*		Lo									Lo
28	9/24/77	Black progress	Black caucus	Hi											Lo
29	9/26/77	World economy	Economic conference		Hi	Hi	Lo		Lo	Lo			Hi		
30	10/7/77	Democratic goals	Democratic party conference		Lo		Hi			Hi	Hi		Hi		
31	10/12/77	Housing development	Governmental officials			Lo	Lo			Lo					
32	10/19/77	Nuclear fuel	Science conference	Lo	Hi*	Hi				Lo	Lo	Hi	Hi		
33	10/22/77	Panama Canal	Press conference		Hi	Hi	Lo	Lo		Hi					
34	10/24/77	Veterans' Day	Memorial observance	Hi	Lo	Lo									
35	11/2/77	Mid-East situation	Jewish conference		Lo		Hi	Hi		Lo					
36	11/8/77	Energy plan	National (address)		Hi*	Lo	Lo	Lo	Lo*	Lo					
37	11/15/77	Iran/U.S. relations	Diplomatic dinner	Lo	Hi	Hi	Hi	Hi		Lo	Lo		Hi	Lo	Hi*
38	11/22/77	Medal of Science	Award ceremony	Lo	Lo	Hi	Hi	Hi		Hi		Hi		Hi	Hi

Profile of Jimmy Carter's Presidential Addresses (1978)

#	DATE	TOPIC	SITUATION	Activity	Realism	Certainty	Optimism	Symbolism	Self-Reference	Familiarity	Human Interest	Embellishment	Variety	Complexity
1	1/4/78	Visit to France	Diplomatic dinner	Hi	Hi		Lo		Lo		Hi			
2	1/19/78	State of the Union	National (State of the Union)			Lo	Hi	Hi		Lo			Hi*	Lo
3	1/20/78	Salute to the south	Georgia dinner	Hi*		Lo	Hi		Hi	Hi		Lo		Lo
4	1/27/78	National goals	Democratic National Committee	Lo					Hi			Hi		Lo
5	2/1/78	Panama Canal	National (address)	Hi		Lo	Lo		Lo	Hi		Lo		
6	2/6/78	Polish Americans	White House reception						Hi	Hi*	Hi			
7	2/20/78	Democratic party	Delaware rally			Lo			Hi	Lo			Lo	
8	3/17/78	International affairs	Wake Forest University	Hi	Hi*	Hi				Lo	Hi	Lo	Lo*	
9	3/17/78	St. Patrick's Day	Society dinner	Hi		Lo*	Hi		Hi*	Lo*	Hi	Lo	Hi	Lo*
10	4/11/78	Anti-inflation policy	Newspaper conference	Hi				Hi			Lo	Lo		
11	4/28/78	Democratic party	Democratic women's conference		Hi*		Hi			Hi			Hi	Lo
12	5/2/78	Small business	Award ceremony	Hi						Lo				Lo
13	5/3/78	Solar energy	Researchers' conference	Hi	Lo*		Lo		Lo	Lo	Lo*	Lo*	Lo	
14	5/26/78	Democratic party	West Virginia rally	Lo*					Hi				Hi	
15	6/1/78	National Art Gallery	Dedication ceremony						Hi	Lo			Lo	
16	6/7/78	Military preparedness	National (U.S. Naval Academy)	Lo	Hi	Hi*	Hi	Hi	Lo			Hi	Lo	Hi

#	Date	Topic	Event											
17	6/16/78	Civil rights	Brotherhood commission	Lo								Hi		Hi
18	6/30/78	Nation's leadership	YWCA conference	Lo					Lo			Hi		
19	6/30/78	International affairs	Military ceremony				Hi*				Hi	Hi		
20	7/20/78	American agriculture	Farmers' meeting	Lo	Hi			Lo	Hi		Hi*	Hi		Lo
21	8/5/78	U.S.S. Mississippi	Commissioning ceremony	Lo	Hi		Hi				Hi	Hi		
22	8/5/78	American agriculture	Growers' Warehouse	Hi	Hi		Hi		Hi		Hi		Hi	
23	8/16/78	Central Intelligence Agency	Agency employees	Lo	Lo		Hi		Hi		Lo	Lo		
24	9/18/78	Mid-East situation	National (congress)	Lo			Lo		Lo		Lo			
25	9/22/78	Nation's progress	North Carolina rally	Lo			Hi		Lo		Lo	Lo		Hi
26	9/23/78	Democratic goals	Ohio rally	Hi	Hi		Hi*		Hi		Hi			
27	10/1/78	Space exploration	Awards ceremony	Hi	Hi		Hi		Lo		Lo	Lo		Hi
28	10/28/78	Democratic party	New York rally	Hi	Hi		Hi		Hi				Lo	
29	10/28/78	Democratic party	Maine rally		Hi	Lo*		Hi						
30	11/11/78	American history	Veterans Day ceremony	Lo					Lo		Hi			Hi*
31	11/16/78	Anti-inflation program	White House briefing	Lo	Lo				Hi					Hi
32	11/27/78	Family unity	Mormon church ceremony								Lo		Hi	Hi
33	12/5/78	Higher education	Educators' conference				Hi		Hi					Hi
34	12/6/78	Human rights	White House ceremony						Lo		Lo	Hi	Hi	Hi
35	12/5/78	New York politics	Fundraising rally	Lo	Lo		Hi				Lo			
36	1/16/78	Hubert Humphrey	National (funeral services)	Hi	Hi		Lo		Lo			Hi*	Lo	
37	12/9/78	National accomplishments	National (Tennessee rally)	Lo					Lo		Lo			
38	12/13/78	Crime	Government conference	Lo	Lo		Lo		Hi		Lo*		Hi	Hi

PROFILE OF JIMMY CARTER'S PRESIDENTIAL ADDRESSES (1979)

#	DATE	TOPIC	SITUATION	Activity	Realism	Certainty	Optimism	Symbolism	Self-Reference	Familiarity	Human Interest	Embellishment	Variety	Complexity
1	1/18/79	Moral values	Prayer breakfast		Lo		Lo			Hi				Hi*
2	1/23/79	Domestic problems	National (State of the Union)	Lo	Lo			Hi		Lo	Hi	Hi	Hi	Hi
3	1/29/79	Asian affairs	Welcoming ceremony								Hi*			Lo*
4	2/12/79	Inflation	National (press conference)				Lo			Lo	Lo		Hi*	
5	3/26/79	Middle East peace	National (ceremony)	Lo	Lo			Hi		Lo	Lo			Lo
6	3/31/79	Administration's accomplishments	Political dinner		Hi	Hi		Hi	Lo					
7	4/4/79	Hospital costs	Legislative briefing	Lo		Lo	Hi							
8	4/5/79	Energy	National (address)	Hi	Lo					Lo*				Hi
9	4/10/79	Energy	National (press conference)	Lo						Hi	Lo			Lo
10	4/24/79	Victims of the holocaust	Commemorative ceremony		Hi*	Lo	Lo			Lo		Hi		Lo
11	5/10/79	Trade policies	Retail Federation	Hi	Lo					Hi	Lo	Lo		Lo
12	5/1/79	American justice	Law Day reception	Lo	Lo		Hi					Hi		
13	5/3/79	Women and politics	League of Women Voters			Lo*			Hi	Lo	Lo			
14	5/11/79	Care for the aged	Senior citizens' group				Hi		Hi			Lo		
15	5/17/79	Segregation	Commemorative ceremony							Hi*	Lo		Hi	
16	5/20/79	Civil rights	Cheney State College		Lo	Lo	Hi				Hi		Hi	Hi

#	Date	Topic	Setting													
17	5/25/79	Democratic leadership	Democratic National Committee	Hi	Hi			Lo	Hi*		Hi		Hi	Hi	Lo	Hi
18	5/29/79	Energy	National (press conference)				Hi			Hi				Hi	Hi	
19	6/18/79	Disarmament	National (congress)	Hi	Hi	Hi		Hi				Hi	Hi	Hi	Hi	Lo
20	6/30/79	Military excellence	Welcoming ceremony	Hi	Lo	Lo		Lo			Hi*					
21	7/15/79	Crisis of confidence	National (address)	Lo	Hi	Hi					Hi*	Hi*	Lo	Lo		
22	7/16/79	Energy	Association convention	Hi*							Lo*	Lo*	Lo	Hi	Hi	
23	7/20/79	Family problems	Conference on the family	Lo							Hi	Hi	Hi	Hi		
24	7/25/79	Domestic problems	National (press conference)	Hi		Hi	Lo*		Hi			Lo*	Lo	Lo	
25	8/22/79	America's attributes	Iowa town meeting	Hi	Hi	Hi		Hi	Hi		Hi	Hi	Lo	Lo	Hi
26	8/30/79	National values	Emory University					Hi	Lo	Hi	Hi	Hi	Lo	Lo	Hi
27	9/26/79	Administration's strengths	Democratic National Committee	Lo	Lo	Lo		Hi	Lo	Lo				Hi	
28	10/1/79	Cuban/Russian troops	National (address)	Hi	Lo*	Hi	Lo*					Lo*	Lo*	Hi
29	10/11/79	American industry	Labor convention				Lo		Hi		Hi	Lo	Lo	Lo	
30	10/23/79	Equal rights amendment	White House reception					Hi	Hi	Hi	Hi	Lo	Lo	Lo
31	10/24/79	Administration's accomplishments	Fundraising dinner	Lo	Lo	Lo	Hi			Hi	Lo	Lo	Hi
32	11/15/79	Iranian crisis	Labor convention	Lo	Hi	Hi		Hi	Lo				
33	11/16/79	Conservation	White House briefing				Lo				Lo	
34	11/28/79	Iranian crisis	National (press conference)	Lo	Hi	Hi	Hi*		Hi		
35	12/2/79	Candidacy for office	National (address)			Lo		Hi	Lo	Hi	Lo
36	12/12/79	National defense	Business council		Lo					Lo	Lo
37	12/20/79	Rural economy	White House briefing	Hi		Lo	Lo			Lo	Lo	Lo
38	12/21/79	Iranian crisis	White House briefing	Lo*	Hi	Hi*	Hi	Hi	Hi	Lo	Hi*	Lo

Profile of Jimmy Carter's Presidential Addresses (1980)

#	DATE	TOPIC	SITUATION	Activity	Realism	Certainty	Optimism	Symbolism	Self-Reference	Familiarity	Human Interest	Embellishment	Variety	Complexity
1	1/4/80	Invasion of Afghanistan	National (address)	Hi		Hi				Lo	Lo		Lo	
2	1/13/80	Energy policy	Business conference		Lo	Lo					Lo	Hi	Hi*	Hi*
3	1/23/80	Middle East hostilities	National (State of the Union)				Hi		Lo	Lo				
4	1/27/80	Human rights	Humphrey award dinner				Lo			Hi			Lo	
5	2/19/80	International tensions	American Legion conference	Hi	Lo		Hi			Lo	Hi	Hi		
6	3/14/80	Inflation	National (report)		Lo*		Lo			Lo	Lo	Hi		
7	3/26/80	Administration's agenda	Democratic dinner	Lo					Lo*		Hi	Hi	Hi	
8	4/10/80	Russian aggressiveness	Newspaper convention	Hi	Lo	Hi	Lo		Lo*	Hi	Lo*		Lo	
9	4/25/80	Iran crisis	National (address)		Lo	Hi			Hi	Hi	Hi			
10	5/1/80	Human services	Committee for the handicapped						Hi	Hi		Hi		
11	5/9/80	Middle East problems	World Affairs Council				Hi		Lo	Lo	Hi	Hi	Hi	
12	5/15/80	Equal rights amendment	White House briefing			Lo*				Hi				
13	5/19/80	Administration's goals	Democratic committee	Lo		Hi					Hi	Hi		Lo
14	5/26/80	Military greatness	Military tour				Lo				Lo	Lo		
15	6/5/80	Family life	Family conference	Lo					Hi		Hi	Lo	Hi	Lo
16	6/9/80	Youth and work	Labor conference	Hi							Lo	Lo		

No.	Date	Topic	Event										
17	6/10/80	Human services	Mayors' conference	Hi									Lo
18	6/12/80	Democratic opportunities	Democratic National Committee	Hi*	Hi								Lo
19	6/18/80	Administration's accomplishments	Fundraising dinner	Hi	Lo	Lo					Hi		Lo
20	7/1/80	Bravery in battle	Bill signing ceremony	Lo									Hi
21	7/3/80	Public education	Education association			Hi	Lo						Hi
22	7/4/80	Civil rights	Civil rights conference	Hi		Lo							Hi
23	7/17/80	Democratic achievements	Democratic fundraiser	Lo		Hi		Hi					
24	7/18/80	American values	Youth conference	Hi*	Hi*		Hi			Lo	Hi		
25	7/22/80	Natural resources	Bill signing ceremony		Lo	Lo				Lo			
26	7/25/80	American values	Democratic reception	Hi	Hi	Lo	Hi				Lo		
27	7/30/80	Sports and politics	Medal presentation ceremony	Lo		Hi*	Lo		Hi*				
28	8/4/80	Billy Carter	National (press conference)	Hi	Lo		Hi	Hi*	Hi*	Lo	Lo*		Hi
29	8/5/80	Courage and injustice	Medal presentation ceremony		Lo			Hi		Lo			
30	9/4/80	Middle East peace	B'nai Brith conference		Lo		Hi	Lo		Lo	Hi		
31	9/9/80	Economic progress	Dedication ceremony	Lo	Hi								
32	9/23/80	World peace	Democratic fundraiser		Hi	Hi		Lo	Lo				
33	10/6/80	Business advances	Political rally	Hi				Lo	Lo				Lo
34	10/6/80	Nation's challenges	Voter registration rally	Lo	Hi	Hi		Lo*		Lo*			
35	10/28/80	National opportunities	National (debate)	Lo*	Hi	Hi*	Hi	Lo		Lo			Lo*
36	11/1/80	Experiences as President	Political rally	Hi	Lo	Hi		Lo			Lo		Lo
37	11/4/80	Experiences as President	Georgia residents		Lo*	Hi	Hi	Hi		Lo*			Hi
38	11/4/80	Election results	National (rally)	Hi	Hi*	Hi*	Hi	Hi*		Lo			Lo

Profile of Ronald Reagan's Presidential Addresses (1981)

#	DATE	TOPIC	SITUATION	Activity	Realism	Certainty	Optimism	Symbolism	Self-Reference	Familiarity	Human Interest	Embellishment	Variety	Complexity
1	1/20/81	National values	Inaugural (t.v.)	Lo	Hi	Hi*	Lo	Hi*			Hi		Lo	Hi*
2	1/27/81	Iranian hostages	White House ceremony (t.v.)		Lo	Lo	Hi				Hi*	Hi		Lo
3	2/5/81	Economy	National (address)		Lo		Lo				Lo	Lo	Hi	
4	2/18/81	Economy	National (Joint Session)							Lo	Lo*			
5	2/26/81	Britain/U.S. relations	White House ceremony	Lo	Hi		Hi		Lo		Hi	Hi*		
6	3/20/81	National solidarity	Conservative conference			Lo					Hi		Hi	
7	4/30/81	Holocaust	Commemorative ceremony		Hi	Hi	Lo	Hi			Hi	Lo*	Lo	
8	5/27/81	National solidarity	West Point graduation			Hi								
9	6/16/81	National problems	Press conference (t.v.)											Lo
10	6/22/81	Athletics & spirit	White House reception		Lo	Lo	Hi*		Hi*		Lo*	Hi		Lo*
11	6/29/81	Racial integration	N.A.A.C.P. conference		Hi	Hi	Lo	Hi						
12	7/7/81	Supreme Court appoint.	Briefing (t.v.)	Lo					Hi	Hi			Hi	
13	7/27/81	Economy	National (t.v.)				Hi			Lo*		Hi	Lo*	
14	9/10/81	National defense	Military ceremony	Hi			Hi							
15	9/18/81	Ford presidency	Dedication ceremony	Hi	Hi	Hi		Hi	Lo*	Hi*		Hi	Hi	
16	9/22/81	Multiple Sclerosis	Fund-raising ball	Lo	Lo			Hi						

#	Date	Topic	National (t.v.)							
17	9/24/81	Economy	Lo						Lo	Lo
18	9/28/81	International crime	Police convention	Lo						Hi
19	10/1/81	National problems	Press conference (t.v.)	Hi	Lo	Hi	Lo	Lo	Lo	Hi*	Lo
20	10/13/81	U.S./Spanish relations	State dinner	Lo	Lo						Hi
21	10/15/81	Foreign policy	World Affairs Council	Hi	Lo	Hi	Lo	Lo	Hi	Hi
22	11/6/81	Irish heritage	Historical Society	Hi	Hi		Hi			Hi
23	11/13/81	Americanism	Texas Republican meeting	Hi*	Lo	Hi	Hi	Hi	Lo	Hi*	Hi
24	11/18/81	Republicanism	Republican dinner	Hi*	Hi	Hi	Hi	Lo	Lo

DESCRIPTIVE STATISTICS FOR *DICTION*-PROCESSED LANGUAGE SAMPLES

TABLE B.1

OVERALL STATISTICAL DATA FOR LANGUAGE SAMPLES

Variable	Presidential sample (N = 380)				All samples (N = 861)			
	Mean	Standard deviation	Minimum	Maximum	Mean	Standard deviation	Minimum	Maximum
Activity	200.6	20.3	146.5	269.5	202.5	19.1	132.0	269.5
Realism	192.3	16.2	157.9	255.0	187.0	16.7	124.3	255.0
Certainty	185.5	18.7	134.5	251.4	186.8	19.5	124.9	252.0
Optimism	218.7	17.3	161.6	256.2	214.2	18.0	161.6	264.8
Complexity	5.11	0.79	3.90	7.60	5.39	0.83	3.90	8.20
Variety	.489	.037	.324	.584	.492	.039	.324	.604
Self-Reference	8.01	7.19	0.0	39.0	6.91	6.89	0.0	49.0
Familiarity	102.1	10.8	68.0	133.0	104.1	11.0	68.0	106.0
Embellishment	.067	.061	0.0	.500	.061	.057	0.0	.500
Human Interest	27.5	9.8	2.0	86.0	28.5	10.8	0.0	86.0
Symbolism	4.99	5.06	0.0	25.0	—	—	—	—

TABLE B.2

Institutional Correlates of Presidential Style

	Presidents (N = 380)	Corporation executives (N = 50)	Social activists (N = 50)	Political campaigners (N = 129)	Religious leaders (N = 160)	F	P
Activity	200.6	205.3	206.2	202.1	204.1	1.92	.10
Realism	192.4	176.2	184.9	186.2	178.8	27.90	.00
Certainty	185.5	182.4	183.2	188.9	192.3	5.12	.00
Optimism	218.7	205.9	201.3	211.4	212.8	17.39	.00
Complexity	5.11	5.33	5.51	5.31	5.60	14.32	.00
Variety	.488	.507	.504	.503	.485	8.06	.00
Self-Reference	8.01	4.78	6.88	5.27	5.85	6.49	.00
Familiarity	102.1	103.4	104.9	102.2	110.3	17.85	.00
Human Interest	27.5	22.4	26.3	27.8	31.2	7.91	.00
Embellishment	.066	.060	.050	.058	.060	1.28	.27

TABLE B.3

SITUATIONAL ASPECTS OF RICHARD NIXON'S STYLE

	Speech location[a]				Speaking format[a]				Time period			
	Domestic (N = 19)	Foreign (N = 5)	t	p	Impromptu (N = 12)	Prepared Text (N = 12)	t	p	Presidential (N = 38)	Vice-presidential (N = 29)	t	p
Activity	202.0	205.7	.43	.67	194.4	211.1	2.04	.05	205.8	203.8	.50	.62
Realism	190.3	204.9	3.12	.00	197.0	189.6	1.19	.24	204.3	193.2	2.53	.01
Certainty	189.9	200.6	.99	.36	197.3	187.0	1.27	.22	190.2	190.2	.01	.99
Optimism	209.5	221.3	1.47	.16	217.1	206.7	1.19	.24	215.6	215.6	.01	.99
Complexity	5.72	5.60	.32	.76	5.53	5.85	1.35	.19	4.53	4.73	3.13	.00
Variety	.459	.432	2.12	.06	.429	.457	2.77	.01	.453	.489	3.71	.00
Self-Reference	7.79	9.20	.46	.66	9.08	7.08	.95	.35	10.1	5.1	3.29	.00
Familiarity	107.5	112.4	1.19	.27	110.5	106.6	1.17	.25	109.1	103.3	2.46	.01
Human Interest	28.9	40.0	2.10	.03	31.8	30.8	.21	.42	29.7	32.5	1.12	.13
Embellishment	.056	.058	.10	.93	.066	.047	1.03	.31	.044	.052	.95	.34
Symbolism	4.26	9.00	1.13	.30	5.33	5.16	.06	.95	6.79	6.27	.37	.71

[a]Speeches on international topics only.

TABLE B.4

SITUATIONAL ASPECTS OF LYNDON JOHNSON'S STYLE

	Congressional speeches (N = 30)	Presidential speeches (N = 38)	t	p
Activity	198.5	202.8	1.03	.16
Realism	184.4	195.4	3.21	.00
Certainty	186.3	185.4	.20	.84
Optimism	208.0	219.2	2.95	.00
Complexity	6.83	4.46	15.05	.00
Variety	.492	.489	.45	.65
Self-Reference	5.20	7.68	1.96	.03
Familiarity	101.2	97.0	1.94	.03
Human Interest	36.1	29.4	2.94	.00
Embellishment	.0506	.0556	.56	.58
Symbolism	4.27	5.08	.57	.54

TABLE B.5

SIGNIFICANT CORRELATIONS BETWEEN VARIABLES
FOR ASSORTED LANGUAGE SAMPLES ($p < .01$)

Correlated variables	Presidents	Political candidates	Religious leaders	Corporation executives	Social activists
Activity—Optimism	−.224	−.226			
Activity—Familiarity			.202		
Activity—Variety					−.250
Realism—Variety	−.418	−.356	−.306		−.408
Realism—Optimism				.258	−.243
Realism—Self-Reference				.226	.257
Realism—Embellishment			−.200		−.240
Realism—Certainty	.204				.254
Certainty—Embellishment					−.369
Certainty—Human Interest					
Certainty—Complexity		−.218			
Optimism—Embellishment	.200				
Optimism—Self-Reference				.223	
Optimism—Human Interest		.339			
Optimism—Variety		−.222			
Embellishment—Familiarity			−.326	−.253	
Embellishment—Complexity			.205		
Embellishment—Variety					.326
Embellishment—Self-Reference					−.306
Embellishment—Human Interest					−.463
Variety—Complexity	.229	.299	.263		
Variety—Familiarity	−.326		−.333		−.331
Variety—Human Interest	−.247	−.290	−.262		−.329
Variety—Self-Reference	−.214	−.289			−.227
Self-Reference—Human Interest				.230	.267
Symbolism—Realism	.286	—	—	—	—
Symbolism—Certainty	.228	—	—	—	—
Symbolism—Variety	−.251	—	—	—	—
Symbolism—Human Interest	.223	—	—	—	—

TABLE B.6
Developmental Correlates of Presidential Style

	Presidential era				Time during administration			
	Early modern (N = 114)	Later modern (N = 266)	t	p	First half (N = 190)	Second half (N = 190)	t	p
Activity	201.7	200.1	.66	.51	199.9	201.4	.69	.49
Realism	193.0	192.1	.53	.59	193.6	191.1	1.48	.13
Certainty	192.8	182.3	4.72	.00	182.9	188.0	2.69	.00
Optimism	216.1	219.7	1.82	.07	219.7	217.6	1.15	.25
Complexity	4.64	5.31	11.13	.00	5.01	5.21	2.43	.01
Variety	.492	.486	1.40	.16	.489	.487	.42	.67
Self-Reference	4.43	9.54	8.12	.00	9.23	6.79	3.35	.00
Familiarity	102.8	101.8	.89	.37	101.9	102.3	.32	.75
Human Interest	26.1	28.0	1.80	.04	27.4	27.5	.09	.93
Embellishment	.0696	.0654	.65	.51	.069	.064	.91	.36
Symbolism	3.22	5.78	5.23	.00	4.62	5.41	1.52	.13

TABLE B.7

Generic Differences within Presidential Language Sample

	Political rally (N = 29)	Inaugural (N = 8)	State of the Union (N = 18)	College commencement (N = 14)	Ceremonial (N = 23)	F	p
Activity	194.8	206.9	206.3	194.4	200.9	1.297	.27
Realism	202.9	197.1	190.0	197.4	199.5	1.357	.25
Certainty	187.8	212.9	178.3	197.2	193.0	5.691	.00
Optimism	222.7	224.6	221.4	219.9	226.7	0.415	.79
Complexity	4.655	4.650	5.055	4.871	4.739	1.505	.20
Variety	.471	.476	.521	.504	.478	5.172	.00
Self-Reference	11.20	1.12	5.38	3.28	9.39	5.750	.00
Familiarity	109.2	99.6	93.1	102.7	104.6	6.083	.00
Human Interest	28.6	38.01	27.8	25.1	31.9	3.411	.01
Embellishment	.0487	.0840	.0788	.0722	.0877	1.145	.34
Symbolism	6.27	6.78	4.11	6.14	6.60	0.789	.53

TABLE B.8

Personality Correlates of Presidential Style

	Truman (N = 38)	Eisenhower (N = 38)	Kennedy (N = 38)	Johnson (N = 38)	Nixon (N = 38)	Ford (N = 38)	Carter (N = 152)	Reagan (N = 24)	F	p
Activity	201.9	199.3	203.9	202.8	205.8	199.5	198.3	209.9	1.63	.12
Realism	194.2	186.6	198.4	195.4	204.3	191.2	188.4	182.0	8.33	.00
Certainty	196.9	191.6	190.0	185.4	190.1	176.1	181.1	175.9	7.35	.00
Optimism	218.5	216.7	213.1	219.2	215.6	218.9	221.2	220.4	1.31	.24
Complexity	4.63	4.73	4.58	4.46	4.52	4.65	5.89	5.72	89.75	.00
Variety	.480	.504	.493	.489	.453	.502	.490	.518	10.62	.00
Self-Reference	3.97	4.65	4.68	7.68	10.05	12.89	9.04	8.38	8.31	.00
Familiarity	107.9	98.2	102.4	97.1	109.1	97.7	102.1	101.4	7.37	.00
Human Interest	27.4	24.9	26.0	29.4	29.7	25.2	28.0	28.3	1.31	.24
Embellishment	.073	.065	.070	.056	.044	.072	.072	.034	2.15	.03
Symbolism	4.50	2.97	2.21	5.08	6.79	4.02	6.15	3.91	4.80	.00

TABLE B.9

Situational Effects Upon Presidents' Styles[a]

	Topic	Audience	Time	Audience × Time	Audience × Topic	Topic × Time	Topic × Audience
Activity	————	5.341(DDE) 12.700(←)	3.875(JEC)	————	3.284(JEC)	4.238(DDE)	————
Realism	————	4.238(DDE) 5.402(RMN)	4.209(LBJ) 15.006(JEC)	————	————	————	3.258(GRF)

Certainty	4.417(JFK) 10.213(JEC) 3.800(↔)	------	7.050(↔) 3.905(GRF) 6.675(JEC)	------	6.652(LBJ) 7.113(RWR)	------	------
Optimism	7.948(HST) 3.260(↔)	11.070(↔)	------	4.667(DDE) 3.870(↔)	------	------	------
Complexity	3.690(↔) 3.157(JFK) 3.257(LBJ)	6.550(LBJ) 6.292(RMN) 22.030(↔)	8.730(↔) 8.634(HST) 4.945(LBJ) 29.673(JEC)	8.820(↔)	4.861(RWR)	------	------
Variety	3.182(JFK)	8.470(RMN)	------	6.087(JFK)	------	------	3.179(JEC)
Self-Reference	3.273(JFK) 4.110(JEC) 7.420(↔)	4.076(JFK) 5.916(RMN) 6.200(↔)	5.522(JFK) 17.273(GRF) 11.190(↔)	4.312(LBJ) 8.609(JEC) 7.080(↔)	4.626(LBJ)	4.223(HST)	------
Familiarity	4.845(JFK) 4.647(LBJ)	4.799(JFK) 8.720(↔)	------	7.657(LBJ) 7.098(RWR)	3.059(JEC) 7.130(↔)	3.844(LBJ)	------
Human Interest	3.204(JFK) 4.008(JEC) 9.136(RWR)	4.502(LBJ) 4.857(RMN) 9.910(↔)	------	4.809(RWR)	3.205(LBJ) 6.970(RWR)	------	5.895(GRF) 3.630(↔)
Embellishment	3.520(JFK) 6.552(JEC) 5.220(↔)	------	4.820(JEC)		9.466(JEC) 12.420(↔)	4.192(JEC)	3.719(JEC)
Symbolism	5.722(RWR) 4.762(HST)	6.225(RWR) 5.793(HST) 9.091(LBJ)	7.149(JEC)	------	9.432(RWR) 3.456(LBJ) 7.528(JEC)	------	------

[a] In all F values reported, $p < .05$. ↔ Overall effect for all presidents.

TABLE B.10

MAJOR CORRELATIONS BETWEEN VARIABLES FOR PRESIDENTIAL LANGUAGE SAMPLES (P < .01)

Correlated Variables	All presidents	Truman	Eisenhower	Kennedy	Johnson	Nixon	Ford	Carter	Reagan
Activity–Realism	.223					-.342		-.229	
Activity–Optimism							-.407	-.240	
Activity–Variety			-.393			.442		.234	
Activity–Human Interest	.204		.308			.292	-.407	-.202	
Realism–Certainty		.382							
Realism–Optimism								.225	
Realism–Self-Reference				.504					
Realism–Variety	-.418			-.637		-.516	-.324	-.272	
Certainty–Embellishment									
Certainty–Optimism					.308			.227	-.711
Optimism–Human Interest	.200	.336					.503	.236	
Optimism–Embellishment	.229							.193	
Complexity–Variety			.649	.757	.454	.561	.576		
Complexity–Self-Reference				-.389	-.378		-.400	-.299	
Complexity–Familiarity				-.469			-.529		
Complexity–Human Interest	-.213	-.392	-.402		-.439	-.700			
Variety–Self-Reference	-.326			-.394				-.292	
Variety–Familiarity	-.291			-.416				-.375	
Variety–Human Interest						-.423	-.389		
Self-Reference–Familiarity				.414				.304	.272
Self-Reference–Embellishment								-.249	-.380
Familiarity–Embellishment			-.353						-.370
Human Interest–Embellishment									.368
Symbolism–Realism	.206		.399						
Symbolism–Certainty	.228	.451	.389			.564		.242	.642
Symbolism–Optimism									-.608
Symbolism–Variety	-.252			-.410		-.391		-.197	
Symbolism–Human Interest	.204				-.388				
Symbolism–Complexity				-.362					

TABLE B.11

STYLISTIC DIFFERENCES BETWEEN AMERICAN PRESIDENTS AND THEIR POLITICAL RIVALS: PART 1

	Truman–Dewey				Eisenhower–Stevenson				Kennedy–Nixon			
	Truman	Dewey	t	p	Eisenhower	Stevenson	t	p	Kennedy	Nixon	t	p
Activity	205.7	199.9	1.01	.31	192.3	199.5	1.05	.30	208.3	203.8	.97	.33
Realism	193.2	188.7	1.29	.20	179.4	187.3	1.72	.09	198.4	193.1	.79	.43
Certainty	194.5	197.0	.46	.64	184.8	189.6	.78	.44	184.1	190.1	1.11	.27
Optimism	220.4	209.1	2.06	.04	218.4	215.1	.64	.52	213.9	215.6	.37	.71
Complexity	4.74	5.09	2.71	.01	4.75	4.63	6.11	.00	4.62	4.73	1.36	.18
Variety	.487	.495	.66	.51	.512	.498	1.31	.19	.497	.489	.69	.49
Self-Reference	4.78	3.10	1.53	.13	7.10	4.84	.94	.35	6.21	5.06	.77	.44
Familiarity	107.9	106.6	.39	.70	102.1	98.7	1.04	.30	101.3	103.2	.61	.54
Human Interest	25.8	27.7	.03	.97	26.1	26.7	.37	.71	26.7	32.4	1.33	.19
Embellishment	.0681	.0688	.05	.96	.0779	.0667	.93	.35	.0578	.0520	.37	.72

TABLE B.12

Stylistic Differences Between American Presidents and Their Political Rivals: Part 2

	Johnson–Goldwater				Nixon–Humphrey				Nixon–McGovern			
	Johnson	Goldwater	t	p	Nixon	Humphrey	t	p	Nixon	McGovern	t	p
Activity	200.8	206.7	1.06	.29	205.3	201.6	.68	.50	206.2	207.2	.22	.82
Realism	191.5	179.8	3.38	.00	208.6	188.9	2.91	.00	199.9	183.7	2.80	.00
Certainty	185.9	194.5	1.67	.10	190.6	191.2	.10	.92	189.6	174.8	2.56	.01
Optimism	217.9	204.7	2.72	.01	216.6	215.0	.29	.77	214.6	206.7	1.30	.20
Complexity	4.54	5.19	4.45	.00	4.43	5.69	6.48	.00	4.61	5.67	9.89	.00
Variety	.492	.509	1.97	.05	.445	.501	3.74	.00	.460	.517	5.10	.00
Self-Reference	7.47	4.20	1.82	.08	10.60	6.65	1.70	.10	9.52	5.65	1.95	.06
Familiarity	95.2	100.2	1.80	.08	109.1	99.4	1.71	.00	109.1	101.5	2.26	.03
Human Interest	28.7	22.8	2.46	.01	31.4	27.0	1.71	.09	27.9	28.7	.87	.39
Embellishment	.0551	.0439	.85	.39	.0405	.0559	1.67	.10	.0484	.0511	.19	.84

TABLE B.13

STATISTICAL DATA FOR CARTER LANGUAGE SAMPLES
($N = 152$)

Variable	Mean	Standard deviation	Minimum	Maximum
Activity	198.3	20.9	146.5	252.2
Realism	188.4	13.8	161.8	233.0
Certainty	181.1	14.7	134.5	217.3
Optimism	221.1	15.8	173.0	255.2
Complexity	5.89	0.67	4.30	7.60
Variety	.491	.029	.416	.558
Self-Reference	9.0	7.57	0.00	37.0
Familiarity	102.1	9.9	68.0	126.0
Embellishment	.071	.075	0.00	.500
Human Interest	28.1	9.64	9.00	86.0
Symbolism	6.01	5.52	0.00	25.0
Approval rating[a]	45.1	12.3	26.0	66.0

[a] CBS/*New York Times* Polls (figures are percentages).

MAJOR EVENTS DURING
THE CARTER PRESIDENCY

MAJOR EVENTS IN CARTER PRESIDENCY

Time period	International events	National events	Administration events	N.Y. Times/CBS news poll (approval rating) (%)
Winter 1977	Rabin wins election in Israel. U.S. aid to Argentina, Ethiopia, and Uruguay cut because of human rights violations. Indira Gandhi resigns in India.	Draft evaders pardoned. Tax cut bill sent to Congress. Natural gas shortages occur. Soviet dissident received at White House.	Carter conducts phone-in with American citizens. Senate confirms new cabinet. Carter attends first "town meeting."	66
Spring 1977	U.S. and Cuba negotiate fishing rights. Likud Party wins in Israel.	Senate adopts ethics code. Tax rebate plan scotched by Carter. Carter signs public works bill. Rosalynn Carter tours Latin America. B-1 bomber plan scotched by Carter.	Carter speaks on energy. Carter's problems with congressional relations reported.	64
Summer 1977	OPEC raises oil prices. Panama and U.S. reach agreement on canal. U.S. and Canada reach agreement on pipeline.	Dept. of Energy created. Welfare reform bill sent to Congress. Deregulation of natural gas filibustered in Senate.	Bert Lance's financial practices scrutinized. Lance resigns as Director of the Budget. Blacks accuse Carter of nonsupport	62

(continued)

287

MAJOR EVENTS IN CARTER PRESIDENCY (*Continued*)

Time period	International events	National events	Administration events	N.Y. Times/CBS news poll (approval rating) (%)
Fall 1977	Begin invites Sadat to Israel. Carter arrives in Poland to begin six-nation tour.	Carter signs human rights treaties. SALT pact announced. Senate passes energy plan. Carter vetoes nuclear-reactor funding. Coal strike announced. Carter signs social security bill.	"Georgia Mafia" held up for criticism by congressional insiders.	55
Winter 1978	Sadat visits U.S. U.S. sells warplanes to Egypt, Saudi Arabia, and Israel. Israel invades Lebanon. Panama Canal treaty approval by U.S. Senate.	Carter's first state of the Union speech. Coal miners strike. Plan for revitalization of U.S. cities announced by Carter.	Bert Lance turns in diplomatic passport.	51
Spring 1978	U.N. troops stand guard in Lebanon.	Carter administration sells gold to protect the dollar. Postal rates increase sharply. California voters approve Proposition 13.	Camp David meeting on administration's priorities. Rafshoon added to White House staff. Democrats resist Carter campaign help.	46

Summer 1978	U.S. resumes direct economic aid to India. Shah of Iran appoints new government. Cuba agrees to let 1000 prisoners emigrate to U.S. Carter meets Sadat and Begin at Camp David.	Carter signs bill for loans to New York City. Carter vetoes defense procurement bill.	Dr. Peter Bourne forced to resign White House job. Rosalynn Carter defends White House accomplishments. George Meany attacks Carter administration. Tip O'Neill and Carter wrangle over Griffin appointment. Carter campaigns for congressional candidates.	38
Fall 1978	John Paul II named Roman Catholic pontiff. Sadat and Begin named Nobel Prize winners. OPEC announces oil price hikes.	Congress passes oil control bill. Carter announces voluntary wage-price guidelines. Republicans make modest gains in off-year elections. Carter announces U.S./China accord.	Women's group upbraids Carter record on women's rights. Nixon attacks Carter on human rights. Media report Carter's rise in polls.	45
Winter 1979	Shah leaves Iran. Chinese Deputy Premier vists U.S. Ayatollah Khomeini returns to Iran. Egypt-Israel peace treaty signed.	Carter sends Congress an "inflation-curbing" budget. Bureau of Labor statistics report highest inflation in 4½ years.	Carter dismisses Bella Abzug from Advisory Commission. Billy Carter makes "anti-Semitic" remarks. Jerry Brown attacks Carter record. Carter warns staff to demonstrate loyalty.	42

(continued)

MAJOR EVENTS IN CARTER PRESIDENCY (*Continued*)

Time period	International events	National events	Administration events	N.Y. Times/CBS news poll (approval rating) (%)
Spring 1979	Carter signs bill for unofficial U.S./Taiwan relations. U.S./Soviet exchange of political prisoners. State of Siege declared in El Salvador. Carter and Breshnev sign SALT II treaty.	Carter announces plans for windfall profits tax. Gas rationing begins in California. Carter approves development of MX missile.	Black officials meet to discuss administration's progress on racial matters. Carter defends record to Democratic National Committee. Polls reveal Carter is seen as likable but incompetent.	37
Summer 1979	Andrew Young resigns as U.N. representative. Justice Department ends "Koreagate" probe. Soviet troops in Cuba revealed by U.S.	Carter conducts Camp David domestic summit meeting. Carter delivers "crisis of confidence" speech. Congress creates Department of Education.	Hamilton Jordan becomes Chief of Staff. Carter accepts several Cabinet resignations. Carter announces fewer press conferences. Carter hosts picnic for organized labor. Carter conducts "town meeting" in New York City.	37

Fall 1979	Pope arrives in U.S. Shah of Iran arrives in U.S. U.S. embassy in Iran taken by students. Soviets invade Afghanistan. Shah leaves U.S. for Panama.	Federal Reserve tightens U.S. money supply. Carter approves Chrysler loan guarantees. Kennedy, Reagan, and Carter announce candidacies.	Secretaries of Commerce and Education appointed.	31
Winter 1980	Grain shipments to Russia curtailed. U.S. "mistakenly" condemns Israeli settlements.	Carter cancels U.S. Olympic participation. Price of gold hits $875 an ounce. Carter gives state of Union address. Reagan and Carter win New Hampshire primaries. Carter announces anti-inflation program.	Carter refuses to campaign around U.S. Ted Kennedy attacks Carter administration in several major speeches.	52
Spring 1980	Cuban refugees arrive in U.S. U.S. rescue mission fails in Iran. Carter tours Europe.	Banks raise interest rates to 20%. John Anderson announces independent candidacy. Unemployment reaches 7.8%. Draft registration bill passes.	Hamilton Jordan leaves White House to run reelection campaign. Cyrus Vance resigns. Muskie named Secretary of State. Carter makes first public appearance in over 6 months.	40

(continued)

MAJOR EVENTS IN CARTER PRESIDENCY *(Continued)*

Time period	International events	National events	Administration events	N.Y. Times/CBS news poll (approval rating) (%)
Summer 1980	Carter meets Chinese Premier in Tokyo. Polish workers strike. Iran/Iraq battle escalates.	Federal Reserve ends credit controls. Carter announces auto industry assistance. Carter, Reagan nominated. Draft registration begins. Reagan/Anderson conduct debate.	Bill Carter's Libyan ties revealed. Carter approves special panel for investigation of Billy Carter.	30
Fall 1980–Winter 1981	Iraqi troops surround Iran oil fields. Iran sets conditions for release of hostages. Iran releases hostages.	Carter and Reagan hold debate. Ford Motor Company reports largest losses ever. Reagan wins the presidency.	Justice Department accuses Carter of non-cooperation in brother's investigation.	26

SEMANTIC COMPONENTS OF *DICTION* PROGRAM

Notes

1. On the following pages, asterisks (*) indicate homographic terms. Counts for such terms were differentially weighted within the various subdictionaries by applying statistical norms for usage of those terms. Thus, for example, when the word "state" was used in a given passage, 33.3% of its occurrences were recorded in the Activity subdictionary termed Communicativeness (as in "Please state your opinion") and 33.3% of its occurrences were recorded in the Realism subdictionary termed Concreteness (as in "the state of California"). Had DICTION contained a subdictionary called Philosophical Abstraction, the remaining 33.3% of the occurrences of "state" would have been assigned to that variable (as in "the state of uncertainty"). The sourcebook used to assign these differential weightings is referenced in the Notes of Chapter One, n. 38.

2. Scores for the Major Dictionaries were generated by standardizing all subdictionary totals and then combining them as follows:

Certainty = [Rigidity + Leveling + Collectives + Power Factor] − [Numerical Frequency + Qualification + Self-Reference + Variety]

Optimism = [Praise + Satisfaction + Inspiration] − [Adversity + Negation]

Activity = [Aggressiveness + Accomplishment + Communicativeness] − [Intellectuality + Passivity + Embellishment]

Realism = [Familiarity + Spatial Awareness + Temporal Awareness
+ Present Concern + Human Interest + Concreteness]
− [Past Concern + Complexity]

Definitions of Subdictionaries

Rigidity: Treats all forms of the verb "to be" as indicators of complete certainty.

Leveling: Words used to ignore individual difference or distinctiveness.

Collectives: Singular nouns connoting plurality that function to decrease specificity.

Power Factor: A measure of code restriction; a high Power Factor indicates repeated use of a finite number of terms. Calculated by Hart to be a measure of linguistic "contentedness."[1]

Numerical Frequency: Any sum, date, or product that serves to specify the facts in a given case. (Includes both numerals and verbal constructions.)

Qualification: Conditional or ambivalent words that assist a speaker in stepping away from a verbalization.

Self-Reference: Signals one's refusal to speak ex cathedra and a willingness to acknowledge the limitations of one's opinions. (Includes all first-person pronouns)

Variety: Johnson's type-token ratio, which divides total different words by total words.[2] A high TTR indicates a speaker's unwillingness to repeat himself or herself and, presumably, a desire for linguistic precision.

Praise: Verbal affirmations of some person or idea.

Satisfaction: Words normally associated with a positive, affective state.

Inspiration: Abstract virtues deserving of universal respect.

Adversity: Reference to negative feelings or dangerous events.

Negation: Verbal constructions that function to deny.

Aggressiveness: Words indicating assertiveness or competition.

Accomplishment: Connotations of movement or completion of a task.

Communicativeness: Reference to social interaction.

Intellectuality: Remarks about cerebral, reflective processes.

Passivity: Words implying lack of motor or psychic acivity.

Symbolism: A list of the nation's sacred terms, containing both designative as well as ideological language.

---

1. R. P. Hart, "Absolutism and Situation: Prolegomena to a Rhetorical Biography of Richard M. Nixon," *Communication Monographs,* 43 (1976), pp. 204–228.

2. W. Johnson, *People in Quandries* (New York: Harper, 1946).

Embellishment: A selective ratio of adjectives to verbs based, in part, on Boder's conceptualization that heavy use of adjectival constructions "slows down" a verbal passage.[3]

Familiarity: Consists of Ogden's "operation" and "direction" words that he calculates to be among the 750 most frequently encountered terms.[4]

Spatial Awareness: Practical words referring to geographical boundaries or physical distances.

Temporal Awareness: Terms that fix an event or person within a specific time frame.

Present Concern: A selected list of present-tense verbs that recur frequently in everyday talk.

Human Interest: An adaptation of Flesch's notion that a heavy concentration on human beings gives discourse a life-like quality.[5]

Concreteness: References to physical objects, sociological or geographical units, or natural forces.

Past Concern: Past-tense constructions of the present-tense verbs described above.

Complexity: A simple measure of the average number of characters-per-word of a given passage (also known as MLU, or Mean Length of Utterance). Borrows Flesch's notion that linguistic convolutions make it difficult for listeners to extract concrete meaning from a dense statement.[6]

Certainty Dictionaries

Rigidity	shall	anyhow
am	she's	anyone
are	was	anything
be	were	anyway
been	*will	anywhere
*being		each
he's		entire
I'll	*Leveling*	everlasting
I'm	all	evermore
is	any	every
it's	anybody	everybody

3. D. P. Boder, "The Adjective-Verb Quotient: A Contribution to the Psychology of Language," *Psychological Record*, 3 (1940), pp. 310–343.

4. C. K. Ogden, *Basic English: International Second Language* (New York: Harcourt, 1968).

5. R. Flesch, *The Art of Plain Talk* (New York: Collier, 1951).

6. Flesch (1951).

everyone
everything
everywhere
least
most
none
nothing
only
whole

Collectives

*administration
alliance
army
*association
*board
brotherhood
bureau
cabinet
campaign
church
city
civilization
committee
community
company
conference
congregation
congress
council
country
day
decade
department
economy
education
enemy
family
food
generation
globe

government
*group
housing
humanity
industry
leadership
legislation
legislature
majority
man
mankind
military
minority
month
movement
nation
navy
*organization
*party
police
*press
property
*public
*race
republic
society
staff
*state
union
week
world
year

Numerical Frequency

billion(s)
eight (een) (h) (y)
    (eenth)
eleven (th)
fifteen (th)
fifth
fifty

first
five
forty
four (teen) (th)
half
hundred(s)
million(s)
nine (teen) (ty) (teenth)
ninth
second
seven (th) (teen) (ty)
    (teenth)
six (th) (teen) (ty)
    (teenth)
ten (th)
thirteen (th)
thousand
three
third
twelfth
twelve
twentieth
twenty
two
(Plus all integers)

Qualification

*about
almost
although
appears
but
can
could
feel(s)
guess (ed) (es)
hesitate (d) (s)
hope (d) *(s)
I'd
if
*may

*might
much
ought
perhaps
seem (ed) (s)
should
some
somebody
someone
sometime
somewhat
somewhere
think (s)
though
*tried

tries
try
unless
wonder (ed) *(s)
would

Self-Reference

I
I'd
I'll
I'm
me
*mine
my (self)

Power Factor

Number of nouns or noun-derived adjectives (appearing three or more times per passage) × their number of occurrences ÷ 10.

Variety

Type-token ratio: number of different words in passage) divided by total words in passage (which in all cases was 500).

Optimism Subdictionaries

Praise

alert
beautiful
best
better
blessed
bright
*clean
*clear
conscientious
correct
*dear
easy
effective
*fair
*fine
*free
generous
genuine
good
great
happy

healthy
holy
important
innocent
*kind
laudable
loyal
mighty
moral
necessary
noble
perfect
positive
powerful
profitable
reasonable
*right
safe
smart
special
splendid
strong
successful

sweet
true
valuable
wise
wonderful

Satisfaction

amaze (d) (ment)
bravery
care (d) (s)
caring
cheer (ful)
comfort (able)
confident
courage
delight (ed)
determination
determined
enjoy (ed) (s) (ment)
excite (d) (ment)
exciting
friendly

friendship
fun (ny)
glad
grateful
gratitude
happily
happy
hope (ful)
hoping
joy
liking
love (d)
loving
pleased
pleasure
pride
proud
safe (ty)
secure
security
surprise (d)
surprising
welcome (d)

Inspiration

ability
assistance
authority
*beauty
brotherhood
charity
comfort
commitment
*concern
confidence
courage
dedication
democracy
determination
devotion
dignity
*duty

education
*employment
exploration
friendship
faith
freedom
health
*help
*honor
hope
humility
independence
initiative
inspiration
integrity
justice
knowledge
leadership
liberty
*love
patriotism
patience
peace
power
pride
principle
productivity
progress
prosperity
prudence
*reason
*respect
responsibility
rights
*sacrifice
safety
sense
success
*support
thrift
trust
truth
values

virtue
wisdom
*work (ing)

Adversity

adversary
adversaries
afraid
aggression
alienation
alone
anger
angry
annoyed
annoying
anxious
assault (s)
attack (s)
bad
battle (s)
blame
burden (s)
challenge (s)
coercion
combat
conflict (s)
contempt (ible)
contrary
controversy
cowardly
crime
crises
crisis
cruel
danger (s)
dangerous
deadly
death (s)
difficult
deficit (s)
depression
despair (ed)

desperate
desperation
dislike (d) (s)
disease (s)
disgust (ed) (ing)
dispute
disruption
doubts
enemies
enemy
envy
evil (s)
failure
false
fear (s)
fight (ing) (s)
grief
guilt
hate (d) (ful) (s)
hating
hatred
hazard
horrible
hostile
hostilities
hostility
hunger
illegal
illness (es)
impossible
injuries
injury
jealous (y)
loneliness
lonely

loss (es)
obstacle (s)
offensive
opponents
opposition
painful
panic (ed) (s)
peril (s)
pity
poor
poverty
problem (s)
rash
rebellion
recession
resistance (s)
revolution
risk (s)
ruin
sacrifice (s)
sad (ness)
scare (d)
sick (ness) (nesses)
sorrow
starvation
strife
struggle (s)
stupid
suffering
terrible
terrified
terror
threat (en) (ened) (s)
tragic
trouble (s)

ugly
unfair
unemployment
vice
war (fare) (s)
weapon (s)
weak (ness) (nesses)
worry (ing)
worried
worse
worst
wrong

Negation

aren't
cannot
can't
didn't
doesn't
don't
hasn't
haven't
isn't
neither
never
no
none
nor
not
nothing
nowhere
without
won't
wouldn't

Activity Subdictionaries

Accomplishment

accomplish (ed) (es)
achieve (d) (s)

*advance (d) *(s)
*approach (ed) *(es)
attempt (ed) *(s)
became

become (s)
began
begin
bring (s)

brought
build (s)
built
came
carried
carries
carry
*change (d) (s)
come (s)
conclude (d) (s)
continue (d) (s)
deliver (ed) (s)
establish (ed) (es)
expand (ed) (s)
explore (d) (s)
find (s)
follow (ed) (s)
found
get (s)
go (es)
gone
got
grew
grow (s)
hit (s)
improve (d) (s)
*leap (ed) *(s)
*leave *(s)
*left
*march (ed) (es)
*move (d) *(s)
plunge (d) (s)
*produce (d) (s)
pull (ed) (s)
*push (ed) (es)
ran
*reach (ed) *(s)
*rise (s)
*run
send (s)
sent
*start (ed) *(s)

strengthen (ed) (s)
strive (s)
strove
*thrust (ed) *(s)
tried
tries
try
*walk (ed) *(s)
went
*work (ed) *(s)

Aggressiveness

abolish (ed) (es)
arrest (ed) (s)
attack (ed) (s)
break (s)
broke
confront (ed) (s)
compete (d) (s)
defend (ed) (s)
destroy (ed) (s)
eliminate (d) (s)
fight (s)
force (ed) (s)
fought
hurt (s)
kill (ed) (s)
oppose (d) (s)
overcame
overcome
prevent (ed) (s)
reduce (d) (s)
reject (ed) (s)
resist (ed) (s)
ruin (ed) (s)
strive (s)
struggle (d) (s)
take (s)
took
wreck (ed) (s)

Communicativeness

inform (ed) (s)
insist (ed) (s)
invite (d) (s)
listen (ed) (s)
*mention (ed) (s)
negotiate (d)
*order (ed) *(s)
persuade (d)
propose (d) (s)
publish (ed)
read (s)
recommend (s)
report (ed) *(s)
respond (ed) (s)
said
say (s)
speak (s)
spoke
taught
teach (es)
tell (s)
testified
testifies
testify
told
urge (d) (s)
write (s)
wrote

Intellectuality

*believe (d) (s)
choose (s)
compare (d) (s)
comprehend (ed) (s)
concentrate (d) (s)
consider (s)
decide (d) (s)
discover (ed) (s)
*doubt (ed) *(s)
examine (d) (s)

expect (ed) (s)
forget (s)
forgot
interpret (ed) (s)
knew
know (s)
learn (ed) (s)
pray (ed) (s)
prove (ed) (s)
*realize (d) *(s)
recognize (d) (s)
remember (ed) (s)
solve (d) (s)
studied
*studies
*study
think (s)
*thought
understand (s)
understood

Passivity

acceptable
acceptably
accept (ed) (s)
agreeable
agreeably
*calm (ly)
careful (ly)
cautions
cautious (ly)

contented
continue (d) (s)
*delay (ed) *(s)
dormant
*fixed
gentle
gently
gradual (ly)
hesitant (ly)
hesitate (d) (s)
keep (s)
kept
*lay *(s)
*maintain (ed) (s)
meek (ly)
mild (ly)
moderate (ly)
normal (ly)
passive (ly)
*patient (ly)
*pause (d) *(s)
peaceful (ly)
permanent (ly)
preserve (d) (s)
*quiet (ly)
*refrain (ed) *(s)
regular (ly)
relax (ed) (es)
remain (ed) (s)
*rest (ed) *(s)
*safe (ly)
same

satisfactory
satisfied
secure
*set
sit (s)
*sleep (s)
slept
slow
*stable
stand (s)
*stay (ed) *(s)
*still
stood
stop (s) (ped)
submit (s) (ted)
*surrender (ed) (s)
tame
tired
tolerate (d) (s)
*wait (ed) (s)
*yield (ed) (s)

Embellishment

Sum of "Praise" and
"Adversity" category
(adjectives) divided
by sum of "Present
Concern" and "Past
Concern" categories.

Realism Subdictionaries

Spatial Awareness

aboard
*area *(s)
*capital *(s)
cities

city
*close (r)
communities
community
continent (s)
countries

country
distance (s)
district (s)
domestic
earth
east

eastern
everywhere
far
farm (s)
federal
*field *(s)
foreign
frontier
globe
hemisphere
here
home (s)
homeland (s)
inch (es)
indoor
international
island (s)
isolate (d)
isolation
*land *(s)
local
locale (s)
location (s)
mile (s)
national
nation (s)
nationwide
near
neighborhood (s)
northern
outdoor
outside
*place *(s)
private (ly)
properties
property
*public (ly)
region (s)
remote (ly)
republic (s)
room

rural
societies
south
southern
space (s)
sphere *(s)
*states
street
territories
territory
there
town (s)
universe
urban
valley (s)
vicinity
west
western
where
world (s)
zone (s)

Familiarity

about
across
after
against
am
among
at
are
be
been
before
between
by
came
come
comes
did

do
does
done
down
for
from
gave
get (s)
give (s) (n)
go (es) (ne)
got
had
has
have
he
he'd
he'll
her
in
is
keep (s)
kept
let (s)
made
make (s)
of
off
on
put (s)
said
say (s)
see (s)
seem (ed) (s)
send (s)
sent
take (s) (n)
through
to
took
under
up

was
went
were
with

Temporal Awareness

age (s)
ago
already
always
ancient
begin (s)
beginning
brief
century
day
decade (s)
delay (s)
duration
during
early
end
epoch (s)
era (s)
finally
first
forever
former
future
generation (s)
hour (s)
hurry
immediate (ly)
immortal
instant (ly)
late
minute (s)
modern
moment (s)
month (s)

morning (s)
never
next
new
night (s)
noon
now
occasional (ly)
old
past
perpetual (ly)
prompt
quick (ly)
recent (ly)
remember (ed)
sometime (s)
soon
stop
sudden (ly)
summer
temporary
then
time
today
tomorrow
tonight
tradition (al)
until
wait (ed)
week (s)
when
while
winter
year (s)
yesterday
young

Present Concern

become (s)
bring (s)

*call *(s)
*change *(s)
come (s)
do
does
fail (s)
*fight *(s)
give (s)
go
goes
keep (s)
know
*live *(s)
make (s)
*need *(s)
provide (s)
require (s)
say (s)
*state *(s)
take (s)
tell (s)
want (s)
write (s)

Human Interest

aunt
baby
boy
brother
child
cousin
dad
daddy
daughter
family
father
fellow
folks
friend
gentleman

girl
guy
hers
he's
him
himself
his
husband
lady
man
mister
mother
Mr.
Mrs.
nephew
niece
our
ourselves
parent
people
she'd
she'll
she's
sir
son
their (s)
them (selves)
they
they'd
they'll
they're
us
we
we'd
we'll
we're
wife
woman
you
you'd
you'll
your (s)

you're
yourself
yourselves

Concreteness

*administration
Africa
*air
aircraft
America
Americans
*arms
armament (s)
*arms
army
automobile
Asia
bank (s)
bible
*board *(s)
brother (s)
*building (s)
car (s)
child
Catholics
cent (s)
chairman
chairmen
children
Christians
church (es)
cities
citizen
city
college (s)
committee (s)
communists
computer (s)
congress
congressman
congressmen

council (s)
countries
country
*criminal (s)
democrats
doctor (s)
dollar (s)
earth
enemies
enemy
Europe
*face *(s)
factory
family
families
farmer (s)
father (s)
*fellow (s)
field (s)
fire (s)
floor
food
friend
furniture
*globe
governor (s)
gun
*hand *(s)
heart
hemisphere
home (s)
hospital
house (s)
housewife
human (s)
*jet *(s)
Jew (s)
king (s)
*land *(s)
lady
ladies
lawyer (s)

leader (s)
letter (s)
market (s)
mayor (s)
member (s)
money
moon
*mother *(s)
nation (s)
navy
negro (es)
neighbor (s)
office (s)
officials
partner
*people (s)
*plane *(s)
*plant *(s)
police
person (s)
president (s)
prisoner (s)
*press
Protestants
railroad (s)
*relative (s)
republicans
river (s)
room (s)

*school (s)
senator
*ship *(s)
sister (s)
soldier (s)
son (s)
*state *(s)
station (s)
student (s)
sun
table
taxpayer (s)
teacher (s)
*train *(s)
troop (s)
union (s)
university
universities
valley (s)
veteran (s)
voter (s)
water
weapon (s)
wife
wives
woman
women
worker (s)
world (s)

Past Concern

became
brought
called
changed
did
done
failed
fought
gave
kept
knew
lived
made
needed
provided
required
said
stated
told
took
wanted
went
wrote

Complexity

Mean character length
of words used in pasage.

Symbolism

America (n)
country
Democracy
freedom

government
law (s)
nation
peace

people
rights

INDEX

Numbers in italics refer to pages on which the complete references are given.

O

P

Computerized language analysis; DIC-
TION program; Language statistics;
Speech samples
Reston, J., *173,* 198
Revenue sharing, 136
Rhetoric, *see* Presidential persuasion; Presi-
dential speechmaking
Rhetorical attitudes, 10
Rhetorical determinism, 151, 198
Rhetorical perspective, 5–8, 25
Rhetorical presidency, 3–4, 96, 208–209,
234–236
Ribicoff, A., 20
Rice University, 98
Richardson, E., 89, *93,* 127
Right to Life movement, 218
Rigidity (in DICTION), 294, 295
Rochester, N.Y., 144
Rockwell, N., 72
Role, *see* Presidential role
Roman Catholicism, 23, 107, 172, 185, 209,
289–290
Roosevelt, E., 70
Roosevelt, F. D., 10, 12, *25,* 34, 68–69, 73,
87, 90, 102, 145, 151, 214, 223
Roosevelt, T., 5, 155
Roseberry, Earl of, *see* Primrose, A. P.
Rose Garden strategy, 183
Rosenfield, L. W., *148*
Rosenman, D., *91–92*
Rosenman, S., 68, *91–92*
Ross, C. G., 71–72, 76
Rossiter, C., 32, *64*
Rourke, F., *64*
Rowe, J. H., *123*
Rubicon River, 123
Russia, *see* Soviet Union

S

Sadat, A., *288–289*
Safire, W., 198
St. Louis, Mo., 292
Salinger, P., 108, *125*
SALT Treaty, 185, 288, 290
San Antonio, Tex., 76
Sanders, K., *26*
Satisfaction (in DICTION), 294, 297–298

Saudi Arabia, 288
Sausalito, Calif., 77
Schell, J., 144, *149*
Schlesinger, A., Jr., 12, *26,* 98–100, 107,
124–125, 150, *172,* 228, *237*
Scott, R. L., *149*
Sears, J., 152
Sedelow, S. L., *28*
Sedelow, W. A., Jr., *28*
Self-monitoring, 141
Self-Reference (in DICTION), 16, 19, 21,
27, 45–49, 51–53, 55–56, 58, 62, 87–90,
100–102, 110–111, 113–114, 120, 141,
143, 155, 163–164, 169–170, 184–191,
196–197, 209, 219, 221–222, 250–284,
293–295, 297
Sellers, P., 105
Senoff, A. P., *236*
Settings of speeches, 12–13, 58–61, 240,
275, 279; *see also* specific speech type
(ε.g., Ceremonial speaking)
Sevareid, E., 239
Shah of Iran, *see* Pahlavi, M. R.
Sherrill, R., *125–126*
Shrum, R., 164
Shull, S. A., *25, 174*
Sickels, R., 86, *93*
Sidey, H., 9, *25*
Siffin, W., *173*
Silent Majority, 61
Simons, H., *65*
Sioux City, Iowa, 76–77
Skau, L., *92*
Smith, A., 167
Smith, C., *149*
Smith, H., *175,* 193, *210,* 215, 217, *236,*
240–241
Smith, H. K., 239
Smith, Mm., 84, 86, *93*
Smith, Mr., *26*
Social activists' speaking, 23, 32, 35–36, 38,
40, 45, 52, 274, 277
Social Security, 115; *see also* Human ser-
vices; Medical problems
Somerset, Mass., 76
Sorensen, T., 9, *25,* 97–98, 101, 103–104,
109, 122, *124–126*
South Africa, 207
South Florida Bar Association, 161
Southern Baptist Convention, 187, 197

Y

PN4055 U53 P643 1984